MW00639790

A CONCISE HIS

This book tells the story of humankind as producers and reproducers from the Paleolithic to the present. Renowned social and cultural historian Merry E. Wiesner-Hanks brings a new perspective to world history by examining social and cultural developments across the globe, including families and kin groups, social and gender hierarchies, sexuality, race and ethnicity, labor, religion, consumption, and material culture. She examines how these structures and activities changed over time through local processes and interactions with other cultures, highlighting key developments that defined particular eras, such as the growth of cities or the creation of a global trading network. Incorporating foragers, farmers, and factory workers along with shamans, scribes, and secretaries, the book widens and lengthens human history. It makes comparisons and generalizations, but also notes diversities and particularities, as it examines the social and cultural matters that are at the heart of big questions in world history today.

MERRY E. WIESNER-HANKS is Distinguished Professor and Chair of the History Department at the University of Wisconsin-Milwaukee. She is the author or editor of twenty books, including editor-in-chief of the multi-volume *Cambridge World History* (2015), *Early Modern Europe 1450–1789* (Cambridge, 2nd edn. 2013), *Women and Gender in Early Modern Europe* (Cambridge, 3rd edn. 2008), *Christianity and Sexuality in the Early Modern World: Regulating Desire, Reforming Practice* and *Gender in History: Global Perspectives*. She has also written a number of innovative source books for use in the college classroom, including *Discovering the Global Past: A Look at the Evidence*, a book for young adults, *An Age of Voyages, 1350–1600*, and a book for general readers, *The Marvelous Hairy Girls: The Gonzales Sisters and their Worlds*.

CAMBRIDGE CONCISE HISTORIES

This is a series of illustrated "concise histories" of selected individual countries, intended both as university and college textbooks and as general historical introductions for general readers, travellers, and members of the business community.

A full list of titles in the series can be found at:
www.cambridge.org/concisehistories

A Concise History of the World

MERRY E. WIESNER-HANKS
University of Wisconsin-Milwaukee

for Kathy
best wishes on
this global journey
Merry

CAMBRIDGE
UNIVERSITY PRESS

CAMBRIDGE
UNIVERSITY PRESS

32 Avenue of the Americas, New York NY 10013-2473, USA

Cambridge University Press is part of the University of Cambridge.

It furthers the University's mission by disseminating knowledge in the pursuit of education, learning and research at the highest international levels of excellence.

www.cambridge.org
Information on this title: www.cambridge.org/9781107028371

First published 2015

Printed in the United States of America by Sheridan Books, Inc.

A catalogue record for this publication is available from the British Library

Library of Congress Cataloguing in Publication data
Wiesner, Merry E., 1952–
A concise history of the world / Merry Wiesner-Hanks,
University of Wisconsin-Milwaukee.
pages cm
Includes bibliographical references and index.
ISBN 978-1-107-02837-1 (Hardback : alk. paper) –
ISBN 978-1-107-69453-8 (Paperback : alk. paper)
1. World history–Textbooks. I. Title.
D21.W64 2015
909–dc23 2015020010

ISBN 978-1-107-02837-1 Hardback
ISBN 978-1-107-69453-8 Paperback

CONTENTS

FIGURES

MAPS

Introduction

There are many ways to tell the history of the world. Oral histories that were later written down, including the Book of Genesis, the Rig Veda, and the Popul Vuh, focused especially on the actions of gods and on human/divine interactions. The ancient Greek historian Herodotus drew on such oral traditions along with eyewitness testimony to provide deep background for his story of the war between the Persians and the Greeks, setting this within the context of the world as he knew it. The ancient Chinese historian Sima Qian told history through an encyclopedic presentation of events, activities, and biographies of emperors, officials, and other important people, beginning with the semi-mythical first sage rulers of China. The tenth-century Muslim historian Abu Ja'far al-Tabari began before the creation of Adam and Eve, and used biblical, Greek, Roman, Persian, and Byzantine sources to present history as a long and unbroken process of cultural transmission. Dynastic chroniclers in medieval Europe and Mughal India often began their accounts with the creation of the world to devise "universal histories," then moved quickly through the millennia, slowing down as they neared the present to focus on political developments in their own locale. Histories that had a broad scope were among the flood of books produced after the development of printing technology in the fifteenth century, most written by highly learned male scholars, but some by poets, nuns, physicians, obscure officials, former slaves, and others. With the expansion of literacy in the eighteenth and nineteenth centuries, authors wrote world histories full of moral lessons, some of them designed specifically for children or female readers.

Throughout much of the twentieth century scholarly history focused on nations, but world history did not disappear. For example, right after the devastation of World War I, and in part as a response to the slaughter, H.G. Wells wrote *The Outline of History*, which told the history of the world as a story of human efforts to "conceive a common purpose in relation to which all men may live happily." Readers could buy this in cheap bi-weekly installments, just as they had Wells' earlier novel *The War of the Worlds*, and millions did. By the last quarter of the twentieth century, the increasing integration of world regions into a single system through globalization led to a re-emergence of scholarly history conceptualized on a global scale, and the intensifying flows and interactions of people, goods, and ideas across national borders inspired histories that focused on those flows and interactions themselves. So today there are imperial histories, transnational and borderlands histories, postcolonial histories, histories of migrations and diasporas, and global histories of individual commodities such as salt, silver, or porcelain.

SOCIAL AND CULTURAL WORLD HISTORY

This book thus draws on long traditions and recent developments. Like all world histories, it highlights certain things and leaves many others out, for there is no way to tell the whole story within the pages of a book that could be read (to say nothing of written) within one lifetime. It tells the story of humans as producers and reproducers, understanding these terms in a social and cultural as well as material sense. My notion of humans as "producers" incorporates not only foragers, farmers, and factory workers, but also shamans, scribes, and secretaries. Discussions of family and kin structures, sexuality, demography, and other issues that are often seen as "reproduction" examine the ways these are socially determined and change with interactions between cultures. The book also underlines the constant connections between production and reproduction throughout human history, as changes in the modes or meaning of one led to changes in the other. It does not ignore political and military developments, but examines the way these shaped and were shaped by social and cultural factors. Doing this provides a fuller and more accurate picture of both politics and war than does analyzing these more traditional topics as somehow divorced from society.

This social and cultural focus brings a new perspective to a brief world history. Along with global history, social and cultural history—and related fields that have developed within them—have been the most important new approaches in history over the last half century. Through them, the focus of history has broadened from politics and great men to a huge range of topics—labor, families, women and gender, sexuality, childhood, material culture, the body, identity, race and ethnicity, consumption, and many others. The actions and ideas of a wide variety of people, and not simply members of the elite, have become part of the history we know. World history was developing as a field during the same time, but it generally emphasized political economy, and focused on large-scale political and economic processes carried out by governments and commercial leaders. It has had a powerful materialist tradition, in part because material objects seem relatively unproblematic to compare and connect across regions. By contrast, social and cultural forms and categories appear more particular to individual societies, and have a very different meaning in different places. Thus trying to compare them or make generalizations seems to require glossing over differences and reducing complexities, the opposite of what social and cultural historians generally seek to do. In addition, in the world histories of the nineteenth and early twentieth centuries, making comparisons among social and cultural forms was often part of ranking them—groups were "primitive" or "advanced," cultures were "civilizations" or they were not—and most contemporary historians try to avoid such rankings.

Comparing does not have to mean ranking, however, and historical analysis always involves comparison, if only the comparison between something at one point in time and at a later point, or between the past and the present. No question about change, continuity, causation, or connections can be answered without making comparisons. History also always involves generalization and a selection of evidence. Even histories that look very closely at one event or one individual leave out things that the historian judges to be less important, and suggest parallels with developments in different places or times. The search for patterns is what allows historians to create categories that can organize and make sense of the past. (Anyone who tells a story about past events, including us as we talk to our friends about our own experiences yesterday, does the same thing.) There are categories based on chronology, including large ones such as ancient, medieval, and modern, and smaller ones such as the Song dynasty or the 1950s. There are categories based on geography—Australia, the Amazon basin; on politics—Brazil, Berlin; on occupation—doctor, data processor; on religion—Muslim, Mormon; on social group—noble, nun; and on many other things. Most of these categories are human constructions, of course, although sometimes this is forgotten and they come to be seen as self-evident, divinely created, or naturally occurring. Their boundaries are frequently contested, and blurry lines of division are more common than sharp borders. And all of these categories—even the geographic ones, as we see in our era of rising ocean levels and dried-up rivers—change over time. In examining social and cultural developments on a global scale, this book will make comparisons and generalizations just as earlier world histories of trade, commodity flows, and empires have done, but also note diversities and counter-examples. You might think of this in musical terms, as a theme and variations.

Social and cultural matters are at the heart of big questions in world history today, from the Paleolithic (Did early *Homo sapiens* begin creating social institutions, art, and complex language as the result of a sudden cognitive revolution, or was this a gradual process?) to the present (Are technology and globalization destroying local cultures through greater homogenization or providing more opportunities for democratization and diversity?). Social and cultural matters are also part of issues in world history that might seem to be about political economy, such as whether European dominance of most of the world in the nineteenth century was the result of accidents like easy access to coal or learned behaviors like a Protestant work ethic or competition.

This book differs from other world histories in its social and cultural focus, but it shares certain basic aspects of world history as a field. Most obviously, world historians use a wide spatial lens, although they do not always take the entire world as their unit of analysis. They tend to de-emphasize individual nations or civilizations, and focus instead on regions defined differently, including zones of interaction, or on the ways in which people or goods or ideas moved across regions. Oceans are just as important as continents, or perhaps even more important, especially in the era before mechanized transport, when travel by sea was far easier and cheaper than travel by land. Islands are interesting, as are the beaches on those islands, often the first place that interactions occurred.

As with any history, some world history has a very narrow temporal framework, examining developments around the world in a single decade or even a single year: 1688, for example, saw dramatic events in many places, as did the 1960s. Other world history has a broader temporal framework, and stretches far back into the past. Just as they have de-emphasized the nation as the most significant geographic unit, most global historians have also de-emphasized the invention of writing as a sharp dividing line in human history, separating the "prehistoric" from the "historic." With this the border between archaeology and history disappears, and the Paleolithic and Neolithic become part of history. Some expand their time frames even further, and begin history with the Big Bang, thus incorporating developments that have usually been studied through astrophysics, chemistry, geology, and biology within what they term "Big History." Others are not willing to go this far, but most world historians agree that history should be studied on a range of chronological and spatial scales, including, but not limited to, very large ones.

World historians also agree that we should always be conscious and careful about how we divide history into periods and determine which events and developments are key turning points between one era and another, although they often disagree about those periods and turning points. Some argue, for example, that the modern world began with the establishment of the Mongol Empire in the thirteenth century, while others would say that this happened in 1492, with Columbus' voyages, and still others in 1789, with the French Revolution. Other world historians would say that the search for one single point is misguided, because it implies there is only one path to modernity, or that the whole notion of "the modern" is so value-laden that we should stop using the term.

Along with disagreeing about when history starts and how it should be periodized, historians who study the whole world also disagree about what to call their field. Some draw a distinction between world history and global history, and guard the borders of one or the other, or the borders of other related approaches, such as transnational or diasporic history. I do not find guarding borders very interesting or fruitful, and I use "world" and "global" interchangeably, choosing one or the other sometimes simply because of the structure of a sentence. "World" can be used both as an adjective (world literature, world music) or a noun (a history of the world), while "global" is always an adjective. To most people "a history of the globe" would be a history of spherical maps.

You might be asking why all this matters, why you need to know about my approach in this book. Because writing history (or producing it in other ways, such as films, television programs, websites, or museum displays) is a selective process of inclusion and exclusion, it is important for you as its reader or viewer to think about the conscious or unconscious assumptions and perspective of whoever produced it. These were themselves shaped by historical processes, for the questions we (as historians or just as human beings) think are interesting and important about the past change, as do the ways we try to answer them. It is no surprise that social and labor history developed when working-class students entered universities and graduate programs in larger numbers, nor that women's and gender history did when women did. It is no surprise that world, global, transnational, postcolonial, and diasporic history have become increasingly common approaches in the interconnected world of the twenty-first century. It would have been strange had it been otherwise.

THE PLAN

The book is arranged chronologically in five chapters, each covering a shorter time frame than its predecessor. Each chapter includes some discussion of the way people have thought about the era covered by the chapter and the important forms of evidence they have used in order to learn about it. Thus you will get a sense not only of what happened, but also of how people have discovered what happened and how they have given it meaning. For every chapter except Chapter 1, this includes writings of people living at the time about their own society and era. Because world history can be studied on many different scales, each chapter contains a few embedded micro-histories, specific examples that use a narrower range of focus.

Certain topics emerge in most chapters— families and lineages, food production and preparation, social and gender hierarchies, slavery, cities, organized violence, religious practices, migration—because these were structures that men and women created or activities they engaged in that were spread widely across time and space and had significant impact everywhere. None of these was static, however, and each chapter notes how they changed, sometimes through internal developments, sometimes through encounters with others, and most often through a combination of these. Each chapter also centers on one or two particular developments that mark the era covered in the chapter, such as the growth of cities or the creation of a global trading network. These developments are those generally viewed as central by world historians, but their social and cultural aspects have sometimes been ignored.

Reflecting the view among world historians that writing was not the beginning of history, Chapter 1, "Foraging and farming families (to 3000 BCE)," discusses the Paleolithic and Neolithic, thus covering the vast majority of human history. It examines the more complex social structures and cultural forms that plant and animal domestication enabled, as the simple stone hand axes of the Paleolithic were replaced by more specialized tools, small kin groups gave way to ever larger villages, egalitarian foragers became stratified by gender distinctions and divisions of wealth and power, and spirits were transformed into hierarchies of divinities worshipped at permanent human-built structures. The basic social pattern set in early agricultural societies—with the majority of people farming the land and a small elite who lived off their labor—was remarkably resilient, lasting well into the twentieth century for most of the world.

Villages became cities and city-states, which grew in some places into larger-scale states and empires. That process is traced in

Chapter 2, "Cities and classical societies (3000 BCE–500 CE)," with a focus on the social institutions and cultural norms that facilitated these developments, including hereditary dynasties, hierarchical families, and notions of ethnicity. Writing and other means of recording information were invented to serve the needs of people who lived close to one another in cities and states. Oral rituals of worship, healing, and celebration in which everyone participated grew into religions, philosophies, and branches of knowledge presided over by specialists, including Judaism and Confucian thought. Social differences became formalized in systems that divided slave and free, or that grouped people into castes or orders, distinctions that were maintained through marriage and cultural ideologies. Hinduism, Buddhism, and Christianity were created and then expanded in the cosmopolitan worlds of classical empires, shaping family life and social practices.

Most of the classical empires collapsed in the middle of the first millennium, but despite this collapse various regions of the world became more culturally, commercially, and politically integrated in the millennium that followed, a process traced in Chapter 3, "Expanding networks of interaction (500 CE–1500 CE)." Mercantile and religious networks, including Islam, linked growing cities and glittering courts, where hereditary rulers and their entourages of elites developed institutions and ceremonies that strengthened royal authority, and created courtly cultures with distinctive codes of behavior. All of these relied for their wealth on a spread and intensification of agriculture, which happened in both the eastern and western hemispheres, and was interwoven with changes in social and gender structures. Cites such as Constantinople, Tenochtitlan, and Hangzhou grew into large metropolises, and religion, trade, and diplomacy motivated people to travel, creating regional and transregional zones of exchange in goods and ideas.

The voyages of Columbus and his successors linked the two hemispheres, and Chapter 4, "A new world of connections (1500 CE–1800 CE)," surveys the positive and negative biological, cultural, and social consequences of this "Columbian Exchange." Among these were the spread of disease and the transfer of plants, animals, and consumer goods, along with economic changes that led to social protests, revolts, warfare, and forced migrations in an increasingly interdependent world. Religious transformations, including the Protestant and Catholic Reformations and the creation of Sikhism, were interwoven with all of these developments, as religions, too, migrated and morphed. New urban social settings and cultural institutions, such as coffee and tea houses, theatres, and salons, offered men—and sometimes women—opportunities for entertainment, sociability, consumption, and the exchange of ideas, but the increasing contacts among peoples also resulted in more rigid notions of human difference.

The transformations of the modern era have led to today's vast social divisions between wealth and poverty, but also created a human community that is interconnected on a global scale, processes that are examined in Chapter 5, "Industrialization, imperialism, and inequality (1800 CE–2015 CE)." Major economic and political changes, such as industrialization and de-industrialization, imperialism and anti-imperialism, the rise and collapse of communism, and the expansion of nationalism, have intersected with social and cultural changes within a framework of rapidly increasing population and human impact on the environment. International movements for social justice have called for greater egalitarianism and understanding, while ethnic, religious, and social divisions have led to brutality, genocides, and war. Technological developments in agriculture, medicine, and weaponry have both extended human life and extinguished it at levels unimagined in earlier eras, simultaneously challenging and reinforcing long-standing social hierarchies and cultural patterns.

One of those mass wars led H.G. Wells to write *The Outline of History* a century ago, as he sought examples in history of the search for happiness and a common purpose to counteract the misery and carnage he had just witnessed. My aims with this book are not as sweeping, but, like all global historians, I hope to widen (and lengthen) your view of the human past, and, like all social and cultural historians, to make it a more complicated (and more interesting) story.

FURTHER READING

As I was writing this book, I was also serving as the editor-in-chief of the *Cambridge World History* (2015). Its seven volumes provide an excellent overview of the dynamic field of world history today, with essays by historians, art historians, anthropologists, classicists, archaeologists, economists, sociologists, and area studies specialists from universities around the world; their insights are reflected in the pages of this book. For one-volume introductions to world and global history as a field, see: Bruce Mazlish and R. Buultjens, eds., *Conceptualizing Global History* (Boulder, CO: Westview Press, 1993); Ross Dunn, ed., *The New World History: A Teacher's Companion* (New York: Bedford/St. Martin's, 2000); Patrick Manning, *Navigating World History: Historians Create a Global Past* (New York: Palgrave Macmillan, 2003); Marnie Hughes-Warrington, ed., *Palgrave Advances in World Histories* (New York: Palgrave Macmillan, 2005); Douglas Northrop, ed., *A Companion to World History* (Oxford: Wiley-Blackwell, 2012); Kenneth R. Curtis and Jerry H. Bentley, eds., *Architects of World History: Researching the Global Past* (Oxford: Wiley-Blackwell, 2014). For studies of how history has been written around the world, see: Eckhardt Fuchs and Benedikt Stuchtey, eds., *Across Cultural Borders: Historiography in Global Perspective* (Lanham, MD: Rowman & Littlefield, 2002); Dominic Sachsenmaier, *Global Perspectives on Global History: Theories and Approaches in a Global World* (Cambridge: Cambridge University Press, 2011); Prasenjit Duara, Viren Murthy, and Andrew Sartori, eds., *A Companion to Global Historical Thought* (Oxford: Wiley-Blackwell, 2014).

Useful surveys of historical practice today that include consideration of world and global history are: David Cannadine, ed., *What Is History Today?* (London: Palgrave Macmillan, 2003); Ludmilla Jordanova, *History in Practice*, 2nd edn. (London: Hodder Arnold, 2006); Ulinka Rublack, *A Concise Companion to History* (Oxford: Oxford University Press, 2012). The website "Making history: the changing face of the profession in Britain" developed by the Institute of Historical Research in London has some excellent short essays on current approaches: www.history.ac.uk/makinghistory/themes/.

No overview of social history has been published recently, but for cultural history see Peter Burke, *What Is Cultural History?* (Cambridge: Polity Press, 2004) and Alessandro Arcangeli, *Cultural History: A Concise Introduction* (London: Routledge, 2011). Susan Kingsley Kent, *Gender and History* (London: Palgrave Macmillan, 2011) provides an introduction to gender history, which has been an important component of both social and cultural history. For global gender history, see Teresa A. Meade and Merry E. Wiesner-Hanks, eds., *A Companion to Gender History* (Oxford: Wiley-Blackwell, 2004).

I

Foraging and farming families (to 3000 BCE)

About ten thousand years ago, a group of young people entered a cave in the valley of the Pinturas River in what is now southern Argentina. They held their hands up to a wall of the cave and, using pipes made of bone, blew paint made with different colors of mineral pigments around their hands to create silhouettes. They, or someone else who lived at roughly the same time, also painted hunting scenes with humans, animals, birds, and bolas made of stones on the ends of cords, with which humans captured those birds and animals. Someone also painted geometric and zigzag patterns, and, judging by the dots of paint on the ceiling of the cave, tossed bolas dipped in paint upwards. We know these were young people because the hands are slightly smaller than adult hands, and we know it was a group because they are all different. Most are left hands, which indicates that most of these individuals were right-handed, since they would have held the pipe for blowing in the hand they normally used for tasks. What occasioned this group project in the Cueva de las Manos (Cave of the Hands), as this site has become known, is unknown. It could have been a coming-of-age ceremony for adolescents led with solemnity by adults, or it could have been a less formal coming-of-age ritual conducted by adolescents themselves, akin to graffiti tagging. It could have simply been play. No matter why it was painted, the cave provides powerful evidence for many aspects of early human society: technological inventiveness, symbolic thinking, social cohesion. It, and similar hand prints found all over the world, suggest that the urge to say "I was here" and "we

1.1 Hand prints from the Cueva de las Manos, Argentina, made about 8000 BCE, from mineral pigments blown through pipes made of bone to create silhouettes.

were here" is very old. People would later convey this in writing, and place themselves and their group within larger scales of space and time, but the young people who left their hand prints in the Cueva de las Manos knew these would be seen by those who entered the cave later. They were intentionally creating a record of past events for people in the future, what we would call a history.

Along with their handprints, the people who painted the Cueva de las Manos also left tools made of bone and stone. Tools made from hard materials are the most common type of evidence that survives from the early human past, and they shape the way we talk (and think) about that past. In the nineteenth century the Danish scholar C.J. Thomsen, studying collections of such tools in Copenhagen, devised a system for dividing human history into eras. Thus the earliest human era became the Stone Age, the next era the Bronze Age, and the next the Iron Age. The Stone/Bronze/Iron progression does not work very well in many parts of world, particularly if it is used as a general measure of technological advance: in some places iron was the first metal to have a major impact, and in many places very complex technologies developed without metals. It also ignores tools made from softer materials (such as plant fibres, sinew, and leather) or from organic materials that generally decayed (such as wood) that were important parts of the human toolkit. And it centers on tools, and not on other material objects or non-material factors. Despite its limitations, however, Thomsen's three-age system has survived. A later scholar further divided the Stone Age into the Old Stone Age, or Paleolithic era, during which food was gained largely by foraging, followed by the New Stone Age, or Neolithic era, which saw the beginning of plant and animal domestication. More recent archaeologists have further divided the Paleolithic into Lower-Middle-Upper (if they work on Europe and Asia), or Early-Middle-Later (if they work on Africa), again based primarily on the tools that have survived, with further subdivisions and geographic variations.

Along with tools and paintings, other physical evidence also survives in some places, including fossilized bones, teeth, and other body parts; evidence of food preparation, such as fossilized animal bones with cut marks or charring; or holes where corner-posts of houses once stood. Fortunate accidents have preserved materials in a few places when most are long gone: they are deep in the earth in caves, or landslides prevented them from being worn away by wind and water, or the chemical nature of bogs prevented their decay. To all of this evidence, scholars increasingly apply chemical and physical tests along with close observation. These include, among others, analysis of the wear patterns on stone tools (termed microwear analysis), chemical analysis of bones or of fossilized feces to determine food sources and other things (termed stable isotope analysis), genetic testing to examine DNA, and various methods of dating, such as the thermoluminescence dating of sediments, electron spin resonance dating of teeth, and carbon-14 dating of organic materials. To this, they add evidence from comparative linguistics, primatology, ethnography, neurology, and other fields.

Putting this information together, archaeologists, paleontologists, and other scholars have developed a view of early human history whose basic outline is widely shared, although just as in physics or astronomy, new finds spur rethinking. This chapter traces that history, beginning with the evolution of hominids and the various species in the genus *Homo*, examining the lifeways, kin structures, art, and rituals of early foragers, and assessing the ways in which plant and animal domestication enabled the creation of larger-scale hierarchical social structures and more elaborate cultural forms.

Interpreting the partial and scattered remains of the human past involves speculation, and this is particularly true for social and cultural issues. By themselves, tools and other objects generally do not reveal who made or used them (though sometimes this can be determined from the location in which they were found), nor do they indicate what they meant to their creators or users. Because evidence gets rarer and more accidental in its preservation the further back one goes, controversies about how much we can draw from it are especially sharp among those who study the earliest human history.

SOCIETY AND CULTURE AMONG OTHER HOMINIDS

Those controversies include a very basic question that seems to be about periodization, but is actually philosophical: when should the story of society and culture start? The eighteenth-century European scientists who invented the system we now use to classify living things placed humans in the animal kingdom, the order of Primates, the family Hominidae, and the genus *Homo*. The other surviving members of the hominid family are the great apes—chimpanzees, bonobos, gorillas, and orangutans—and some primatologists who study them are quite comfortable talking about, say, chimpanzee society or even chimpanzee culture. All of the great apes—and certain other animals and birds as well—use tools and live in complex social hierarchies, and one bonobo, Kanzi, who now lives with a small group of his relatives at the Iowa Primate Learning Sanctuary in Des Moines, can make sharpened stone tools, gather wood, light a fire, and cook his food after watching the humans who care for him do this. He has been taught to recognize, respond to, and choose symbols on a screen representing objects or ideas, but whether he can recombine symbols to produce new ideas, or recognize that both he and the humans surrounding him are doing this, is hotly debated.

These two characteristics—combining symbols in new ways, and understanding that both oneself and others have internal lives and consciousness—are currently the core of what most scientists see as the divide between humans and other species. (Other characteristics that have been proposed, such as tool-making, awareness of death, suffering, altruism, and counting, are now known to be shared with other animals.) Symbolic thought involves creating a symbolic or syntactic language, that is, a way of communicating that follows certain rules and that can refer to things or states of being that are not necessarily present. This can be oral or gestural or written or a combination of these, but it must be shared with at least one other being to be a language. Symbolic communication allows better understanding and manipulation of the world, and can be passed from one generation to the next, thus leading to multi-generational collective explanations for that world. A consciousness of consciousness—what philosophers call a "theory of mind"—is also both cognitive and social. It involves not only responding to what others are doing (which animals clearly do), but also reasoning about what others think or feel, recognizing that they have aims, and making abstractions about why they might be doing something.

The primatologists who work with Kanzi affirm that he does both of these, but others who observe him think that this is anthropomorphizing. The scholars who study early hominins—the subfamily division within the hominid family that includes us (but excludes the great apes)—are similarly divided. Some think that any discussion of culture among hominins of the past that were not users of symbolic language is also a kind of anthropomorphism, projecting our ways of thinking onto beings that were not like us, or at least not enough like us to have such a thing as "culture." Clive Gamble and others assert that this is too limited a view, and see symbolic thought expressed through objects and the human body itself millions of years before it was expressed orally, connecting hominins in social webs of shared understanding.

All sides in these debates about *when* to start agree about *where* to start, however: humans evolved in Africa, where between 7 and 6 million years ago some hominids began to walk upright at least some of the time. Initially these hominids combined two-limbed movement on land and four-limbed movement in trees, but over many millennia the skeletal and muscular structures of some of them evolved to make upright walking easier. This included groups that lived in southern and eastern Africa beginning about 4 million years ago, whom paleontologists place in the genus *Australopithecus*, small hominids with bodies light enough to move easily in trees, but with hind limbs that allowed efficient bipedal motion. About 3.4 million years ago, some australopiths began to use naturally occurring objects as tools to deflesh animals, as evidenced by cutmarks and scrapes on fossilized animal bones. This gave them greater choice about when and where they would eat, as they could cut meat into portable portions. At some point, certain groups in East Africa began to make tools as well as use them; the earliest now identified are 2.6 million years old, but archaeologists suspect that older ones will be found. Hominids struck one stone against another to break off sharp flakes that contemporary archaeologists have found are capable of butchering (though not killing) an elephant, and carried the rocks to make these stone tools from one place to another.

Like making anything, making these stone flakes required intent, skill, and physical capability, the latter provided by a hand that was able to hold the "hammer" stone precisely, with an opposable thumb and delicate muscles that can manipulate objects. Why australopiths developed this hand that was very different from the less flexible (but much stronger) hands of other primates is not clear, but what *is* clear is that they already had it when they began making tools. The human hand did not evolve to use or make tools, but used tools because it had already evolved. It is thus what paleontologists call an "exaptation": something that evolved randomly or for a reason that we do not yet understand, but was then used for a specific purpose. Other structures within the body that became essential in later developments—such as the larynx, about which more below—were also exaptations. (Many social structures and cultural forms were exaptations as well—they developed for reasons that are unknown, or perhaps simply as experiments, but then became traditions; explanations for how they originated were invented later that probably have little to do with how they had actually developed.)

Australopiths seem to have eaten anything available, and fossilized animal bones, fossilized teeth, and other types of evidence indicate that this included meat. Paleontologists think this meat was most likely scavanged; australopiths may have stolen carcasses that leopards had hidden in trees, or engaged in "power scavanging"—throwing rocks with their flexible hands to drive off other predators. This suggests that they lived in larger groups than just a few closely related individuals. Living in larger groups would have also enabled them to avoid predators more effectively—for hominins were prey as well as predators—and may have encouraged more complex communications.

These new tools and the innovative behaviors that went with them emerged among australopiths, who also branched out into different species in various parts of Africa. Around 2 million years ago, one of these branches developed into a different type of hominin that later paleontologists judged to be the first in the genus *Homo*. Which of the fossil remains that have been found in East Africa should be categorized as the very first *Homo* is disputed, because this depends on exactly which anatomical features or behavioral patterns indicated in the scattered bones and stones of the fossil record one sees as making a hominin clearly *Homo* (and thus the ancestor of us). Among the contenders are *Homo habilis* ("handy human") and *Homo ergaster* ("working human"), names that indicate that the essence of being human to the archaeologists who invented these terms in the 1960s and 1970s was the ability to make things. And make things *Homo* did: first multipurpose sharpened stone tools generally called hand axes and then slightly specialized versions of these. This suggests greater intelligence, and the skeletal remains support this, for these early members of the genus *Homo* had a larger brain than did the australopiths. They also had narrow hips, longer legs, and feet that indicate they were fully bipedal, but here there is an irony: the slender upright pelvis made giving birth to a larger-brained infant difficult. Large brains also take more energy to run than other parts of the body, so that large-brained animals have to eat more calories than small-brained ones.

This disjuncture between brain and pelvis had many consequences, including social ones, which might have begun with *Homo ergaster*. The pelvis puts a limit on how much the brain can expand before birth, which means that among modern humans much brain expansion occurs after birth; humans are born with brains that are only quarter of the size that they will be at adulthood. Humans thus have a far longer period than do other animals when they are completely dependent on their parents or others around them. Those parents also have a long period during which they must tend an infant or it will die. Judging by brain size, that period was shorter in *Homo ergaster* than in modern *Homo sapiens*, but it may still have been long enough that groups developed multi-generational social structures for the care of infants and children. Perhaps *Homo ergaster* mothers might have even helped one another to give birth, just as they (and the males as well) helped one another gather, hunt, and prepare food, activities that are clearly evident in the fossil record.

Along with a larger brain and narrower pelvis than austrolopiths, *Homo ergaster* also had other physiological features with social implications. Their internal organs were small, including those for digestion. Thus, in order to obtain enough energy to survive, they had to eat a diet high in fat and protein, most easily obtainable by eating animals and animal products—insects, reptiles, fish, eggs, and birds along with mammals. Catching some of those animals may have necessitated walking or running significant distances in the hot sun, which is difficult for most mammals because they only lose body heat through panting. *Homo ergaster* probably had the ability to cool down by sweating, a process made easier by the fact that they were relatively hairless. Studies of human body lice support this idea, for our hairy heads support a type of louse found only in humans and our hairy pubic regions another, which we share with other animals. The former is the descendant of the louse we have been home to since our ancestors had hair everywhere, and the latter we picked up from later contacts with other species.

This loss of body hair facilitated cooling (and thus hunting), but it also meant that infants could not cling as easily to their mothers as could those of other primate species. How *Homo ergaster* mothers handled this problem is not evident in the fossil record. Perhaps they did not hunt when they had small children or they left their children briefly, as sites indicate that groups sometimes had a home base to which they returned. Perhaps they devised slings made of plant or animal material to help carry their children, though like any tool made from soft materials these have left no trace.

Another solution to the problem of a short digestive tract is to transfer some digestion outside the body, through cooking. Raw meat is hard to chew and digest, as are many raw plant products; other primates spend many hours a day chewing. Cooking allows an outside source of energy—fire—to do much of this work, breaking down complex carbohydrates and proteins to increase the energy yield of food; it also detoxifies many things that would otherwise be dangerous to eat. There are a few shreds of evidence of fire at early *Homo ergaster* sites, and some scholars, including Richard Wrangham, argue that even without fossil evidence of actual cooking, the larger brains, smaller and less pointed teeth, and shorter guts that developed about 2 million years ago would only have been possible with cooked food. Other scholars see cooking as an invention of hominin species that developed more recently, perhaps beginning around 780,000 BCE, the date of the first widely accepted evidence of controlled fire at a site in Israel. Or perhaps regular use of fire came as late as 400,000 years ago, when hearths become a common part of the archaeological evidence in many areas.

Wherever and whenever it occurred, cooking had enormous social and cultural consequences. Cooking causes chemical and physical reactions that produce thousands of new compounds and make cooked foods more aromatic and more complex in their flavors than raw foods. As descriptions of roasted coffee or chocolate put it, they develop "overtones" or "flavor notes" of completely different things. Because members of the genus *Homo* were omnivores, they may have been genetically predisposed to prefer complex flavors, so that cooked food tasted (and smelled, which is essential in taste) better. Thus cooking led to eating together in a group at a specific time and place, which increased sociability. Because it expands the range of possible foodstuffs, cooking encouraged experimentation in other aspects of food preparation. For example, the site in Israel with the earliest hearths also provides evidence of tools used for cracking nuts and seeds, which expanded the ways they could be eaten. Cooking may also have encouraged symbolic thought, as cooked foods often make us think about something that is not there, and both cooking and eating can be highly ritualized activities. Plus cooking involved fire, which itself has deep meaning in later human cultures.

The evidence for cooking among *Homo ergaster* is very thin, but the evidence for migration is unequivocal. Gradually small groups migrated out of East Africa onto the open plains of Central Africa, and from there into northern Africa. From 1 million to 2 million years ago the earth's climate was in a warming phase, and *Homo ergaster* ranged still farther, moving into western Asia by as early as 1.8 million years ago. Here some developed into a species that many paleontologists call *Homo erectus* ("upright human"), although others see *ergaster* and *erectus* as two names for the same species. (*Homo ergaster* and *Homo erectus* are currently broad and variable species categories, encompassing many subgroups.) They continued to migrate: bones and other materials from China and the island of Java in Indonesia indicate that *Homo erectus* had reached there by about 1.5 million years ago, thus migrating over large landmasses as well as along the coasts. (Sea levels were lower than they are today, and Java could be reached by walking.) *Homo erectus* also walked west, reaching what is now Spain by at least 800,000 years ago, and then further north in Europe. In each of these places, *Homo erectus*

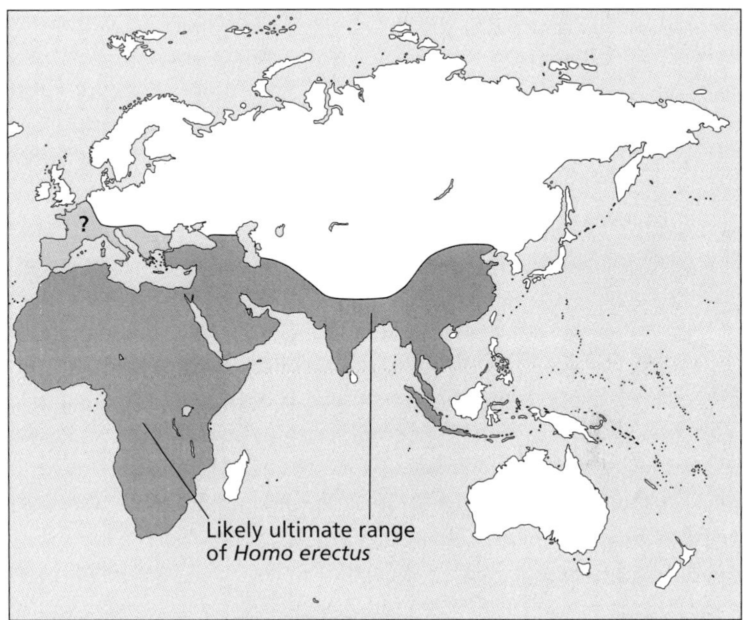

Map 1.1 *Homo ergaster/Homo erectus* migrations

adapted gathering and hunting techniques to the local environment, learning about new sources of plant food and how to best catch local animals.

A *Homo erectus* site in the modern country of Georgia dating from about 1.8 million years ago provides the first evidence of compassion or social concern in the fossil record. One of the skulls recovered was that of an aged man who had lost all but one of his teeth, but lived for a number of years after this. This would only have been possible had those who lived with him helped him.

There is no clear evidence in the fossil record of symbolic thought among *Homo ergaster/erectus*—no decorations, no artwork, no sign of body adornment. Those who take a more expansive view of culture point out, however, that hand axes found over a huge area and a long period of time were symmetrical and uniform, which may simply have been a matter of practicality and usefulness, but may also have represented a conceptualization of what was "good." They were often made in great quantities at a single site, which again may have simply been a practical matter of locations with especially good stone, but suggests some degree of specialization of labor or social roles. At a few of these sites thousands of hand axes remain and a few are far too large to have been tools; might these have been ritual or ceremonial objects, or the maker showing off unusual talent?

Suggestions about social differentiation or culture among *Homo erectus* are very controversial, but those about slightly later species of hominins are a bit less so. One of these was *Homo heidelbergensis*, found throughout much of Afroeurasia between 600,000 and 250,000 years ago, with a brain close to that of modern humans in size. Some built simple shelters, and, as noted above, after 400,000 BCE many sites show evidence of controlled fire. One of these is Terra Amata in what is now southern France, where there were also pieces of red and yellow clay carried in from far away. These were probably used as pigment, again suggesting some notion about what was attractive or important. A bog in Germany has yielded evidence of cooking hearths and the oldest preserved wooden tools (long sharpened wooden spears and what look like wooden handles for stone blades) from about 400,000 years ago, the earliest indication of composite tools. A pit at the bottom of a deep shaft within one of the caves in the Atapuerca region of Spain contains remains of at least twenty-eight individuals, dating from at least 350,000 and perhaps as early as 600,000 years ago. These individuals must have been put there intentionally after they died, which makes Sima de los Huesos (the pit of bones) the earliest known site of burial, a practice with huge cultural implications. At a site in Kenya, archaeologists have found disks of ostrich eggshell from about 280,000 years ago with holes bored in them, so that they could have been worn on a strand, and in Israel archeologists discovered what some argue is the first evidence of artistic production—a small stone shaped like a female torso, from about 230,000 years ago.

The group at Sima de los Huesos appears to have been the ancestors of the most famous non-*Homo sapiens* species of hominins, the Neanderthals (named after the Neander Valley in Germany, where their remains were first discovered). Neanderthals lived throughout Europe and western Asia beginning about

170,000 years ago, thus initially alongside *Homo heidelbergensis*. They had brains as large as those of modern humans, although dental evidence suggests that they matured earlier, so had a period of dependence on others—and thus perhaps of learning—shorter than ours. They used complex tools, including spears and scrapers for animal skins, that enabled them to survive in the diverse environments and climates in which their bones have been found, from the shores of the Mediterranean to Siberia. Judging by wear and tear on skeletal remains, both males and females engaged in the same type of hard physical labor, and died at similar ages. They built free-standing houses, and controlled fire in hearths, where they cooked animals, including large mammals (as evidenced by stable isotope analysis) and many kinds of plants (as evidenced by their tooth plaque). Their tools appear to have changed somewhat over time, and show signs of being made in several stages, not just on the spot as need required. Thus Neanderthals exhibited technological inventiveness and long-range planning, characteristics that scholars such as Francesco d'Errico have described as part of "behaviorial modernity," even if anatomically they were not *Homo sapiens*.

Evidence from one 50,000-year-old Neanderthal site in Spain has yielded intriguing suggestions about Neanderthal society. Here twelve individuals of various ages appear to have been killed and eaten by another group, during a period—judging by the tooth enamel of the victims—of food scarcity. DNA evidence shows that these twelve individuals were related, and that the adult males were more closely related than the females. Thus the men had most likely stayed with their birth family, while the women had come from other families, a pattern that would be replicated later among *Homo sapiens* of many eras and places. Two of the children were offspring of the same woman, and were about three years apart in age; this birth interval, perhaps the result of long breast-feeding, is also something that would be replicated among many later foragers. This site provides an unusual opportunity to glimpse Neanderthal social relationships, both hostile and caring.

Materials unearthed in many locations also indicate that Neanderthals sometimes buried their dead carefully, and occasionally decorated objects and themselves with red ochre, a form of colored clay. Burial and body decoration seem so characteristic of modern

1.2 Sculpted model of a female Neanderthal, based on anatomy from fossils and DNA evidence, which reveals some Neanderthals carried genes for red hair and blue eyes. The artists chose the facial expression they did to reflect the harsh conditions of life, and added decorative body painting because lumps of pigment have often been found at Neanderthal sites.

humans that Neanderthals were originally categorized as a branch of *Homo sapiens*, but DNA evidence from Neanderthal bones now indicates that they were a separate species that developed from a different line of *Homo erectus* than we did.

In the last few years, DNA evidence has also been used to provide further details about non-*Homo sapiens* hominins. It suggests, for example, that Neanderthals and *Homo sapiens* occasionally had sex with one another, for between 1 and 4 percent of the DNA in modern humans living outside of Africa likely came from Neanderthals. Bones and teeth dating from about 40,000 years ago found in the Denisova cave in Siberia in 2010 have yielded DNA that is distinct from both Neanderthals and *Homo sapiens*, although the Denisovans also shared some genetic material with both groups, thus suggesting that they interbred with them. Whether they also shared social organization or ideas is not revealed by anything remaining at the site.

The last evidence of Neanderthals as a separate species comes from about 30,000 years ago, and until very recently they were thought to be the last living hominins that were not *Homo sapiens*. In 2003, however, archaeologists on the Indonesian island of Flores discovered bones and tools of three-foot-tall hominids that dated from only about 18,000 years ago, which they nicknamed "hobbits." (Lawyers for the Tolkien estate are trying to block the use of that nickname to describe these small individuals, arguing that it is copyrighted.) They appear to be a distinct species, probably descended from *Homo erectus* just as were Neanderthals, and to have lived on the island for more than 800,000 years. Like the DNA evidence from Siberia, the physical evidence from Flores has just begun to be interpreted and has occasioned much controversy, but few dispute that these and other recent finds demonstrate that the human evolutionary path is more complex and multi-branched than we used to recognize, more of a bush than a pine tree.

THINKING HUMANS

Neanderthals, Denisovans, *Homo floresienses* and other species and sub-species of hominins not discussed above or yet to be discovered, classified, and named lived in many parts of Afroeurasia. A few scientists think that *Homo sapiens* ("thinking humans") evolved from several of these branches, but the majority think that, like hominid evolution from earlier primates, this occurred only in Africa. The evidence is partly archaeological, but also genetic. One type of DNA, called mitochondrial DNA, is inherited through the maternal line and can be traced far back in time. Mitochondrial DNA indicates that modern humans are so similar genetically that they cannot have been evolving for the last million or 2 million years, but only for about 250,000 years or perhaps even as little as 200,000 years. Because there is greater human genetic variety today in Africa than in other parts of the world, the evidence also suggests that *Homo sapiens* have lived there the longest, so that Africa is where they first emerged and all modern humans are descended from a relatively small group in East Africa. (Picking up on the biblical story of the first humans, some scientists have given the name Mitochondrial Eve to the most recent common matrilineal ancestor from whom all living humans are descended.)

Archaeologists distinguish *Homo sapiens* from other hominins by a number of anatomical features, most notably a relatively slender build, a head with a large cranium (and forebrain) with a face tucked underneath this, small teeth and jaws, and a larynx situated lower in the throat. The earliest fossilized remains showing these features come from two sites in Ethiopia, and have been most recently dated as about 195,000 and 160,000 years old. The younger of these two finds includes skulls that had been deliberately polished, a mortuary practice that several scholars have interpreted as evidence of ritualizing or decoration, and thus perhaps of symbolic thought. The tools found with these skulls are not very different from those found with other hominins, however, nor are those found at other early *Homo sapiens* sites.

This disjuncture between anatomy and tools has led to sharp disputes among paleontologists and archaeologists about the process of human evolution at this key point. One group, including Richard Klein and Chris Stringer, asserts that although early *Homo sapiens* were *anatomically* modern, they were not *behaviorally* modern. Behavioral modernity, which they see as including long-range planning, rapid development of new technologies such as the bow and arrow, behaviors to deal with changing environments, wide use of symbols in burials and personal adornment, and broad networks of social and economic exchange, developed only about 50,000 years ago, in what is termed the Upper Paleolithic or Later Stone Age. At this point there was a "cognitive revolution"—sometimes dubbed the "Human Revolution" by those who take this position—a sudden flowering of creative activity within one small group that led to symbolic thought and then to everything else that is part of behavioral modernity. This may have been the result of a random, but selectively advantageous, genetic mutation that increased the mental capacity for syntactic language, allowing this group to take full advantage of changes in the vocal tract through which speech could be produced. Historical linguists such as Christopher Ehret see oral language as the key driver of this dramatic change rather than one of its results, noting that changes in vocal tract configuration and facial musculature about 70,000 years ago allowed the intricate manipulation of consonantal and vowel sounds that is human speech. (These and a few other small anatomical changes are what led paleontologists to differentiate this group as a sub-species: *Homo sapiens sapiens*.) Linguistic evidence suggests that human languages all descend from a small cluster of interacting languages that emerged first in Africa. Language developed in tandem with new technologies, in this point of view, and is what really allowed modern human behavior to develop.

In opposition to those arguing for a sudden and quite recent cognitive or language "revolution" are those who take more gradualist views. Among these are scholars such as Gamble who find symbolic thought evident in material objects, bodily gestures, and social relationships that long preceded speech, and those such as d'Errico who suggest that some "modern" behavior can be found among Neanderthals. The archaeologists Sally McBrearty and Alison Brooks—among others—take a slightly less expansive view, but still assert that evidence of everything labeled "behaviorally modern" emerges gradually in different parts of Africa over the Middle Stone Age, the period from about 250,000 years ago to about 50,000 years ago. For example, pieces of obsidian (a volcanic rock favored for its ability to take and hold a sharp edge) found at Sanzako in northern Tanzania in a site dating from 100,000–130,000 years ago came from more than 300 km away, suggesting that the group at Sanzako traded for this stone rather than traveling that long distance to collect it. Red ochre and ochre-stained stones on which it was ground to make pigment date from sites in Israel, Morocco, and South Africa older than 100,000 years ago (and perhaps much older). In caves near the coast of southern Africa, archaeologists have found shells with holes bored in them (suggesting they were worn as beads), stone tools that had been hardened in a fire through a multi-stage process to keep an edge better, and pieces of ochre with a cross-hatched pattern cut into them, all of which date from around 75,000 years ago. Thus there are indications of trade, long-range planning, and symbols developing separately in different parts of Africa, and then gradually assembled into the modern human cognitive and material toolkit.

Although both revolutionaries and gradualists view social and cultural matters as key *markers* of behavioral modernity, the gradualists (and to some degree the historical linguists) tend to see social and cultural factors as possible *causes* for the growth in brain complexity and symbolic thought, or at least for the better survival of hominins that exhibited this. Thus they see the development of cognition as a cultural as well as a neurological process. Some of this operated at the individual level: Individuals who had better social skills were more likely to mate than those who did not — this has been observed in chimpanzees and, of course, in humans from more recent periods — and thus to pass on their genetic material, creating what biologists term selective pressure that favored the more socially adept. For humans, being socially adept includes being able to understand the motivations of others—that is, recognizing that they have internal lives that drive their actions. Such social skills were particularly important for females: Because the period when human infants are dependent on others is so long, mothers with good social networks to assist them were more likely to have infants who survived. Cooperative child rearing required social skills and adaptability, and may itself have been an impetus to increasing complexity in the brain. Selective pressure may have also operated in the realm of language. As we know from contemporary research on the brain, learning language promotes the development of specific areas of the brain. Neurological research thus supports the argument of paleolinguists that gradually increasing complexity in language led to more complex thought processes, as well as the other way around.

Some of these social and cultural factors operated at the group level: As it developed, speech and other forms of communication allowed for stronger networks of cooperation among kin groups and the formation of larger social groupings. Family bands that were more socially adept had more contacts with other bands, and developed patterns of exchange over longer distances, which, as with trade in later periods, gave them access to a wider range of products and ways of using them and thus greater flexibility to meet any challenges to survival, including dramatic changes in climate. This was also the case with less utilitarian products, such as pigments and beads, which might have stimulated better forms of communication and higher levels of creativity as well as reflecting these. As Marcia-Anne Dobres and others have pointed out, new technologies and ways of using them were (and are) invented not simply to solve problems or address material needs, but also to foster social activities, convey world views, gain prestige, and express the makers' ideas and sense of identity.

At the moment, the archaeological record, particularly of human remains, in Afroeurasia for the key period from about 100,000 to about 50,000 years ago is sparse. Further research in many fields—including neurology, comparative linguistics, and genetics as well as archaeology—will no doubt provide firmer support for the revolutionary or gradualist perspective, or perhaps allow them to be combined.

Genetic evidence has already shown that human evolution is not the story of steady and inevitable progress that the developments related above might make it appear to be. About 70,000 BCE, so about the time oral symbolic language seems to have been initially developing, the total population of the ancestors of all people living today shrank to about 10,000 people, and perhaps to only a few thousand. One proposed explanation for this genetic bottleneck was a volcanic mega-explosion near today's Lake Toba in Indonesia, which led, according to some scholars, to a multi-year volcanic winter that drastically reduced food sources and thus the hominin (and animal) population. Another explanation is more cultural and social: perhaps the *Homo sapiens* that were beginning to use symbolic language were increasingly picky about mates, choosing them from only among other language users rather than from among all *Homo sapiens* in an early example of the endogamy that would become such a common feature of later human groups. Or these two could have operated together, with both climate change and intentional endogamy reducing the genetic stock.

However and whenever behaviorally modern humans emerged, at just about the time of the Toba explosion *Homo sapiens* were doing what *Homo ergaster* did before them and what they have done ever since: moving. First across Africa, and then into Eurasia, initially sporadically and then more regularly. They used rafts or boats to reach what is now Australia by at least 50,000 years ago and perhaps earlier, which required traveling across nearly 40 miles of ocean even when sea levels were at their lowest during the last ice age. By 20,000 years ago humans were living in northern Siberia above the Arctic Circle, and by at least 15,000 years ago they had walked across the land bridges then linking Siberia and North America at the Bering Strait and had crossed into the Americas. Because by 14,000 years ago humans were already in southern South America, 10,000 miles from the land bridges, many scholars now think that people came to the Americas much earlier, perhaps 20,000 or even 30,000 years ago, using rafts or boats along the coasts when water prevented walking.

Homo sapiens moved into areas where there were already other types of hominins. This included Neanderthals, who appear to have lived side by side with the immigrants in Europe and western Asia for millennia, hunting the same types of animals and gathering the same types of plants. Eventually the Neanderthals may have all been killed, or they may simply have lost the competition for food as the climate worsened in a period of increasing glaciation that began around 40,000 years ago. So far no evidence of interactions between *Homo sapiens* and any other hominin group has been discovered (other than DNA), but we know the outcome: *Homo sapiens* survived, others did not. The rest of this book is thus the story of these thinking humans.

African: L, L1, L2, L3
Near Eastern: J, N
Southern European: J, K
General European: H, V
Northern European: T, U, X
Asian: A, B, C, D, E, F, G (*M is composed of C, D, E, and G*)
Native American: A, B, C, D, and sometimes X

Map 1.2 DNA evidence of global *Homo sapiens* migration

FORAGING LIFEWAYS

The final retreat of the glaciers occurred between 15,000 and 10,000 years ago, and with the melting of glaciers sea levels rose. Parts of the world that had been linked by land bridges, including North America and Asia as well as many parts of Southeast Asia, became separated by water. This cut off migratory paths, but also spurred innovation. Humans designed and built ever more sophisticated boats and learned how to navigate by studying wind and current patterns, bird flights, and the position of the stars. They sailed to increasingly remote islands, including those in the Pacific, the last parts of the globe to be settled. The western Pacific islands were inhabited by about 2000 BCE, and other island groups long after this; the traditional dating of the first settlements of Hawai'i,

Rapa Nui (Easter Island), and New Zealand put these in the last half of the first millennium CE, but more recent studies suggest that these may have been as late as the thirteenth century CE. In areas where food resources were rich, such as along seacoasts, people built structures and lived relatively permanently in one place.

Eventually human cultures became widely diverse, but in the Paleolithic period people throughout the world lived in ways that were similar to one another, in small groups of related individuals—what anthropologists often refer to as "bands" —who moved through the landscape in search of food. Paleolithic peoples have often been called hunter-gatherers, but recent archaeological and anthropological research indicates that both historical and contemporary hunter-gatherers have depended much more on gathered foods than on hunted meat. Thus it would be more accurate to call them "gatherer-hunters," and most scholars now call them foragers, a term that highlights the flexibility and adaptability in their search for food. Most of what foragers ate was plants, and much of the animal protein in their diet came from foods gathered or scavenged rather than hunted directly: insects, shellfish, small animals caught in traps, fish and other sea creatures caught in weirs and nets, and animals killed by other predators. Gathering and hunting probably varied in importance seasonally or from year to year depending on environmental factors and the decisions of the group.

Paleolithic peoples did hunt large game. Groups working together forced animals over cliffs, threw spears, and, beginning about 17,000 BCE, used bows and atlatls—notched throwing sticks made of bone, wood, or antler—to launch arrows and barbs with flint points bound to wooden shafts so that they could stand farther away from their prey while hunting. The warming climate that accompanied the final retreat of the glaciers was less favorable to the very large mammals that had roamed the open spaces of many parts of the world. Wooly mammoths, mastodons, and wooly rhinos all died out in Eurasia in this megafaunal extinction, as did camels, horses, and sloths in the Americas and giant kangaroos and wombats in Australia. In many places, these extinctions occurred just about the time that modern humans appeared, and increasing numbers of scientists think that they were at least in part caused by human hunting.

Most foraging societies that exist today or did so until recently have some type of division of labor by sex, and also by age, with children and older people responsible for different tasks than adult men and women. Men are more often responsible for hunting, through which they gain prestige as well as meat, and women for gathering plant and animal products. This has led scholars to assume that in Paleolithic society men were also responsible for hunting, and women for gathering. Human remains provide some evidence for this, as skeletons and teeth indicate the type of tasks the person did while they were alive. At Chinchorro on the north coast of Chile, for example, male skeletons from the period 7000–2000 BCE often show bone growths in the ears, the result of diving in the cold coastal waters for seals and shellfish (today this condition is called "surfer's ear"), while female skeletons show changes in the ankle bones resulting from prolonged squatting, perhaps to process the marine products or gather and process terrestrial foods. Such a division of labor is not universal, however: in some of the world's foraging peoples, such as the Agta of the Philippines, women hunt large game, and in numerous others women are involved in certain types of hunting, such as driving herds of animals toward a cliff or compound or throwing nets over them. Where women hunt, they either carry their children in slings or leave them with other family members, suggesting that cultural norms, rather than the biology of lactation, is the basis for male hunting. In many Paleolithic sites male and female skeletons show little evidence of sexually differentiated work, and the stone and bone tools that remain from the Paleolithic period give no clear evidence of who used them. The division of labor was most likely flexible, particularly during periods of scarcity, and also changed over time.

Both hunted and gathered foods were cooked, generally by roasting them directly over or near a fire or placing them in a pit-oven along with heated stones or smoldering wood. Grains and nuts were ground, mixed with water, and baked on stones into flat breads, the earliest direct evidence of which comes from about 30,000 years ago; later grinding became a women's task in almost all of the world's societies, but there is less evidence for this in the Paleolithic. Cooking stones, which have been found at some Paleolithic sites and continued to be used into recent times by some groups, may have also been put in bags made from animal skins along with liquids and other ingredients, thus introducing a new method of cooking—boiling. That new method was made easier with the invention of clay pots, themselves "roasted" in a fire at a temperature high enough to make them watertight. The earliest surviving example of a fired clay object is a figurine of a woman from today's Czech Republic that dates from about 29,000 BCE (about which more below), but fired clay pots have been found in Japan that date from about 15,000 BCE, and China and eastern Russia from somewhat after that. These were made either in an open fire or more likely in a pit that was filled with combustible materials, somewhat covered, and set on fire. Cooking in bags with heated stones (and later with fired clay balls that served the same function) or in pots expanded the repertoire of possible foodstuffs to those that were too hard to process or eat otherwise, including legumes and certain kinds of grains and shellfish. It also provided those who did not have good (or any) teeth, such as infants and the elderly, with softer foods.

Because organic materials from the Paleolithic survive only very rarely, it is difficult to speculate about clothing and other soft material goods, although bone needles for sewing and awls for punching holes in leather can give us some indications. Clothing and headgear were often decorated with beads made from shells, ivory, teeth, and other hard materials, and from the placement of these in undisturbed burials archaeologists can see that the clothing of men and women was often different, as was clothing in some places at different stages of life. Thus gender and age had a social meaning.

The oldest direct evidence of weaving comes from the same area of the Czech Republic that has yielded the earliest fired clay, and is itself clay: fragments with impressions of knotted cordage and woven basketry or cloth made of plant fibre, dating from around 30,000 years ago. (Some scholars suggest that the 75,000-year-old cross-hatched pattern in pieces of ochre found in South Africa mentioned above also represents netting, though it is not an impression made by an actual net.) Along with clothing and bags, weaving, plaiting, and cording (twisting plant fibres together to make string and rope) may have been used to make nets and snares that were

1.3 The Venus of Brassempouy, a small head carved from mammoth ivory carved about 25,000 years ago in what is now southern France. The decoration on the head is usually interpreted as a patterned hood, or perhaps a representation of netting or woven cloth.

more delicate than those that could be made out of leather or sinew, and to make slings to carry infants. Weaving, plaiting, and cording were developed independently in many parts of the world, as objects made of materials that have survived demonstrate: ivory objects show textile motifs; clay figurines wear clothing and headgear; the placement of beads and ornaments found in burials shows they were originally strung on corded necklaces or sewn onto clothing.

Obtaining and processing food was a constant preoccupation, but it was not a constant job. Studies of recent foragers indicate that, other than in times of environmental disasters such as prolonged droughts, people need only about ten to twenty hours a week to gather food and carry out the other tasks needed to survive, such as processing food, locating water, and building shelters. The diet of foragers is varied and—especially compared to today's diet of highly processed foods loaded with fat, sugar, and salt—nutritious: low in fat and salt, high in fiber, and rich in vitamins and minerals. The slow pace of life and healthy diet did not mean that Paleolithic life spans approached those of the modern world, however. People avoided such contemporary killers as heart disease and diabetes, but studies of skeletal remains indicate that they often died at young ages from injuries, infections, animal attacks, and interpersonal violence. Mothers and infants died in childbirth, and many children died before they reached adulthood.

Total human population thus grew slowly during the Paleolithic, to perhaps half a million about 30,000 years ago. By about 10,000 years ago this number had grown to 5 million — ten times as many people. This was a significant increase, but it took 20,000 years. (By contrast, the earth's population today is more than 7 billion; it was slightly under one billion a mere three hundred years ago.) The low population density meant that human impact on the environment was relatively small, although still significant.

FAMILY, KINSHIP, AND ETHNICITY

Small bands of humans — twenty or thirty people was a standard size for foragers in harsh environments — were scattered across broad areas, but this did not mean that each group lived in isolation. Their travels in search of food brought them into contact with one another, not simply for talking, celebrating, and feasting, but also for providing opportunities for the exchange of sexual partners, which was essential to group survival. Today we understand that having sexual relations with close relatives is disadvantageous because it creates greater risk of genetic disorders. Earlier societies did not have knowledge of genetics, but most of them developed rules against sexual relations among immediate family members, and sometimes very complex rules about allowable partners among more distant relatives. Some natural scientists argue that incest taboos have a biological or instinctual basis, while most anthropologists see them as cultural, arising from desires to lessen intergroup rivalries or increase opportunities for alliances with other lineages. Whatever the reasons, people sought mates outside their own band, and bands became linked by bonds of kinship, which in a few places has been traced through the study of bone chemistry. Mating arrangements varied in their permanence, but many groups seem to have developed a somewhat permanent arrangement whereby a person—more often a woman than a man—left her or his original group and joined the group of a mate, what would later be termed marriage. Judging by later ethnographic parallels, how kin groups were defined and understood varied tremendously, but they remained significant power structures for millennia, and in some areas still have influence over major aspects of life, such as an individual's job or marital partner.

Stereotypical representations of Paleolithic people often portray a powerful fur-clad man holding a club and dragging off a (usually attractive) fur-clad woman by her hair, or men going off to hunt while women and children crouch around a fire, waiting for the men to bring back great slabs of meat. Studies of the relative importance of gathering to hunting, women's participation in hunting, and gender relations among contemporary foraging peoples have led some analysts to turn these stereotypes on their heads. They see Paleolithic bands as egalitarian groups in which the contributions of men and women to survival were recognized and valued, and in which both men and women had equal access to the limited amount of resources held by the group. This may also be a stereotype, overly romanticizing Paleolithic society as a sort of vegetarian commune. Social relations among foragers were not as hierarchical as they were in other types of societies, but many foraging groups from more recent periods had one person who held more power than others, and that person was almost always a man. In fact, anthropologists who study such groups call them "Big Man" societies. This debate about gender relations is often part of larger discussions about whether Paleolithic society — and by implication "human nature" — was primarily peaceful and nurturing or violent and brutal, and whether these qualities are gender-related. Like much else about the Paleolithic, sources about gender and about violence are fragmentary and difficult to interpret; there may simply have been a diversity of patterns, as there is among more modern foragers.

Whether peaceful and egalitarian, violent and hierarchical, or somewhere in between, heterosexual relations produced children, who were fed as infants by their mothers or by another woman who had recently given birth. Breast milk was the only food available that infants could easily digest, so mothers nursed their children for several years. Along with providing food for infants, extended nursing brings a side benefit: it suppresses ovulation and thus acts as a contraceptive. Foraging groups needed children to survive, but too many could tax scarce food resources. Many groups may have practiced selective infanticide or abandonment. They may also have exchanged children of different ages with other groups, which further deepened kinship connections between groups. Other than for feeding, children were most likely cared for by other male and female members of the group as well as by their mothers, as they are in modern foraging cultures.

Within each band, and within the larger kin group, individuals had a variety of identities; they were simultaneously fathers, sons, husbands, and brothers, or mothers, daughters, wives, and sisters. Each of these identities was relational (parent to child, sibling to sibling, spouse to spouse), and some of them, especially parent to child, gave one power over others. Along with age, gender, and position in a family, people were also no doubt differentiated by personal qualities such as intelligence, courage, and charisma. Burials provide evidence of social differentiation and social connections. The people who buried a young adult woman near Bordeaux in southern France about 19,000 years ago, for example, dressed her in clothing, covered her with ochre pigment, and placed her in a container made of stone slabs, along with a few perforated shells, a bead, some tools made of bone and stone, bones of antelope and reindeer, and 71 red deer canine teeth that had holes drilled in them for stringing and may have been on a necklace. Red deer did not live near Bordeaux at this time of worsening climate, so the teeth had most likely been brought there over many years through networks of exchange, perhaps given as gifts in marriages or in trade for other goods. Something about this young woman or her death led those who buried her to decide to include so many valuable grave goods; through this they referenced both her individual identity (and perhaps high social position) and her links to a social network that ranged across time and space.

Bands of foragers may have been exogamous, but as humans spread out over much of the globe, kin groups and larger networks of interrelated people often became isolated from one another, and people mated only within this larger group. Thus local exogamy was accompanied by endogamy at a larger scale, and over many generations humans came to develop differences in physical features, including skin and hair color, eye and body shape, and amount of body hair, although genetically there is less variety among them than among chimpanzees. Language also changed over generations, so that thousands of different languages were eventually spoken; more than eight hundred have been identified, for example, in contemporary Papua New Guinea alone. Groups created widely varying cultures and passed them on to their children, further increasing diversity among humans.

Over time, groups of various sizes came to understand themselves as linked by shared kinship and culture, and as different from other groups. Words were devised to describe such groups, which in English include people, ethnic group, tribe, race, and nation. Shared culture included language, religion, foodways, rituals, clothing styles, and many other factors, whose importance in defining membership in the group changed over time (though language was almost always important). Because of extensive intermarriage within the group over many generations, the differences between groups were (and are) sometimes evident in the body, and were (and are) often conceptualized as blood, a substance with deep meaning. Kinship ties included perceived and invented ones, however, as adoption and other methods were devised to bring someone into the group, or traditions developed of descent from a common ancestor. At the heart of all such groups was a conscious common identity, which itself enhanced endogamy as people chose (or were required) to marry within the group. These groups came into being, died out, morphed into other groups, split, combined, lost and gained in significance, and in other ways changed, but their fluidity and the fact that they were constructed through culture as well as genetics does not make them any less real. They came to have enormous significance later in world history, but developed before the invention of writing and appear to have been everywhere. No doubt the people who traced their hands on the Cueva de los Manos had a word to describe their own group, and to distinguish themselves from those not in the group.

RITUALS

Like painting the Cueva de los Manos, the burial of the young woman in southern France was a social occasion, but it was also a way to express ideas and beliefs about the material world and perhaps an unseen world beyond. Paleolithic mortuary rituals created social and political messages, and conveyed (and possibly distorted) cultural meaning. (As have funerals ever since.) They marked membership in a group, which might have been understood to continue after death took one from the realm of the living. Bodies were handled in a wide variety of ways: buried upright, prone or flexed, alone or with others, and with widely varying grave goods; placed in jars, under the floors of houses, or in locations far away; defleshed, beheaded, or the bones disarticulated, with some parts (especially the skull) placed somewhere else in a second ritual; painted, plastered, covered in ash or ochre. What these all meant is hard to determine, but they must have meant *something*, as it took time and effort to treat the deceased in whatever way was considered appropriate. Archaeologists often mark the spatial or chronological boundary between one group and another by differences in the style of burial. Together with paintings and decorated objects, burials suggest that people thought of their world as extending beyond the visible. People, animals, plants, natural occurrences, and other things around them had spirits, an animistic understanding of the spiritual nature and interdependence of all things. The unseen world regularly intervened in the visible world, for good and ill, and the actions of dead ancestors and the spirits could be shaped by living people.

Rock art from around the world and a wide array of ethnographic evidence suggests that ordinary people were thought to learn about the unseen world through dreams and portents, while messages and revelations were also sent more regularly to shamans, spiritually adept men and women who communicated with or traveled to the unseen world. Shamans created complex rituals through which they sought to ensure the health and prosperity of an individual, family, or group. These included rituals with gender and sexual imagery, and shamans in some places may have constructed a transgender role through which they harnessed power that crossed gender boundaries, just as they crossed the boundary between the seen and unseen world. Many cave paintings show groups of prey or predator animals, and several include a masked human figure usually judged to be a shaman in a gesture or pose assumed to be some sort of ritual. Sometimes the shaman is shown with what looks like a penis, and such figures used to be invariably described as men. More recently the suggestion has been made that these figures may have been *gendered* male, but could have been a woman wearing a costume, as gender inversions are often part of many types of rituals and performances. Or the figure—and the actual shaman who it may have represented—was understood as a third gender, neither male nor female, or both at the same time. Shamans in many cultures wore masks that gave them added power, and were understood to take on the qualities of the animal, creature, or spirit represented by the mask; transcending boundaries was thus their role. They also operated as healers; burials of individuals assumed to be shamans often include bundles of plant, animal, and mineral products, which were eaten, sniffed, or rubbed on the skin, most likely in conjunction with chants, songs, and prescribed movements. Judging by practices from later periods, the rituals and medicines through which shamans and healers operated were often closely guarded secrets, but they were passed orally from one spiritually adept individual to another. Gradually they built a body of knowledge about the natural world, as well as how best to communicate with supernatural forces.

Interpreting what certain objects that appear to have ritual purposes might have meant to those who made or possessed them is just as contentious as other aspects of early human history. For example, small stone, ivory, bone, or clay figures of women, often with enlarged breasts, buttocks, and/or stomach, dating from the later Paleolithic period (roughly 33,000–9,000 BCE) have been found in many parts of Europe. These were dubbed "Venus figures" by nineteenth-century archaeologists, who thought they represented Paleolithic standards of female beauty just as the goddess Venus represented classical standards. Some scholars have interpreted them, as well as later Neolithic figurines of women, as fertility goddesses, evidence of people's beliefs in a powerful female deity. Others view them as aids to fertility, carried around by women hoping to have children—or perhaps hoping not to have more. Perhaps they were made by women looking at their own bodies in mid-life, with the rounded form of most women who have given birth, and represent hopes for good health during aging. Or they

1.4 Paleolithic rock art from Tanzania shows shamans somersaulting over animals. The dotted and hatched lines may represent visual hallucinations, and the animals might also be visions seen in a trance rather than real prey.

were sexualized images of women carried around by men, a sort of Paleolithic version of the centerfold in a men's magazine. Or perhaps, taking into account the emphasis in cultural history on multiple and shifting meanings, they might have represented different things to different people. Small clay figurines of women from Mesoamerica and coastal Ecuador in the second millenium BCE have been similarly interpreted in a range of ways: as fertility emblems, ritual objects, models of sexuality, and aids to pregnancy.

In both the Old World and the New, figurines of women—and of men or people whose gender is not clearly indicated, along with animals and animal/human hybrids—have most commonly been found in household debris, which suggests that domestic and ritual spaces were not separate from one another. Instead, ordinary actions were ritualized, that is, carried out as performances with certain conventions and formality that gave them added meaning. Paleolithic rituals might have involved special locations and objects, but they also involved the materials of everyday life, such as food, tools, or the materials out of which houses were made, and took place in the house or in unaltered places in the landscape.

Ascribing ritual purposes to ordinary objects does not mean that these do not reflect other aspects of life as well. The painted, carved, and otherwise decorated objects and locations from the later Paleolithic are also products of imagination, reason, pride, mischievousness, and a range of emotions (including boredom). The body itself could be a canvas for social and cultural values, as skeletons and corpses whose skin and hair have been preserved show bodily modifications of all types: piercings, tattooing, removal of various parts, binding, scarification, tooth filing, elongation, skull deformations, and others. The body of a man frozen in the Alps from about 5300 years ago, for example, has both pierced ears and tattoos. (The latter may have been done in part for therapeutic reasons, as the tattoos are in locations on the spine, knees and ankles often used for acupuncture.) Objects modified in a particular way or by talented individuals—what we might now call "luxuries" or "art"—conveyed status and prestige, which is why they show up in burials or the mounds of refuse left from feasts.

Funerals, feasts, and other public occasions were events where certain individuals could show off their wealth (and generosity) to a large audience, but they were also times during which community leaders could stress social cohesion and egalitarianism. Using ethnographic parallels, scholars stress that egalitarian social systems are not "simpler" than hierarchical ones, nor are they "natural," but require complex social rules and their continual reinforcement to maintain.

SEDENTISM AND DOMESTICATION

Foraging remained the basic way of life for most of human history, and for groups living in extreme environments, such as tundras or deserts, it was the only possible way to survive. In some places, however, the natural environment provided enough food that people could become more settled. Moderate temperatures and abundant rainfall allowed for verdant plant growth; or seas, rivers, and lakes provided substantial amounts of fish and shellfish. About 15,000 years ago, as the earth's climate entered a warming phase, more parts of the world were able to support sedentary or semi-sedentary groups of foragers. Archaeological sites in many places begin to include storage pits, bins, and other sorts of containers, as well as grindstones and the skeletons of rats and mice who also ate stored food. They show evidence that people were intensifying their work to get more food from the surrounding area, preparing a wide range of foods out of hundreds of different ingredients, acquiring more objects, and building more permanent housing.

Sedentism used to be seen as a result of the plant and animal domestication that scholars use to separate the Neolithic from the Paleolithic, but in many places it preceded intentional crop-raising by thousands of years, so the primary line of causation runs the other way: people began to raise crops because they were living in permanent communities. Thus people were "domesticated" before plants and animals were. They developed socio-economic and socio-political structures for village life, such as ways to handle disputes or to make decisions about community resources, which they then adapted when they changed their subsistence strategies to agriculture.

The archaeological site of Hallan Çemi in what is now eastern Turkey provides a good example of these developments. About

11,000 years ago, people here were foragers: they ate wild sheep and goats, along with wild plants including almonds, pistachios, and legumes. These were abundant enough to support a small permanent village, and the people built houses, but in contrast to the normal living arrangements of groups of foragers, the entrances to these faced away from the central communal space. Thus they would have given the families who lived in them some degree of privacy. The inhabitants of Hallan Çemi also built several larger structures, with hearths and benches and floors that they replastered many times. These buildings contained fragments of imported copper and obsidian, and in one of them an aurochs skull was hung on the wall facing the entrance. These buildings could have held many members of the community for public events over a number of years, and the aurochs skull suggests that these events included rituals. Those events certainly included feasting, as decorated stone bowls, sculpted pestles, and burnt animal bones appear in great numbers, suggesting ritualized preparation and consumption of food and drink. The feasts appear to have been so large, in fact, that they must have included people living in other communities, perhaps those who facilitated the trade in copper and obsidian, though whether these feasts were designed to promote cooperation with other communities or competition with them is impossible to tell from the evidence. (And they might have done both.) Along with bowls and pestles, residents also made small stone batons that were notched in what look like tallies. Michael Rosenberg, who has closely studied this site, suggests that these could be counts of things done, things given, or perhaps things owned. Whatever they represent, the fact that something is being formally counted is a departure from the more egalitarian and reciprocal norms common among foragers. Thus, in this foraging village, there are clear indications of some type of social differentiation and sociopolitical structures beyond the kin group, along with cultural norms to support these.

Eastern Turkey is within the part of the world in which sedentary villagers first began intentional crop-planting—the area archaeologists call the Fertile Crescent, which runs from present-day Lebanon, Israel, and Jordan north to Turkey and then south to the Iran–Iraq border. At just about the time the villagers of Hallan Çemi were building their houses and public buildings, residents of other villages began to use the digging sticks, hoes, and other tools with which they gathered wild wheat and barley to plant the seeds of these crops, along with seeds of legumes such as peas and lentils, and of the flax with which they made linen cloth. They selected the seeds they planted in order to get crops that had favorable characteristics, such as larger edible parts or kernels clustered together that ripened all at one time and did not just fall on the ground, qualities that made harvesting more efficient. Through this human intervention, certain crops became domesticated, modified by selective breeding so as to serve human needs. Archaeologists trace the development and spread of plant-raising by noting when the seeds and other plant parts they discover show evidence of domestication.

By about 9000 BCE, many villages in the Fertile Crescent were growing domesticated crops, and a similar process—first sedentism, then domestication—happened elsewhere as well. By about 8000 BCE, people were growing sorghum and millet in parts of the Nile River Valley, and perhaps yams in western Africa. By about 7000 BCE, they were growing domesticated rice, millet, and legumes in China, yams and taro in Papua New Guinea, and perhaps squash in Mesoamerica. In each of these places, crop-raising occurred independently, and it may have happened in other parts of the world as well. Archaeological evidence does not survive well in tropical areas like Southeast Asia and the Amazon Basin, which may have been additional sites of plant domestication. Within several centuries of initial crop-planting, people in the Fertile Crescent, parts of China, and the Nile Valley were relying on domesticated food products alone. Farming increased the division of labor within communities, as families and households became increasingly interdependent, trading food products for other commodities or services.

Farming villages were closer together than were communities of foragers, and in many places the division of labor between communities grew as well, as local, regional, and sometimes long-distance trade networks handled a growing variety of commodities. These included raw materials such as obsidian and jade that could be made into utilitarian, ceremonial, and decorative items, and metals, including gold, silver, copper, and lead, which were hammered into beads and other jewelry. By about 5500 BCE people in the Balkans had learned that copper could be extracted from ore by heating it in a

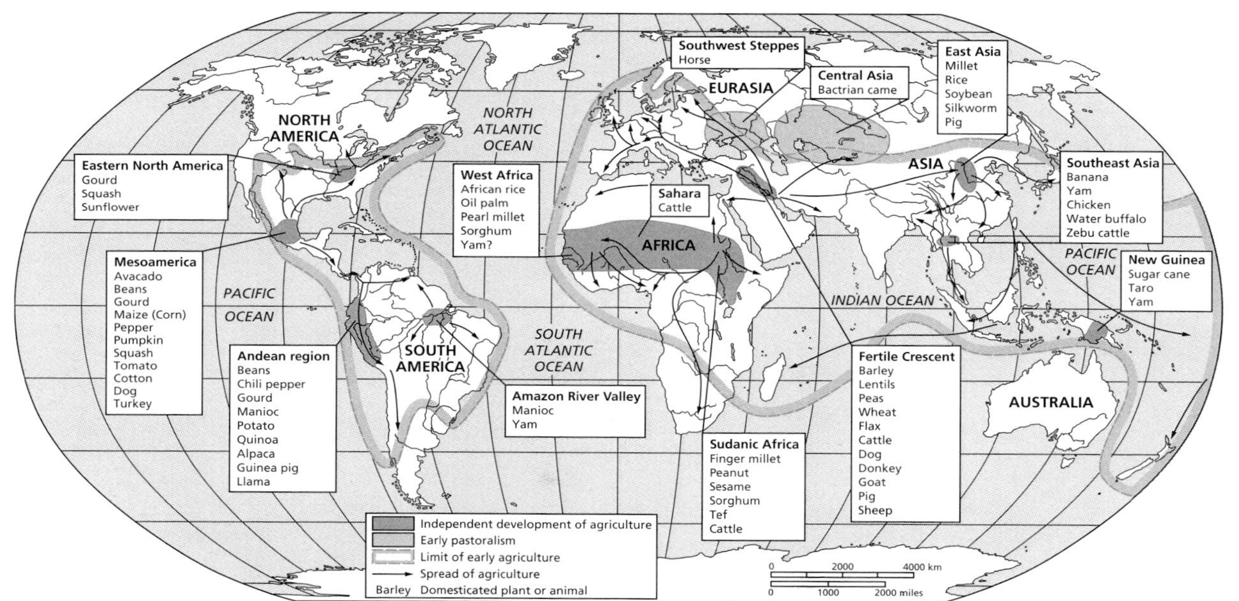

Map 1.3 Plant and animal domestication

smelting process. Smelted copper was poured into molds and made into spear points, axes, chisels, and other tools along with jewelry.

People adapted crops to their local environments, choosing seeds that had qualities that were beneficial, such as drought resistance. They also domesticated new kinds of crops. In the Indus Valley of South Asia people were growing dates, mangoes, sesame seeds, and cotton along with grains and legumes by 4000 BCE. In the Americas by about 3000 BCE corn was domesticated in southern Mexico and potatoes and quinoa in the Andes region of South America, and by about 2500 BCE squash and beans in eastern North America. These crops then spread, so that by about 1000 BCE people in much of what is now the western United States were raising corn, beans, and squash.

At roughly the same time that they domesticated certain plants, people also domesticated animals. The earliest animal to be domesticated was the dog, which separated genetically as a subspecies from wolves at least 15,000 years ago and perhaps much earlier. The mechanism of dog domestication is hotly debated: did it result only from human action, as foragers chose and bred animals that would help them with the hunt rather than attack them, or was it also caused by selective pressure resulting from wolf action, as animals less afraid of human contact came around campsites and then bred with one another? However it happened, the relationship provided both with benefits: humans gained dogs' better senses of smell and hearing and their body warmth, and dogs gained new food sources and safer surroundings. Not surprisingly, humans and domestic dogs migrated together, including across the land bridges to the Americas and on boats to Pacific islands.

Dogs fit easily into a foraging lifestyle, but humans also domesticated animals that fit with a sedentary way of life. In about 9000 BCE, at the same time they began to raise crops, people in the Fertile Crescent domesticated wild goats and sheep, probably using them first for meat and skins, then for milk, and eventually shearing the sheep for wool. They learned from observation and experimentation that traits are passed down from generation to generation, and they began to breed the goats and sheep selectively for qualities that they wanted, including larger size, greater strength, better coats, increased milk production, and more even temperaments.

Sometimes they trained dogs to assist them in herding, and then selectively bred the dogs for qualities that were advantageous for this task. The book of Genesis in the Bible, written in the Fertile Crescent sometime in the first millennium BCE, provides an early example of selective breeding. Jacob makes a deal with his father-in-law to take only those goats and sheep that are spotted, but he secretly increases the number of spotted animals in the flock by placing a spotted stick "before the eyes ... of the strongest of the flocks ... whenever they were breeding" so that more and stronger spotted animals were born (Genesis 30:41). This method was based on the idea—accepted for a very long time—that what a pregnant animal or woman saw during pregnancy would influence the outcome; although this has been firmly rejected in modern science, the Bible notes that it was successful, and that Jacob "grew exceedingly rich, and had large flocks." People also domesticated other animals, including pigs, guinea pigs, and various sorts of poultry, using the latter for eggs as well as meat.

Neolithic villages increasingly included spaces for domesticated animals as well as storage places for crops. In warmer climates people contructed pens and in colder climates they built special buildings or took animals into their houses. They learned that animal manure increases crop yields, so they gathered the manure from enclosures and used it as fertilizer. Increased contact with animals and their feces also increased human contact with various sorts of disease-causing pathogens, including minor illnesses such as the common cold and deadly killers such as influenza, bubonic plague, and smallpox. This was particularly the case where humans and animals lived in tight quarters, for diseases spread fastest in crowded environments. Thus farmers developed illnesses that had not plagued foragers, and the diseases became endemic, that is, widely found within a region without being deadly. Ultimately people who lived with animals developed resistance to some of these illnesses, and foragers' lack of resistance to many illnesses meant that they died more readily after coming into contact with new endemic diseases, as was the case when Europeans brought smallpox and other diseases to the Americas in the sixteenth century. (Discussed in detail in Chapter 4.)

Domesticated animals eventually far outnumbered their wild counterparts. For example, in the United States today (excluding

Alaska), there are about 77 million dogs, compared to about 6,000 wolves. The United Nations estimates that worldwide there are more than 2 billion cattle, and more than 20 billion chickens, with enormous consequences for the environment. Animal domestication also shaped human evolution; groups that relied on animal milk and milk products for a significant part of their diet tended to develop the ability to digest milk as adults, while those that did not remained lactose intolerant as adults, the normal condition for mammals.

Demographic, social, and cultural factors appear to have operated together in the turn from gathering wild plants to growing domesticated ones, and from hunting and snaring wild animals to raising domesticated ones. In terms of demography, although the warming climate allowed levels of foraging that were sufficient for sedentary villages to develop, population may have slowly grown beyond the readily available food supply. This increase in population resulted from lower child mortality and longer life spans, and perhaps also from higher fertility rates. Naturally occurring foods often included cereals or other crops that could be ground and cooked into a mush soft enough for babies to eat. This mush—for which there is widespread archaeological evidence—allowed women to decide to stop nursing their children at a younger age and instead put their energies elsewhere. Skeletal evidence from California, for example, shows that as groups living there around 2500 BCE increasingly relied on acorns for food—which must be boiled or roasted and ground before they are edible—women's work load increased, and they weaned their children earlier. By doing this, women lost the contraceptive effects of breast-feeding, and children were born at more frequent intervals. But instead of moving to a new area—the solution that foragers relied on when faced with the problem of food scarcity—people chose to stay with or near the physical and social structures of the sedentary villages they had built. So they developed a different way to increase the food supply to keep up with population growth—plant and animal domestication—thus beginning cycles of expanding population and intensification of land use that have continued to today.

Cultural factors interwove with these demographic and social ones. One example of this can be seen at Göbekli Tepe, a site not far from Hallan Çemi in present-day Turkey, where around

1.5 A predator eyes a boar on one of the huge limestone pillars at Göbekli Tepe, which were carved, arranged in rings, and then buried about 9000 BCE. Most carvings are of dangerous animals such as lions, snakes, and scorpions rather than prey, and the structure required great skill and effort to build.

9000 BCE hundreds of people came together to build rings of massive, multi-ton elaborately carved limestone pillars, and then covered them with dirt and built more. The people who created this site lived some distance away, where archaeological remains indicate that, at the time they first carved the pillars, they ate wild game and plants, not crops. Once these pillars were carved and raised in place, however, their symbolic, cultural, or perhaps religious importance may have made people decide to adopt a subsistence strategy that would allow them to stay nearby. Studies of other sites in the area show that in some population was *not* outstripping the food supply obtained by foraging, so that the new economy was primarily the result of deliberate cultural choice, not food scarcity.

Nowhere do archaeological remains alone answer the question of who within any group first began to cultivate crops, but the fact that, among many foragers, women have been primarily responsible for gathering and processing plant products suggests that they may also have been the first to plant seeds in the ground. In many parts of the world, crops continued to be planted with hoes and digging sticks for millennia, and crop-raising remained primarily women's work, while men hunted or later raised animals. In these places, which include large parts of North America and Africa, women appear to have retained control of the crops they planted, sharing them with group members or giving them as gifts.

A field of planted and weeded crops yields ten to one hundred times as much food — measured in calories — as the same area of naturally occurring plants, a benefit that would have been evident to early crop-planters. It also requires more labor, however, which was provided both by the greater number of people in the community and by those people working longer hours. In contrast to the twenty hours a week foragers spent on obtaining food, farming peoples were often in the fields from dawn to dusk, particularly during planting and harvest time, but also during the rest of the growing year because weeding was a constant task. Neolithic farmers were also less healthy than foragers were; although crop-raising gave them a more reliable food supply, their narrower range of foodstuffs made them more susceptible to disease and nutritional deficiencies such as anemia.

Foragers who lived at the edge of farming communities may have recognized the negative aspects of crop-raising, for they often adopted this new way of life quite slowly. In some places farming spread through migration. Studies of bone chemistry have revealed that sometimes farming villagers moved to a different area, built a new village, cleared land, and planted seeds, or sometimes only men moved, intermarrying with women from foraging groups. These migrations could be accompanied by violence; judging by cemetery remains, the number of people who died violent deaths increased in the period of intensifying foraging and early agriculture in some parts of the world, and both weapons and armor became more prevalent. Because the population of farming communities grew so much faster than that of foragers, however, the balance shifted. By about 6500 BCE farming had spread northward from the Fertile Crescent into Greece and by 4000 farther northward into Europe all the way to Britain. Crop-raising spread out from other areas in which it was first developed, and slowly larger and larger parts of Asia, Africa, and the Americas became home to farming villages.

The most common global pattern for crop-raising involved sedentary villages, but this was not the case everywhere. In some parts of the world, including Amazonia, Papua New Guinea, and many parts of North America, crop-raising was combined with gathering and hunting. Especially in deeply wooded areas, people cleared small plots by chopping and burning the natural vegetation—a method termed "slash and burn" —and planted crops in successive years until the soil eroded or lost its fertility. They then moved to another area and began the process again, perhaps returning to the first plot many years later, after the soil had rejuvenated itself. Groups using shifting slash-and-burn cultivation remained relatively small and continued to rely on the surrounding forest or jungle for much of their food, practices that continued into the twentieth century.

Animal-raising was also not sedentary everywhere. In drier areas, flocks of sheep and goats need to travel long distances from season to season to obtain enough food, and a new form of living was created based on herding and raising livestock: pastoralism. Some pastoralists became nomadic, relying primarily on their flocks of animals for food, but also gathering wild plant foods. Pastoralism was well-suited to areas where the terrain or climate made crop-planting difficult, such as mountains, deserts, dry grasslands, and tundras. Eventually other grazing animals, including cattle, yaks, and reindeer, also became the basis of pastoral economies in central and western Asia, many parts of Africa, and far northern Europe.

PLOW AGRICULTURE AND FOOD PROCESSING

Crop-raising and pastoralism brought significant changes to human ways of life, but the domestication of certain large animals had an even bigger impact. Cattle and water buffalo were domesticated in some parts of Asia and North Africa in which they occurred naturally by at least 7000 BCE, and horses, donkeys, and camels by about 4000 BCE. Cattle and water buffalo were used for their meat, and also perhaps for their blood, which was tapped and either drunk or mixed into cooked foods. More importantly, all of these animals can be trained to carry people or burdens on their backs and pull against loads dragged behind them, two qualities that are rare among the world's animal species. In many parts of the world, including North America and much of South America and sub-Saharan Africa, no naturally occurring large species could be domesticated. In the mountainous regions of South America, llamas and alpacas were domesticated to carry packs, but the steep terrain made it difficult to use them to pull loads, and they were not large enough to ride. The domestication of large animals dramatically increased the power available to humans to carry out their tasks, which had both an immediate effect in the societies in which this happened and a long-term effect when these societies later encountered societies in which human labor remained the only source of power. The biologist and environmental scientist Jared Diamond has proposed, in fact, that large domesticated animals provided Eurasian societies with advantages that resulted in the differences of wealth and power in the modern world, a very long legacy of these early endowments.

In terms of food production, the pulling power of animals came to matter most. Sometime in the seventh millennium BCE, people attached wooden sticks to frames that animals dragged through the soil, thus breaking it up and allowing seeds to sprout more easily. These simple scratch plows were pulled first by cattle and water buffalo, and later by horses and mules. (Donkeys and camels were used primarily as pack animals, but occasionally for plowing as well.) Over millennia, moldboards — angled pieces that turned the soil over, bringing fresh soil to the top — were added, which reduced the time needed to plow and allowed each person to work more land.

Using plows, people produced a significant amount of surplus food. Certain planted crops eventually came to be grown over huge areas of land, so that some scientists describe the development of agriculture—like the domestication of dogs—as a process of codependent domestication: humans domesticated crops, but crops also "domesticated" humans so that they worked long hours spreading particular crops around the world. Of these, wheat, rice, and corn have been the most successful. The United States Department of Agriculture estimates that today wheat is planted in over 800,000 square miles around the world, and represents a fifth of all calories in the human diet, while rice is planted in over 600,000 square miles. A further 600,000 square miles are now planted in corn, with one-quarter of the nearly 50,000 items in the average American supermarket containing corn, not even counting the corn eaten by the chickens, pigs, and cattle whose meat is also found in that supermarket.

Technologies of storing and cooking developed alongside those of food production, varying according to the raw materials that were available. People in many parts of the world developed techniques of weaving baskets from the rushes and reeds found along seacoasts, lakes, and rivers. Baskets were used for storage (and also for catching fish and other aquatic animals), and those that were woven tightly enough could also be used to make soups and stews by placing hot cooking stones in them. The invention of kilns—which happened independently in many places—allowed clay pots and the glazes painted on them to be fired at higher temperatures so that the pots became completely impermeable to liquids, thus making them useful as vessels for long-term storage as well as cooking. Sometime in the fifth millennium BCE pot-makers in Mesopotamia invented the potter's wheel, a technology for making higher-quality pots that both spread and developed independently elsewhere. Cooking in pots allowed people to blend foods in new ways, which led to greater distinctions in eating habits both among different groups and within one group based on the differing abilities of families to obtain more unusual or expensive ingredients. Food preparations for celebrations and feasts became more elaborate, and the consumption of food acquired added ceremonies and rules.

Clay pots were also used for preparing, storing, and transporting fermented food and beverages. Fermentation is a natural process that, like cooking, makes food more nutritious and easier to digest; it makes things rot, but also preserves many foods from spoiling and kills off pathogens in water. Pastoralists discovered one particular type of fermentation when they learned that the lining of a baby animal's stomach curdles milk into a more digestible, easy-to-transport, and longer-lasting product—cheese—and began to control this process in leather bags and containers. When humans first began to control fermentation is not clear. Evolutionary biologists using DNA evidence have determined that the primary yeast used in the fermentation that produces alcohol, *Saccharamyces cerevisiae*—one of many yeasts present naturally in the air—shows signs of human selection beginning more than 10,000 years ago, thus perhaps even before wheat. Significant wine and beer making began about the same time as farming itself, although people were most likely making mead from honey and small amounts of wine and beer before this.

Alcohol should perhaps be added to the list of reasons for the development and spread of crop-raising, as humans sought to obtain a reliable supply of raw material they could transform into this high-energy substance that also became their principal pain-killer. Evidence from skeletal remains in South America supports this idea, as people living there about 6000 BCE consumed the corn they had begun to grow as alcohol (most likely as a type of quicha, a beer made by chewing grain and then spitting it into a pot, which allows the fermentation process to begin) before they turned to eating it. Like the domestication of milk-producing animals, the production of fermented beverages also shaped human evolution, as a larger share of the population developed the ability to metabolize alcohol, which is actually a poison. Alcohol became part of social events and its consumption was often ritualized, with beer and wine among the offerings given to spirits and deities, or consumed by shamans, priests, and worshippers as a means of gaining access to the world beyond the visible or honoring the gods.

Just as foragers continually improved their tools and methods, pastoralists and farmers did as well. They adapted the wheel invented to make clay pots for use on carts and plows pulled by animals. Wheeled vehicles led to road-building, and wheels and roads together made it possible for people and goods to travel long distances more easily, whether for settlement, trade, or conquest.

SOCIAL AND GENDER HIERARCHIES

In many parts of the world, foragers showed signs of increasing social differentiation in their material goods and mortuary practices, and in some the concentration of power by a "Big Man" coalesced into a chiefdom, in which power was more formalized. These processes occurred more often in agricultural communities.

Certain people were buried with significant amounts of jewelry, shells, household goods, fancy fabrics, weapons, and other objects, while others were buried with very little. Graves and other evidence also show greater differentiation based on gender, with men becoming more associated with the world beyond the household and women with the domestic realm. These social and gender hierarchies varied in their intensity, changed over time, and blended with more egalitarian practices, but no agricultural society was without them. Lines of causation in these changes are difficult to trace; written sources do not provide a clear answer because social and gender hierarchies were already firmly in place by the time writing was invented.

Most likely the causes were complex and intertwining, with multiple pathways leading to prominence and power. Within foraging groups, some individuals already had more authority because of their links with the world of gods and spirits, positions as heads of kin groups or tribes, or personal characteristics. This power became more significant over time as there were more resources to control. Priests and shamans developed more elaborate rituals and became full-time religious specialists, exchanging their services in interceding with the gods for everything else that they needed to live. In many communities, religious specialists were the first to work out formal rules of conduct that later became oral and written codes of law, generally explaining that these represented the will of the gods. The codes threatened divine punishment for those who broke them, and they often required people to accord deference to priests as the representatives of the gods, so that they became an elite group with special privileges.

Individuals who were the heads of large families or kin groups, or who had unusual leadership talents, had control over the labor of others. They were the "Big Men" who made decisions about how group resources should be used, which became more significant when these included material goods that could be stored for long periods of time. Material goods — plows, sheep, cattle, sheds, pots, carts — gave one the ability to amass still more material goods, and the gap between those who had them and those who did not widened. Storage also allowed goods to be handed down from one family member to another, so that over generations small differences in wealth grew larger.

Human and animal power could be used for destruction as well as production, and war enhanced social and political hierarchies. It allowed some communities to conquer others, and the threat of war convinced people within a community to accept the authority of leaders in the hopes of avoiding being conquered themselves. Higher levels of armed struggle may have been a cause as well as a result of the spread of agriculture, as leaders advocated subsistence strategies that would increase the population (and thus provide more soldiers), and as the larger populations of agricultural communities allowed them to conquer their forager neighbors.

Signs of greater wealth and power included prestige goods such as gold and copper jewelry, precious stones, carved jade, and feathers, which then marked their owners—in life and death—as different from most people, thus creating as well as reflecting prominence. Prestige goods were given away or exchanged locally and regionally, allowing their owners to gain supporters or build networks of mutual obligation. These ties might be expressed in egalitarian or even familial terms, so that exisiting ideologies of egalitarianism were not ignored or refuted, but instead put to new uses.

Wealth could command labor directly, as individuals or families could buy the services of others to work for them or impose their wishes through force, hiring others to threaten or carry out violence. Eventually some individuals bought others outright. As with social hierarchies in general, slavery predates written records, but it developed in almost all agricultural societies. Like animals, slaves were a source of physical power for their owners, providing them an opportunity to amass still more wealth and influence. In the long era before the invention of fossil fuel technology, the ability to exploit animal and human labor was the most important mark of distinction between elites and the rest of the population. Land ownership was often what distinguished elites from others, but that land was valuable only if there were people living on it who were required to labor for the owner.

Along with hierarchies based on wealth and power, the development of agriculture was intertwined with a hierarchy based on gender. In every society in the world that has left written records men have more power and access to resources than women and some men are dominant over other men. This patriarchal gender system came before writing, and searching for its origins involves interpreting many different types of sources. Some scholars see the origins of gender inequality in the hominid past, noting that male chimpanzees form alliances to gain status against other males and engage in cooperative attacks on females, which might have also happened among early hominids. Other scholars see the origins in the Paleolithic, with the higher status of men in kin groups.

The development of plow agriculture and the resultant increase in the ability to amass food and other goods heightened patriarchy. Although farming with a hoe was often done by women, plow agriculture came to be a male task, perhaps because of men's upper-body strength, or because plow agriculture was more difficult to combine with care for infants and small children than was farming with a hoe or digging stick. Depictions of plowing on Mesopotamian cylinder seals invariably show men with the cattle and plows. At the same time that cattle began to be raised for pulling plows and carts rather than for meat, sheep began to be raised primarily for wool rather than meat or hides. Spinning thread and weaving cloth came to be seen primarily as women's work; the earliest Egyptian hieroglyph for weaving is, in fact, a seated woman with a shuttle, and a Confucian moral saying from ancient China asserts that "men plow and women weave." Spinning and weaving were generally done indoors and involved smaller and cheaper tools than plowing; they could also be taken up and put down easily, and so could be done at the same time as other tasks. Though in some ways this arrangement seems complementary, with each sex doing some of the necessary labor, men's responsibility for plowing and other agricultural tasks took them outside the household more often than women's duties did, enlarging their opportunities for leadership.

The earliest written records and later ethnographic evidence suggest that village structures of power were almost always gender and age related, and in most parts of the world adult male heads of household or heads of families had the most power. In some groups, men at (or near) the top of the social heap used their greater wealth to acquire more wives, which both increased their family's ability to produce and raised their status when compared with other men, as wives were a "prestige good."

1.6 In this clay and wood model from Middle Kingdom Egypt (*c.* 2000 BCE–1700 BCE), a man plows with a scratch plow pulled by two oxen. Egyptian depictions of plowing always show men at this task, though women are sometimes shown seeding.

Warfare and other forms of organized violence also gave men power. Like slavery, armed conflict predates written records, but from its earliest occurrences it was profoundly gendered. Battle was perceived as the ultimate test of both individual and collective manhood, and justified in part because it was a defense of those who could not defend themselves, especially children and women. Victors were portrayed in images and oral traditions, and later in writing, as masculine and virile, and losers as unmanly, feminized, and weak. Conquests sometimes ended with the symbolic or actual rape of the defeated soldiers as well as women who were on the losing side. War sometimes created alterations in gender structures, as it broke down traditional norms of conduct, turning women into booty but also creating emergency situations in which women carried out tasks normally done by men. Because war was viewed as an extraordinary situation calling for great sacrifices and bravery from all, however, this did not lead to permanent change in gender roles.

As with other social hierarchies, gender hierarchies and ideas about the proper roles of women and men may have shaped subsistence strategies as well as been shaped by them. Farming with a hoe is every bit as physically demanding—or perhaps even more so—than farming with a plow, so that men's association with large animals and plowing may have been rooted more in culture than in physiology. Visual and verbal depictions of men plowing and women weaving may initially have been prescriptive, not descriptive, designed to teach people what tasks they were supposed to do. The exchange of women by men for their procreative power and the prestige they conferred suggests that women (or at least some women) were understood to be property, perhaps preceding other forms of private property, such as land ownership or slavery.

Whether women were the first form of private property has been debated since the nineteenth century, but there is no debate that the inheritance systems through which goods passed from generation to generation tended to favor men. This was particularly the case with land and the right to farm communally held land, which was most often passed down through the male line. In some places inheritance was traced through the female line, but in such systems women themselves did not necessarily inherit goods or property; instead a man inherited from his mother's brother rather than from his father. Accordingly, over generations, women's independent access to resources decreased, and it became increasingly difficult for women to survive without male support. Skeletal studies from Southwest Asia indicate that although farming brought a decrease in health and nutritional status for everyone, women's physical health deteriorated more, perhaps because they lost access to resources.

As inherited wealth became more important, men wanted to make sure that their sons were theirs, so they restricted their wives' movements and activities. This was especially the case among elite families. Among foragers, women needed to be mobile for the group to survive; their labor outdoors was essential. Among agriculturalists, the labor of animals, slaves, and hired workers could substitute for that of women in families that could afford them. There is evidence that women spent more and more of their time within the household, either indoors or behind walls and barriers that separated the domestic realm from the wider world. Thus although the lines of causation are not clear, the development of agriculture was accompanied by the increasing subordination of women in many parts of the world.

Social and gender hierarchies were enhanced over generations as wealth and power were passed down unequally, and they were also enhanced by rules and norms that shaped sexual relationships, particularly heterosexual ones. (Early rules and laws about sex did not pay much attention to same-sex relations because these did not produce children who could disrupt systems of inheritance.) However their power originated, elites began to think of themselves as a group apart from the rest with something that made them distinctive—such as connections with a deity, military prowess, and natural superiority. They increasingly understood this distinctive quality to be hereditary, and, like membership in an ethnic group, to be carried in the blood. High-status people were often thought to have superior blood; in parts of today's Indonesia, for example, nobles were referred to as "white-blooded" and married only those with similar blood, as did those who had "noble blood" elsewhere. Traditions—later codified as written laws—stipulated which heterosexual relationships would pass this quality on to children, along with passing on wealth. Relationships between men and women from elite families were formalized as marriage and generally passed down both status and wealth. Relationships between elite men and non-elite women generally did not do so, or did so to a lesser degree; the women were defined as concubines or mistresses, or simply as sexual outlets for powerful men. The 1780 BCE Code of Hammurabi, for example, one of the world's earliest law codes, sets out differences in inheritance for the sons a man had with his wife and those he had with a servant or slave, and did not mention inheritance by daughters at all. Again judging by later law codes, relations between an elite woman and a non-elite man could bring shame and dishonor to the woman's family and sometimes death to the man.

Thus along with distinctions *among* the groups thought of as tribes, peoples, ethnicities, or nations that resulted from migration and endogamy, distinctions developed *within* groups that were reinforced by social endogamy, what we might think of as the selective breeding of people. Elite men tended to marry elite women, which in some cases resulted in actual physical differences over generations, as elites had more access to food or to more nutritious foods, so were able to become taller and stronger. No elite can be completely closed to newcomers, however, because the accidents of life and death, along with the genetic problems caused by repeated close intermarriage, make it difficult for any small group to survive over generations. Thus just as mechanisms were devised to incorporate people into ethnic groups, methods were also developed in many cultures to adopt boys into elite families, legitimate the children of concubines and slave women, or allow elite girls to marry men lower on the social hierarchy. All systems of inheritance also need some flexibility. The inheritance patterns in some cultures favored male heirs exclusively, but in others close relatives were favored over those more distant, even if this meant allowing daughters to inherit. The drive to keep wealth and property within a family or kin group often resulted in women inheriting, owning, and in some cases managing significant amounts of wealth, a pattern that continues today. Hierarchies of wealth and power thus intersected with hierarchies of gender in complex ways, and in many cultures age and marital status also played roles. In many later European and African groups, for example, widows were largely able to control their own property, while unmarried sons were often under their father's control even if they were adults, a pattern that may have begun with the first settled agriculture.

MONUMENTS AND MENTALITIES

Objects were not the only things traded over increasingly long distances during the Neolithic period, for people also carried and circulated ideas, symbols, and symbolic behavior with them as they traveled on foot, boats, or animals, and in wagons or carts. Knowledge about the seasons and the weather, for example, was vitally important for those who depended on crop-raising, and agricultural peoples in many parts of the world began to calculate recurring patterns in the world around them, slowly developing calendars. People built circular structures of mounded earth or huge upright stones called megaliths to help them predict the movements of the sun and stars, including Nabta Playa, erected about 4500 BCE in the desert west of the Nile Valley in Egypt, and Stonehenge, erected about 2500 BCE in southern England. Megalithic arrangements are particularly common in some regions, such as Brittany, suggesting ideas about how and why to make them were transmitted across regions.

The sites of these mounds and megaliths, and graves and trash heaps as well, often yield carved objects or pottery with motifs from the agricultural and pastoral world: shepherds' crooks, sheep, cattle and cattle horns, plowing with yoked cattle, plowed fields, buildings that may be houses or sheds or granaries. Small model houses made from pottery have been found in Neolithic settlements in many parts of eastern Europe and western Asia. Such decorated objects suggest that now, instead of hunting, the growing and storing of food was ritualized; animals are still there, but they are the domesticated animals that are now human property.

Along with megaliths that may have been calendars, agriculturalists in some areas also built other large structures that were likely monuments, shrines, and sanctuaries, giving new meaning to already significant natural places. Thus the landscape was altered not only by farming, but also by the construction of many more human-made objects in it. These structures sometimes included tombs built above ground, in the walls of houses, with tombstones over graves, or with many skulls decorated and gathered together, constant visual reminders of a group's lineage and collective ancestors. Symbolic archaeologists such as Jacques Cauvin have argued that these large buildings and new funerary customs are evidence of a different way of thinking—a new mentality—in which spirits became more clearly divinities distinct from humans to be prayed to and worshipped, and humans became more clearly separate from the environment. He proposes, in fact, that mental transformations and changes in symbolic uses of material culture preceded any change in subsistence strategy, and are a better explanation for the development of farming than population pressures or resource depletion. Others have also noted that domestication involves a new attitude toward linear time as well as cyclical, and greater separation from nature. Those who raise crops and animals must look beyond an annual cycle and plan for the longer term, keeping seed corn for the next year and deciding which animals to keep and which to kill. The separation between humans and animals, and between wild and tame, was not absolute, however; humans continued to live in intimate relations with animals, and archaeological evidence provides examples of attitudes of trust and respect, as well as domination, of animals and the natural world.

The rhythms of the agricultural cycle and new patterns of material and cultural exchange also shaped other ritualized aspects of life. Among foragers, human fertility is a mixed blessing, as too many children can overtax food supplies, but among crop-raisers and pastoralists, fertility—of the land, animals, and people—is essential. Figurines, carvings, and paintings from the Neolithic include clearly pregnant women, women giving birth, and men (or individuals gendered male) with erect penises. Shamans and priests developed ever more elaborate rituals designed to assure fertility, in which spirits were often given something from a community's goods in exchange for their favor, such as food offerings, fermented beverages, animal sacrifices, or sacred objects.

In many places spirits also became more obviously deities: gods and goddesses who took human form that came to be associated with patterns of birth, growth, death, and regeneration. Gods and goddesses could bring death and destruction, but they also created life. Like humans, the gods came to have a division of labor and a social hierarchy. There were rain gods and sun gods, sky goddesses and moon goddesses, gods that assured the health of cattle or the growth of corn, goddesses of the hearth and home. Thus as human society was becoming more complex and hierarchical, so was the unseen world.

PREHISTORIC PATTERNS

By 3000 BCE, humans were the only surviving hominins, and had migrated to all of the large land masses of the world (except Antarctica), and many of its islands. Whether foragers, farmers, or a combination of these, they brought with them symbolic language, kinship structures, technological inventions, food preferences, aesthetic and moral values, rituals, and divisions of labor, creating distinct cultures reinforced by endogamy. Everywhere humans migrated, from Argentinian caves to sub-Arctic tundra, they left their tools, trash, and marks on the world.

All the aspects of human society that people carried with them played a role in the domestication of people, plants, and animals that marked the Neolithic, and were themselves affected by that domestication. Agriculture and animal domestication allowed the populations of farming communities to grow much faster than those of foragers, and resulted in a widespread common social pattern in which a small elite of landowners, religious specialists, and military leaders lived from the labor of the vast majority, who spent their lives raising crops. Like boundaries between cultures, social and gender hierarchies within cultures were reinforced by endogamy and other marital and inheritance patterns, and also by force, religion, and oral traditions. Soon other human creations, including writing and states, would further enhance the possibilities for differentiation among and within cultures, but the basic social patterns set in the Neolithic would not change dramatically for thousands of years.

FURTHER READING

Ian Tattersall, *Masters of the Planet: The Search for Our Human Origins* (London: Palgrave Macmillan, 2013) provides an excellent brief survey of both human evolution and the field of paleoanthropology. He emphasizes a quite sudden change to behavioral modernity, as do Richard Klein and B. Edgar, *The Dawn of Human Culture* (New York: Wiley, 2002) and Chris Stringer, *Lone Survivors: How We Came to Be the Only Humans on Earth* (New York: Times Books, 2012), which was published in England with the less dramatic title *The Origin of Our Species*. For the more gradualist view, see Sally McBrearty and Alison S. Brooks, "The Revolution That Wasn't: A New Interpretation of the Origin of Modern Human Behavior," *Journal of Human Evolution* 39, no. 5 (2000): 453–563. For an even *more* gradualist view that sees symbolic thought emerging very early, see Clive Gamble, *Origins and Revolutions: Human Identity in Earliest Prehistory* (Cambridge: Cambridge University Press, 2007). For

Kanzi the bonobo, see Kathy Schick *et al.*, "Continuing Investigations into the Stone Tool-making and Tool-using Capacities of a Bonobo (*Pan paniscus*)," *Journal of Archaeological Science* 26 (1999): 821–32. For some of the new thinking on Neanderthals, see Francesco d'Errico, "The Invisible Frontier: A Multiple Species Model for the Origins of Behavioural Modernity," *Evolutionary Anthropology* 12 (2003): 188–202 and J. Zilhão, *Anatomically Archaic, Behaviorally Modern: The Last Neanderthals and Their Destiny* (Amsterdam: Stichting Nederlands Museum voor Anthopologie en Praehistorie, 2001).

On the importance of cooking to human evolution, see Richard Wrangham, *Catching Fire: How Cooking Made Us Human* (New York: Basic Books, 2009). Felipe Fernández-Armesto, *Near a Thousand Tables: A History of Food* (New York: Free Press, 2002), Martin Jones, *Feast: Why Humans Share Food* (Oxford: Oxford University Press, 2007), and Rachel Landau, *Cuisine and Empire: Cooking in World History* (Berkeley: University of California Press, 2013) all provide fascinating overviews of the significance of food preparation and consumption across time.

Nicolas J. Allen *et al.*, eds., *Early Human Kinship: From Sex to Social Reproduction* (Oxford: Wiley-Blackwell, 2008) is a series of essays that examine the transformation of biological kinship into social kinship systems. Other recent work on kinship and the life course include Kristen Hawkes and Richard R. Paine, *The Evolution of Human Life History* (Sante Fe: School of American Research Press, 2006) and Sarah Blaffer Hrdy, *Mothers and Others: The Evolutionary Origins of Mutual Understanding* (Cambridge, MA: Harvard University Press, 2009). Allen Johnson and Timothy Earle, *The Evolution of Human Societies: From Foraging Group to Agrarian State*, 2nd edn. (Stanford: Stanford University Press, 2000) argue that cultural and social evolution is rooted in the exchange of goods and services between families. For more on the role of culture, see Peter J. Richerson and Robert Boyd, *Not by Genes Alone: How Culture Transformed Human Evolution* (Chicago: University of Chicago Press, 2006). On migration as key to the formation and transmission of language, material culture, and other aspects of human society, see Peter Bellwood, *First Migrants: Ancient Migrations in Global Perspective* (Oxford: Wiley-Blackwell, 2013).

Ian Kuijt, ed., *Life in Neolithic Farming Communities: Social Organization, Identity, and Differentiation* (New York: Kluwer Academic, 2000) provides a series of essays that examine the development of sedentism, including the article by Michael Rosenberg and Richard W. Redding on Hallan Çemi discussed in the chapter. For more on Neolithic society, see Jane Peterson, *Sexual Revolutions: Gender and Labor at the Dawn of*

Agriculture (Walnut Creek, CA: AltaMira Press, 2002) and Alasdair Whittle, *The Archaeology of People: Dimensions of Neolithic Life* (London: Routledge, 2003). W.K. Barnett and J.W. Hoopes, eds., *The Emergence of Pottery: Technology and Innovation in Ancient Societies* (Washington, DC: Smithsonian Institution Press, 1995) and Marcia-Anne Dobres, *Technology and Social Agency* (Oxford: Blackwell, 2000) provide excellent analyses of the invention and transmission of technologies. On rituals, symbols, and spirituality, see Jacques Cauvin, *The Birth of the Gods and the Origins of Agriculture* (Cambridge: Cambridge University Press, 2000), Richard Bradley, *Ritual and Domestic Life in Prehistoric Europe* (London: Routledge, 2005), and David Lewis-Williams and David Pearce, *Inside the Neolithic Mind: Consciousness, Cosmos, and the Realm of the Gods* (London: Thames & Hudson, 2005). Ian Hodder, *Entangled: An Archaeology of the Relationships between Humans and Things* (London: Wiley-Blackwell, 2012) presents a fascinating theory of connections between humans and material objects from the Neolithic community of Çatalhöyük to today.

On the development of hierarchies within and among societies, see Timothy Earle, *How Chiefs Came to Power: The Political Economy in Prehistory* (Stanford: Stanford University Press, 1997), Jared Diamond, *Guns, Germs, and Steel: The Fates of Human Societies* (London: Vintage, 1998), and especially the magisterial Kent Flannery and Joyce Marcus, *The Creation of Inequality: How Our Prehistoric Ancestors Set the Stage for Monarchy, Slavery, and Empire* (Cambridge, MA: Harvard University Press, 2012).

Essays on many of the topics in this chapter may be found in David Christian, ed., *Introducing World History, to 10,000 BCE* and Graeme Barker and Candice Goucher, eds., *A World with Agriculture, 12,000 BCE–500 CE*, Volumes 1 and 2 of the *Cambridge World History*.

2

Cities and classical societies (3000 BCE–500 CE)

In 113 CE, when she was nearly seventy years old, the historian, poet, and scholar Ban Zhao accompanied her son to his new position in a rural district away from Luoyang, the eastern capital of Han dynasty China. Recounting the trip in a poem, she tells of her uneasiness and sadness as they pass through small fields and rundown villages, and writes:

> Secretly I sigh for the Capital City I love, (but)
> To cling to one's native place characterizes a small nature,
> As the histories have taught us.

She pulls herself out of this mood by pouring a cup of wine and thinking about the philosopher Confucius, who had lived in a "decadent, chaotic age," but had urged "truth and virtue, honor and merit," and at the end of the poem writes stirringly that "Muscles stretched, head uplifted, we tread onward to the vision ... and turn not back."

Ban Zhao's love for the city was shared by her brother Ban Gu, also a historian, poet, and scholar, who wrote an ode in praise of Luoyang that became a classic of Chinese literature. Poets and scholars living at the other end of Eurasia in the cities around the Mediterranean shared this preference for urban life, especially those in Rome, the largest city in the world at the time Ban Zhao was writing. Here as well, educated urban residents generally saw the city as a place of rational behavior and the good life, and viewed themselves as more advanced and sophisticated than rural folk. They were more "civilized," a word that comes from the Latin adjective *civilis*, meaning of or pertaining to citizens, and the origin as well of the English words "civic" and "civil." The opposite opinion could also be found, however. In much of the Old Testament—and in some Greek, Roman, and Christian works—cities are portrayed as dens of iniquity and materialism, autocratic hierarchies ruled by tyrannical despots. Only by escaping to the pastoral countryside or to the wilderness could a person escape oppression and live a moral and pious life. Ban Gu himself expresses this opinion in a poem about the Western Han capital Changan, which he criticizes for wastefulness and extravagance. Both value judgments can be found in written commentaries from other parts of the ancient world as well (and in discussions about cities today), but what their writers agree on is that cities were *different* from the countryside that surrounded them. They represented something new, a view that is widely shared by archaeologists and historians.

The process of urbanization was not simply a matter of higher population densities and new political forms, but involved a restructuring of social institutions and cultural practices, which this chapter examines. Social and gender hierarchies became more formalized in cities and the larger-scale states and empires that developed from them. These were increasingly ruled by hereditary dynasties, that is, lineages of elites maintained by careful marriage strategies whose authority was bolstered by ideologies connecting them to heroic figures or gods. Families and kin groups further down the social scale also arranged marriages strategically to maintain or enhance their status and wealth, which often included individuals owned as slaves. In some places, writing and other information technologies transformed the oral communication of ideas into written law codes, religious texts, and philosophical systems, creating distinctive and long-lasting cultural traditions that were later labeled "classical." Although politically classical societies ranged from tiny city-states to giant empires, cities, writing, and formalized social hierarchies were important features of all of them. From the growth of the first cities about 3000 BCE to what is traditionally viewed as the end of the classical period about 500 CE, most people continued to live in small agricultural villages, or moved around the landscape as foragers or pastoralists. But for those who wanted change, cities were the place to be.

PATHS OF URBANIZATION

Cities first appeared in Mesopotamia and Egypt at the end of the fourth millennium BCE, in South Asia in the middle of the third millennium BCE, and in China at the end of the third millennium BCE. In Africa outside the Nile Valley, cities were founded early in the first millennium BCE, and in Southeast Asia late in that millennium. In the New World, cities appeared early in the first millennium BCE in Mesoamerica, slightly later in South America, and in the first millennium CE in North America. In each of these regions, cities developed independently, and in many places urbanism spread, with cities multiplying and growing, but also shrinking and disappearing.

Cities grew where they did for a variety of reasons, often intertwined. Some were established by people seeking safety and security from frequent armed conflicts or from natural disasters such as floods. Others were villages along rivers or land trade routes that gradually grew in size. Some cities were founded through a deliberate political choice. Around 2300 BCE, King Sargon conquered much of Mesopotamia with what was probably the world's first permanent army, and according to sources written at the time built a new capital at Akkad. (Akkad has not yet been identified archaeologically.)

Ideological and religious forces often played important roles in the establishment and expansion of cities, and they became ceremonial as well as economic centers. Cities often had special buildings or sacred precincts for regular public performances and rituals, to which people gained access through routes between buildings and monuments that enhanced their awe. Certain rituals were held in temples before a select few, but processions could involve vast numbers and were watched by even more. During the fifteenth and fourteenth centuries BCE in Egypt, for example, kings and nobles built temples and tombs at the city of Thebes and linked them by grand ceremonial ways using rivers, canals, and roads on land. Buildings within a city might be constructed according to cosmic principles and alignments, and the city itself might be laid out along certain lines and patterns to form a cosmogram—a model of the heavens and earth. Maya cities built in the late first millennium BCE, for example, often had a building complex consisting of a carefully leveled elevated square with a pyramid on the west side and a low platform running north and south on the east, which oriented them toward the rising sun on the eastern horizon; these complexes were also designed to replicate sacred mountains and bring them within the community and thus under the control of its rulers. Such geometric forms are allowing archaeologists today to discover buildings and sometimes whole cities in deeply forested areas of Mesoamerica through the use of Lidar—a technology that analyzes reflected light from a laser carried in a small plane over the treetops. Lidar imagery can be used to create three-dimensional digital maps of the forest floor, with human-made structures evident from their straight lines, regular placements, and distinctive shapes.

However they originated, cities began to assert control over the surrounding hinterland, forcing residents to supply some of their agricultural surplus to the city. Villages in the hinterlands often became economically dependent on the cities they surrounded, so that urbanization was accompanied by "ruralization," and village societies were different than they had been before. Cities were crowded with people and animals, and they became breeding grounds for diseases. Mortality levels were higher than fertility levels, and cities required in-migration to maintain their population. Most migrants were young adults, who came seeking opportunities or as conscripted laborers or slaves. Thus as cities pulled in agricultural surpluses from neighboring villages, they also pulled in young adults in the prime of life, and village populations skewed older. (The same demographic pattern can be found when comparing urban to non-urban populations today.) Cities and villages were not completely separate, however; there was often much back and forth between the city and the countryside as residents left the city to work in fields during the day or during certain seasons.

Cities all faced the same central challenge: reliably feeding a large population in a sustainable fashion. To do this, they developed structures of power and authority that ranged from highly centralized to less hierarchical, with most having multiple nodes of decision-making. A closer examination of two very different patterns of urbanization—Sumer and Jenne-jeno—can reveal ways in which these political arrangements were intertwined with social and occupational hierarchies, and with cultural practices.

The earliest cities in the world were in Sumer, the southern part of Mesopotamia, where the soil was fertile but the rainfall inadequate for regular crop-raising. In this arid climate farmers developed irrigation on a large scale, which demanded organized group effort, but allowed the population to grow. Beginning about 4000 BCE, several agricultural villages, beginning with Uruk, expanded into cities housing tens of thousands of people, with massive hydraulic projects including reservoirs, dams, and dikes to prevent major floods and to enable trading with one another, defensive walls, marketplaces, and large public buildings. Each one came to dominate the surrounding countryside, becoming city-states independent from one another, though not very far apart.

The city-states of Sumer relied on irrigation systems that required cooperation and at least some level of social and political cohesion. The authority to run this system initially seems to have been an assembly of elders, and priests also began to have greater power. Temples grew into elaborate complexes of buildings with storage space for grain and other products, staffed by priests and priestesses who carried out rituals to honor the city's primary god or goddess, who often represented cosmic forces such as the sun, moon, water, and storms. People believed that humans had been created to serve the gods and generally anticipated being well treated by the gods if they served them well. Surrounding the temple and other large buildings were the houses of ordinary citizens, each constructed around a central courtyard.

Exactly how kings emerged in Sumerian city-states is not clear. Scholars have suggested that during times of emergency, a chief priest or sometimes a military leader assumed what was supposed to be temporary authority over a city. He established an army, trained it, and led it into battle, making increasing use of bronze weaponry. Temporary power gradually became permanent kingship, and sometime around 2500 BCE kings in some Sumerian city-states began to hand down the kingship to their sons, establishing patriarchal hereditary dynasties in which power descended through the male line. They built palaces, which came to rival the temples in their size and magnificence. This is the point at which written records of kingship begin to appear, which, unsurprisingly, highlight the importance of kings and their connections with the gods. Priests and kings in Sumerian cities used force, persuasion, and threats of higher taxes to maintain order, keep the irrigation systems working, and keep food and other goods flowing. Urban residents inevitably found ways to subvert or resist their orders, however, such as exchanging surplus food directly with a neighbor for cloth or pots, or worshipping family or household gods rather than at state temples.

The king and other members of the elite held extensive tracts of land, as did the temple; these lands were worked by the palace's or the temple's clients, free men and women who were dependent on the palace or the temple. They received crops and other goods in return for their labor. Although this arrangement assured the clients of a livelihood, the land they worked remained the possession of the palace or the temple. Some individuals and families owned land outright and paid their taxes in the form of agricultural products or items they had made. At the bottom rung of society were slaves; the law code of the Sumerian king Ur-Nammu from 2100 to 2050 BCE—the world's oldest surviving law code—distinguishes between free persons and slaves in laws regarding marriage, rape, and injuries, and orders owners of fugitive slaves to reward those who return them.

Each of these social categories included both men and women, but their experiences were not the same, for Sumerian society made distinctions based on gender. Most elite landowners were male, but women who held positions as priestesses or as queens ran their own estates, independently of their husbands and fathers. Some women owned businesses and took care of their own accounts. Sons and daughters inherited from their parents, although a daughter received her inheritance in the form of a dowry, which technically remained hers but was managed by her husband or husband's family after marriage. The Sumerians established the basic social, economic, and intellectual patterns of Mesopotamia, and influenced their neighbors to the north and east.

Because Sumerian cities are the oldest in the world, and because after 3000 BCE written records add to the evidence provided by archaeological sources, they have had a tremendous influence on ideas about what a city is and how ancient cities functioned. Many ancient cities in other parts of the world *did* resemble those of Sumer in important ways. The Olmec city of San Lorenzo, built around 1400 BCE in what is today southern Mexico—the first city in the western hemisphere—had large temples with plazas, gigantic statues, substantial residential structures for the city's elite, a drainage system that brought in fresh water, and trading networks through which prestige materials such as jade, magnetite, and obsidian were imported and then fashioned by artisans into luxury goods and weapons. In 1200 BCE the largest city in the world was probably Anyang on the Huang He (Yellow) River in China, with perhaps 100,000 residents. It contained palaces and temples, along with elaborate underground tombs where rulers from the Shang dynasty that controlled this area and their wives were buried along with hundreds of exquisite bronze ceremonial vessels, ivory and jade ornaments, bronze weapons and armor, and a group of people who would serve them after death. In the first centuries CE the largest city in the world was undoubtedly Rome, with a population somewhere between half a million and a million. Here the emperors built beautiful temples, huge athletic arenas, triumphal arches celebrating their victories, stately palaces, and hundreds of miles of aqueducts to bring fresh water into the city, although most people lived in shoddily constructed houses and some depended on public distributions of bread and oil to survive. In the western hemisphere the largest city in the first centuries CE was Teotihuacan in the Valley of Mexico, where over 100,000 residents under the rule of kings understood to be divine built hundreds of temples, including the magnificent Pyramid of the Sun, developed a writing system, and traded jade, obsidian, and other goods with distant Maya cities.

Other urban centers looked and operated very differently from those in Sumer, however, sometimes so much so that they were not even recognized as cities until quite recently. One of these was Jenne-jeno, on the Middle Niger River floodplain in what is today Mali, initially built in the third century BCE, expanded over many centuries and then abandoned about 1400 CE. First excavated in the 1970s, Jenne-jeno was not a single city, but a clustered urban complex, with each node of the cluster specializing in the

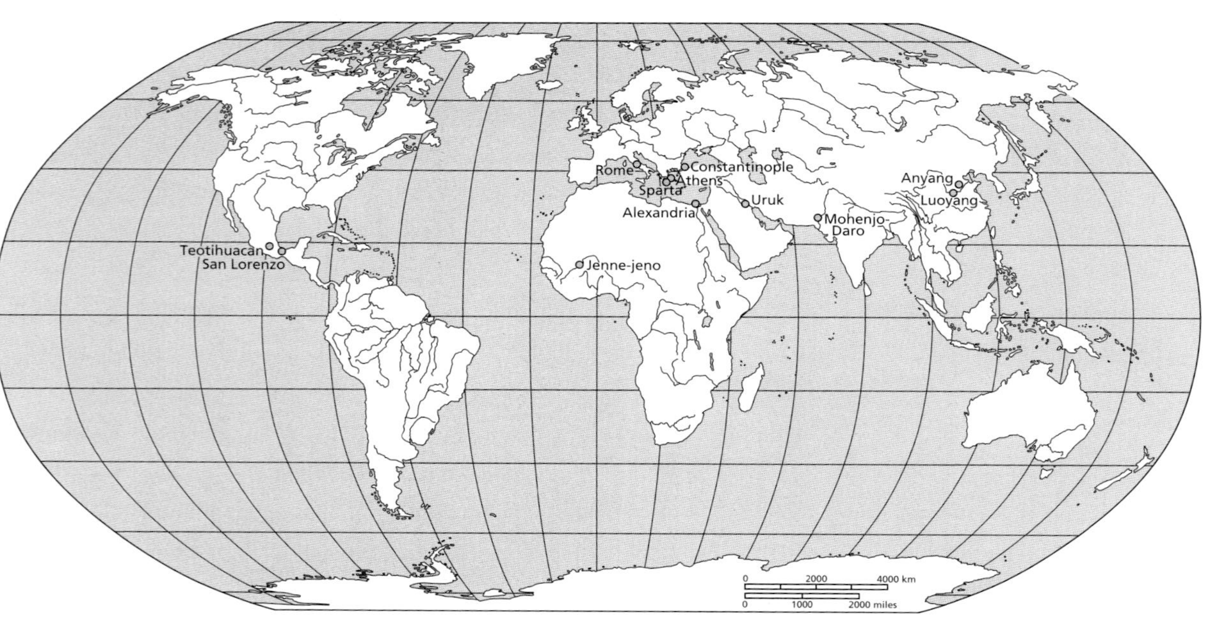

Map 2.1 Ancient cities mentioned in the chapter

production of one particular item that was then traded with others. Thus the groups living in some locales produced pots, others iron tools, others fishing nets (as evidenced by the weights that would have been attached to the nets), and so on. People raised and herded sheep, goats, and cattle, and also hunted wild animals and fish. Plant foods included rice, millet, sorghum, and vegetables grown in fields along the Middle Niger in a system that most likely took advantage of the seasonal fluctuations of the river just as farmers living in Egypt at the same time did with the Nile. Jenne-jeno became a transshipment point where merchandise arriving by camel or donkey from across the Sahara was traded for metals and local goods, and then sent by boat along the Niger.

No temples or palaces or other large buildings have been found at Jenne-jeno, leading Rod and Susan McIntosh and others who have studied this urban cluster to posit that decisions were made about the exchange of goods and services through a system of reciprocity among occupational groups rather than through a strong central authority. In this intertwined system of mutual dependence, rules and norms created expectations of the behavior needed to maximize reciprocal relationships, and were backed up by consequences—administered by the groups themselves—if the rules were not followed.

Jenne-jeno was not the only ancient city in which alternative mechanisms of authority constrained hierarchical structures and prevented them from becoming the primary exercisers of power. In the Indus River Valley, Mohenjo-Daro was built as a planned city about 2500 BCE, with straight streets, bricks made to a standard proportion, large ventilated granaries, and a drainage system that connected an indoor toilet in each house with a sewer under the street. The elaborate and dense architecture and sophisticated hydraulic infrastructure would have required coordination in building and maintenance, but there are no large buildings that are unambiguously palaces and temples, no elaborate royal burials, and no other evidence of kingship or warfare. Thus in Mohenjo-Daro and perhaps in other cities within the Indus River Valley such as Harappa, power may have been distributed among competing and fluid social or economic groups rather than being highly centralized within a single ruling dynasty.

Ancient cities were often divided into quarters, districts, or neighborhoods; these may reflect pre-existing social divisions such as kin groups, but they also grew out of new divisions fostered by the city itself, such as craft specialization or allegiance to a particular temple. In Teotihuacan, for example, some neighborhoods seem to have been reserved for merchants and traders. Even the practical necessities of urban life could generate new social groups and ideologies that underpinned these. The sewer system of Mohenjo-Daro, for example, required people to clean it so that it continued to function; they most likely took the human waste to the fields near the city to be used as fertilizer, along with animal wastes that had ended up in city streets. In other cities as well, trash collectors gathered refuse and knackers picked up dead animals, which they rendered into a variety of products, including leather, glue, and bone meal. Such activities were essential in densely populated urban spaces, but they came to be seen not only as smelly and unpleasant, but also as socially undesirable and ritually unclean. When social hierarchies later became more formalized, people who handled waste or dead animals were often the lowest group, unthinkable as marriage partners or even as neighbors by those who did other sorts of work. Cities provided opportunities for social and economic mobility, but this could be up or down.

Among the social divisions and new identities fostered by cities was that of the "citizen," understood to be the permanent resident of a specific area who had certain duties and privileges. (In time this understanding of "citizen" would also apply in larger political units such as empires and nations.) The idea that residence in a specific urban area gave one a distinct identity appears very early in the development of cities. In Mesopotamia of the third millennium BCE, for example, both members of the elite and workers named in temple ration lists were known by their city of origin.

In the cities of first-millennium BCE Greece, the distinction between citizen and non-citizen, combined with a commitment to male egalitarianism among citizens, created forms of governance that were unusual in the ancient world. Although Athens and Sparta are often contrasted, both were places where free adult male citizens shared in determining diplomatic and military policies, and where leadership appointments circulated. Women were citizens for religious and reproductive purposes, but their citizenship did not give them the right to participate in government. Citizenship was not completely distinct from kin structures, however, as almost all Greek cities defined a citizen as an adult man with at least one citizen parent, or at some times and places two. In classical Athens, resident foreigners and their sons and grandsons—termed "metics," and numbering perhaps half of the free population of the city—had to perform military service and pay taxes, but had no political voice. They could be enslaved for certain offenses—which citizens could not—and only very occasionally were granted citizenship. Thus citizens shared ancestry as well as a place of residence. As with other changes brought by cities, new civic identities overlay but did not eliminate what had existed before.

WRITING AND OTHER INFORMATION TECHNOLOGIES

Rock art in many parts of the world includes spectacular pictures of humans and animals, and it also sometimes includes tally marks, which may record days, or distance, or people, or some other thing the maker wanted to count. Tallies also show up on sticks, shells, and other objects that could be carried around, and it is these tallies that are the origins of the world's earliest writing system, which developed in Sumerian cities. Writing began not as a way to record speech, but to record data: it was an information technology that later became a communications technology. Writing was invented independently in at least three places—Sumer, China, and Mesoamerica—and perhaps in many more, and it spread from the places it was invented just like any other technology, through conquest, trade, and imitation.

Writing systems—and other forms of information technology—were invented or adopted as a way to organize and run cities that had become too large to administer by word of mouth, and to store, sort, and retrieve information across space and time. Tangible records did not depend on human memory, but were external to the individual; they transcended particular contexts and could be inspected and verified. As cities grew and their populations became more diverse and interdependent, creating and maintaining common and consistent means of measurement, and assigning collective meaning to events and structures, became more important. Conversely, writing also

2.1 Sumerian clay tablet with cuneiform characters from the ancient city of Girsu (now Tello), in modern Iraq, shows a tally of sheep and goats. Tens of thousands of cuneiform tablets have been taken, legally and illegally, from this site.

depended on cities, on the high degree of uniformity and control that cities made available, and on the specialization of labor in cities that allowed some individuals to spend time learning to write. As with the domestication of dogs, urbanization and the development of record-keeping was a process of co-evolution.

In Sumer, writing began sometime in the fourth millennium BCE as pictures drawn with a sharpened stylus on small clay tablets about the size of a cell phone, which then hardened in the sun. To the pictures people gradually added symbols, which linguists call ideograms or logograms, to represent other words and ideas. The system became so complicated that scribal schools were established, which by 2500 BCE flourished throughout Sumer. Students at the schools were all male, and most came from families in the middle range of urban society. Scribal schools were primarily intended to produce individuals who could keep records of the property and goods of temple officials and nobles. Thus writing concentrated knowledge and power in the hands of urban elites—and primarily the men among them. Hundreds of thousands of Sumerian clay tablets have survived, the oldest dating to about 3200 BCE. In them historians can see the evolution of writing from its earliest beginnings, and also learn about many aspects of everyday life, including taxes, wages, trade, and employment. A clay tablet from the city of Uruk in about 3000 BCE, for example, records the rations of beer that workers on temple agricultural lands were paid, and others record payments of bread, fish, and oil, along with outputs of wool spun into yarn, and grain harvested from fields.

In China, the oldest surviving writing is on ox shoulder-bones and turtle shells from about 1200 BCE, many of which come from the tombs of Shang rulers. Diviners at the royal court carved hollows in bones and shells, and applied heat to them with a bronze rod until cracks formed. The cracks were then interpreted by diviners—including the king himself—as an omen sent from the gods answering a question about the future. They sometimes carved the question and interpretations of the omen onto the shell, with characters that are an archaic form of modern Chinese writing; this gave the writing a ritual purpose and sacred power. Oracle bone inscriptions sometimes record actual events such as battles, floods, harvests, and royal births, so they provide information about these as well as about what rulers hoped and feared.

Oracle bones sometimes specify the source of authorization for certain actions— "The king orders so-and-so to carry out such-and-such a task"—allowing a brief glimpse at the way power was (at least in theory) disbursed. Such commands and proclamations from political leaders became a common type of written record wherever writing was introduced, allowing the dictates of the ruler to transcend the immediacy of face-to-face interaction and become, literally, the law of the land. Law codes themselves were also among the earliest form of written records, often prefaced by a statement about their being the will of the king, or the gods, or both. The Babylonian ruler Hammurabi, for example, issued a law code governing many aspects of life in 1790 BCE, and ordered it inscribed on huge stone pillars set up in public throughout his realm; at the top was often a sculpture of Hammurabi receiving the scepter of authority from the sun-god Shamash, the god of law and justice.

In Mesoamerica the development of writing also appears to have been associated with rulers and with secret knowledge. The earliest surviving example of writing comes from the Olmecs in around

900 BCE, and by about 200 BCE fully developed writing systems were in use in a number of different cities. In the Classic Period, 200–900 CE, the Maya developed the most complex writing system in the Americas, a script with nearly a thousand characters (termed "glyphs") that represent concepts and sounds, which over the last fifty years has been largely deciphered. Classic Maya writing was painted or inscribed with large glyphs in public places where it could be easily seen, on books made of treated tree bark, and on smaller objects made of valuable materials designed to be worn or diplayed, such as carved shells, ceramic vessels, hairpins, and jade ornaments, whose value was further enhanced by the artistic quality of the writing. As in Mesopotamia, students learned to write in schools, where they probably began by copying models onto perishable bark and palm leaves.

Many of the surviving large-scale inscriptions are historical documents recording the births, accessions, marriages, wars, and deaths of Maya kings and nobles counted in a linear fashion forward from a specific date. Others relate to the two cyclical calendars used by the Maya to determine the proper times for religious rituals, one of which they had perhaps inherited from the Olmecs and the other devised through their own careful observation of the earth's movements around the sun. Such public writing communicated the links between a city's rulers and the gods even to those who did not read (or who did not read very well), so it served as a form of propaganda for public consumption, assuring the city's residents that the rulers had fulfilled their obligations to the gods.

Mesopotamian, Chinese, Maya, and other early forms of writing combined symbols that stood for words and ideas with a few that stood for sounds, and sometime around 1800 BCE workers in the Sinai peninsula, which was under Egyptian control, began to use only phonetic signs to write their language, with each sign designating one sound. This system vastly simplified writing and reading and spread among common people as a practical way to record things and communicate. Phoenicians—sea-going traders from the cities of the Mediterranean coast of modern Lebanon—adopted the simpler system for their own language and spread it around the Mediterranean. The Greeks modified this alphabet,

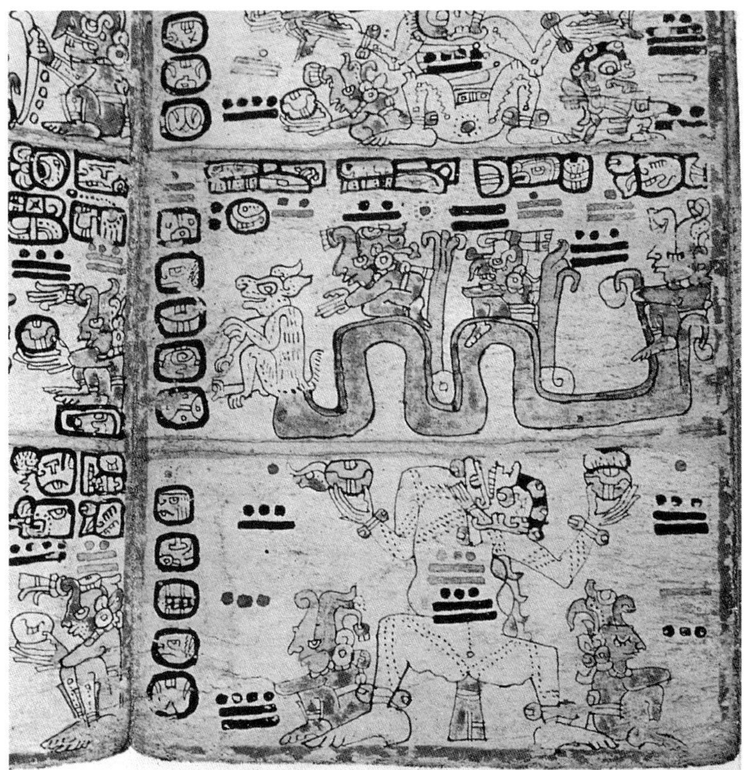

2.2 A page from the Maya book known as the Madrid Codex, painted in the thirteenth century on paper made from fig tree bark, which presents almanacs, horoscopes, and astronomical tables related to the 260-day ritual calendar used throughout Mesoamerica for divination and prophecy. The images include rituals and ordinary activities, and are bordered by glyphs.

especially by adding vowels, and beginning in the eighth century BCE used it to write their own language. The Romans later based their alphabet—the script we use to write English today—on Greek, which was also the basis for the Cyrillic script of eastern Europe and the runic script of northern Europe. Alphabets based on the Phoenician alphabet were also created in the Persian Empire and formed the basis of Hebrew, Arabic, and various alphabetic scripts of South and Central Asia. The system invented by ordinary people and spread by Phoenician merchants is the origin of most of the world's alphabetic scripts in use today.

Even after alphabetic systems became more common, however, learning to read and write took a number of years, which meant that until quite recently this was generally limited to three sorts of people: members of the elite who did not have to engage in productive labor to support themselves; clergy and other religious personnel for whom reading and writing were spiritually meritorious tasks; and those who could hope to support themselves by writing or for whom writing was required as part of their work. The first two groups comprised both women and men, for some elite women have been literate in all of the world's cultures that have writing, as have some nuns in certain religious traditions. The third group was predominantly male: professional scribes, copiers, record-keepers, artisans in certain trades, officials, and administrators whose parents had been willing and able to pay for schooling, or who had found a patron to support them in this.

The functions to which writing was put in early cities, and in the larger states that developed out of them, were multiple and varied: economic administration, the performance of power, the recording and commemoration of ritual, the transmission of divine instructions. Was the invention of writing a revolution? For scholars in the nineteenth and much of the twentieth centuries, the answer to that question was a resounding yes: Writing marked the beginning of history, with the human past before writing regarded as prehistory, and groups that did not have writing were dismissed as uncivilized "people without history." In the 1960s and 1970s, the British anthropologist Jack Goody and the North American cultural theorists Walter Ong and Marshall McLuhan developed more nuanced versions of this, rejecting the sharp civilized versus uncivilized dichotomy, but arguing that changes in modes of communication brought dramatic changes in every other realm of life, external and internal. For Goody, writing (especially the alphabetic writing of the Greeks) encouraged abstract thought, formal logic, and a distinction between myth and history. For Ong and McLuhan, when writing moved language from the world of sound to the world of sight, it restructured human cognition and consciousness.

Many social historians and anthropologists saw these assertions as too sweeping. They emphasized that, until the last several centuries, only a tiny share of the population could read or write, and most people's worlds were oral ones. Institutions to support oral culture were created and expanded long after writing was invented: high altars, pulpits, and towers were constructed in or on religious buildings so that people could hear priests or the call to prayer more clearly; outdoor platforms and balconies were built on palaces and town halls where laws and rules were proclaimed; theatres were established for oral performances. Even in classical Athens—the prime example in Goody's argument about the revolutionary impact of writing—adult male citizens gathered for speeches and debate at the assembly known as the *ekklesia*, which was held outdoors on a hill in central Athens. Written texts became central in certain religions, including Buddhism, Christianity, and Islam, but the monks, priests, merchants, and teachers who spread these might not have been able to read themselves.

World historians, especially those who concentrate their research on parts of the world where writing did not develop, have also disputed the idea that there was a sharp divide between oral and written cultures. They note that oral traditions could also be formal and ritualized and require a long period of training, giving those with this training social and political power, or close connections to those with power. In the Mande societies of West Africa, for example, oral historians known as *griots* preserved and transmitted cultural memory, serving as advisers to kings and promoters of royal authority, and among the Luba of Central Africa, *bana balute* ("men of memory") did this as well.

Oral traditions might also be enhanced by physical mnemonic devices that were not writing, but served many of its functions. The bana balute used *lukasa*, hourglass-shaped wooden memory boards covered with beads, shells, and incised symbols that helped them remember royal genealogies, events, places, and migration routes. Peruvian peoples, most prominently the Inca, used *khipu* (also spelled *quipu*), knotted string devices with sometimes hundreds of cords, to record information. Spanish colonial-era records indicate that these were used to keep track of tax and labor obligations, the output of fields, land transfers, census records, and other numeric data. They were created and read by older male specialists, and were carried by runners and officials on the vast highway system of the Inca, proving to local communities that whoever carried them had authorization from above for his demands, and allowing the official to report back with more detail to his superiors. Scholars have decoded the way numbers were recorded on khipu, and are currently working on deciphering words, which may have been recorded in numbers, similar to the way postal codes today represent places and various types of identification numbers represent persons. Khipu were not connected to spoken language, and knowledge of how to read them died out after the Spanish conquest. Spanish officials and soldiers destroyed khipu in the Andes because they thought they might contain religious messages and encourage people to resist Spanish authority. About 600 Inca khipu survive today, more than half in museums in Europe or the United States. They—and other aids to memory—suggest to those who study them that writing may not have been such a dramatic change, that other types of recording systems also provided their users with the ability to sort, quantify, keep order, and assert power.

Since the 1990s, media and cultural studies scholars and some neurologists have returned to viewing writing as revolutionary, however. Not only did writing lead to greater cultural uniformity, tighter political control, and new social institutions, but it also shaped the human brain itself, affecting left brain/right brain lateralization and other brain features. Media scholars tend to focus on today (and tomorrow) rather than the past as they examine what the first issue of *Wired* magazine in 1993 described as "the Digital Revolution [that] is whipping through our lives like a Bengali typhoon," but their assertions that the way in which we acquire information shapes (or, as some would argue, determines) us as individuals and as societies supports the view that writing really mattered.

STATES AND LINEAGES

Just as writing has been judged a major break in the human past, so have the political forms that first emerged in the cities of Sumer: these were the world's first states, the sociopolitical form in which a small share of the population is able to coerce resources out of everyone else in order to gain and then maintain power. States are large and complex; they coerce people through violence, or the threat of violence, and also through bureaucracies and systems of taxation. In contrast to kin groups and chiefdoms, states have formalized rules, norms, and ways of distributing power, more elaborate social and gender hierarchies through which certain groups are privileged and others subordinated, and cultural institutions and practices that have allowed them to be judged "civilizations."

States grew in scale in the ancient world. In Southwest Asia, the individual city-states of Sumer grew into kingdoms controlling more than one urban center such as that of Sargon of Akkad, and then into empires, large multi-ethnic states created by military force. The kingdom established by Sargon collapsed, perhaps because of a period of extended drought, and this area became part of various other kingdoms and empires over the next several millennia: Babylonian, Assyrian, Hittite, Neo-Babylonian, Neo-Assyrian, Persian, Alexandrian, Seleucid, Roman. In between eras in which empires unified large territories under their rule were periods of instability and decentralization. Other parts of the world saw similar long-term political patterns. In China, armies of the Shang rulers were defeated in about 1050 by those of the Zhou, who expanded the size of Chinese territory significantly; Zhou rule fell apart in what became known as the "Warring States Period" (403–221 BCE), then the Qin and Han rulers (221 BCE–220 CE) restored unity and increased the size of China's empire still further, but then this also collapsed into the "Age of Division" (220–589 CE). In Egypt, unity and disunity structure the entire understanding of history, which is described as three periods of stability and expansion—the Old (2660–2180 BCE), Middle (2080–1640 BCE) and New (1570–1070 BCE) Kingdoms—each followed by a time of fragmentation and disorder: the First, Second, and Third Intermediate Periods. On the western coast of South America and in the Andes, urban societies ruled by kings built monumental architecture and became regional powers that dominated ever-larger territories, but then collapsed: Caral (2500–1600 BCE), Chavin (1000–200 BCE), Moche (200 BCE–700 CE), Tiwanaku (100 CE–1100 CE).

Accounts of the rise and fall of city-states, kingdoms, and empires, and their conflicts and rivalries with one another, have been the primary story told by historians since the invention of writing. This is understandable: empires did become empires through conquest. But empires only *stayed* empires by establishing some means through which power was handed on, and almost all of the states established in the ancient world—first in Southwest Asia and the Nile Valley, and then in India, China, the Mediterranean, Central and South America, and ultimately other areas—did so in the same way. They were hereditary monarchies, in which those who held power were regarded as members of one kin group, and the legitimate handing on of authority was understood to proceed through a dynastic succession. Chinese history came to be told as a series of named dynasties (Shang, Zhou, Qin, Han, Sui, Tang, Song, Yuan, Ming, Xing) and Egyptian as a series of thirty-one numbered ones, a system invented in the third century BCE by the Egyptian historian Manetho from existing king lists. Even in those few states that were *not* hereditary monarchies, such as the city-states of classical-era Greece or the Roman Republic (in which authority was exercised by a Senate of aristocratic landowners), membership in the group that made political and military decisions was determined by birth. Thus the rise and fall of states is also a story of the rise and fall of lineages, that is, social groups maintained through sexual relationships that produced children who could legitimately inherit. This connection between politics and (hetero)sexuality in most of recorded history is so close that it has often been invisible to historians, but it was not to those who held power.

The idea that authority should proceed within a lineage was so compelling that when there was no heir (or no competent heir) available or on the horizon, one was often created, with a ruler adopting a likely young man as his son. Norms of succession were also flexible; brothers or nephews inherited, and sometimes a royal lineage passed down to the male children of daughters if there were no sons. Although in most places women were excluded from actual rule, in extraordinary cases there were female rulers. Even rules regarding legitimate birth could be malleable. In some hereditary monarchies, having a mother who was not officially a wife of the ruler barred a son absolutely from inheriting the throne, but in others it did not. His mother's status was simply ignored, or he might be adopted by an official wife as hers. Just as kin relations within ethnic groups were sometimes invented, so were those in hereditary dynasties, but this is evidence of the power, not the weakness, of the state/lineage link.

China provides an excellent example of how this connection operated in both theory and practice. In both the Shang and the Zhou dynasties, rulers carried out rituals to a range of deities, which they declared included their own ancestors, from whom they sought guidance and assistance. The Zhou also portrayed their victory over the Shang in 1050 BCE as justified by the fact that the sky deity Heaven (*Tien*) had removed support from the Shang because they were oppressive and inept, and transferred legitimate rule to the virtuous Zhou. The king is understood to be the Son of Heaven in Zhou documents, but Heaven gives him the mandate to rule only as long as he rules wisely and in the interests of the people. This political theory of the Mandate of Heaven was new, and it lasted for millennia. Succession was hereditary and kings were linked in a family relationship with divine forces, but there was also a sense that kings were to act ethically, or Heaven would take the mandate away and entrust it to a ruler who was virtuous.

Along with religious rituals and political theories, both the Shang and the Zhou cemented their dynastic rule through more prosaic methods. Kings married multiple times, with the size of their households a demonstration of their wealth and power. The majority of their wives came from other states, for marriage was an important tool in forming political networks and consolidating territory. Gradually the Lineage Law (*zongfa*) system coalesced, which privileged the eldest son of the principal wife, and the pattern became one primary wife along with concubines, who were legal spouses but of lower rank. This patrilineal system came to encompass other elite families as well; for great nobles and the lower ranks of the aristocracy known as *shi*, family and clan names were transmitted along patrilineal lines, as were administrative positions, property, titles, and traditions of sacrificing to the ancestors.

Neither military superiority nor smart marriage alliances last forever, and China broke apart into rival states about 400 BCE. The next long-lasting dynasty, the Han, was established in 206 BCE by a charismatic leader from a relatively ordinary family, but he and his advisers and successors successfully linked the Han dynasty with earlier strong rulers. They promoted the veneration of Huangdi (the Yellow Emperor)—a remarkable early ruler now known to be mythical—as the founder of China, and claimed descent from him

2.3 A lacquered basket from the Han dynasty (206 BCE–222 CE) shows model sons whose names are taken from the *Xiao Jing*, a Confucian classic giving advice on filial piety. This basket was found in a tomb in the Chinese colony of Lelang in northern Korea.

through one of his twenty-five sons. They also promoted the philosophical system known as Confucianism, based on the ideas of the fifth-century BCE thinker Confucius as recorded and spread by his followers. Confucius considered the family the basic unit of society, and emphasized the importance of filial piety, and the reverence and obedience that children owe their parents, and in particular that sons owe their fathers. The father/son relationship was one of the key hierarchies in society, along with those of ruler/subject, husband/wife, and elder brother/younger brother, all of which reflected the cosmic hierarchical relationship between Heaven and earth. In these hierarchies one element is clearly superior and the other inferior, but both are necessary, and harmony and order depend on the balance between the two.

In Confucian teachings, the ultimate goal for a man—at least for those who could afford it—was to become a sage, a highly educated and wise individual who, in words attributed to Confucius, "seeks also to enlarge others," that is, to serve the broader political order. In addition, men were expected to carry out specific rituals honoring their ancestors and parents throughout their lives, have sons so that these rituals could continue, and place the interests of the family line above their own. The ultimate goal for a woman was to be regarded as a "Treasure of the House," who willingly submitted to the "three obediences" to which women were subject: to her father as a daughter, to her husband as a wife, and to her son as a widow. Han rulers recruited men such as Ban Gu trained in the Confucian classics as officials to run their growing empire. These scholar-officials in turn wrote commentaries emphasizing that the emperor alone connected Heaven and earth, and that all proper human relationships were hierarchical and orderly. Confucianism became a state ideology, and a publicly acknowledged ethical system for many elite families as well. All aspects of family relationships had proper etiquette and rituals attached, which became more elaborate over the centuries.

Unfortunately Han rulers were not always as blessed with sons as Huangdi had been, nor were all relationships what Confucian scholars wanted them to be. The wife of the first Han emperor had a son, but he was a child when he inherited the throne, and his mother served as regent (termed an "empress dowager" in China), ruling on his behalf. The reign of Empress Dowager Lü was apparently stable and popular, but historians at the courts of later Chinese emperors invented stories that she killed all her rivals, and the "Evil Empress Lü" became a prime example of the terrible things that would happen when a woman ruled.

The collapse of the Han dynasty provides another instance of the close relationship between sexual reproduction—or its absence—and the state. In the late second century CE a succession of Han rulers died without leaving an adult son, and the mothers of the boy-emperors served as regents. The empresses and their families formed one faction at court, scholar-officials another, and a third faction was made up of eunuchs—castrated men—who held important official positions. Eunuchs appear in historical records nearly as early as states, with the first in Sumerian cities about 2000 BCE.

They were common in the ancient world in the Assyrian, Persian, and Eastern Roman empires as well as in China, and later in other states as well. Some were captives of war or rebels castrated as punishment, but others had been castrated as boys by their families because this opened up opportunities for employment. In China and elsewhere, eunuchs were granted positions in the bureaucracy, army, and royal palace in part because they could not marry and father children; as the theory went, they would be more loyal to the ruling family than to their own, so could be trusted. Eunuchs sometimes rose to high rank and had illustrious careers; the fifteenth-century Chinese admiral Zheng He, for example, who led several enormous expeditions to the Indian Ocean, was a eunuch, castrated as a boy after being taken as a prisoner of war. Eunuchs were not always as reliable as rulers hoped, however, as they still had broader family connections and personal ambitions. In the case of the Han dynasty, eunuchs, empresses, and court officials all plotted against one another, and engaged generals with armies to back up their aims. Those generals had their own ambitions, however, and by the early third century China was torn apart and the Han dynasty was no more.

The state/lineage connections developed in other hereditary monarchies show many of the same characteristics as those in China. Ruling lineages elsewhere also justified their authority through ties with an ancestral heroic figure. Rulers worked closely with religious authorities and relied on ideas about their connections with the gods, as well as the rulers' military might, for their power. Rulers everywhere used marriage as a way to make or cement alliances, and as a symbol of conquest. They often had large numbers of wives, concubines, slaves, and other types of female dependants as a sign of status, a pattern termed "resource polygyny." Rulers depended on their family members for many aspects of government.

The growth of hereditary monarchies and larger-scale states affected relations between power and gender in ambiguous and sometimes contradictory ways. In many cases it led to restrictions on women and greater gender differentiation. Because the right to rule—or for nobles, other privileges of rank—was handed down through inheritance, it was extremely important to male elites that the children their wives bore were theirs. Elite women in many states were thus increasingly secluded, and strict laws were passed regarding adultery, which in some cases affected non-elite women as well. Women's own kin connections often became less important than those of their husbands, which made their status more derivative and dependent than it had been in tribes or chiefdoms.

The development of hereditary monarchies did not uniformly limit women's power and status, however, but increased those of a small group of women and occasionally gave them legitimately sanctioned authority as members of a lineage.

In Egypt, the ruler—who was eventually called the pharaoh—was regarded as divine, and the divine force was found in all members of his family. Rulers or rulers-to-be occasionally married their sisters or other close relatives in order to increase the amount of divine blood in the royal household, and to imitate the gods, who in Egyptian mythology often married their siblings. The familial connection with the divine allowed a handful of women to rule in their own right in Egypt's long history, including Hatshepsut (r. 1479–1458 BCE), the daughter of King Thutmose I, and the half-sister and wife of King Thutmose II. Just as male rulers did, she had herself depicted in ceremonial representations with the standard pharaonic regalia—a kilt, a false beard, and a headdress topped by a cobra—or as the god Osiris, although in other official portraits she wears the normal clothing of a wealthy Egyptian woman, and she made no attempt to hide the fact that she was a woman in any inscriptions. Her adopting the same garb that male rulers did suggests that she understood her lineage to be more important than her gender, as would later female rulers throughout the world.

Several women, including empresses Hamiko and Jingu, are mentioned among the early rulers of Japan, gaining power through both their family connections and their role as shamans capable of hearing and transmitting the advice of the gods; accounts of their lives mix myth and history, but they became important parts of Japanese national traditions. In Mesoamerica, Lady Ahpo-Katun, Lady Ahpo-Hel, Lady Zac Kuk, and other women ruled Maya city-states on their own. Reliefs sometimes show them dressed as male gods, just as Hatshepsut was in some of her portraits, or wearing costumes that blended male and female clothing in ways that suggest a range of gender and transgender possibilities. The wives of Maya rulers participated along with their husbands in the blood-letting rituals that were a key symbol of royal power. Ceremonies involving actual royal blood could be found in other places as well, and in even more places royal blood was understood to be a real substance whose power trumped other distinctions.

MARRIAGES AND FAMILIES IN CITIES AND STATES

Rulers' families were different from other families in some ways, but in other ways they were not, because urbanization, writing, and the growth of the state shaped family life at all social levels. Conversely, the aims and actions of families and kin groups influenced larger-scale socio-economic structures, government policies, and cultural patterns. Families in the ancient world (and beyond) were both sites and agents of historical transformation.

Certain trends can be seen wherever cities and states developed, which written records can allow us to trace in greater detail, particularly for urban dwellers of middling status and above. These patterns were remarkably long-lived, with many of them continuing for millennia and some still evident today. For urban families, as for hereditary rulers, procreation and property were the family's intertwined core threads. Because marriage linked two families as well as two persons, the choice of a spouse was much too important a matter to be left to young people to decide. Marriages were most often arranged by one's parents, other family members, or marriage brokers. They assessed the possible marriage partners and chose someone appropriate, whom they hoped would produce children and enhance or at least maintain the family's socio-economic status. Families consulted astrologers or diviners or other types of people who predicted the future for advice about a suggested spouse and the most propitious time for the wedding. In the Roman Empire, June was a favored month, as it was named after Juno, the goddess of marriage and childbirth, and as children conceived in June would be born in the spring, increasing their chances of survival.

Marriage had aspects of a business agreement: the groom or his father offered the prospective bride's father a gift, and if this was acceptable the bride's father or other family members provided his daughter with a dowry, which generally technically remained hers, though her husband administered it during the course of the marriage. Dowries might consist of land, movable goods, jewelry, slaves, and later also coinage or promissary notes for future payments. Like other business arrangements, a marriage might be formalized by a written contract, signed by the fathers of the spouses or by the groom and the bride's father. No religious or public official played any role in this; marriage was a legally and culturally recognized tie, but it was a private familial agreement. Weddings were central occasions in a family's life, with much of a family's resources often going to pay for the ceremony and setting up the new household. In most urbanized societies, living arrangements for spouses were patrilocal: the bride came to live in or near the ancestral home of the groom, or in a place determined by his family rather than hers.

Sexual relations finalized the marriage; if they did not occur for some reason, negotiations generally began to return the gifts and dissolve the contract. In South Asia, religious ideas about the importance of family life and many children led to a pattern in which all men and women were expected to marry. Women in particular married very young, and widows and women who had not had sons were excluded from wedding festivities. Anything that interfered with procreation, including exclusively same-sex attachments or religious vows taken early in life, was frowned upon. The domestic fire had great symbolic importance, with husband and wife making regular offerings in front of it. Children, particularly boys, were shown great affection and developed close attachments to their parents, especially their mothers. These mothers often continued to live in the house of their eldest son upon widowhood, creating stresses between mothers-in-law and daughters-in-law. Cruel and angry mothers-in-law were standard figures in the stories of classical India, reflecting what was often harsh treatment of young women in real life. (In the Mediterranean and the rest of Europe, widowed mothers generally did not live with their married sons, so the spiteful old woman in stories is generally a stepmother rather than a mother-in-law.)

Arranged marriage did not always preclude the possibility of spousal affection and romantic love. Among the tax lists and legal codes that are the most common records left from ancient societies, there is also some erotic love poetry, although we have no way of knowing whether this poetry was written as a prelude to marriage, during a marriage, to someone not the author's spouse, or perhaps even as a metaphor for love of a god. Material evidence is a bit firmer: Men's tomb inscriptions from New Kingdom Egypt and the Roman Republic occasionally refer affectionately to their wives, and couples were sometimes portrayed standing close to one another or arm in arm.

Marriage itself was a private agreement, but as soon as states were established they attempted to regulate aspects of family life. Early written law codes often included provisions regarding dowries, inheritance, and other types of property transfer within families, and also provisions about sexual behavior. About a third of the several hundred provisions in the law code of the Babylonian king Hammurabi from 1790 BCE, for example, concerned families and sex, including laws regarding adultery, desertion, separation and divorce, the husband's sex with servants or slaves and his treatment of the children that resulted from this, rape within the family, premarital sex, incest, breach of marital contract, second marriages after divorce or death, adoption, and the complexities of inheritance and ownership of property that could result from all of these.

The code of Hammurabi clearly envisions the husband/father as the dominant person economically and socially in the household. His decisions were expected to determine the economic (and thus marital) fate of his children by his wife or servants. If he could prove that his wife "wishes to leave it [the household], plunges into debt, tries to ruin her house, neglects her husband, and is judicially convicted," he could divorce her without returning her dowry. That clause, and others in the code, provide evidence that women were perhaps not as dependent as the male, educated, well-to-do Babylonian lawmakers hoped they would be, however. If a wife "plunges into debt," someone had to loan her the money, and other provisions of the code discuss women contracting debts before and during marriage, husbands giving their wives "fields, gardens, and houses," and mothers choosing which of their sons to favor in handing on property. (The ability to decide who gets your property after you die, called "testamentary freedom," was often restricted by gender, birth position in a family, and other factors; the

Babylonian code is unusual in the amount of testamentary freedom it gives to married women.) Although women are always a tiny minority of those who appear in the sparse records of actual legal and financial transactions, sources from many parts of the ancient world suggest that women may have made more family decisions and controlled more of what went on in the household than laws alone would indicate.

Women were particularly active in the Greek city-state of Sparta, which developed family structures very different from those anywhere else in the ancient world. In Sparta between the eighth and the fifth centuries BCE, all activity was directed toward military ends. Citizen boys left their homes at seven years old and lived in military camps until they were thirty, eating and training with boys and men their own age. They married at about eighteen to women of roughly the same age, but saw their wives only when they sneaked out of camp. Military discipline was harsh—this is the origin of the word "spartan"—but severity was viewed as necessary to prepare men both to fight external enemies such as Sparta's rival city Athens and to control the slaves who lived in the city and the dependent farmers who lived in the rural area around it, groups that vastly outnumbered the citizens.

In this militaristic atmosphere, citizen women were remarkably free. As in all ancient societies, there was an emphasis on childbearing, but the Spartan leadership viewed maternal health as important for the bearing of healthy, strong children, and so encouraged women to participate in athletics and to eat well. With men in military service most of their lives, citizen women owned property and ran the household, and were not physically restricted or secluded. Despite the emphasis on procreation, same-sex attachments were widely accepted, with male same-sex relationships in particular viewed as militarily expedient, leading men to fight more fiercely in defense of their male lovers and comrades, as well as their wives and children.

The unusual family and gender structures of Sparta did not leave much of a legacy, however, for the dominant city-state in classical Greece culturally, politically, and intellectually was Athens. As noted above, Athenian democracy made a sharp distinction between citizen and non-citizen, with citizenship handed down from father to son, symbolized by a ceremony held on the tenth day after a child was born in which the father laid his son on the floor of the house and gave him a name; this ceremony marked a boy's legal birth. It was thus very important to Athenian citizen men that their sons be their own, so that their wives were increasingly secluded in special parts of the house. Female citizens participated in religious festivals and funerals, and may have attended some theatre performances and other public events, although the extent to which they did so is debated. In contrast to most classical societies, Athenians regarded the individual man, rather than the family, as the basis of the social order; an adolescent was to learn how to be a citizen in a hierarchical tutorial relationship with an older man. That relationship might involve sex, with the older man taking the active (penetrator) role viewed as appropriate for adult male citizens, but it was supposed to become intellectualized and "platonic" once the adolescent became an adult. (How often actual sexual relationships between men or between men and women approached the ideal in Athens is difficult to say, as most of the surviving sources are prescriptive, idealized, or fictional.)

Athenian norms and ideas were carried widely around the Mediterranean and beyond by the armies of Alexander the Great in the fourth century BCE and by the Hellenistic states set up as hereditary monarchies ruled by Greeks after his death. In some places these clashed with existing practices. In Egypt, for example, women had long done business and worked in public without head coverings, managed their own property, served as guarantors for the loans of others, and acted on their own behalf in legal matters, including appearing in court. This was startling to Greek conquerors, and some Egyptian men attempted to take advantage of the more restrictive Greek laws and deprive female family members of their property. Egyptian legal records from the third century BCE include cases in which women fought such moves, and demanded to remain under the more gender-egalitarian Egyptian legal codes.

Marriages in the ancient world sometimes ended with divorce, but much more often with the death of one spouse. Law codes include stipulations about what would happen when either the man or the woman died first, but because a woman's economic situation, social position, and legal standing were generally more dependent on her husband's than his was on hers, a husband's death

2.4 On this krater used to mix wine and water, made in fifth-century BCE Athens and attributed to the anonymous vase painter known as the Kleophrades painter, a discus thrower gets tips from his trainer. Athenian vases and dishes often depict young male athletes, who generally competed in the nude, as festivals celebrated both athletic prowess and the male body.

was a more dramatic rupture in the family. At his death, a wife became a widow, a word for which there is no male equivalent in many ancient languages and one of the few words in English and other modern languages in which the male, widower, is derived from the female instead of the other way around. Her situation varied considerably from place to place, and it changed over time. In much of South Asia and China, when a husband died his widow came under the legal authority of her eldest son or her husband's brother or other family members. One of the articles of the Manusmrti ("Laws of Manu"), a long text detailing social and ritual obligations compiled between 200 BCE and 200 CE in India, states: "In childhood a female must be subject to her father, in youth to her husband, and when her lord is dead, to her sons; a woman must never be independent." Among Central Asian nomads, the widow was expected to marry the brother of her dead husband—a practice called levirate marriage—which appears to have been a common practice in other areas as well. This was a way to provide for her and her children, keep them within the clan, and assure that a sexually experienced woman came quickly under a husband's authority. The Hebrew Bible mandates levirate marriage if the widow was childless, with her firstborn son considered the child and heir of her dead husband, but it also provides a way for the man to opt out of this. Levirate marriages never seem to have been very common among Jews, however, and grew even less so over time.

In contrast to places where widows quickly came under the control of male family members, in other places a woman's ability to act independently increased after her husband died. There were no categorical statements prescribing or praising this to parallel Confucian texts or the Manusmrti—perhaps because the authors of such texts were all male—but records from Egypt, cities around the Mediterranean in the Hellenistic period (336–100 BCE), Imperial Rome, and even the Bible show widows buying and selling land, making loans, giving charitable donations, or providing support for religious establishments. Widows were somewhat suspect because they were not under direct male control, but such actions were acceptable because widows were often guardians for their children and so in control of family finances. Even in China and India, descriptive sources suggest that some widows were more economically active than prescriptive sources imply, managed the assets of their dowries and gave donations to Buddhist monasteries.

FAMILY PATTERNS IN KIN-BASED SOCIETIES

Family life in the ancient period is harder to examine for parts of the world in which there were few cities and where traditions and norms were transmitted orally. Historians and anthropologists use a variety of means to study kinship organizations, marital patterns, living arrangements, and other aspects of family structure: written records from later periods, reports of outsiders, direct interviews and oral histories with living individuals, archaeological remains, and linguistic analysis of words denoting family and kin. All of these provide evidence, but they also have limitations. What is described as "traditional" may often be quite new, for family patterns are not static, and groups living in areas without strong written traditions developed very diverse family forms and arrangements.

Some patterns of family structure and function appear to have been fairly common among agriculturalists, pastoralists, and foragers who did not live in states. Those considered kin tended to include a fairly wide group of relatives, and this kin group had a voice in domestic and other matters, such as who would marry and when they would do so, who would have access to land, animals, or other economic resources, or whose conduct was unacceptable and worthy of censure or punishment. These decisions were arrived at through a process of negotiation and discussion within the family, with the influence of each member dependent on the situation. The opinions of older family members generally carried more weight than those of younger, the opinions of first born more than later born, and the opinions of men more than women. These two hierarchies—age and gender—interacted in complex ways dependent on the issue at hand, with older women sometimes having control of younger men on certain matters. Death did not end one's authority, for the ancestors now inhabiting the unseen world could also intervene in family life.

Marital patterns and the resultant living and ownership arrangements varied. In agricultural areas of Africa, many marriages were polygynous, and families lived in house-compounds in which each wife had her own house, cattle, fields, and property. In eastern and southern Africa, groups such as the Khoisan and Nilotes were pastoralists, with the men typically caring for cattle, the higher-status animals, and the women caring for smaller ones such as goats. Cattle often formed the bridewealth that husbands presented to their wives' families on marriage, with fathers and male elders retaining control over young men's marriages through their control of the cattle. Among Germanic and Slavic peoples in Europe and Western Asia, wealthy and powerful men had several wives, but they all lived in the same household; polygamy was not common among ordinary people, nor was female property ownership as widespread as it was in Africa.

Many cultures in Africa, the Americas, and the Pacific were matrilineal, in which membership in a kin group was traced through the female line and a man's heirs were his sister's children. This meant not necessarily that women were economically or legally autonomous, but that they depended more on their brothers than their husbands. Their brothers also depended on them, however, for many of these cultures also had systems of marriage in which a husband brought a bridewealth to his wife's family. A man often used the money, land, or goods that the family had received as the bridewealth at the marriage of his sister as his own bridewealth, so that his marriage was dependent on his sister marrying well. A prospective groom also frequently performed brideservice for the family of his future wife, working for his future father-in-law either before the wedding or in a period of trial marriage. Matrilineal inheritance systems encouraged close lifelong relations among siblings, with women relying on their birth families for support if they came into conflict with their husbands. This was particularly true in groups that were also matrilocal, such as those in eastern North America, in which husbands came to live with their wives' clans and related women lived together. Relations with one's mother's kin were thus more important than those with one's father's kin or even one's spouse, and children often regarded their mother's brothers with particular respect.

Matrilineal, matrilocal systems allowed for the relatively easy in-marriage of men from other groups, because the men could not claim immediate control over their wives' property. This became particularly important in places where men traveled long distances for trade or settlement. For example, Austronesian men sailed large outrigger canoes west across the Indian Ocean from southern Borneo and other parts of contemporary Indonesia to the east coast of Africa between about 100 CE and 700 CE, bringing with them food crops, including bananas, coconuts, and sugar cane, which began to be cultivated in Africa. They also appear to have intermarried with local women, as, judging by genetic evidence, the people who began to settle the large and previously uninhabited island of Madagascar off the East African coast shortly after this have ancestry that is about half Austronesian and half East African. The Malagasy language spoken on Madagascar is an Austronesian language similar to those spoken on Borneo, and the material culture on the island combined Austronesian and African elements.

Although we do not know definitively that this means East African groups were matrilineal, similar examples of in-marrying men from more recent periods in other places suggests this is likely. Wherever it occurred, in-marriage of outside men facilitated trade and cultural exchange, thus providing a good example of the way in which family structure shaped society beyond the household.

Matrilineal inheritance systems and bridewealth made some family relationships stronger, but they also created problems. Just as patrilineal inheritance could lead to tensions, so could bride-service. Men objected to the influence of their wives' families, and, in areas where wives moved to their husband's households, intentionally chose wives who came from far away, which also lessened the degree to which their sons could rely on their maternal uncles. Conflict between fathers and sons was exacerbated by polygyny and bridewealth, as families had to decide whether their resources would best be spent acquiring a first wife for a son or another wife for the father. Some scholars have seen this generational conflict as a source for harsh initiation rituals that unmarried young men often had to undergo; only those who had gone through such rituals would be allowed to marry and join the ranks of fully adult men.

Some groups in Africa and the Americas had bilateral inheritance. Among many peoples living in the Andean region, for example, lines of descent appear to have been reckoned through both sexes, with girls inheriting access to resources such as land, water, and animals through their mothers, and boys through their fathers. In other groups with bilateral inheritance, only men inherited, but they did so from both their fathers and their mothers' brothers.

Some form of divorce or marital separation appears to have been widely available. In later periods, among matrilocal groups in North America, a man who wished to divorce simply left his wife's house, while a woman put her husband's belongings outside her family's house, indicating she wished him to leave; the children in both cases stayed with the mother and her family. Among some groups divorce was frowned upon after children had been born, however, or because it would involve complicated financial transactions, such as the return of bridewealth.

Descriptions of family relationships in the vast parts of the world outside of states and empires in the ancient period must remain

2.5 Pottery effigy jar of a mother and child, from the Moche culture that flourished on the coast of Peru from about 100 CE to about 800 CE. Moche ceramics served as funerary offerings in burials, but were also used in households for everyday purposes, where they communicated cultural values.

tentative, which is also true for the majority of people who lived inside states. Written records tell us little about the families or personal relationships of people who owned no property, and even less about the families of people who were themselves property. As families or as individuals, lower-status people generally appear in the records only when for some reason they were not fulfilling their obligations to their higher-ups: when drought or floods destroyed agricultural surpluses; when famine or epidemics slowed the stream of migrants into cities; when they rebelled or fled.

SOCIAL HIERARCHIES AND CASTE

The written records produced by cities and states reflect the concerns of those at the top of the social heap, and among these was the maintenance of that hierarchy itself. States generated new patterns of social inequality, expanding on those that emerged in agricultural villages, and often codifying these in written law. In early Roman history, for example, the most significant social division was that between the hereditary ruling group of families known as patricians and the free common people known as plebeians. Philosophical and religious texts discussed these hierarchies, justifying them with reference to the gods or to nature.

Among the most complex and enduring of these social hierarchies was the system that developed in South Asia after the mid second century BCE. In the earliest sources the Sanskrit term *varna* ("color") was used to identify social categories, but Portuguese traders later called them *casta* from their own word for hereditary social divisions, and this became the English word caste. The caste system originated during the millennium from 1500 to 500 BCE, in which people who called themselves Aryans (from "noble" in Sanskrit) came to dominate northern India politically and culturally. They created a body of sacred works, epics, hymns, philosophical treatises, and ritual texts called the Vedas, from which this period draws its name—the Vedic Age—and which serve as the primary source of information about this era. The traditional view is that the Aryans came into India from the north using the superior military technology of chariots and bronze weaponry, and conquered the indigenous tribal population. Although archaeological evidence for the Aryan invasion is slim, this is the story told in the Vedas, which present their leaders as heroic figures aided by priests and warriors, who became the two highest castes, the Brahmin and the Kshatriya. Merchants formed the third caste (Vaishya) and peasants, laborers, and conquered peoples the fourth and largest caste (shudra). The Vedas portray this system as created by the gods, who divided the original cosmic being into four parts corresponding to parts of the body; this gave caste divisions religious sanctions. As elsewhere in the ancient world, in the Aryan kingdoms priests supported the expanding power of rulers, who in return confirmed the superior status of the Brahmins as ritual specialists whose ceremonies could assure divine favor.

The high status of Brahmins was further affirmed in the Upanishads, cosmological texts composed between 750 and

500 BCE in which the universe was understood to be an endlessly repeating cycle in which souls were reincarnated through a continual process of rebirth known as *samsara*. Actions performed in one's life—known as *karma*—determined one's status in the next life, with good deeds leading to higher status and bad deeds to lower. The ultimate goal of life was to escape this relentless cycle of birth and rebirth and achieve *moksha*, a state of liberation, bliss, and awareness in which one achieved union with the ultimate unchanging reality that is the source of the universe, called *brahman*.

Originally, true spirituality could only be achieved through strict asceticism and was open only to men in the Brahmin caste, but by the third century BCE the quest for *brahman* was increasingly understood to include personal devotion to one or more of the many gods and goddesses who were manifestations of *brahman*. Personal gods could be honored through devotional practices such as saying prayers, singing hymns, dancing, presenting offerings, and making pilgrimages, and also by living an honorable life in one's own situation, what became known as *dharma*, a Sanskrit word with many shades of meaning, involving piety, moral law, ethics, order, duty, mutual understanding, justice, and peace. Prosperity and pleasure were legitimate aspects of *dharma*, for all the deities were sexually active and generally very attractive. The family was *dharma*'s central setting; all men and women were expected to marry, with sexual pleasure, fulfilling religious obligations, and having children regarded as the three purposes of marriage. These moral and spiritual teachings, later termed Hinduism, were widely appealing because they offered direct contact with the gods and guidance for everyday life. They validated the caste system and provided a source of social stability, but because devotion to one god did not mean rejection of others, they also allowed for the incorporation of new deities, doctrines, and rites. Following rules of behavior and performing ceremonies associated with one's caste and favored god might lead to being born in a higher caste in the next life, while not following them could result in social ostracism or even death.

Skin color may have played a role in the origins of caste—Aryan epics describe those who opposed them as dark-skinned savages—but function in society was the key source of differentiations. Thus attitudes toward certain types of work underlay them: memorizing religious texts and engaging in intellectual debates was honored work, while farming or making things with one's hands were demeaning. Over time, occupational and geographic distinctions were elaborated into an increasingly complex system of thousands of hereditary sub-castes known as *jati*—which literally means "births"— each understood to have a common identity and ancestors, and with roles, rituals, and status prescribed by custom and tradition. As new occupations developed because of technological change or cultural interactions, or as groups migrated in or invaded, new *jati* were created for them or older ones redefined, so the system was both stable and flexible. Scholars debate the limits of this flexibility, and other aspects of the caste system, at different historical points; some argue that British rule in India in the nineteenth century made the system far more rigid and authoritative than it had been earlier because it codified the system in writing, while others stress that unwritten norms can be just as powerful, or perhaps even more so, than written law.

Certain tasks were regarded as beneath the dignity of even the lowest sub-group within the shudra caste, and those who did them were viewed as outside of the caste system, a social classification that developed into the notion that certain groups were "untouchable" because they were impure. That designation became a circular one: untouchables were scorned because their occupations polluted them, but certain occupations polluted all who did them.

Notions of purity and pollution shaped relations between castes and *jati* as well—members of some groups came to avoid eating with one another, walking near one another, and, most importantly, marrying one another. Over generations, this endogamy reinforced ties within the group, as members increasingly shared common ancestors in reality as well as tradition. (The 1950 Indian Constitution officially prohibited discrimination based on caste, and since then India has taken various affirmative action measures to improve the status of historically discriminated groups, which in turn have led to charges of reverse discrimination. The power of caste in contemporary Indian society is a sharply disputed political issue, although most commentators agree that it has become less important in urban areas but that marital endogamy remains the norm.) Elements of Indian caste divisions spread to Nepal and Sri Lanka, where they blended with indigenous social stratifications into distinct systems.

Religious and social practices associated with Hinduism spread into Southeast Asia as well, carried across the Indian Ocean by merchants and sailors on ships that generally originated in small coastal trading states along the Malay peninsula and the islands of Sumatra and Java. After about 100 CE Indian priests and officials traveled to Southeast Asia on Malay ships as well, where they married into powerful families and were appointed as advisers by rulers attempting to build up their authority on the Indian model. In these Indianized kingdoms of Southeast Asia, including Langasuka, Funan, and Champa on the mainland and Taruma and Sunda on Java, imported traditions fused with local ones. Some groups understood themselves to be members of specific Indian castes, especially lineages within the warrior Kshatriyas, and huge stone temples were built to Hindu deities, but rituals also continued to indigenous gods and spirits, who retained their power over the rice harvest, daily life, and cosmic order. Among the Cham people in what is today southern Vietnam, inheritance was matrilineal, and women appear to have played a more active role in public life than they did in either China or India, a pattern that would continue in much of Southeast Asia. Other than among South Asian migrants, the impact of caste was limited, and locally created social hierarchies remained the most important.

SLAVERY AND SLAVE SOCIETIES

Along with the distinctions between elites and commoners, and men and women, the most pervasive social distinction in the ancient world was that between slave and free. Sometimes, in fact, it was the only distinction. In the law code of the Sumerian king Ur-Nammu everyone other than the king is divided into two groups, slave and free. In Sumeria and elsewhere, slavery clearly predated the growth of cities and the creation of written records, increased with urbanization, and increased even more with the development of the state. The coercive powers of states allowed owners to live safely amidst many slaves, and rulers sometimes used slaves in military, police, and administrative roles to enhance their power. Slavery was a recognized social status in the law codes of every state in the ancient world for which these survive, including those of Southwest Asia, Egypt, China, India, and the Mediterranean, and is evident from different sources in many other states as well. Slavery was also present in many tribal societies, including those of Central Asia, Europe, Africa, the Americas, and many parts of Oceania. Slaves came from every ethnic group, and included captives of war, raids, piracy, and abductions, as well as people enslaved for debt, sold by their families, or who sold themselves into slavery because of extreme poverty. In some places slaves were largely from nearby areas, while in others organized slave trading existed across huge distances. Slaves were a major component of trade, and were used—along with horses, camels, oxen, donkeys, and mules—to carry other items of trade. Slave markets existed at many nodes in trading networks, which meant that war captives, criminals, and rebels could be sold away instead of killed or imprisoned.

The labor that slaves did was highly variable, and in most places slaves did every kind of work that free people did, often alongside them: they farmed small plots of land, carried out domestic work, produced goods for sale, worked for wages, cared for children, and so on. Gangs of slaves also mined silver and copper and quarried stone in conditions of extreme brutality. Slaves functioned as items of conspicuous consumption as well. Owning many slaves marked one as a person of wealth, particularly in status-conscious cities such as Alexandria, Rome, or Chang'an, while slaves from far away indicated that one was able to afford exotic luxury goods. The households of rulers had particularly large numbers of slaves, who could range from male slaves who had positions of power and influence as government officials and royal advisers to female slaves who wove cloth or bore and cared for the emperor's children to slaves of both sexes who entertained, cooked, tended animals, and maintained the palace.

Slavery was thus diverse and flexible, but everywhere it depended on the communal recognition that some individuals owned others as property, which gave them the authority to sell and transport them, and to discipline them or otherwise control their behavior. Laws enforced the fact that slaves were property, but also viewed them as individuals able to act on their own and to engage in relationships with other individuals. This complexity was already there in the Code of Ur-Nammu, in which one provision lists selling a slave as the first option to pay off a debt, but another notes, "If a man's slave-woman, comparing herself to her mistress, speaks insolently to her, her mouth shall be scoured with one quart of salt." Similarly, in Hammurabi's code slaves are property that is bought, sold, and inherited, but they are also sellers and buyers of property.

In most states in the ancient world, the proportion of slaves in the population was not very great and most work was carried out by persons who were legally free; even the Egyptian pyramids appear to have been built largely by wage laborers. This was also the case in South Asia and in Han China, where peasants who owned their own land or who farmed the same piece of rented land for generations were the vast majority of the population. Land was generally divided equally among the sons, and as the population grew, the landholding of any one family shrank. Using iron tools and cattle-drawn plows if they could afford them, peasant families farmed these small plots intensively, with frequent weeding, cultivation, fertilizing, and thinning, to which women added weaving as a subsidiary activity that generated income to pay taxes and rents. Slavery was not conducive to intensive agriculture, and slaves may have constituted less than 1 percent of the booming population of Han China. The official Confucian social hierarchy placed peasants after scholar-bureaucrats in prestige, above artisans and merchants. Though this had little impact on the lives of actual peasants, it did mean that honor was accorded to agricultural labor and rural life in the abstract. More important for real people was the fact that because free peasants contributed both taxes and labor services to the state, the government made efforts to keep them productive, and it kept land taxes low.

A few ancient states were true slave societies. In classical Athens, slavery was central to the social structure, economy, and culture, just as it would be in the later slave societies of the Caribbean, Brazil, and the southern United States. Along with household slaves who carried out a variety of tasks, slaves worked in large artisanal workshops, as soldiers and sailors in the Athenian army and navy, as the low-status prostitutes known as *pornai*, in the countryside raising crops, and as laborers in mines and quarries. Determining numbers is difficult, but perhaps as much as a third or even a half of the population of Athens was enslaved. Most citizen households owned at least one slave—to have none was to be seen as poverty-stricken—and it is estimated that the average was three or four. The philosopher Plato (427–347 BCE) owned five, and the ideal state he envisioned in *The Republic* includes slaves who do most of the manual labor, leaving citizens time for thinking and governing. As distinctions among free male citizens were played down in the ideology of Athenian democracy, the distinction between free and slave came to be of special concern. In the *Politics*, the Athenian philosopher Aristotle (384–322 BCE) developed the idea of "natural slavery," arguing that those who can apprehend reason but not practice it were "slaves by nature." Such a man had "only so much moral virtue as will prevent him from failing in his duty" to his master. Aristotle does not explain how those slaves who were able to purchase their freedom or whose masters emancipated them, or conversely those resident foreigners who were enslaved as a punishment or for debt, came to gain or lose their rational capacity or moral virtue in the process.

Athens may provide the best example from the ancient world of the conceptualization of slavery proposed by the Jamaican-born historical sociologist Orlando Patterson, who has argued that slavery everywhere was "social death." Slaves were not simply owned by others, but lost the identity and relations that a person usually possesses by virtue of birth, a process Patterson terms "natal alienation." Slaves were not acknowledged to be members of a family, lineage, clan, or community, but were dishonored persons with only one acknowledged tie, that of subordination to their masters, enforced by violence. Patterson's thesis has been criticized as overly totalizing and dichotomous, because many societies had a range of servile and dependent relationships. It has also been seen as insufficiently attentive to the vibrant cultures that often developed among enslaved persons, but has been influential in its focus on the role of violence and social isolation in slave systems.

In Rome, slavery became an increasingly important social and economic system, and the survival of a wide range of sources allows us to examine many aspects of this development in more detail than we can elsewhere in the ancient world. Although there had always been slaves in the city of Rome and its environs, the expansionary wars of the second century BCE led to a dramatic growth of slavery in several interrelated processes. The prolonged fighting drew men into the army and away from their farms; their wives managed the farms in their absence, but they did not have enough workers to keep them under full cultivation and so could not pay all their taxes or rents. When the soldiers returned, they were often forced to sell their farms at low prices to the wealthy, who included military contractors and others who had become rich through the wars. These wealthy landowners also rented land won by conquest, and created huge agricultural estates termed *latifundia*, where crops could be raised at a lower cost than on small farms. The owners of the *latifundia* occasionally hired free people as day laborers, but they preferred to use slaves, who had no legal identity and could not be drafted into the army. Those slaves were provided by the conquests; slave dealers accompanied Roman armies, and brought back slaves of every conquered population, particularly boys and young men, favored as workers on *latifundia*. Gradually agriculture in Italy was transformed from subsistence farming to an important source of income for the Roman ruling class. Large labor gangs of slaves worked under the supervision of overseers, who might themselves be slaves. Estimates are difficult, but by the end of the first century BCE perhaps one-third of the population of Italy were slaves.

Slaves on *latifundia* raised all types of crops, but the most important of these was wheat, the staple of the Roman diet. Romans may have eaten some wheat in the form of sheets of fried dough akin to pasta (the idea that Marco Polo brought pasta to Italy from China in the thirteenth century is a legend), but they—and other Mediterranean peoples—ate their wheat primarily in the form of bread, flat if necessary and leavened if possible. Breads of various types became foods with great nutritional, cultural, and ultimately religious importance.

Slaves were also engaged in other occupations besides farming in Roman Italy. They ranged from highly educated household tutors and widely sought out sculptors to gladiators forced to fight and

2.6 In this first-century CE Roman wall fresco, slaves slaughter a small animal, perhaps a fawn, in preparation for a meal, while a nearby tray holds imported species and a bulb of garlic. In most wealthy households all the kitchen staff, including the head cook, would have been slaves.

convicts condemned to work in the mines, and their living conditions were similarly varied. Slaves could not marry and had no legally recognized family ties—here Patterson's thesis fits well—and the children of a female slave belonged to her owner. Some household slaves did enter into marriage-like relationships, but these could be broken up at the will of the owner, and sources indicate that very young enslaved children were regularly sold by themselves from one house to another.

Slaves sometimes attempted to flee, and those who failed in their attempts were returned to their masters and often branded on their foreheads. There were occasional small slave revolts, and one major one, in 73 BCE, which began when a group of gladiators escaped from one of the gladiatorial schools near Mount Vesuvius in southern Italy. Led by Spartacus and several others, the armies of escaped slaves eventually numbered in the tens of thousands. They defeated several Roman army units sent to quash them, and finally a large army of regular soldiers put down the revolt. Spartacus was apparently killed on the battlefield, and the slaves who were captured were crucified, with thousands of crosses lining the main road to

Rome. The rebellion had a significant impact on Roman politics, as the commanders who had defeated the slaves took their own armies to Rome and began to shape the Roman Republic to fit their ambitions, eventually leading to its downfall at the hands of Julius Caesar and the establishment of the Roman Empire by his grandnephew (and adopted son) Augustus.

The effects of the Spartacus revolt on Roman slavery are less clear. The use of slaves on *latifundia* began to decline in the first and second centuries CE, but this appears to have resulted primarily from the fact that, as the military expansion of the Empire slowed and the influx of new slaves lessened, hiring poor free families as sharecroppers became cheaper than purchasing and maintaining slaves. More people freed their slaves in these centuries than had earlier—so many that in 4 CE Emperor Augustus in the *Lex Aelia Sentia* regulated the practice—with motivations that ranged from philosophical to economic. Manumitted slaves, or those who had purchased or otherwise gained their own freedom, belonged to a legal class in Rome called *libertini* (singular *libertus/liberta*). Their position varied depending on the circumstances of their becoming free and changed over time, but in general the men among them had a limited political voice, and their children were full citizens.

Roman laws about slavery—as about many things—became increasingly complex over the centuries, and were always connected to other social practices and aims. For example, in the *Lex Aelia Sentia*, a *libertus* who would normally only have received limited citizenship rights was made a full citizen as long as he married a freewoman or a *liberta* and she had a son. The woman herself could claim these rights for herself and her son if the *libertus* had died, and if she had given birth to a certain number of children she could petition to be released from male legal guardianship. Augustus promoted these measures not because he was a champion of slaves or women, but because he was worried about the Roman birthrate and what he perceived as a decline in traditional Roman values centered on the family, and because he was positioning himself as the real source of authority in Rome during this period of transition from republic to empire. In his efforts at social control, he also passed a series of other laws regarding marriage and morality, among them a restriction on the inheritance of property by free men and women who were unmarried or had no children, and a transformation of adultery from a private family matter into a public crime.

Rome was unusual in the ancient world in its dependence on slave labor, but not in its concern with the sexual actions of slaves and ex-slaves, which appear in law codes, edicts, and commentaries from other areas as well. Although in Athens adult male slaves were specifically prohibited from engaging in relations with free male adolescents because this would upset the proper power hierarchy of male–male sexual relations, in most places the primary concern of lawmakers was sexual relations that could produce children. In the law codes of the Germanic tribes that conquered Roman lands from the third to the fifth century CE, for example, enslaved men who engaged in sex with free women were generally liable to death (as were the women), and freed women (that is, former slaves) who had sex with or married slaves could be enslaved again. Different rules and laws were issued in other areas, although everywhere policing the boundaries between various social groups depended on traditions and norms as much as on statutes.

TEXT-BASED RELIGIONS AND CULTURAL INTERACTIONS

In the middle of the first millennium BCE, those traditions and norms were themselves being systematized and often written down for the first time. The period from about 600 BCE to about 350 BCE encompasses the life-spans of Confucius and Laozi (viewed as the founder of Daoism) in China, the Greek thinkers Thales, Heraclitus, Socrates, Plato, and Aristotle, the Hebrew prophets Jeremiah, Ezekiel, and the second Isaiah, and the Buddha and Mahavira (the founder of the Jain faith) in South Asia. In the mid twentieth century the scholars Karl Jaspers and Shmuel Eisenstadt posited that this period—which they later extended from 800 to 200 BCE—was also a crucial turning point in human history, to which they gave the name "Axial Age," from the German word *achse*, which means both axis and pivot. They saw this as a time when (in Jaspers' words) "the spiritual foundations of humanity were laid" because for the first time self-reflective thinkers became skeptical about received truths, argued that the individual has worth, stressed moral conduct and compassion, and drew lessons from history. The concept of an Axial Age has been very influential among sociologists interested in typologies of human experience and among scholars of religion, who sometimes extend it forward in time to encompass the development of Christianity. Some historians point out, however, that six hundred years (or more) is a long time for a turning point, and that what made the Axial Age thinkers most distinctive is that their ideas came to be written down. Earlier thinkers, or those in societies that did not leave written records, or women, or illiterate rural dwellers, may have had similar ideas, they note, but no record of them survives. Whether or not you find the notion of an Axial Age persuasive, the fact that the ideas of these thinkers were recorded, and, more importantly, copied and recopied, studied, commented on, and expanded until they became foundational cultural traditions does make them extremely significant.

Among these written traditions are those created by the Hebrews, a group of people who briefly established two small states in the area between the Mediterranean and the Jordan River known as Canaan. Politically unimportant when compared with the Egyptians or the Babylonians, the Hebrews created a new form of religious belief, a monotheism based on the worship of an all-powerful god they called YHWH, Anglicized as Yahweh. Beginning in the late 600s BCE, they began to write down their traditions, laws, history, and ethics, which were edited and brought together in the five books known as the Torah. More history and traditions, and other types of works—advice literature, prayers, hymns, and prophecies—were added, to form the Hebrew Bible, which Christians later adopted and termed the "Old Testament" to parallel specific Christian writings termed the "New Testament." These writings became the core of the Hebrews' religion, Judaism, a word taken from Judah, the southern of the two Hebrew kingdoms and the one that was the primary force in developing religious traditions.

Fundamental to an understanding of the Jewish religion is the concept of the Covenant, an agreement that people believed to exist between themselves and Yahweh. According to the Hebrew Bible, Yahweh appeared to the tribal leader Abraham, promising him that he would be blessed, as would his descendants, if they followed

Yahweh. (Because Judaism, Christianity, and Islam all regard this event as foundational, they are referred to as the "Abrahamic religions.") The Bible recounts that Yahweh next appeared to a charismatic leader named Moses during a time he was leading the Hebrews out of enslavement in Egypt, and Yahweh made a covenant with the Hebrews: if they worshipped Yahweh as their only god, he would consider them his chosen people and protect them from their enemies. Early leaders such as Abraham and Moses and later individuals such as Jeremiah, Ezekiel, and Isaiah who acted as intermediaries between Yahweh and the Hebrew people were known as "prophets." Much of the Hebrew Bible consists of writings in their voices, understood as messages from Yahweh to which the Hebrews were to listen.

Worship was embodied in a series of rules of behavior, the Ten Commandments, which Yahweh gave to Moses. These required certain kinds of religious observances and forbade the Hebrews to steal, kill, lie, or commit adultery, thus creating a system of ethical absolutes. From the Ten Commandments a complex system of rules of conduct was created and later written down as Hebrew law. Like the followers of other religions, Jews engaged in rituals through which they showed their devotion. They also were to please Yahweh by living up to high moral standards, and by worshipping him above all other gods. Increasingly this was understood to be a commandment to worship Yahweh alone. The later prophets such as Isaiah created a system of ethical monotheism, in which goodness was understood to come from a single transcendent god, and in which religious obligations included fair and just behavior toward other people as well as rituals. Religious leaders were important in Judaism, but personally following the instructions of Yahweh as recorded in sacred texts was the central task for observant Jews in the ancient world. Political and military developments led Jews to scatter widely, first throughout the Mediterranean and then beyond. They maintained their cohesion as a group through intermarriage, and only rarely actively sought converts.

Other religious traditions were spread by their adherents, becoming what are often called "universal religions" or "portable religions"—religious traditions not identified with particular locations or ethnic groups as were most in the ancient world, but that appealed across cultural boundaries. Migrations, invasions, trade, and intentional missionary work carried religious ideas and practices from place to place in the first millennium BCE, and they became transformed in the process.

Buddhism was the first religious tradition to spread widely, to Southeast Asia alongside Hinduism and in many other directions as well. Buddhism was based on the ideas of a north Indian prince, Siddhartha Gautama (*fl. c.* 500 BCE), called the Buddha ("enlightened one"). As related in later Buddhist texts, Prince Gautama had a pampered and sheltered early life, but gradually learned about the reality of pain, suffering, and death. He left his wife and family to go off as a wandering ascetic, but while meditating had a revelation in which he achieved enlightenment, that is, insight into the cosmic truths that underlay the universe. He began to teach his central insights, laid out as the Four Noble Truths and the Eightfold Path: life is suffering arising from desire and attachments, but people can overcome their desires and weaknesses by deciding to liberate themselves from them, living morally, being compassionate, and searching for enlightenment through contemplation. Those who gain enlightenment are freed from the cycle of birth and death, and enter into a state called nirvana, a blissful nothingness akin to the Hindu concept *moksha*. In theory, the Buddhist path to enlightenment was (and is) an individual journey open to all regardless of caste or gender, although other early texts present women as dangerous threats to men's achieving enlightenment. The Buddha taught that a life of monasticism—renouncing the world in favor of a life of prayer and meditation in a community—could make one spiritually superior, but that lay believers gained spiritual merit by supporting the monastic community (*sangha*). He allowed women to become nuns—and many did—but placed them in a subordinate status to monks.

Although Buddhist teachings emphasized that withdrawal from the world was the best way to lessen desire, political leaders adopted Buddhism. Among the earliest was Ashoka (ruled *c.* 270–232 BCE), who ruled the Mauryan Empire founded by his grandfather that controlled a large part of the Indian subcontinent. Ashoka became a Buddhist at some point in his life—by tradition after being revolted by the slaughter and suffering involved in one of his military campaigns—built monasteries and mounds called *stupas* to house Buddhist relics, sent missionaries beyond the borders of his territory, and erected large pillars proclaiming his devotion to *dharma* and instructing his officials and subjects on how to act according to its principles of justice and ethics, which included toleration of other traditions.

The Mauryan Empire collapsed shortly after Ashoka's rule, and northern India came to be ruled by groups that originated elsewhere and brought with them other traditions. Among these were the Kushans, a Central Asian nomadic people who established an empire that by the second century CE stretched from western China to the Ganges Valley and west to modern-day Afghanistan and Pakistan, with cities at the oases along the trading routes that crossed Asia known as the Silk Roads. Judging by archaeological evidence and sources from outside—no textual works have survived from Kushan itself—the Kushans followed a range of religious practices and blended aspects of many cultures. Their empire included small states that had been ruled by Greek-speaking kings since the time of Alexander the Great in the fourth century BCE, including Gandhara, where several rulers had become Buddhists, and Hellenistic Greek ideas, religious traditions, and artistic styles blended with Indian ones.

The Kushans adopted the Greek alphabet for their own language and began minting gold, silver, and copper coins on the Greek model, which showed a Kushan ruler on one side and a god or mythological figure on the other, including the Greek hero Hercules, the deified Buddha, the Hindu god Shiva, and the Egyptian god Sarapis. Coins also depicted the Iranian god Ahuramazda, which suggests that some Kushan rulers had adopted the teachings of Zoroaster, a prophet and thinker whose ideas had gained wide acceptance centuries earlier in the Persian Empire, which along with Indo-Greek kingdoms was now the western part of Kushan. Zoroastrianism taught (and teaches) that Ahuramazda was the source of all good, and that individuals had the responsibility to choose between good and evil in their thoughts, words, and actions. At the end of time Ahuramazda would preside over a last judgment to determine each person's eternal fate. Veneration was owed to Ahuramazda alone, and not to other deities.

2.7 Relief sculpture showing the Buddha surrounded by devotees, from Mathura, one of the capitals of the Kushan Empire, in about the second century CE. Anthropomorphic representations of the Buddha appeared first in Kushan, where Hellenistic Greek styles, including flowing robes and defined musculature, combined with Buddhist devotional forms.

Buddhism grew in this setting of cultural mixture, and over centuries divergent traditions developed. The Buddha's teachings began to be written down by his followers in the second or first century BCE in sacred texts called *sutras*. Monastic communities recited and studied the sutras, and came to stress different ones among them and to write new texts. Many of these texts focused on *bodhisattvas*, compassionate beings who were far along on the path to enlightenment and nirvana but who stayed in the world to help other sentient beings on their own paths. Bodhisattvas were understood to be both in time and timeless, and their lives and powers absorbed aspects of local deities and religious traditions. The bodhisattva Guanyin, for example, was originally depicted as a young man, but became increasingly associated with the goddess of mercy and kindness worshipped in local religions, and came to be shown primarily as a beautiful young woman in a flowing robe. Bodhisattvas became objects of veneration, as did the Buddha himself, who was more and more viewed as a transcendental and eternal being, and the chief among a group of celestial buddhas. Among the celestial buddhas was Amitabha ("the buddha of infinite light"), who had been a bodhisattva over countless lives, and had created a paradise beyond the bounds of the world called the Pure Land, open to all who call on him in death. The earliest known inscriptions and sutras referring to Amitabha come from the Kushan Empire in the second century CE, at which point the Kushan emperor Kanishka the Great (r. 127–151) was actively promoting the spread of Buddhism, the Kushan Buddhist monk Lokaksema was translating sutras into Chinese, and merchants and pilgrims were traveling along the Silk Roads through Central Asia and other well-established trade routes.

The veneration of bodhisattvas and celestial buddhas, and the notion that every sentient being is on the path to buddhahood in a celestial realm, became the center of one of the primary traditions within Buddhism, Mahayana, which means "Great Vehicle," a term reflecting the idea among its followers that it is broadly inclusive. This branch of Buddhism—which because it was open to new texts had many different schools and traditions within it—spread from northern India and Kushan into other parts of South Asia, Central Asia, China, the Himalayas, and ultimately Korea, Japan, and much of Southeast Asia. Texts were translated, beautifully decorated temples and stupas were built, and tens of thousands of people became monks and nuns in monasteries, which sometimes grew wealthy on the gifts from pious believers. In China, the decision to enter a monastery and forgo family life conflicted with traditional Confucian aims, but in the unstable political environment after the fall of the Han dynasty, even rulers and officials, along with countless ordinary people, were attracted to Buddhist teachings of ethics, charity, and spiritual meaning. Buddhism also fit well with another Chinese philosophical tradition, Daoism, which taught that the best life was one that does not seek to change anything, but passively yields to the *dao*, the "way of nature" that underlies everything. Translators of Buddhist texts used Daoist terminology, and Daoist rituals of fasting and meditation were adapted to include Buddhist concepts, as were traditional rituals of divination and ancestor veneration. Confucian hierarchies also shaped translations of Buddhist texts and made them seem less foreign: "husband supports wife" became "husband controls wife" and "wife comforts husband" became "wife reveres husband."

Some monasteries and religious thinkers emphasized different sutras, rules, and practices, and a different tradition became more common in southern India and Sri Lanka, termed Theravada, the "Teaching of the Elders," which put particular emphasis on the oldest texts. In Theravada understandings, only one buddha could appear in a cosmic age, so the ultimate ideal is to become not a buddha but rather an *arhat*, an individual who achieves full enlightenment in nirvana and is thus completely freed from material existence and will never be reborn in any world. Monasticism was viewed as the superior way of reaching this state because it allowed for a life of meditation, morality, and study, although lay people gained merit by reciting scriptures and supporting monks. (This respect for monks continues among contemporary Theravada Buddhists; they disagree about whether women can become fully ordained nuns, and historically there have been far more monks than nuns.) From southern India and Sri Lanka, monks took Theravada Buddhism to Southeast Asia, where it gradually supplanted other forms of Buddhism and remains the dominant form of Buddhism today.

In all of its variants, Buddhism came to encourage travel: people often went on pilgrimages to the holy places associated with the life of the Buddha, to monasteries and temples that contained relics or particularly impressive images, or to shrines associated with bodhisattvas. Some of these travelers wrote about the peoples they met along their journeys, and their works are an early form of world history.

Like Buddhism, Christianity also took root and expanded in a cosmopolitan world with a great mixing of cultures, languages, and traditions, and when it was fairly easy to move around and exchange ideas and practices on roads and sea routes. It appeared in the early Roman Empire, in which people followed and combined a variety of spiritual traditions, including religions devoted to the traditional Roman gods of the hearth, home, and countryside, syncretistic religions that blended Roman and indigenous deities, and mystery religions that offered the promise of life after death. Christianity developed initially in the Roman province of Judaea, where the civil wars and turmoil that ended the Roman Republic and created the Empire had led to a climate of violence. Movements in opposition to the Romans spread among Jews, and many Jews came to believe that a final struggle was near and that it would lead to the coming of a savior, or Messiah, who would destroy the Roman legions and inaugurate a period of happiness and plenty for Jews.

Into this climate of Roman religious blending and Jewish Messianic hope came Jesus of Nazareth (c. 3 BCE–29 CE). According to Christian Scripture, he was born to deeply religious Jewish parents and raised in Galilee, stronghold of those opposed to Rome and a trading center where Greeks and Romans interacted with Jews. His ministry began when he was about thirty, and he taught by preaching and telling stories. Like the Buddha, Jesus left no writings. Accounts of his sayings and teachings first circulated orally among his followers and beginning in the late first century were written down to help build a community of faith. Discrepancies within early texts indicate his followers had a diversity of beliefs about Jesus' nature and purpose, but they agreed that Jesus preached of a heavenly kingdom of eternal happiness in a life after death and of the importance of devotion to God and love of others. His teachings were based on Hebrew Scripture and reflected a conception of God and morality that came from Jewish tradition, but he deviated from this in insisting that he taught in his own name, not in the name of Yahweh. He said that he was the Messiah (*Christus* in Greek, the origin of the English word Christ), but also asserted that he had come to establish a spiritual kingdom, not an earthly one based on wealth and power. Worried about maintaining peace and order in Jerusalem, the Roman official Pontius Pilate arrested Jesus and condemned him to death, and his soldiers carried out the sentence. On the third day after Jesus' crucifixion, some of his followers said that he had risen from the dead, an event that became a central element of faith for Christians.

The memory of Jesus and his teachings survived and flourished. Believers in his resurrection and divinity met in small assemblies or congregations, often in one another's homes, to discuss the meaning of Jesus' message and to celebrate a ritual (later called the Eucharist or Lord's Supper) commemorating his last meal with his disciples before his arrest. Because they expected Jesus to return to the world very soon, they regarded earthly life and institutions as unimportant. Marriage and normal family life should be abandoned, and followers of Jesus should depend on their new spiritual family of co-believers. Early Christians often called each other brother and sister, a metaphorical use of family terms that was new to the Roman Empire.

The catalyst in the spread of Jesus' teachings was Paul of Tarsus, a well-educated Jew who was comfortable in both the Roman and the Jewish worlds. After a conversion experience, Paul became a vigorous promoter of Jesus' ideas, traveling all over the Roman Empire and writing letters of advice that were copied and widely circulated, transforming Jesus' ideas into more specific moral teachings; Paul's letters later became part of Christian Scripture. The breadth of the Roman Empire enabled early Christians to spread their faith easily throughout the world known to them, as Jesus had told his followers to do. Paul urged that Gentiles, or non-Jews, be accepted on an equal basis, and the earliest Christian converts included men and women from all social classes who learned about Christian teachings through family contacts, friendships, and business networks. People were attracted to

Christian teachings for a variety of reasons: they offered the promise of a blissful life after death for all who believed; stressed the ideal of striving for a goal; urged concern for the poor; and provided a sense of identity, community, and spiritual kinship welcome in the often highly mobile world of the Roman Empire.

At first most Roman officials largely ignored the followers of Jesus, but slowly some came to oppose Christian practices and beliefs. They considered Christians to be subversive dissidents because they stopped practicing traditional rituals, objected to the cult of the emperor that was becoming an important part of Roman political ideology, and seemed to be trying to destroy the Roman family with their claim that salvation was more important than family relationships. Persecutions of Christians, including torture and executions, were organized by governors of Roman provinces and sometimes by the emperor; although most were local and sporadic, some were intense, and accounts of heroic martyrs provided important models for later Christians.

By the second century CE Christianity was changing. The belief that Jesus was soon coming again gradually waned, and as the number of converts increased, permanent institutions were established instead of simple house churches. These included large buildings for worship and a hierarchy of officials—priests, bishops, archbishops—often modeled on those of the Roman Empire. Christianity also began to attract more highly educated men who developed complex theological interpretations of issues that were not clear in early texts. Often drawing on Greek philosophy and Roman legal traditions, they worked out understandings of such issues as how Jesus could be both divine and human and how God could be both a father and a son (and later a spirit as well, a Christian doctrine known as the Trinity). These interpretations became official doctrine through decisions made at church councils, large gatherings of bishops and other clergy, which also decided which books circulating among believers would be canonical, that is, officially part of Christian Scripture. Not everyone agreed with these decisions, however, and major splits over doctrinal issues led to the formation of variant branches. Bishops and theologians also modified Jesus' teachings about wealth, power, and family, downplaying those that seemed socially disturbing and bringing them more in line with Roman values.

Christianity was thus becoming more formal and centralized, and it was also spreading. Christian missionaries, sometimes sent by bishops, and Christian merchants or other travelers ventured beyond the borders of the Roman Empire. They brought Christianity to the kingdom of Kush along the Nile south of Egypt and then further south to the empire of Aksum in the Ethiopian highlands, which was already home to a sizable Jewish community and the center of a trading network that reached from the Mediterranean to India. In the fourth century, King Ezana of Aksum (r. *c.* 320–360) made Christianity the official religion of his kingdom and his primary Christian adviser Frumentius became a bishop. Texts were translated into Ge'ez, the local language, churches were built (sometimes hewed out of a single block of rock), and monasteries were established, creating the Ethiopian Church that has continued to today with practices and doctrines somewhat different from other branches of Christianity, including dietary rules similar to those in Judaism and a slightly different group of books in its biblical canon.

Missionaries, merchants, and soldiers took Christian teachings eastward and northward as well, into the tolerant Parthian Empire centered in Persia and to the tribal Celtic and Germanic peoples of Europe. Bishop Ulfilas (*c.* 310–383), himself a member of the Germanic Ostrogoths, translated the Bible from Greek into the Gothic language, creating a new Gothic script in order to write it down. Over the next several centuries this text was recopied many times and carried with the Gothic tribes as they migrated throughout southern Europe. Rituals were more important than texts in the transmission of Christian teachings, however, and the veneration of saints became especially important. Saints were people who had lived (or died) in a way that was spiritually heroic or noteworthy; like bodhisattvas, they were understood to provide protection and assistance, and objects connected with them, such as their bones or clothing, became relics with special power that linked the material and spiritual world. Churches that housed saints' relics became places of pilgrimage for those seeking help, comfort, or blessing. Missionaries and converts often fused existing local religious customs with Christian teachings. For example, landscape features such as lakes or mountains sacred to indigenous gods became associated with specific saints, as did various aspects of ordinary life, such as traveling, planting crops, and childbirth. Saints' days came to punctuate the calendar, providing days of rest or celebration with rituals of veneration and worship.

The third century brought civil war, invasions, and economic chaos to the Roman Empire. Hoping that Christianity could be a unifying force in an empire plagued by problems, Emperor Constantine (r. 306–337) ordered toleration of all religions in the Edict of Milan, issued in 313. He supported the Christian Church throughout his reign, expecting in return the support of church officials in maintaining order, and late in his life he was baptized as a Christian. Constantine also freed the clergy from imperial taxation, called and appeared at councils that decided theological issues, and endowed the building of Christian churches, especially in the new capital he was building for the Roman Empire at Byzantium, an old Greek city on the Bosporus, a strait on the boundary between Europe and Asia. He named the city the "New Rome," though it was soon called Constantinople. Constantine also declared Sunday a public holiday, choosing it over the Jewish holy day of Saturday because it fit with his own worship of the sun god, a practice shared by many Romans. The annual celebration of the birthday of Jesus was set at midwinter, when Romans were already celebrating the rebirth of the sun at the winter solstice. Thus Roman as well as Germanic and other pre-Christian religious traditions were assimilated into Christianity. Christians altered their practices to follow the emperor's decrees; worship became increasingly elaborate, and clergy began to wear ornate clothing and use expensive symbols of authority modeled on those of the emperor.

Some Christians objected to these close connections between church and state, wondering if Christianity could be both powerful and holy. Men and women who thought this way sometimes left cities and went into the Egyptian desert to live as ascetics, or formed themselves into monastic communities somewhat cut off from the world, similar to the monasteries that emerged in Buddhism.

Helped in part by its favored position, Christianity slowly became the leading religion in the empire, and emperors after Constantine continued to promote it. In 380 the emperor Theodosius

(r. 379–395) made Christianity the official religion of the Roman Empire. He allowed the church to establish its own courts and to use its own body of law, called "canon law." With this he laid the foundation for later growth in church power.

Christianity was not able to hold the whole Roman Empire together, but capable military leadership and powerful fortifications protecting the city of Constantinople and some border areas allowed the eastern half of the empire to withstand attacks and remain in existence for another thousand years, becoming what people later termed the Byzantine Empire. (Those who actually lived in the Byzantine Empire called themselves "Romans" and their state the "Roman Empire," thus emphasizing cultural and political continuities.) The western half of the empire gradually disintegrated, as the emperors ruling from Constantinople could not provide enough military assistance to repel invaders, which included Germanic peoples such as the Goths and Vandals and nomadic central Asian steppe peoples, especially the Huns. In 476, a Germanic chieftain, Odoacer, deposed the Roman emperor in the west and did not take on the title of emperor, calling himself instead the king of Italy. This date marks the official end of the Roman Empire in the west, although much of the empire had come under the rule of various barbarian tribes well before that.

THE END OF A CLASSICAL WORLD?

In the fifteenth century, humanist scholars in the growing cities of northern Italy began to think that they were living in a new era, one in which the literary, philosophical, and artistic glories of ancient Greece and Rome were being reborn. What separated their golden age—later dubbed the Renaissance, French for rebirth—from those of Greece and Rome was a long period of darkness and decline, to which a seventeenth-century professor gave the name "Middle Ages." In this conceptualization, the history of Europe was divided into three periods, ancient, medieval, and modern, with the fall of the Western Roman Empire seen as a great turning point when the glorious culture of the Romans was replaced by barbarism.

Historians of other parts of the world have also pointed to the collapse of large-scale empires and classical societies in roughly the

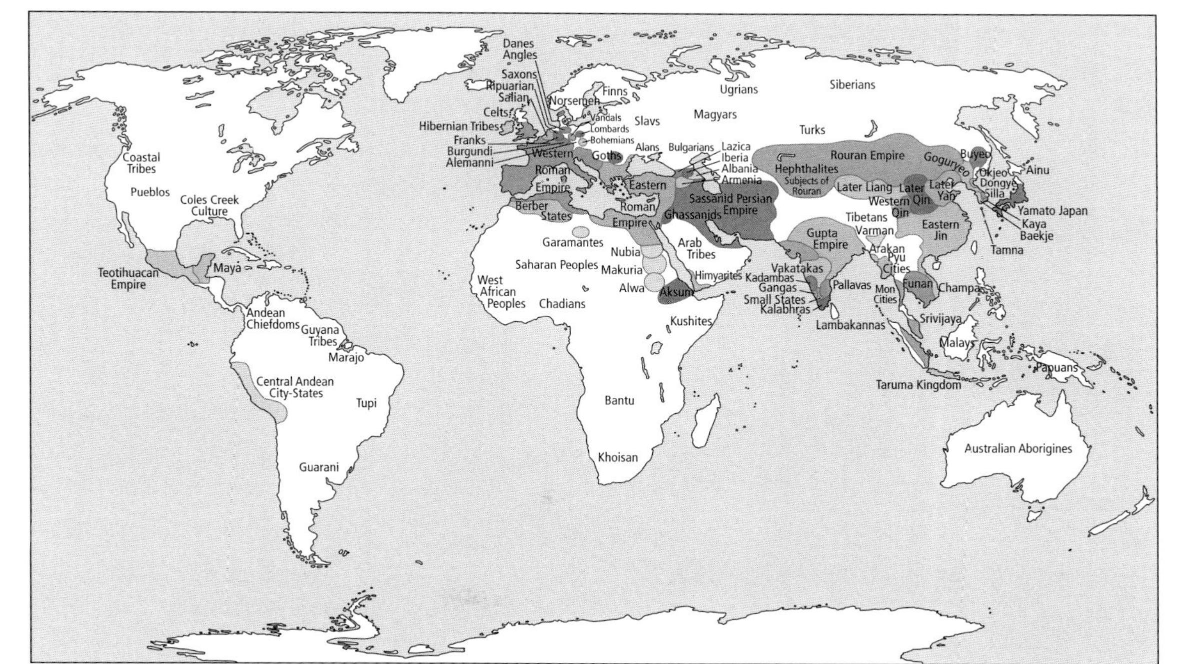

Map 2.2 The world in about 400 CE

same period. The Han dynasty of which Ban Zhao and Ban Gu were so proud ended in 220 CE when the son of a general deposed the reigning emperor, but provincial military leaders refused to recognize his authority and the empire broke into warring factions, while waves of invaders—including the Xiongnu, known in the West as the Huns—swept across the frontiers. Centuries of disunity followed. The Kushan Empire fragmented into two parts in the third century, and outsiders overwhelmed each of these shortly afterward. Those outsiders included the Gupta Empire, which brought large parts of northern India under its control in the fourth century, but then broke apart in the fifth century because of invasions from the north by steppe people known in Western and Indian sources as the Hepthalites or White Huns. In Mesoamerica, decline came somewhat later but was similarly traumatic: invaders burned down the great city of Teotihuacan in 750, and the urban cores of many southern Maya city-states were abandoned between 800 and 900. Thus in many places the urbanized societies examined in this chapter became less urban, hereditary dynasties were overthrown, and violence disrupted village life.

These collapses are generally described in political and military terms, but they appear to have often had demographic and environmental roots. The Silk Roads across Asia carried Buddhism and trade goods, but they also carried disease pathogens, and what had been separate disease pools were connected, with catastrophic results. Roman soldiers returning from fighting in Mesopotamia in 165 CE brought with them a disease that may have been smallpox or measles, which devastated the city of Rome and then spread to the northern provinces; estimates of deaths in this Antonine Plague over the next decade or so range in the millions, and may have been as much as one-quarter of the Roman Empire. Another pandemic in 250–270 CE, again probably smallpox and named the Cyprian Plague after an early Christian bishop who saw and wrote about it, also killed thousands per day in the city of Rome itself and perhaps hundreds of thousands elsewhere. Both of these epidemics diminished the ranks of the Roman army, created labor shortages in the countryside, and so allowed the migration of Germanic peoples further and further into the empire. A third epidemic in 541–543, called the "Justinian Plague" after the emperor ruling in

Constantinople at the time who contracted it but survived, and which was probably bubonic plague, swept across western Asia and the Mediterranean, weakening both the Byzantine Empire and its enemy the Sassanid Empire in Persia. Similar diseases also destabilized the Han Empire, and were everywhere exacerbated by a fluctuation in the climate cycle that brought colder weather and declining agricultural productivity. Climate change also created ecological crises in the Americas; severe El Niños, the periodic warm weather currents in the Pacific, brought both drought and torrential rains to the Peruvian coast in the fifth century, while drought and the resultant crop failures seem to have been factors in the Maya collapse. Demographers suggest that world population may have dropped from about 250 million in 1 CE to 200 million in 500 CE, with the largest decline in Asia and Europe.

Decreases in population created challenges for ruling hereditary dynasties dependent on the work and taxes of their subjects, and the diseases themselves carried off both rulers and heirs. High rates of death from epidemic disease or from the large-scale violence that accompanied political instability created problems for ordinary families as well. Overcrowded cities became even more deadly, particularly for children, who were already at risk from ordinary infectious diseases. Systems of ownership and inheritance and norms of proper family relationships were confronted by situations that lawmakers and moralists had not envisioned. The in-migration of new peoples brought different ways of organizing society from the family on out, challenging social structures and norms that were understood to be "natural" or rooted in unchangeable divine command.

The social structures and cultural traditions created in the ancient world turned out to be far more resilient than commentators at the time predicted, however. (Dire warnings about the disastrous effects of social change and new practices are one of the traditions that has had a long life.) The Western Roman Empire was never reconstructed, but Greek philosophy and Roman laws, including those concerning slavery and the family, were preserved in the Eastern Roman Empire, eventually reintroduced in western Europe, and from there taken around the world. Sometimes this transmission happened directly when Greek scholars came west, and sometimes it happened indirectly through the work of Muslim and Jewish scholars. Muslim scholars also passed on Greek ideas to the Islamic world, which, as we will see in the next chapter, came to stretch over much of Afroeurasia and to view written texts with particular esteem. Confucianism has survived every political change in China, minor or major, and was exported to Vietnam, Japan, and Korea, where it became a powerful cultural force. Buddhism similarly spread to Korea and Japan, where it developed into new forms that introduced elements from indigenous religious traditions, and was then carried further. Christianity actually benefited from the end of the Western Roman Empire, with its officials assuming a wider range of roles and powers. By 1000 CE, the Christian Church was the wealthiest and most powerful institution in Europe, and "Christian" was people's primary identity beyond their family and village. Hereditary monarchies remained the standard political structure for states until the eighteenth century, and continue to be so in modified form for a significant number of countries today. Slavery and the caste system have officially ended everywhere, but the United Nations estimates that 30 million people are in forced labor situations, often as the result of human trafficking, and that caste discrimination affects more than 200 million people worldwide.

In fact, one might even say that the social forms and cultural traditions created in the urbanized agricultural states of the ancient world and discussed in this chapter are far more powerful today than they were in ancient times. In 500 CE, although the majority of people lived in states, most land was outside of them, and was inhabited by bands of foragers, villagers led by kin leaders, family groups of pastoralists, crop-raisers ruled by chiefs, confederations of clans, or other forms of social organization that later scholars would term "stateless societies." Wherever they lived, the vast majority of people learned the traditions of their culture and their place in the social hierarchy orally. Today, not only do more than half of the world's people live in cities—a milestone reached only in 2008—but every one of them lives in a state, or, as we now term them, a nation. After a brief period dubbed the "new orality," when radio, television, telephones, and other oral and visual media appeared as if they would end the dominance of writing, alphabets have returned in triumph. And like Sumerian scribes, many of us produce our alphabets and symbols on small objects we hold in our hands; among these objects are tablets, on which we sometimes write with a stylus.

FURTHER READING

The best place to find the newest research on cities is Norman Yoffee, ed., *Early Cities in Comparative Perspective, 4000 BCE–1200 CE*, Volume 3 of the *Cambridge World History* (2015); similarly, on the development of states, see Volume 4 of the *Cambridge World History*, Craig Benjamin, ed., *A World with States, Empires and Networks, 1200 BCE–900 CE*. Michael Adas, ed., *Agricultural and Pastoral Societies in Ancient and Classical History* (Philadelphia: Temple University Press, 2001), Bruce D. Trigger, *Understanding Early Civilizations: A Comparative Study* (Cambridge: Cambridge University Press, 2007), and Shelley Hales and Tamar Hodos, eds., *Material Culture and Social Identities in the Ancient World* (Cambridge: Cambridge University Press, 2010) are cross-cultural examinations of recurring social, economic, and cultural patterns. For more on cities, see Joyce Marcus and Jeremy Sabloff, eds., *The Ancient City: New Perspectives on Ancient Urbanism* (Santa Fe: SAR Press, 2008), Monica Smith, ed., *The Social Construction of Ancient Cities* (Washington, DC: Smithsonian, 2010), and Charles Gates, *Ancient Cities: The Archaeology of Urban Life in the Ancient Near East and Egypt, Greece, and Rome*, 2nd edn. (London: Routledge, 2011). For Jenne-jeno, see Roderick J. McIntosh, *Ancient Middle Niger: Urbanism and the Self-Organizing Landscape* (Cambridge: Cambridge University Press, 2005). On states, see Norman Yoffee, *Myths of the Archaic State* (Cambridge: Cambridge University Press, 2005) and Richard E. Blanton and Lane Fargher, *Collective Action in the Formation of Pre-Modern States* (New York: Springer, 2008). Susan E. Alcock, ed., *Empires: Perspectives from Archaeology and History* (Cambridge: Cambridge University Press, 2009) is a collection of essays about pre-modern empires throughout the world, and Jane Burbank and Frederick Cooper, *Empires in World History: Power and Politics of Difference* (Princeton: Princeton University Press, 2010) is a broad analysis that begins with Han China and extends into the twentieth century.

On the development of writing, see Stephen Houston, ed., *The First Writing: Script Invention as History and Process* (Cambridge: Cambridge University Press, 2004). On the implications of writing, see Jack Goody, *The Logic of Writing and the Organization of Society* (Cambridge: Cambridge University Press, 1986), Marshall McLuhan, *The Medium is the*

Massage: An Inventory of Effects (New York: Random House, 1967), and Walter Ong, *Orality and Literacy: The Technologizing of the Word* (London: Methuen, 1982). John Miles Foley, *Oral Tradition and the Internet: Pathways of the Mind* (Urbana-Champaign: University of Illinois Press, 2012) extends this analysis to contemporary media.

On the family, see the enormous edited collection, André Burguière *et al.*, *A History of the Family*, Volume I: *Distant Worlds, Ancient Worlds* (Cambridge, MA: Belknap Press, 1996) and the much more compact Mary Jo Maynes and Ann Waltner, *The Family: A World History* (Oxford: Oxford University Press, 2012). Philip D. Curtin, *Cross-Cultural Trade in World History* (Cambridge: Cambridge University Press, 1984) is a classic work with much information on the ancient period. On slavery, see Keith Bradley and Paul Cartledge, eds., *The Cambridge World History of Slavery*, Volume 1: *The Ancient Mediterranean World* (Cambridge: Cambridge University Press, 2011).

Shmuel N. Eisenstadt, *The Origins and Diversity of Axial Age Civilizations* (Albany: State University of New York Press, 1986) presents a good introduction to the idea of the Axial Age, and Karen Armstrong, *The Great Transformation: The Beginning of Our Religious Traditions* (New York: Anchor, 2007) uses this idea to analyze and compare religious and philosophical traditions in four regions of the world. Richard Foltz, *Religions of the Silk Roads: Premodern Patterns of Globalization*, 2nd edn. (London: Palgrave Macmillan, 2010) examines the transmission of religious culture along the Silk Roads through Central Asia.

3

Expanding networks of interaction, 500 CE–1500 CE

Scholars and poets in the cities of Renaissance Italy viewed ancient Greece and Rome as the height of civilization, a golden age they sought to emulate and revive after a long period of darkness. Scholars and poets in other cities who lived during that period of darkness had a different opinion of their own era, however. One of these was Rashid al-Din (*c.* 1247–1318), a highly learned vizier at the court of the rulers of the Ilkhanate, one of the four divisions of the vast Mongol Empire that had been established by Chinggis Khan (1167–1227). From a family of imperial officials, and a convert from Judaism to Islam, Rashid al-Din was trained as a physician, but was commissioned by two Ilkhan rulers to write a history of "all the people of the world" that would make plain the importance of the Mongols. Such a history was possible, the Ilkhan ruler Öljaitü commented, because "all corners of the earth are under our control and that of Chinggis Khan's illustrious family, and philosophers, astronomers, scholars, and historians of all religions and nations ... are gathered in droves at our glorious court, each and every one of them possesses copies of the histories, stories, and beliefs of their own people." Rashid al-Din relied on those written histories, which included western European and Indian Buddhist chronicles, Hebrew Scripture and other Jewish texts, Persian epics, and Chinese treatises, as well as the oral testimony of merchants and emissaries from many places living in the Ilkhanate capital of Tabriz, to produce an enormous hemispheric history, the *Compendium of Chronicles* (*Jami' al-tawarikh*), which he finished around 1310. Lavishly illustrated copies were made in both Arabic and Persian in a university complex in the city, destined for other cities in the Ilkhanate. In Rashid al-Din's opinion and those of the rulers he worked for, the golden age was not in the past, but now, when the Mongol states encouraged the movement of people and goods and the exchange of ideas across Eurasia. The Ilkhan rulers themselves were active in this exchange, sending emissaries and letters to the pope and the kings of France and England in the hopes of arranging a military alliance against the Turkish Mamluk rulers of Jerusalem and the territory around it. This alliance never happened, but products regarded as Mongol—or "Tatar" as they were often termed—came to be wildly popular among fashionable Europeans, including foods, music, patterned textiles, figured rugs, and children's names.

Like Rashid al-Din, contemporary world historians increasingly view the era in which he lived as a time when various regions of the world became more culturally, commercially, and technologically integrated. The Mongol Empire and other steppe nomads were instrumental in these connections, and so was a new religion, Islam, as well as the older portable religions of Buddhism and Christianity. Trade networks expanded and matured, linking growing cities and glittering courts, which relied for their wealth on the spread and intensification of agriculture, as more and more of the world's land was used for crops. Networks of exchange were larger and denser in the eastern hemisphere than in the western, but products, ideas, and technologies traveled in the Americas as well. Rashid al-Din and his Ilkhan patrons had no knowledge of the other hemisphere, of course—if the Mongols had, they probably would have tried to conquer it. But the knowledge that many people had of places far away grew significantly in this era, and the stories told about distant lands and cities by merchants, pilgrims, soldiers, and returning prisoner of war, enhanced by myths and legends, made them even more desirable as destinations. This chapter examines the ways that, through conquest, trade, migration, conversion, and pilgrimage, networks of interaction expanded and became denser, as people traveled and settled in ever more places.

THE DEVELOPMENT OF ISLAM

Islam, a new religion founded by the religious reformer and visionary Muhammad (*c.* 570–632), created one of the largest and most important of these networks, joining Buddhism and Christianity as a successful portable religion. Carried by its followers over vast distances, Islam blended with local traditions in ways that made it broadly appealing to many ethnic and social groups. Rashid al-Din was a convert to Islam, and so was his patron the Ilkhanate ruler Öljaitü, whose father was a Buddhist and whose mother was a Christian. With their conversions Rashid al-Din and Öljaitü adopted a faith that by the early fourteenth century had spread throughout many of the lands covered in the *Compendium.*

Accounts of the life and teachings of Muhammad first circulated orally and were then written down by his followers, just as were those of the Buddha and Jesus. They relate that the Prophet Muhammad was born in Arabia, where the basic social unit was the patrilineal tribe, became a merchant in the caravan trade, and married a wealthy widow, Khadija. He was a pious man and prayed regularly, and when he was about forty he began to experience religious visions instructing him to preach, which continued for the rest of his life. Muhammad described his revelations in a stylized and often rhyming prose as his *Qur'an*, or "recitation." His followers memorized his words and some wrote them down, most likely on the wide variety of materials used for writing in Arabia at the time, including clay tablets, animal bones, parchment, and palm fronds. Shortly after the Prophet's death, memorized and written materials were collected and organized into chapters, called *suras*, and in 651 Muhammad's political successor arranged to have an official standard version prepared. Copies of that written text were carried wherever Islam expanded, and it serves as the basis for the present form of the Qur'an. Muslims regard the Qur'an as the direct words of God to his Prophet Muhammad and revere it for its prophetic message, divine guidance, and inimitable literary quality. At the same time, other sayings and accounts of Muhammad, which gave advice on matters that went beyond the Qur'an, were collected into books termed *hadith*. Together the Qur'an and the hadith informed Muhammad's followers about the Sunna ("clear and well-trodden path") he had followed, which provided a normative example of how they were to live.

Muhammad's visions ordered him to preach a message of a single God and to become God's prophet, which he began to do in his hometown of Mecca. He gathered followers slowly, but also provoked resistance because he urged people to give up worship of local gods and challenged the power of the local elite. In 622 he migrated with his followers to Medina, an event termed the *hijra* that marks the beginning of the Muslim calendar. At Medina Muhammad was more successful, gaining converts and forming the first *umma*, a community that united his followers from different tribes and set religious ties above clan loyalty.

In 630 Muhammad returned to Mecca at the head of a large army, and he soon united the nomads of the desert and the merchants of the cities into an even larger umma of Muslims, a word meaning "those who comply with God's will." The religion itself came to be called Islam, which means "submission to God," and Mecca became its most holy city. By the time Muhammad died in 632, Muslim forces had taken all of the Arabian peninsula, and during the next century Muslim rule expanded further, from the Iberian peninsula in the west to Central Asia and the Indus River in the east along the trade routes that had long facilitated the movement of people and ideas.

Like the conquests that established the empires of the ancient world, the political authority of Muslim rulers was spread by military victories, but the religious practices and ideas of Islam proved attractive to people both inside and outside Muslim states, partly because of the straightforward nature of its doctrines, and many converted. The strictly monotheistic theology outlined in the Qur'an has only a few central tenets: Allah, the Arabic word for God, is all-powerful and all-knowing. Muhammad, Allah's prophet, preached his word and carried his message. Muhammad described himself as the successor both of the Jewish patriarch Abraham and of Christ, and he asserted that his teachings replaced theirs. He invited and won converts from Judaism and Christianity, although Christians, Jews, and later also Zoroastrians and Hindus in Muslim states came to be regarded as "protected people" (*dhimmis*), who were allowed to maintain their religious practices as long as they recognized the political authority of Muslim rulers and paid their taxes.

All Muslims had the obligation of *jihad* (literally, "self-exertion"), to strive to submit to God, spread God's rule, and lead a virtuous life. According to the Muslim *shari'a*, or sacred law, five practices—the profession of faith in God and in Muhammad as God's prophet, regular prayer, fasting during the sacred month of Ramadan, giving

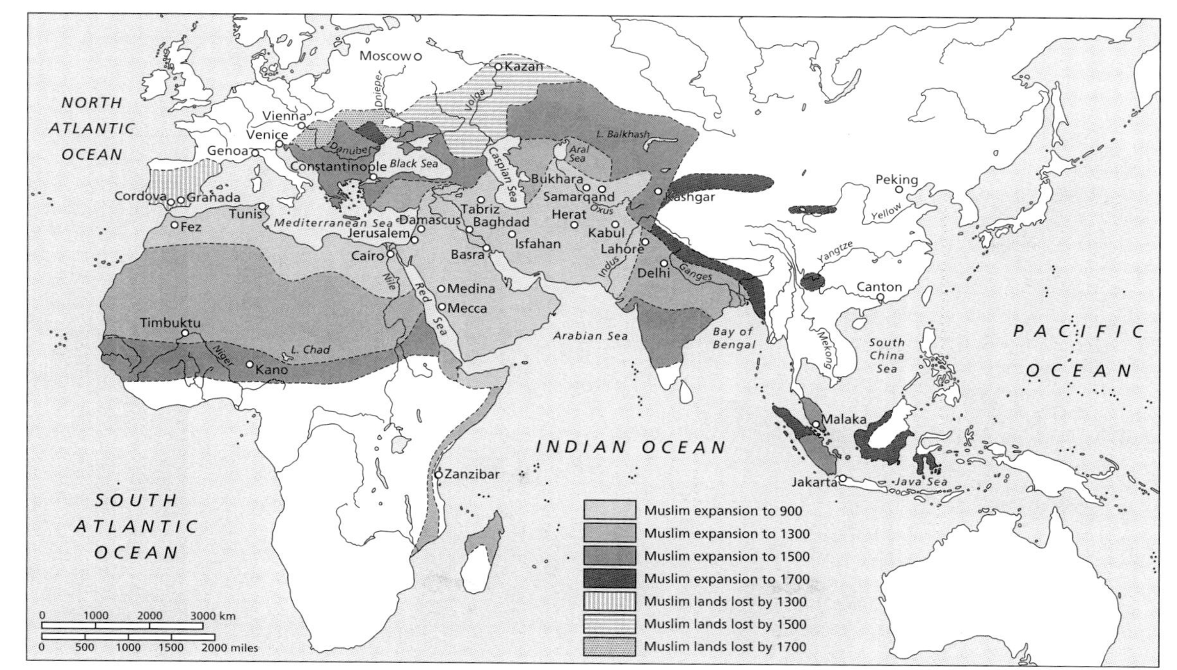

Map 3.1 The spread of Islam

alms to the poor, and a pilgrimage to Mecca if possible—constitute what became known as the Five Pillars of Islam. In addition, the Qur'an forbids alcoholic beverages and gambling, as well as a number of foods, such as pork, a dietary regulation adopted from the Mosaic law of the Hebrews. It condemns business usury—that is, lending money at interest rates—but does not regard material wealth in itself as evil. The hadith discourage the depiction of living beings, and Islamic art tended to favor geometric designs and calligraphy, although in some places—including the Ilkhanate court at Tabriz—figurative art was created as well.

In contrast to Buddhism and Christianity in which a celibate life as a monk or nun was viewed as spiritually superior, the Qur'an and the hadith recommend marriage for everyone, and approve of heterosexual sex within marriage for both procreation and pleasure. As in Judaism, most teachers, judges, and religious leaders in Muslim societies were married men. Men attracted to other men generally married and had children, although in some Muslim societies same-sex love between men was celebrated in poetry and literature. Polygyny was common in Arab society before Muhammad, though it was generally limited to wealthier families. The Qur'an restricted the number of wives a man could have to four, and prescribed that he treat them equitably. As elsewhere, marriages in Muslim societies were generally arranged by the family, and the production of children—especially sons—was viewed as essential, with rituals and prayers devised to help assure the procreation and survival of offspring.

Many scholars note that the Qur'an holds men and women to be fully equal in God's eyes; both are capable of going to heaven and responsible to carry out the duties of believers for themselves. They argue that restrictions on women under Islam came from pre-Muslim practices and are thus not essential to the faith. Men veiled their wives on marriage, for example, as early as the third millennium BCE in the Tigris and Euphrates valleys, and well-to-do women were secluded in Byzantine and Persian lands before Islam developed. They note that Muhammad's first wife, Khadija, convinced him to take his religious visions seriously; she was never veiled and the Prophet did not marry other wives until after her death. Other scholars point out that the Qur'an does make clear distinctions between men and women.

It allows men to have up to four wives and to divorce a wife quite easily, sets a daughter's share of inheritance at half that of a son's, orders that the Prophet's later wives be secluded, and prescribes that wives be obedient to their husbands. Debates about how to interpret the Qur'an are extremely important in Islam because of the book's special stature, but gender distinctions and other social hierarchies also have other bases, including shari'a. Though women played a major role in the early development of Islam—as they had in Christianity—and appear to have prayed and attended religious ceremonies in public, after the first generation the seclusion of women became more common in the Muslim heartland and commentators on the Qur'an interpreted its statements about women in increasingly patriarchal ways. Men were to fulfill their religious obligations publicly, at mosques and other communal gatherings, and women in the home, though they generally had access to a separate section of the mosque unless they were ritually unclean because of menstruation or childbirth. Muslim law did allow women more rights to property than was common in other contemporary law codes, however, and wealthy Muslim women used their money to establish schools, shrines, hospitals, and mosques.

CONFLICT, DIVERSITY, AND BLENDING IN THE MUSLIM WORLD

Muhammad called for unity within the umma, but this was not to be. In both the Arabian heartland and elsewhere, political conflicts and cultural blending led to increasing diversity within Islam, just as they did in Buddhism and Christianity. Shortly after Muhammad's death his followers split over the valid line of succession, which resulted in assassinations and civil war. One faction asserted that Muhammad's cousin and son-in-law Ali was the valid successor because the Prophet had designated him as *imam*, or leader in community prayer. These supporters of Ali—termed Shi'a from Arabic terms meaning "supporters" or "partisans" of Ali—saw Ali and subsequent imams as the divinely inspired leaders of the community and the true successors. The larger body of Muslims thought that other members of Muhammad's extended family chosen by his closest followers as *caliph*—leader and deputy—after his death were the legitimate successors. This group came to be called Sunnis, a word derived from Sunna, the practices of the community based on Muhammad's example. In Sunni Islam, proper interpretation of the Qur'an comes from the consensus of a group of scholars and caliphs who are regarded as having authority over all Muslims, while in Shi'a Islam the statements of an individual imam understood to be invested with divine insight carry great weight. Over the centuries other differences developed, and enmity between Sunni and Shi'a Muslims sometimes erupted into violence, mixing with political and economic disputes to create conflicts that took various forms and continue today.

This split did not halt the expansion of Islam, but as the Dar-al-Islam—the "abode of Islam"—grew, laws and practices that had been developed in the Arabian peninsula mixed with existing traditions and new teachings emerged, creating a broad range of practices, rituals, and norms of behavior among both Sunni and Shi'a Muslims. In the 660s, forceful leaders of the Umayyad clan moved the caliphate to Damascus in Syria and made the position of caliph hereditary, handed down from father to son just as in other ruling dynasties rather than to a leader chosen for his piety and virtue. They were overthrown by the 'Abbasid dynasty (r. 750–1258), who built a new capital with a huge palace and many mosques at Baghdad on the Tigris River. This was in the heart of what had been the Persian Empire, and though the 'Abbasids were Arab, many of their officials were Persian, and the scholars, scientists, poets, philosophers, and mathematicians who mingled in Baghdad came from many different backgrounds. Such cosmopolitan interaction was also true at the other end of the Dar-al-Islam in Spain, where the Umayyads retained power and Córdoba became a center of culture and learning for Muslim, Jewish, and Christian scholars and Europe's largest and most prosperous city. Just as well-educated thinkers in early Christianity drew on Greek philosophy and Roman traditions to develop more complex ideas and institutions, so creative Muslim thinkers in both cities built on Greek, Persian, and Indian knowledge, translating works into and out of Arabic and writing new works. And just as Christian incorporation of classical culture had provoked a reaction by those who thought it had strayed from its original teachings, so did these developments,

3.1 In a thirteenth-century ‘Abbasid illuminated astrological manuscript, the archer associated with the zodiac constellation Sagittarius, flanked by Jupiter and the moon, shoots toward a beast that is his own tail. Astronomy, astrology, science, and medicine flourished at the ‘Abbasid court, where the caliphs supported learning and experimentation.

with conservative moralists urging a return to what they saw as the simpler forms and stricter norms of Muhammad's day. Their calls for a "return" sometimes brought in new ideas that had not actually been part of earlier teachings, but they were described as traditions, a pattern that is common in other conservative religious and political movements as well.

The 'Abbasid caliphate also saw the beginning of the mystical movement known as Sufism, which emphasized personal spiritual experience. Sufis taught that divine revelation could come not only to scholars studying the Qur'an, but also to certain holy individuals who could fully lose themselves and unite with God. This radically different line of thought could have developed into a separate branch of Islam, but most Sufis taught that those who gained knowledge of God through mysticism still had to obey the shari'a, and Sufism became part of orthodox Islam, in both its Shi'a and Sunni branches. Sufis were often wandering ascetics, venerated for their wisdom and austere lifestyle, and some were poets. Religious orders gathered around them or at shrines dedicated to their memory, where people engaged in distinctive rituals and ceremonies, often involving music, dance, or the recitation of sacred texts. Some Sufis came to be regarded as saints, recognized because of miraculous deeds or postmortem communications with the living. Sufi saints were the focus of popular devotion, sometimes over large areas; as in Christianity, people read or heard stories about their lives and miracles, prayed to them for assistance, and made pilgrimages to their shrines. Learned theologians and imams sometimes objected to the emotional rituals and pilgrimages favored by Sufis and their adherents, arguing that they led people away from the essentials of Islam. Sufi orders provided important social links, however, and their ceremonies were generally more popular than the more formal and reserved services in mosques. For these reasons, and because many rulers and other powerful people were members of Sufi orders, opposition to Sufi teachings rarely had much effect.

During the ninth and tenth centuries, Turkic peoples in the steppes of Western and Central Asia converted to Islam. When they subsequently conquered northern India they brought the religion with them, although much of the population remained Hindu, and when they conquered much of the Byzantine Empire they spread

Islam as well, although much of the population remained Christian. The Mongols who conquered much of Asia in the thirteenth century primarily practiced an indigenous shamanist polytheistic religion centered on the sky god Tengri (though some were Buddhist or Christian), but as they settled down to rule many in the western parts of the Mongol realm converted to Islam. Merchants and teachers carried Islam to West Africa on the camel caravan routes that crossed the Sahara, and to the East African Swahili (Arabic for "people of the coast") coast and Southeast Asia on the ships that crisscrossed the Indian Ocean. People living in coastal cities from Melaka on the Malay peninsula to Mombasa in East Africa, or in land-based trading centers from the West African city of Timbuktu to the Silk Road city of Samarkand were attracted by Islam's validation of commerce, spiritual and moral teachings, and global connections. Timbuktu, Samarkand, Córdoba, and other far-flung cities became centers of Islamic learning, where teachers opened schools that taught boys basic reading in Arabic and recitation of the Qur'an, and scholars provided advanced philosophical, theological, and legal training at schools and universities attached to mosques. Thus when Rashid al-Din opened a university in Tabriz, he was following a well-established pattern.

Islam also appealed to many rulers for a combination of religious, political, and commercial reasons. Not only did the rulers of the Ilkhanate become Muslim, but so did those of the West African kingdoms of Ghana, Mali, and Songhai, the city-states along the East African coast, and the coastal states on the Malay peninsula and island Southeast Asia. Intermarriage between Muslim traders from distant lands and local women was often essential to its growth, with women providing access to economic and political power through their kin networks and serving as brokers between indigenous and imported cultures.

When people at any social level converted, they often blended in their existing religious ideas and rituals, which they passed on to their children, and very diverse patterns of Islamic beliefs and practices developed. People carried out rituals to ward off evil spirits or cure illness that invoked the assistance of both local good spirits and Muslim saints, maintained household shrines to their ancestors, honored Hindu gods in ceremonies, or went on pilgrimages to places that were holy to Sufis, Christian saints, bodhisattvas, and local deities. Religious officials denigrated such practices and periodically attempted to prohibit them, but men and women who considered themselves good Muslims believed firmly in their efficacy. Social practices also varied widely. Among Arabs and Persians, women's presence in public was restricted, and in South Asia both Islam and a stricter Hinduism favored the seclusion of women—termed *purdah*. The strictness and exact rules of this varied according to social status and location, however; wealthy urban women were generally the most secluded, while poor rural women—the vast majority of the population—worked alongside male family members. In western Africa, Southeast Asia, and the central Asia steppes, women often worked, socialized, and traveled independently and in public view, sometimes to the horror of male merchants or scholars visiting from areas where women's activities were more restricted.

The spread of Islam was accompanied by political disunity in its heartland. Regional dynasties, some of them Shi'a, broke away from the Sunni 'Abbasid caliphate and established their own Muslim states in Spain, North Africa, Egypt, and elsewhere, which themselves fought with one another and saw ruling families rise and fall. In the eleventh century, Seljuk Turks who had adopted Islam conquered much of the 'Abbasid caliphate, made the caliphs puppets of the ruling Turkish *sultan*—a word that means "he who has authority"—and then divided into smaller states themselves. In the thirteenth century the Mongols reached Muslim lands in their campaign of conquest, and killed the last 'Abbasid caliph. They were stopped in Syria in 1260 by armies of the Turkic dynasty that ruled Egypt and the surrounding area, provoking the outreach to Europe by Öljaitü and other Ilkhanate rulers described at the beginning of this chapter.

SOLDIERS, SLAVES, AND SOCIAL MOBILITY

The expansion and decline of states and empires is a familiar story, but embedded within these developments is a more unusual social feature of the Muslim world. The rulers of Egypt and their troops were Mamluks, slave soldiers of Turkish and other steppe origins who formed a military caste in many Muslim states and sometimes rose to become political as well as military leaders. This slave system was thus very different from those of ancient Athens or Rome. In the Mamluk system, begun in the ninth century by the ‘Abbasid caliphs, non-Muslim boys and young men were purchased or taken as war captives, brought to the ruler’s court, and systematically trained. Although arming slaves as soldiers might seem foolish—and there were examples of Mamluks revolting against their owners—this practice gave the ruler troops who were dependent only on him, not on their own clan leaders, and who as foreigners had no local social or familial ties. Intensive training built up their loyalty to the ruler and to one another, as did the possibilities for advance through the ranks and manumission when they converted to Islam. Regional Muslim rulers in many parts of the Dar-al-Islam and those vying to take over rule increasingly relied on slave soldiers as well, with armies of tens of thousands.

In Egypt, Mamluks became the actual sultans as well as the chief commanders in the middle of the thirteenth century, in a complex set of circumstances that provides an example of the ways in which family and sexual dynamics as well as shifting social hierarchies drove political change. In 1250, Shajar al-Durr, the widow of the previous sultan who had herself originally been a slave, was declared the ruler by Mamluk officers who had assassinated the previous sultan’s son by another wife. She appears to have been an able ruler. During her reign Christian forces on the Seventh Crusade led by King Louis VII of France attacked Cairo, but were defeated; Louis was captured and then ransomed for a huge amount of money that went into the royal coffers. Some regional leaders refused to recognize her as monarch, however, so she married Aybak, one of the Mamluk officers, and made him the sultan. Suspicions grew between the spouses and the Mamluks loyal to each of them and she had him murdered, but the Mamluks loyal to Aybak’s memory installed his son by another woman as sultan. He then had Shajar al-Durr murdered, as the story goes beaten to death by his female slaves and those of his mother. Despite this inauspicious beginning, successive dynasties of Mamluks ruled Egypt from this point until they were defeated by the Ottoman Turks in 1517, and Mamluks continued to have economic and military power in Egypt until thousands of them were killed in a struggle for power in the early nineteenth century.

Unsurprisingly, the story of Shajar al-Durr was retold as part of Egyptian folklore, becoming ever more fantastic, though it actually does not seem to need much embellishment. It is more than a tale of unhappy spouses and bloody palace intrigue, however, as it highlights a distinctive avenue for dramatic social mobility present in some Muslim societies. In other Muslim areas as well, Mamluks who had risen through the ranks to become generals also founded states, including Khwarezm in today's Iran and Afghanistan in the eleventh century, and the Delhi sultanate in northern India in the early thirteenth century, which was also for a brief period ruled by a woman, Raziya, who was killed by male rivals. Only a very few slaves in the Muslim world did become rulers, of course (and even fewer women did). Most male slaves were artisans, agricultural laborers, domestic servants, or ordinary soldiers, while the more numerous female slaves were cooks, servants, nursemaids for children, concubines, or laundresses. Slavery was not a status that extended over generations, however, nor even necessarily over a lifetime. Freeing one's slaves was viewed as a meritorious act in the Qur'an, and female slaves who gave birth to a master's child were to be freed upon the death of the master. Children of Muslim fathers were by definition Muslim and free, and conversion to Islam often brought emancipation. The conditions of labor for many slaves were harsh, but slaves often assimilated into the urban and rural societies to which they had been brought, even if few achieved great power.

Shajar al-Durr's story thus fits within a more general pattern of slavery in the Muslim world, and it also fits within and thus illuminates another, and even broader pattern of this era: the development of courts as centers of power and culture. From one end of Afroeurasia to the other, and also at a few places in the western hemisphere, courts grew up around rulers that shared many features with the Mamluk court in Cairo, including factional intrigue, social climbing, and the tight interweaving of family and politics.

COURTS AND COURTLY CULTURE

The agricultural states and empires of the ancient world had largely been monarchies ruled by hereditary dynasties, and new states created after 500 CE were generally monarchies as well. With monarchies came courts—communities of individuals around a ruler that both exercised and represented power, thus with both practical and symbolic functions. In the era from 500 to 1500, courts could be found in places where they had been earlier—China, Rome, Egypt, the Tigris and Euphrates valleys—and also in Japan, Korea, the Sudanic and Guinea Coast kingdoms of West Africa, the sultanates and caliphates of the Muslim world, the Mongol khanates, the Byzantine Empire, the small kingdoms of western Europe and South and Southeast Asia, the Aztec (Mexica) Empire in Mesoamerica, and the Inca Empire in the Andes. In places such as western Europe where religious leaders held power independent of lay rulers, courts developed around them as well, including a magnificent court around the pope in Rome. Regional or local courts often mimicked central court practices on a smaller scale.

Because land was the chief source of wealth, status, and power in agricultural states, the largest landowners—whom we usually call "nobles" or "aristocrats"—were the top elite; this group included the ruler, although he did not always hold the most land. Aristocratic men generally handed down their status and their land to their sons, and their status and some wealth to their daughters, although rules and patterns of inheritance varied. As populations expanded and economies became more complex, rulers and other members of the elite increasingly turned from forced tribute-taking to more systematic collection of taxes, rents, and labor services in order to extract resources from the people living on their lands. The personnel needed to do this, and to carry out other functions required to administer territories, increased in number and in levels of expertise. Courts became places where authority was delegated through a hierarchy of offices, military and political decisions were made, and decrees and laws were issued.

Courts varied greatly in size, complexity, and structure, but they also showed certain commonalities. As in thirteenth-century Cairo, all were centers of intense competition for power and prestige, as officials, advisers, courtiers, generals, wives, mistresses, and a host of others jostled, plotted, and campaigned with and against one another. Some individuals at court had clearly defined duties—the physical protection or entertainment of the ruler, the maintenance of the royal treasury, the writing of court chronicles—while others had honorific titles and offices with no clear function, but were simply favored by the ruler.

Clever rulers or their chief officials dispensed and rescinded positions strategically, and made decisions about marriage for tactical reasons as well. Marriage to the daughters and sisters of other rulers offered opportunities for alliances, while those to women from powerful local noble families might help secure the loyalty of these families to the ruler. In cultures where powerful men married many wives either at the same time or successively, marriages could accomplish both these goals, and often reflected the changing aims of a ruler. Wives became the mothers of possible claimants to the throne, who sought (often with the assistance of their mothers) to replace rulers or at least secure their own succession. The Frankish king Sigebert I (r. 561–575), for example, married Brunhilda (*c.* 543–613), the daughter of the Visigothic king of what is now Spain; when he was assassinated—perhaps at the order of his brother's wife—Brunhilda became the regent for her son, and later for two of her grandsons and a great-grandson, all in situations of intense courtly intrigue and bloody feuds involving family members and officials. Like Shajar al-Durr, Brunhilda became the stuff of legend, and may have been the inspiration for the character of the same name in the medieval German epic the *Niebelungenlied* and Richard Wagner's opera cycle based on this.

Although many states developed official systems for handing on rule from one generation to the next, these were often more precept than practice, and rulers everywhere needed to show rivals inside and outside their lands just how powerful they and their supporters were. They also needed to demonstrate regularly why people should pay taxes, send their sons to be soldiers, build roads or bridges when ordered to, or carry out other obligations the ruler required. Thus rulers and their officials developed ceremonies, rituals, and other activities that made the special nature of the monarch and his (or occasionally her) connection to the cosmic and social order visible. Monarchies survived in this (or any) era more because people accepted that the hierarchy through which power was administered was legitimate than because of authoritarian or despotic power at the center. Through the creation and repetition of myths of origin and other shared traditions, rituals also reinforced the sense of a conscious common identity among the ruler's subjects, the sense that they were somehow one people.

Courts were thus sites of cultural production and consumption, and of ceremonies and activities through which people at the court simultaneously portrayed unity within the larger society under the beneficent rule of the monarch and showed that they were different from—and superior to—those outside of the court. Certain types of food, clothing, and comportment marked one as a person familiar with courtly life, and trickled down to lesser courts or to other social groups who wished to emulate elites. As their strategies for extracting resources turned more from plunder and tribute to taxes and laws, rulers and nobles had to demonstrate that they were not simply military leaders, but also wise and learned. They became increasingly concerned with culture, literature, and the arts, and what is generally termed "courtly culture" emerged. Sometimes rulers themselves wrote poetry, played music, painted, and danced, and everywhere they determined what forms of each of these would be favored. The 'Abbasid court in Baghdad and the Benin court on the Guinea Coast were centers of musical performance, where highly trained musicians performed for rulers in elaborate palaces. The Khmer rulers in Southeast Asia commissioned artworks, monuments, and temples, including what became the largest religious complex of the era, the elaborately carved stone temple complex of Angkor Wat, originally dedicated to the Hindu god Vishnu. In Europe, rulers and nobles increasingly filled their castles with tapestries, paintings, and lovely furniture, hired musicians and poets, and patronized scholars and scientists.

Rituals performed by the ruler and his entourage were crucial to the identity and role of courts. These included regularly occurring weekly, seasonal, and annual cycles of rites and festivals, along with special ceremonies marking military victories, accessions to the throne, marriages, births, and deaths in the royal family, and a host of other occasions. Some of these were held within the court, with access or participation a mark of favor and prestige. In Byzantium and other Christian courts, for example, the ruler, his family, his closest associates, and a chosen few attended weekly church services, scripted performances accompanied by chanting, incense, prescribed choreography, and the recitation of standardized prayers. Exclusive events included banquets, where huge amounts of exotic imported foods and expensive local delicacies prepared in complex recipes rewarded dignitaries and impressed foreign visitors. Banquets often involved music, dancing, theatrical pieces, puppet shows, or other sorts of entertainment, thus appealing to all five senses. They might also be occasions for gift-giving, creating ties of obligation that linked a ruler and his subordinates.

Other rituals were massive public ceremonies, in which the ruler (or at least an enclosure in which he rode or was carried) was visible to hundreds of thousands of people, moving through a city in an impressive parade along with thousands of officials, soldiers, and slaves. Such processions were designed not only to display royal power and majesty, but also to create a bond between a ruler and his subjects, from the highest to the lowest. Spanish observers described the Inca ruler carried through the streets of Cuzco on a throne made of gold lined with the brightly colored feathers of tropical birds, wearing jewelry of emeralds and gold fitting his status as a son of the sun who defended the cosmic order. Royal parades and visitations to cities were sometimes accompanied by performances that drew on religious, mythological, and literary examples to portray the ruler and his lineage in a heroic or sacred light, and all of this was memorialized in court chronicles and paintings so that its magnificence could be recalled at a later time. Court officials also took care to portray rulers showing the generosity expected of them: Aztec records, for example, tell of Montezuma I (r. 1440–69) distributing 20,000 loads of stockpiled grain when a flood hit his capital city Tenochtitlan.

Courts borrowed practices and values from other courts, which they learned about through written texts, imported material objects, visiting ambassadors, in-marrying wives and concubines, and traveling scholars, merchants, musicians, and monks. The court established in China during the Tang dynasty (618–907 CE) became the model for those that developed in Silla Korea (688–918 CE) and Nara Japan (710–784 CE), with Confucian political ideology, Buddhist religious teachings, and Chinese writing adapted for local use. Muslim forces overthrew the Persian Sassanid dynasty in 651, but Muslim rulers copied many Sassanid ceremonies and rituals,

3.2 In a later copy of a painting on silk by the Chinese court painter Zhang Xuan (712–756), Lady Guo Guo, the sister of the emperor's favorite concubine, rides with a young princess and other members of the Tang court. The relatively simple dress and calm trotting of the horses suggest that this is an informal spring outing rather than a formal procession.

particularly those that emphasized the ruler's exalted status and pre-eminence over his subjects; Byzantine emperors and the popes in Rome copied these as well.

Many of the individuals at court were members of landholding hereditary aristocracies who also had judicial, political, military, and economic responsibilities away from the court, and whose control of land and the people living on it gave them a base of power unconnected to the whims and wishes of the ruler. In a number of places, aristocrats were, in fact, quite independent during this period, and the ruler at the top was not especially powerful himself but was more of a figurehead. In Japan, for example, the emperors—who had ruled since before the earliest written records from Japan in the sixth century CE—were regarded as direct descendants of the sun goddess Amaterasu, the most important deity, but real power was in the hands of landowning aristocrats (*daimyo*). They and their bands of warriors (*samurai*) swore undying allegiance to the emperor, but he was very rarely seen in public and his primary function became siring a son so that the imperial office continued (a task at which emperors were remarkably successful, as the Japanese emperor today is a direct descendant of those of the sixth century). From the sixth century to the nineteenth, often one noble family predominated in Japan; although members of this family never challenged the emperors for the throne, they were granted the title *shogun* (top general), advised the emperors on major decisions, appointed officials to all important government positions, directed the military, and became the center of public courtly life.

In the Byzantine Empire as well, as Arabic, Slavic, and Turkish forces gradually took over more territory beginning in the seventh century, the emperors increasingly relied on the military aristocracy and less on soldiers over whom they had direct power. Those aristocrats engaged in revolts, assassination plots, and court intrigues that sometimes led to the overthrow of an imperial dynasty; these later gave rise to the word "byzantine" in English, meaning overly intricate and entangled. In many Muslim states, although the sultan officially held authority, real power rested with his advisers and generals. In western Europe after the end of Roman Empire in the fifth century there was no strong centralized authority at all. The smaller kingdoms that emerged had weak kings and powerful nobles, who themselves often maintained their own regional courts.

Despite—or perhaps because of—the decentralized and distributed nature of power in reality, various rituals were created to perform the official loyalty of elites to their rulers or other superiors. Japanese nobles and samurai swore loyalty to the emperor, and in western Europe beginning in the tenth century rulers often required nobles to publicly affirm their loyalty in a ceremony that made them the ruler's vassals—from a Celtic word meaning "servant." Such oath-swearing ceremonies of homage and fealty grew out of earlier Germanic oaths of loyalty to a tribal leader, and, like everything in courtly society, became increasingly ritualized and complex. The vassal knelt before the ruler, invoking God and the saints as well as his sense of duty and honor, and the lord responded with prescribed words and actions, generally touching the vassal in a way that physically demonstrated the lord's superiority and magnanimity, such as laying his sword on his vassal's shoulders and head.

The dominant group in most courtly societies in this era remained the hereditary nobility, but courts also housed some men and women from families of lower stature, and a few—as we have seen in Mamluk Cairo—who were from the bottom, or near the bottom, of the social heap. Thus conflicts between individuals and factions were embedded within conflicts between different types of social hierarchies: inherited status, familial relationships with the ruler, wealth, ability, formal training, and physical attractiveness.

For example, beginning in the Tang dynasty, entry into government service and the imperial court bureaucracy in China increasingly occurred through examinations based on the Confucian classics, and by the Song dynasty (960–1279) hundreds of thousands of young men took these examinations after a long period of rigorous study. Aristocratic lineage and patronage still eased one's path to power and influence in China, as about half of the palace bureaucracy rose through their connections, but the examination system provided an alternate route to influence for some able men. Examination systems were also set up in Japan, Korea, and Vietnam in emulation of the Chinese model, although kinship ties and personal connections remained important, and in Japan examinations were soon abandoned. In Byzantium, appointments at court were considered favors of the emperor, not the result of merit or aristocratic pedigree, and were in practice facilitated by a circle of powerful advisers. In the Hindu courts of South and Southeast Asia, religious functions were reserved for Brahmins, but otherwise courts were fluid spaces as far as caste was concerned, and people from many groups sought fortune, employment, prestige, and status through service at court. Elsewhere as well, courts were to some degree socially porous.

CODES OF BEHAVIOR AND TALES OF ROMANCE

Intense rivalry and status insecurity gave rise to particular codes of behavior that sought to teach courtiers—and particularly male courtiers—successful skills to survive and flourish in these challenging settings. Some of these codes, such as Confucianism, revolved around ethical ideals like duty and benevolence, but more often they involved aesthetic and cultural ideals, demonstrated in speech, gestures, clothing, personal grooming, and eating. Although these began among courtiers and court ladies, they eventually spread more widely, becoming the basis of codes of manners and comportment taught in many middle-class families as well. Their courtly origins are evident in words used to describe such behavior, however: ladylike, gentlemanly, courteous.

Those who resided at court—or who hoped to gain a position there—took great care in their appearance, spending large sums on clothing and cosmetics, often imported over vast distances, to make themselves more attractive. They were expected to appreciate literature, music, and art, and perhaps even to produce these, and many did. Chinese courtiers, members of the imperial family, and some emperors wrote poetry and other literary works, produced calligraphy, and painted on silk. In India, rulers sponsored competitions of poetic talents and other types of cultural production.

In Japan, especially during the Heian period (794–1184), aristocrats in the capital city at Kyoto learned Chinese literature and philosophy, wrote poetry, and surrounded themselves with beautiful paintings and objects. They developed an aesthetic ideal called *miyabi*, which emphasized elegance, restraint, sophistication, sensitivity to beauty, and an awareness of the transience of things, and rejected anything uncouth, rough, or rural. This ideal was expressed most fully in the long, complex, and influential novel *The Tale of Genji*, written in the early eleventh century by a lady-in-waiting to the empress at the imperial court whose father had been an ambitious government official. Her real name is unknown, as women in Heian Japan were generally simply referred to by their fathers' or brothers' titles, but she is usually called Murasaki (the name of one of the main female characters in *Genji*) Shikibu (a title once held by her father). The book tells the story of "the shining Genji," the handsome fictional son of the emperor and his favorite concubine in the not-too-distant past, who writes and recites wistful and sensitive poetry, paints, attends elegant ceremonies in even more elegant dress, moves from one romantic affair to another, and talks about all this at great length with his fellow courtiers and court ladies. *The Tale of Genji* was written for just that courtly audience, and because of this was written in *kana*, a syllabic phonetic script devised in the Heian period that was seen as especially appropriate for women, whereas writing in Chinese characters was a masculine pursuit.

The Islamic code of behavior and etiquette, called *adab*, also called for refinement, good manners, and decorum. Young aristocrats who followed it were expected to dress well (though not as beautifully as Genji), know something about Arabic poetry, history, and the Qur'an, act in a dignified way, give and receive gifts gracefully, and be able to converse in an intelligent and witty way on a variety of subjects. In Europe, advice manuals for rulers called "Mirrors for the Prince" and other guides to ideal behavior advised young men on how to live a life pleasing to God, control their anger, handle their rivals, and speak eloquently.

Romantic love became part of the noble ideal in some of these codes of behavior, depicted in poetry, prose, and paintings. Genji and his friends fall in and out of love constantly. In western Europe, although epic poems praising men for valor in battle such as the sagas of the Vikings or the twelfth-century Song of Roland remained popular as courtly entertainment, they were joined by romantic stories of the complicated love life of noble men and women, as in the stories of Tristan and Isolde or the court of King Arthur. In the Muslim world, a group of stories of Persian, Indian, and Arabic origin were brought together and written down in the ninth century, together with a framing story in which a wise bride, Shahrazad, outwits a king who has killed a series of his brand-new wives by telling him a succession of cliff-hangers so that he postpones her execution over and over. These *One Thousand and One Nights* included love stories, trickster tales, fantasies, and murder mysteries filled with bawdy humor, plot twists, and self-fulfilling prophecies. The collection continued to be expanded orally and in written versions over the subsequent centuries, and its stories spread beyond the Muslim world as far as England, where Shakespeare used elements from them as plot devices.

In the epic poetry from the ancient world, men's primary attachments are to their kings, their fellow soldiers, and sometimes their horses, and the values praised are loyalty, comradeship, and bravery in battle. Women only get in the way or keep the hero from his mission. In the stories that became increasingly popular in courtly settings, women still get in the way, but men desire this rather than run from it, and the men themselves are praised for their good looks and charm as well as their valor. This era saw the creation of the conventions of romantic love in the literature of many cultures, the notion that love could be an ennobling and unstoppable force that takes one's breath away, sweeps one off one's feet, makes one a better person, causes time to stand still, and so on. This idealization of love was generally heterosexual, but ardent homoerotic poetry also approvingly depicted male same-sex passion, and male homosexual subcultures developed among officials, intellectuals, and actors in Song China, Japan, and Korea.

Questions remain about who created these romantic conventions, how they were transmitted from one place to another, and why this happened when it did. In the West, one source appears to have been Muslim poets at the courts of both the Muslim rulers of Spain and the Christian rulers of Provence in southern France. Christian Provençal poets who called themselves troubadours then picked up these romantic themes and brought them to courts elsewhere in Europe. Here they blended with courtly conventions about comportment and sensitivity that had developed in bishops' courts in the Rhineland and with literature celebrating noble dynasties and knightly virtues into a European version of this tradition, usually called "chivalry" or "courtly love." In this variant, the male lover is socially beneath his female beloved; her higher status makes her in theory unattainable so his love can remain pure and chaste while he does great deeds in her honor.

This line of transmission does not explain the importance of love as a plot device in *Genji*, however, nor in the poems, stories, and songs in other courtly cultures. Perhaps a better explanation might be that the poets at all of these courts were close observers of the power of sexual and emotional entanglements, and recognized that people wanted to hear about these, particularly if they involved beautiful people and had a tragic ending.

In some places the scholars and officials at those courts also became increasingly concerned with the disruptive power of sexual attraction, but rather than celebrate it they attempted to control it. Laws, strong social sanctions, and sometimes physical barriers were needed, they thought, to shield men from sexual temptation, keep unmarried people apart, and preserve order within the family. Thus at the same time that women became more important characters in stories and poems, restrictions on actual women increased.

Many of these restrictions involved limiting women's mobility, and of these the Chinese practice of footbinding has received the most attention. In order to bind a girl's feet, her toes were forced down and under her heel until the bones in the arch eventually broke. This generally began when she was about six, though a woman's feet needed to remain bound all her life to maintain their desirable small size and pointed "golden lotus" shape. Like many cultural practices, this began at court, first among female entertainers and imperial concubines about 1000; it spread among the elite and middle classes in northern China by about 1200 and eventually to all social classes in this area. Explanations of footbinding have involved a wide range of factors: fantasies among male poets and scholars that eroticized small feet and a swaying walk and linked these with nostalgia for the past; a change in the ideal of masculinity in Song China from warrior to scholar, which meant that the ideal woman had to be even *more* sedentary and refined; a desire to hide the actual importance of women's labor by families eager to prove they were rising socially and economically; Chinese sexual ideas that linked bound feet with improved reproductive capacity and stronger infants. Dorothy Ko has emphasized that no one explanation suffices, and that the reasons for footbinding changed over its thousand-year history and were different for men and women. She notes that women were not simply its victims; they internalized Confucian notions of the importance of self-sacrifice and discipline, and the connections between bound feet, reputation, domesticity, beauty, and self-respect. Thus it was mothers who generally bound their daughters' feet in what became a female rite of passage, and women worked together to make the exquisite embroidered shoes that further represented their high status.

Elsewhere as well, ideologies, norms, and laws prescribing distinct gender roles and male superiority were supported by women as well as men. New norms of masculinity did not bring significant changes in norms of proper female behavior, which continued to revolve around honor and purity. Romantic love was also not tied to marriage in either literature or life in this period. Marriage was far too important as a social, economic, and sometimes political arrangement to leave up to personal passions; if affection developed this was nice, but if it did not people do not seem to have been terribly disappointed.

Whether in *Genji* or the King Arthur stories, romantic love was understood as limited to social elites, just as were other behavioral ideals. People outside the charmed circle of the court were thought to be beneath love in the same way that they were beneath decorum, sophistication, or learning. Their lives were lives of toil, not worth mention in historical chronicles or poetry, a judgment that continued for centuries. Even later historians of labor tended to regard medieval peasants as not especially interesting, when compared with the workers of the modern world. Despite their disdain, however, all courts depended on the surplus provided by villagers, which able monarchs and officials recognized, and sought to increase or at least maintain. The world outside the court may have looked timeless and unchanging to some courtiers, but it was not.

AGRICULTURAL EXPANSION AND VILLAGE SOCIETY

The expansion of sedentary agriculture that began in the Neolithic and continued in the classical period picked up pace in this era, and by 1500 domesticated plants and animals could be found over far more of the globe than they had been in 500, including the islands of the Pacific, eastern North America, and what had been forests, swamps, marshes, and coastal areas in many parts of the world. Rulers and their officials often had a direct hand in this, forcing or providing incentives for people to move to uncleared areas and make the land suitable for farming by cutting down trees, draining swamps, terracing, building dikes and irrigation ditches, or making other alterations in the landscape. Sometimes this was internal colonization, in which spaces between villages and the farmlands that surrounded them were filled in with new villages and farmland, increasing population density. Sometimes it was external colonization, in which villagers followed, or occasionally preceded, armies, or were sent to places where no one had lived before. People also decided on their own to migrate to previously uninhabited or uncultivated land, expand farming into marginal areas, intensify their production, or grow crops that had larger yields or could bring in more income. Rulers and their tax collectors often quickly followed, and as the improvements made to land represented too much of an investment to leave, villagers generally paid their rents, taxes, and labor obligations in the new states that arose in many agricultural areas. Thus states promoted agriculture, and agriculture promoted states.

There were certain commonalities among villages in many places, just as there were commonalities in courts. Sedentary agriculture spread far more widely than did writing, and even in areas where there was writing villagers lived in a largely oral culture. Fathers and mothers taught their children how to carry out the tasks they would be expected to do, and the traditions that otherwise structured their lives. Many of these traditions were undergirded by beliefs about deities, spirits, and sacred beings, whether those of universal religions such as Christianity, Buddhism, or Islam, or of local religions. Villagers joined with neighbors and family members in rituals to express thanks and hopes, celebrate major life transitions such as birth, marriage, and death, and ask for favors and blessings. Like rulers, divine beings and spirits were powerful and sometimes capricious, but they (or at least some among them) were also understood to be beneficent guardians who would protect those who venerated them properly. Within even small villages there was usually

3.3 Inca men and women harvest potatoes, in an illustration from *The First New Chronicle and Good Government*, a handwritten book by Felipe Guaman Poma de Ayala (1550?–1616), who came from a noble indigenous family in Peru. Guaman Poma hoped his history of the Incas and the Spanish conquest would convince the king of Spain to make reforms; the book never reached the king, but it serves as an invaluable source for life in the Andes.

someone who was regarded as having a special connection with the unseen world—a shaman, priest, seer, holy man, "wise woman," or chief with spiritual power. Those individuals engaged in rituals designed to convey the wishes of the unseen world to the village and vice versa, specialized labor for which they received food and other necessities of life, although in smaller and poorer villages they sometimes farmed as well.

Courtiers and scholars often saw villagers as an undifferentiated mass, but social and gender distinctions actually permeated many aspects of village life, including work and property ownership. Men and boys generally cleared new land and built large terraces, and in areas where large animals were used for plowing they did the plowing and cared for oxen and horses; planting, weeding, and harvesting were done by all, including young children. Where crops relied on human labor alone, women sometimes raised most of these, or both sexes did. In cultures where there were ideals of female seclusion, including China and some parts of the Muslim world, women at the top of the village social heap carried out most of their work within the walls of a house or house-compound, while the men of the household along with slaves and servants of both sexes carried out work outdoors. Systems of land inheritance in most agricultural societies tended to favor sons over daughters, although in the absence of sons daughters were sometimes seen as preferable to more distant male family members, as this would keep land in the immediate family. Women's and men's lives were most similar to one another at the bottom of village society, in what historians have called an "equality of misery."

Although aristocratic elites—including the territorial ruler in societies where there was one—demanded taxes and rents from land under their control and sometimes appointed overseers to run things, villages in many places also developed institutions of self-governance that controlled such matters as planting times, crop rotation, the maintenance of irrigation systems, and the use of forests, pastures, or other lands held in common by the village. These local communal bodies also conducted relations with higher levels of government, with their autonomy from these higher levels varying from place to place and over time, as did the ways they fit with clan structures of authority. New agricultural techniques, epidemic diseases, climate change, and cultural developments such as the introduction of new belief systems also had an impact on village institutions. Like structures of power at the top, these communal bodies promoted both solidarity and hierarchy. They represented the village as a whole, but were generally made up only of male heads of households, with younger sons, women, landless individuals, servants, unfree people, and those in various groups understood to be outsiders excluded.

Village authorities generally sought to maximize agricultural output, and because of this emphasis on growth some scholars have seen the roots of current environmental crises in the decisions of villagers in this era. The biogeographer Jared Diamond, for example, uses a number of agricultural societies from this era, including Viking settlements in Greenland, Anasazi towns in the American Southwest, Maya city-states, and Polynesian settlements on Rapa Nui (Easter Island) to argue that societies "choose to fail" by deciding to continue practices that over-exploit the environment and maintaining rigid social mores. That scenario of collapse has been challenged by a number of archaeologists, anthropologists, and historians, who assert persuasively that people in these societies were not stupid and short-sighted, but remarkably resilient and flexible in the face of environmental changes. To view "societies" as undifferentiated wholes making decisions that determined a collective fate is overly simplistic, they note, as it ignores social and political complexities and conflicts within them.

Sometimes these debates about land use have pointed to religious and cultural issues: the Judaeo-Christian tradition has been seen by many as promoting an exploitative and uncaring use of the natural world, while Native American religions that emphasize human connections with the land led to sustainable subsistence strategies that had little permanent impact on the environment. Here as well counter-arguments have been made: within Christianity "the book of nature" was long viewed as a central source of divine revelation, while foraging and agriculture in the pre-Columbian Americas are increasingly recognized as having shaped the flora and fauna in dramatic ways, even in the Amazonian rainforest. Evidence can be found to support all sides of each of these debates, but what most scholars can agree on is that people generally had their natural resources right before their eyes. In contrast to today, those who made decisions about how to use land and resources generally lived on or near that land, and the impact of their decisions was similarly local.

Along with commonalities in village life and social structures across much of the globe, there were also regional variations, which themselves changed with the adoption of new subsistence strategies.

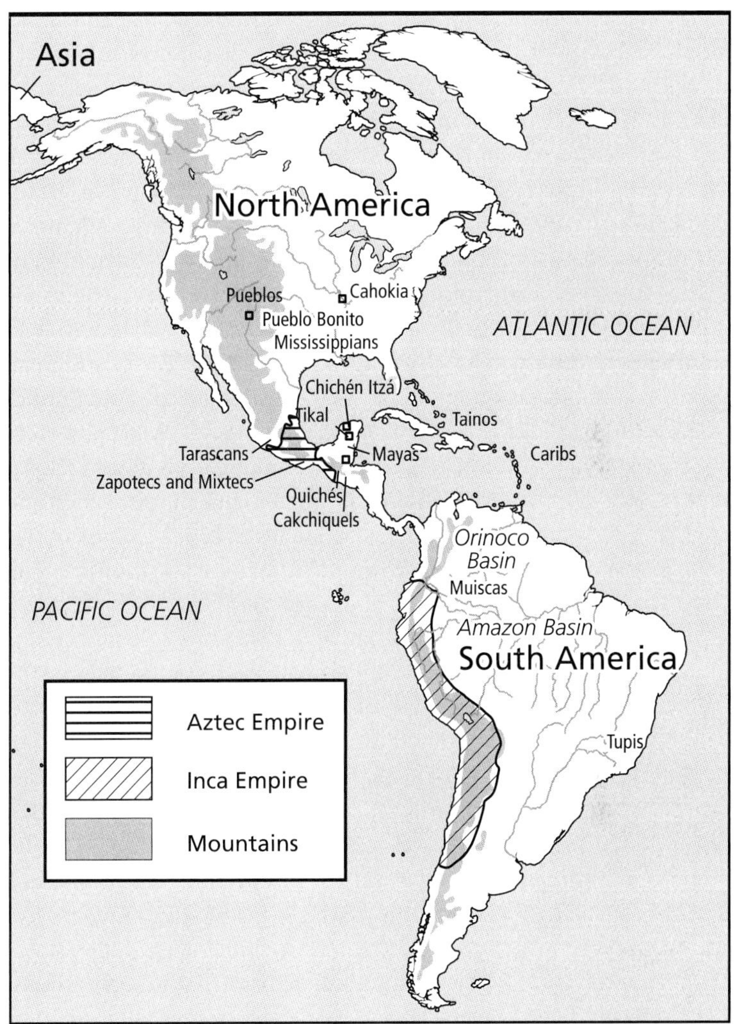

Map 3.2 The Americas before 1492

In North America, trade networks carried maize agriculture from Mesoamerica to the Southwest, into the Mississippi and Ohio River valleys, and then to the Atlantic coast by about 1200 CE. In the Southwest, people also planted desert crops such as agave and cotton, and used large sandstone blocks and masonry to construct thick-walled houses. Across the plains and into the eastern forest, people regularly burned the undergrowth to discourage the growth of brush and trees so that grasslands where bison, elk, and deer fed expanded. These animals were not domesticated, but, through burning, their numbers and range were increased significantly, and hunting was made easier through the enhanced visibility of prairie landscapes. Combined with increasing use of bows and arrow instead of spears after about 600 CE, fire made large game a more reliable food source. In the central river valleys, people used burning and other techniques to clear acres of land to plant maize and other crops, and constructed mounds for burials, ceremonies, and house platforms. Burial chambers filled with valuable artefacts and with individuals sacrificed to accompany the deceased indicate that Mississippian mound culture was hierarchical, and that power was increasingly centralized. Kinship was reckoned matrilineally, but whether this translated into more egalitarian gender structures in this period is difficult to say. By 1500, along riverbanks in the center of North America and along the eastern coastline, fields of maize, beans, and squash and orchards of fruit and nut trees surrounded large, permanent villages containing many houses, all encircled by walls made of earth and timber. The largest of these was Cahokia near the confluence of the Mississippi and Missouri rivers, which at its peak in the thirteenth century was a city of perhaps 40,000 people in a complex of mounds, plazas, and houses that covered five and a half square miles.

Different cultivars of maize were developed for many different climates, but maize was difficult to grow in high altitudes. Thus in the Andes, maize was grown in more low-lying areas and various types of potatoes at higher altitudes. To keep hillsides from sliding and increase the amount of land available for crops, villagers often built terraces separated by stone retaining walls on the steeper slopes, along with irrigation channels and ditches to bring water to the fields. At the time of the Spanish conquest in the sixteenth century, families in most Andean cultures were organized into *ayllus*, groups of related kin that cooperated in farming and ritual activities. Land was owned by the ayllu, not by individuals, with parallel lines of descent; women achieved access to resources such as land, water, and herds through their mothers, and men through their fathers. Ayllus were grouped within one of two moieties, an upper and more prestigious moiety called the *hanansaya* often associated with warfare, and a lower and less prestigious moiety called the *hurinsaya.* After the Inca conquests, members of both moieties and all ayllus owed labor services to the central government in Cuzco, which included working the land, building roads, weaving, and military service.

Maize will also not grow in hot, wet climates very well. Thus in Amazonia, manioc, a tuber that can be cooked in many ways, became the staple food, planted along with other crops, including fruits, nuts, and various types of palm trees, transforming the rainforest into a landscape at least partially managed by humans. People domesticated peach palms, for example, which produce fruit, pulp that is made into flour, heart of palm that is eaten raw, and juice that can be fermented into beer. People throughout the Americas domesticated dogs, but because no native species allowed itself to be harnessed as horses, oxen, and water buffalo did in Asia and Europe, all agricultural labor was human-powered. Judging by later descriptions and depictions, women did much of the crop-raising, or both sexes did, with gender-specific tasks.

In sub-Saharan Africa, Bantu-speaking peoples continued to migrate into forest, savannah, and highland regions, bringing iron tools and crops such as yams and sorghum. In eastern Africa these were joined by bananas and plantains brought from Asia by Austronesian migrants sailing across the Indian Ocean. Because soil quality was poor and draft animals that provided fertilizer as well as power could not survive in many tropical areas because of diseases, farmers generally practiced shifting cultivation, moving to new fields when the soil became less fertile or when population increase required this. Village networks were interwoven with those of clans, religious societies, and age-grade groups (groups of people of about the same age who often underwent rituals that marked stages of life together) into a complex web of associations that stretched beyond a single village to link it to others.

The Austronesians who sailed westward across the Indian Ocean to Africa also sailed eastward into the Pacific Islands beginning about 1500 BCE, carrying domesticated crops and animals along with families, seeds, and religious objects. These intentional settlement

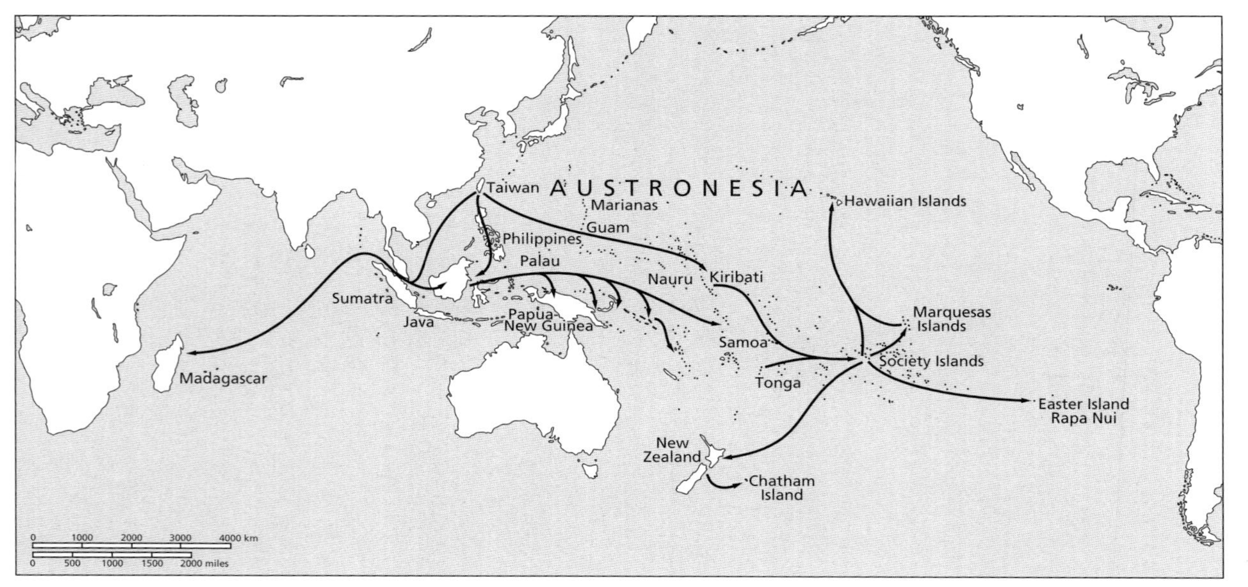

Map 3.3 Settlement of the Pacific

voyages pushed further and further across the Pacific, although the timing of these is currently undergoing revision as radiocarbon dating is becoming more reliable and more widely available. This newer research suggests that Samoa was settled in about 800 BCE, but then voyaging stopped for a long time, and was resumed only about 800–1000 CE, perhaps spurred on by population growth, the invention of the large double-hulled sailing canoe that made long voyages possible, and decisions to explore and colonize made by political leaders. There may have been a particular burst in the thirteenth century when seafarers spread out to the most remote islands of East Polynesia, reaching Hawai'i in the north, Rapa Nui (Easter Island) in the east, and Auckland Island in the south, on some voyages crossing more than 2,000 miles of open ocean, navigating by the stars, sun, currents, wind patterns, and paths of birds. Once islands had been located, navigators also used nautical maps made of palm-fronds and reeds that indicated the time required to sail between islands. By 1500, people lived on almost every inhabitable island in the Pacific, and had brought with them crops such as yams, taro, bananas, coconuts, sweet potatoes, and breadfruit, along with pigs, chickens, dogs, and (unintentionally) rats. On some islands, settlers built terraces and irrigation canals for crops, along with artificial fish ponds where keepers raised plants for fish to eat and then caught them easily in weirs and nets.

Polynesian society was organized into clans under hereditary chiefs, and in many islands there were sharp distinctions between social groups. In Hawai'i, for example, distinctions developed between the highest social group of chiefs (*ali'i*), an elite group of priests, diviners, healers and professionals (*kahuna*), the large body of commoners, and an outcast group. Relations between these groups were regulated by a code of conduct that carried strong religious sanctions in which certain acts such as coming too close to a ruler were *kapu*, ritually forbidden or restricted. (This is the origin of the English word "taboo.") Contact between men and women also had rules of kapu. Men and women were forbidden to eat together, or to prepare food for the other sex; women were prohibited from eating many foods, including pork, bananas, coconuts, and certain types of fish. Other Polynesian island societies also had similar codes of forbidden and expected conduct that were just as complex as those at royal courts, but how and when they developed is not clear. Judging by practices recorded later, many Oceanic cultures accepted some types of same-sex relationships, such as those between older men and boys, or those involving individuals regarded as shamans.

In cold and rainy northern Europe, the introduction of the heavy plow pulled by oxen and suited to clay soils allowed agriculture to spread into areas where the light Mediterranean plow had not. Here people lived in small houses with spaces for their animals attached; villages were set within broad fields, and although families worked their own strips of land within the fields, they often kept the needed oxen collectively. Households generally consisted of one married couple, their children (including step-children), and perhaps one or two other relatives, a neolocal pattern that led to people marrying relatively late, when both spouses had earned or inherited a few resources to establish the household. In southern and eastern Europe, extended families were more likely to live in the same household or near one another, and marriage was earlier, especially for women.

New villages were established in forests, swamps, and coastal areas of Europe that were near to existing villages, but large numbers of people in the twelfth and thirteenth centuries also migrated from one part of Europe to another in search of land, food, and work: the English into Scotland and Ireland; Germans, French, and Flemings into Poland, Bohemia, and Hungary; Christians into Muslim Spain. These long-distance migrants spoke a different language, had different traditions, customs, and laws, and sometimes practiced a different religion than the local population. Chroniclers writing in Latin at the time spoke of differences in terms of *gens* (race or clan) or *natio* (kind or stock); we might now call these "ethnic" differences. If the migrants were predominantly male, they often intermarried with local women, but if women migrated as well, and in some cases even if most migrants were male, laws were sometimes instituted that attempted to maintain distinctions between groups by prohibiting intermarriage. Among these was the 1366 Statute of Kilkenny in Ireland, in which the English who were trying to impose their rule over Ireland and had imposed legal restrictions on the Irish forbade any marriages between English immigrants and Irish, requiring English people to speak English (and not Gaelic), wear English clothing, and ride in the English style (with a saddle), to make which group someone belonged to instantly visible. Laws such as these were variable in enforcement—and they never applied to the upper classes, for whom politically advantageous marriages were made across all kinds of lines—but they contributed to a growing consciousness that certain differences were not simply a matter of customs or language, but were in the body as, for example, "Christian blood" or "English blood."

In southern, eastern, and southeastern Asia, the expansion of agriculture was also a combination of localized intensification and migration to new areas by ethnic groups with a conscious common identity and traditions different from those of the people who already lived there. Whether long-time residents or migrants, villagers diked and leveled forests, swamps and coastal plains, transforming them into irrigated rice paddies that were less dependent on fluctuating rainfall. To grow two crops a year, they grew rice seedlings in a seed bed and then transplanted the seedlings into a flooded field, an extremely labor-intensive process involving every family member. This contributed to an expansion of the food supply that allowed the Chinese population to double from about 50 million in the eighth century to about 100 million in the twelfth, and increased populations elsewhere. Especially in China, villagers also grew cash crops such as sugar, tea, mulberry leaves (for silkworms to eat), and cotton, and women in village households raised silkworms, spun silk thread, and wove textiles. Profits from these household enterprises were used to pay rents and taxes—increasingly in copper coins instead of goods—and to purchase charcoal, tea, oil, pottery, and other consumer goods. Families were generally under the control of the eldest male, who might take several wives, and extended families often lived together in family compounds. Living older family members were to be honored and obeyed, and dead ones venerated.

The spread of agriculture was so extensive as to be nearly global, but it was not unchallenged. Not everyone accepted the new impositions, and in some places people moved to avoid settled farming rather than to spread it. In a process that has been best studied in Southeast and South Asia, some people moved to or remained in rugged and remote terrain, growing root and vegetable crops in small plots of shifting cultivation, and supplementing these by gathering, hunting, and fishing. Commentators from courtly cultures judged such "forest peoples" to be primitive barbarians even less advanced than villagers, but the survival of this less sedentary way of life was in some cases a conscious choice and not simply a holdover.

In some environments, foraging remained the primary subsistence strategy because temperature, rainfall, and terrain prevented agriculture or pastoralism, not because people actively rejected these. Other than some reindeer herding among the Sami people of what is today Scandinavia and Russia, foraging continued as the way of life in the northern zones of boreal forest, taiga, and tundra in Asia, Europe, and North America. Here people such as the Inuit hunted land and sea mammals, birds, and fish, using equipment made of stone, bone, leather, sinew, tusk, and antlers. Foraging also continued in some tropical forests, in deserts and semi-desert areas, and in mountainous regions. Most of the people in Australia were hunter-foragers, although the Guditjmara people who lived in southeastern Australia built an extensive system of ponds, channels, and weirs to farm eels, similar to the fish ponds of Hawaiʻi, which supported a permanent community. Throughout Australia there were sacred sites where men and women gathered to sing, dance, and play musical instruments in ceremonial rituals, and to exchange goods, ideas, and marital partners. Foraging could not support the population that agriculture could; estimates of the entire population of Australia in this era range from 250,000 to 750,000, about the same number of people that lived in one of the larger cities in agricultural states.

NOMADIC PASTORALISTS

While some people resisted agricultural states by moving, others did so militarily, for this was a period in which mounted nomadic pastoralists extended their authority over vast swaths of Eurasia. These nomadic incursions began with the invasions of the Huns (Xiongnu) and the Hepthalites in the fifth century, included the many campaigns of various Turkish peoples, and then those of the Mongols in the thirteenth century under Chinggis Khan (his title, not his name, and which means "universal ruler") and his sons and grandsons. Chinggis Khan combined astute military leadership, personal bravery, and diplomatic shrewdess. He led mobile groups fighting from horseback with compound bows who coordinated their military tactics to overwhelm their opponents, and used psychological strategies against his enemies, sparing them if they surrendered, but killing them ruthlessly, including women and children, if they resisted. Mongol troops leveled cities and slaughtered hundreds of thousands of people. As the troops advanced, the Mongols built roads and bridges, seized arms and their makers, and learned new tactics such as the catapault, thereby laying the groundwork for further expansion. These storms of nomads fully ended only in the fifteenth century when the empire created by the ruthless and charismatic Turkish conqueror Timur (Tamurlane) collapsed. Most of these nomadic pastoralists were from the steppes of Central Asia, but some historians would put the initial expansion of Islam within this framework as well, as much of Muhammad's army of conquest was made up of mounted nomadic Bedouins.

Conflicts between agriculturalists and pastoral steppe nomads are among the big stories of this era, but nomads required sedentary cultures to trade with, plunder, and tax. The Mongols were able to create the largest land-based empire the world has ever seen despite a small population by fully mobilizing the resources—both human and material—that they extracted from the regions that came under their control. Chinggis himself kept conquering new territories until he died, but as he pushed onwards he left behind subordinates and officials to establishment administrative and economic structures in order to keep revenue flowing. They did this primarily by modifying institutions that were already there to promote production and trade, working with Mongolian-approved locals. Some of his commanders suggested turning all of north China into pasture for the horses needed for conquest, but local officials convinced Mongol leaders that it would be far more advantageous to tax the grain, silk, and other commodities produced by farming and artisanal families. The Mongols forcibly moved hundreds of thousands of farmers, artisans, entertainers, hostages, soldiers, and others over vast distances when they judged their labor was needed, and others moved on their own, all of which served to spread agricultural and other types of technology, along with goods and ideas. Chinggis' successors, such as his grandson Khubilai Khan (r. 1260–94) who conquered southern China and Korea, followed a similar pattern: first destruction, and then bureaucracy.

The social structures of Central Asian steppe peoples were also closely connected with this subsistence strategy that combined pastoralism, plunder, conquest, and trade. The steppes were too dry for large-scale agriculture, and there were no good rivers for irrigation, so people and animals followed set migratory paths based on the climate and seasons, living in large round tents called yurts and using horses to herd sheep, goats, and cattle. Men, women, and children learned to ride and care for animals, and ate a diet that relied largely on animal products. Nomadic societies were traditionally organized into clan and tribal groups, with leaders who gained stature through military exploits and the force of their personality.

Chinggis Khan reorganized the Mongol army so that warriors fought not in clan groups, but in groups that combined people from different tribes led by his personal allies chosen on the basis of merit and loyalty rather than tribal chiefs. Because every Mongol man was a soldier (women provided logistical support), this reorganization led to social revolution, as soldiers' loyalty was transferred from their tribe to their commander and up the chain to the Chinggisid family. Mongol practices and rituals also enhanced male self-esteem and soldiers' loyalty to one another. As the Mongols expanded their empire, they took a census of all households and required all male adults to register for military conscription. Some of these men were actually drafted into the army, where they were made distinguishable from the rest of the population by an unusual uniform haircut. That marked them anywhere they went as part of a group of men whose function was fighting, no matter what kind of clothing they were wearing; it made desertion more difficult but also allowed soldiers to recognize one another immediately and encouraged bonding within the group. (Distinctive military haircuts continue to serve all these functions.) The Mongols also had a specific type of male bonding, the *anda* ("sworn friend") bond in which two men pledged to aid one another under any circumstances, creating a permanent spiritual bond between them, ritually consecrated by an oath. Chinggis Khan himself had anda bonds with leaders from

3.4 Chinggis Khan's youngest son Tolui Khan (1192–1232) and his wife Sorghaghtani Beki (*c.* 1198–1252) with courtiers and court ladies, in an illustration from a fourteenth-century manuscript of Rashid al-Din's *Compendium of Chronicles.* Sorghaghtani Beki was a Nestorian Christian, but supported religious institutions of other faiths as well, and helped her four sons become rulers of Mongol states, including Khubilai in China.

other clans, as did his male relatives and descendants, which shaped their military strategies and alliance networks.

Loyalty among men was an important tool in Mongol expansion, and so were other gendered practices. Mongol marital norms forbade marriage to someone from the same clan, so men had to get their wives from other clans and tribes, which they sometimes did by forcibly abducting them. That pattern of exogamy continued as the Mongol Empire grew, and men raped, seized, purchased, and sometimes married women from the groups they conquered. This pattern was particularly evident at the top, as Mongol leaders generally had a number of wives of various ranks and many more women available to them. A widely reported 2003 article from the *American Journal of Human Genetics* noted that over 8 percent of all males in a broad area of Asia from the Pacific Ocean to the Caspian Sea share the same Y chromosome. The twenty-three authors of this article concluded that this pattern most likely resulted from the success that Chinggis Khan and his male descendants had in spreading their Y chromosome across Central Asia. If their sample is representative, more than 16 million men today are direct-line male descendants of Chinggis Khan, surely one of the world's most successful lineages.

The extensive forced and voluntary migrations of men and women within the Mongol Empire led to sexual relationships and marriage across all kinds of lines—linguistic, cultural, tribal, religious—which served as important means of cultural exchange and hybridization. In the western khanates, for example, the first Mongols to accept Islam appear to have been ordinary soldiers who interacted with the largely Muslim indigenous population and married local women. The Mongols who ruled China broke with this pattern, as they wanted to preserve their privileges as conquerors and so avoided many Chinese practices and resisted assimilation. Just as had the English conquerors in Ireland, they forbade Chinese to marry Mongols, and passed other regulations in an attempt to keep Chinese from passing as Mongols and to keep social groups apart. They assigned people hereditary occupations, each of which carried certain tax or labor obligations, and classified the population into four grades, with the Mongols at the top and the southern Chinese at the bottom.

The legacy of the Mongols is complicated and mixed. They slaughtered and moved populations, disrupted agriculture, and plundered wealth across Asia, but they also promoted trade and the exchange of ideas. They were pastoralists, but their forced moving of people helped expand agriculture. They were nomadic, but in the thirteenth century built a new capital city, Dadu (also known as Khanbaliq), that is the heart of modern Beijing and would be the capital of China for all but two brief periods after that. In building this new capital, they broke with their nomadic past, but followed a pattern set by many other rulers, who regarded cities—just as Ban Zhao had in the Han dynasty—as the only place where a cultured and civilized life was possible.

CITY LIFE

The order of a ruler was not the only way that cities were founded in this era. As they had been since they first appeared in Mesopotamia and Egypt at the end of the fourth millennium BCE, cities were built and grew (or were destroyed and abandoned) for many different reasons. Some began as villages along sea coasts, rivers, or trade routes that drew in more and more people because of economic opportunities. Others were, or became, ceremonial and educational centers, with churches, temples, mosques, universities, and schools. Others were places of refuge from armed conflicts, and their residents built strong walls with only a few gates in the hopes of maintaining their safety. Sometimes this worked.

Even today, which of the world's megacities or megalopolises deserves the designation "world's largest city" is disputed, with Tokyo-Yokohama, Jakarta, Seoul, Mexico City, and Shanghai all in the running, depending on how the population is counted and estimated and where the boundaries of the city are drawn. Population estimates for earlier cities are even more difficult, although for the first centuries CE there is no dispute, as the world's largest city was certainly Rome, which may have had more than a million people when it was at its largest. By 500 CE Rome had shrunk to perhaps 50,000 people, however, and it kept shrinking for many centuries after that. (Rome did not reach a million again until the first half of the twentieth century.)

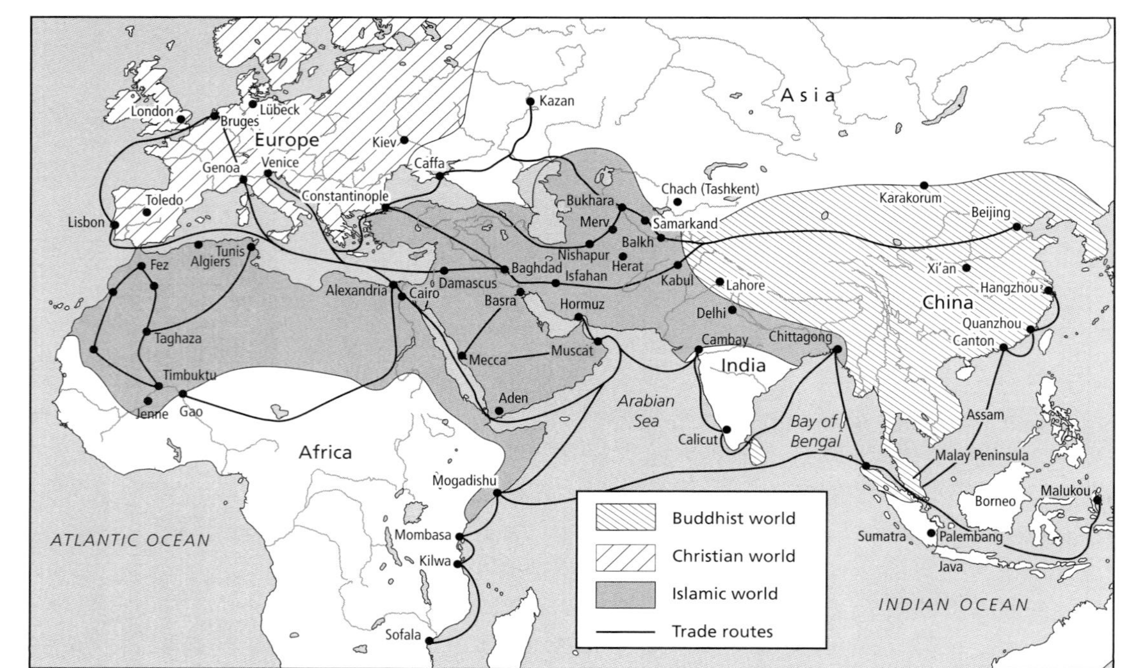

Map 3.4 Trading networks, major cities, and religions in the eastern hemisphere, 500–1500

In 500 the largest cities in the world were most likely Constantinople on the Bosporus and Xi'an in central China, with several hundred thousand residents each. These were joined later in the fifth century by Ctesiphon on the Tigris River, when the Sassanid Persian ruler Khosrau I moved hundreds of thousands of the people he had conquered there and built a new city. Ctesiphon's decline was even faster than Rome's, for when in the eighth century the 'Abbasid caliphs built Baghdad as their capital about 20 miles away, the city was completely abandoned. Other cities in the Muslim world that housed courts also grew to over 100,000 in the centuries before 1500, including Cairo and Córdoba, but the most urbanized part of the world in this era was eastern China, with at least six cities that had more than 100,000 residents. Similar-sized cities, mostly capitals, could be found elsewhere in Asia, including Anghor Thom, Delhi, and Vijiyanagar, the latter growing to perhaps half a million people before it was sacked by invading armies in 1565 and never recovered. In Christian western Europe, only Paris and perhaps Venice and Genoa had 100,000 people before 1500. In the western hemisphere, the largest cities were in Mesoamerica, first Teotihuacan and then Tenochtitlan; in North America, the only large city was Cahokia (see Map 3.4).

Because literate people in this era lived either in cities or in religious institutions (many of which were in cities), urban life has left far more records than has that in the countryside. Visitors to these cities were amazed at what they saw, and their reports and letters provide vivid details that are missing from the often dry bureaucratic records produced by local and royal officials. Universities and other institutions of higher education were established in cities, and their scholars wrote and circulated works of all types, and assembled libraries. Artists and artisans congregated in cities, where wealthy patrons commissioned paintings, sculpture, books, devotional aids, and other objects, and people of all classes purchased whatever they could afford. Thus artistic and material sources augment the rich written record.

Taken together, these sources indicate that cities everywhere had certain things in common. However they began, cities recruited people from the countryside with the promise of greater freedom and new possibilities. Cities provided economic opportunity, which led to greater wealth, a higher standard of living, and upward social mobility for many people, though the numbers of poor swelled as well. Many cities developed a sense of identity, which, like the group identities created by rulers and their courts, was enhanced by myths of origin and regularly occurring public rituals. In Venice, for example, the head of the city's government, known as the doge, was rowed once a year beginning about 1000 on a sumptuous galley at the head of a huge procession of decorated boats and gondolas beyond the lagoon on which the city had been built to the Adriatic Sea, which he both blessed and symbolically married. Throwing a gold ring into the waters, he recited words emphasizing Venice's domination of the sea—the sea was the wife in this ritual—which was to be as indissoluble as Christian marriage. This ceremony, which became larger and more elaborate over time, affirmed to all who watched it that God had lifted the city from the sea for the Venetians and that Saint Mark, whose relics Venetian traders had brought from Alexandria in the early ninth century after the Muslim conquests, protected it. Thus its naval power, commercial success, and opulence were divinely approved, a legend reinforced in other rituals, paintings, operas, and poems. (When Napoleon conquered the city in 1798 the doge abdicated and Napoleon had his ship destroyed; the current mayor of Venice has revived the ceremony, though with a much smaller boat and less pomp.)

Some cities were founded to be capitals of states, or grew up around the court of a ruler, so that royal officials ran the city. Other cities created independent institutions of government, often dominated by major merchants, and the economic, social, and political policies of the city represented the interests of this group. Still others were mixtures of these, with different authorities and factions within them vying for power, and rising and falling over the centuries. Along with the urban government itself, corporate bodies were established in many cities that regulated the production of goods and services, provided support for religious personnel and buildings, patrolled city walls and streets, opened and ran educational institutions, and carried out a variety of other activities. These craft guilds, religious brotherhoods, and civic militias promoted both solidarity and hierarchy: members understood themselves to have a group identity separate from those not in the group, but they were also expected to follow established instructions and rules, and obey orders from the leaders of the group. Guilds and other organized corporate groups provided their members with tangible benefits such as job training and burial plots, and also what sociologists call "social capital," a network of relationships through which they could gain economic and other advantages.

Cities were not egalitarian; the larger they were, the more elaborate the social hierarchy. These ranged from wealthy merchants, officials, and professionals at the top to artisans, students, and shopkeepers in the middle to servants, day laborers, porters, peddlers, and (in some cases) slaves at the bottom. Domestic slavery, reliant largely on women, characterized many cities in the eastern hemisphere, and may have characterized those of the western hemisphere as well. Because many cities were walled, as their populations grew space within the walls became increasingly limited, with narrow streets and alleys. People of all sorts, from beggars to wealthy merchants, regularly rubbed shoulders in the crowded city, but social standing and sometimes occupation were clearly indicated by people's clothing. In many cities, clothing distinctions became a matter of law as well as tradition, with certain costly items—fur in European cities, feathers in Mesoamerican ones—limited to members of the highest social groups.

Because salting, pickling, and drying were the only ways to preserve food, some member of the household had to shop every day, and markets were where they met their neighbors, exchanged information, and talked over recent events, as well as purchasing needed supplies. Markets, streets, and open spaces were also where people gathered for entertainment and relaxation, playing and watching ball games of various types, board and card games, games with dice, tiles, or knucklebones, animal fights, and human sparring matches. All of these were occasions for wagering and gambling, which moralists and officials sometimes condemned but had little power to control. City officials often tried to regulate aspects of urban life, including exchanges at the markets, house construction, street maintenance, and the disposal of waste. Those of the German city of Nuremberg, for example, ordered residents to clean up their pigsties and repair holes in the streets in front of their houses that were large enough for children to drown in them.

3.5 Customers order shoes, inspect cloth, and purchase tableware in this market scene from a fifteenth-century French illuminated manuscript. Although the scene is placed within an archway for stylistic purposes, buildings in European cities did often have covered loggias and passageways where vendors could set up their stands without worrying about rain.

Fire was a constant danger, and because houses were built very close to one another fires spread rapidly. During the thirteenth century, for example, fire burned large sections of Hangzhou in eastern China several times, once taking a reported 30,000 buildings, while major fires in the much smaller city of London destroyed churches, houses, and bridges. (The most devastating fire in London was in 1666, which went on for four days and destroyed most of the old city.) City and royal authorities tried various ways to prevent and fight fires, including prohibiting enclosed ovens and workplaces that used open fire such as smithies and foundries, encouraging the use of non-flammable building materials, establishing systems of watchmen and warning signals, and organizing fire brigades of city residents armed with buckets, ladders, and axes. Sometimes these were effective against small fires, but major conflagrations could overcome them.

Opportunities for work were generally not as plentiful as the number of people flocking into cities, so people supported themselves and their families by activities judged illegal or at least questionable or dishonorable. They stole merchandise from houses, wagons, market stalls, and storage facilities, fencing it to pawnbrokers or taking it to the next town to sell. They stole goods or money directly from people, cutting the strings of their bags or purses. They made and sold mixtures of herbs and drugs claimed to heal all sorts of ailments, perhaps combining this with a puppet show, trained animals, magic tricks, or music to draw customers. They sold sex for money, standing on street corners or moving into houses that in some places were officially sanctioned (and taxed) brothels. Prostitution was especially common in cities where men married late, where there were large numbers of transient merchants, or where certain groups of men, such as university students, soldiers, or clergy, were prohibited from marrying. Both Rome and Paris were known for the quantity (and quality) of the prostitutes who lived there. Most women and men at the bottom of a city's social heap combined all kinds of work in an economy of makeshifts. Religious and charitable institutions provided support for the poor in some cities, but beggars were everywhere.

The economic situation of many people in cities was precarious, and a rise in food prices—on which the poor spent a majority of their income—could be devastating. This sometimes sparked food riots, or attacks on merchants who were perceived to be hoarding or speculating. At times these mixed in suspicion of outsiders: Christians in European towns and cities attacked Jews, while in the Chinese port of Guangzhou rebels in 878 massacred Muslim merchants. Urban unrest and revolts also developed from other causes, including new taxes, higher house rents, changing conditions of work, charismatic religious leaders who urged opposition to authorities, conflicts between corporate groups such as guilds or student organizations, and sometimes even sporting events. In many of these, young unmarried men with no family responsibilities formed the core of the unrest, although women participated in riots over high food prices.

Every city had a slightly different variation on these common themes. Constantinople, built by the Roman emperor Constantine on the site of the smaller city of Byzantium, was initially designed in a distinctly Roman style to reinforce its similarities with the older capital, with colonnaded forums, marble public buildings, and churches that resembled temples. But it was a seaport rather than an inland center, and its well-protected deep-water harbor dominated the city. Constantine walled off the landward side immediately, and later emperors built massive ramparts and sea walls, making it impregnable in both appearance and reality. The city became a frequently copied prototype for later walled cities in Europe and the Mediterranean. Emperors also built churches, monuments, warehouses, race courses, forums, aqueducts, and fountains. As part of his efforts to revitalize the Roman Empire and affirm its Christian identity, Justinian ordered the construction of Hagia Sophia, a colossal domed church dedicated to Holy Wisdom filled with mosaics and relics, and built on the site of an earlier church that had been burnt to the ground in riots between the supporters of two teams in chariot races. Within the walls of the city were huge underground cisterns that provided water, and vast gardens and grazing areas that supplied vegetables and meat, all of which would allow the city to withstand a long siege. Constantinople was probably at its largest in the middle of the sixth century, with about half a million people, before the Plague of Justinian and subsequent epidemics, along with a series of earthquakes and dwindling imperial income because of the spread of Islam, led it to shrink to about a third of this size by the eighth century.

Despite this decline, the city remained an important trade as well as political and religious center, and attracted people from all over the Mediterranean and western Asia. Its foreign quarters were filled with Italians, Jews, Armenians, and Slavs, and even the occasional Persian and Viking. Its markets offered goods from many parts of the world. Furs and timber flowed across the Black Sea, as did slaves across the Mediterranean from northern Europe and the Balkans via Venice. Spices, silks, jewelry, and other luxury goods came to Constantinople from India and China by way of Arabia, the Red Sea, and the Indian Ocean. In return, the city exported glassware, mosaics, gold coins, silk cloth, carpets, and a host of other products, with much foreign trade in the hands of Italian merchants. The typical household in the city included family members and servants, some of whom were slaves. Artisans lived and worked in their shops, while officials and merchants commonly dwelled in multistory buildings, and wealthy aristocrats resided in freestanding mansions that frequently included interior courts, galleries, large reception halls, small sleeping rooms, reading and writing rooms, baths, and chapels. In the homes of the upper classes, women were secluded in separate women's quarters as they had been in ancient Athens.

Like Constantinople, Tenochtitlan was also built to be the center of an empire by people who understood themselves to have a divine mission. Nahuatl-speaking people who called themselves Mexica migrated into the central valley of Mexico beginning in the twelfth or thirteenth century. Here they settled on the shores and islands of Lake Texcoco, and in 1325 on an island in the lake they built the twin cities of Tenochtitlan and Tlatelolco, choosing the location in fulfillment of a prophecy attributed to the warrior-god Huitzilopochtli, who ordered the city built where they found an eagle perched on a cactus growing out of a rock sunk in water and eating a snake. (This origin myth is depicted in the Mexican coat of arms on the center of the Mexican flag.) Tenochtitlan became the larger of the two, and was built with two models in mind: Aztlan, the legendary island home of the Mexica in the north (and the origin of the word Aztec, given to these people by nineteenth-century scholars), and the real city of Teotihuacan about 50 miles north of Lake Texcoco, whose immense pyramids, carefully laid out avenues, residential areas, and vast market compounds were abandoned ruins by the time the Mexica saw them.

To duplicate the scale of Teotihuacan, the Mexica expanded their original island through extensive landfills, and on these built ceremonial centers, pyramids, temples, public buildings, markets, workshops, and houses, all separated by wide, straight streets and canals on which canoes brought goods into the city and took trash and human refuse out. They built a dike to isolate fresh water flowing into brackish Lake Texcoco; constructed terracotta aqueducts from springs in the hills to bring in fresh drinking water and supply fountains in the parks; built four causeways linking the island to the shore, with openings covered by bridges to let boat traffic pass; transformed marshlands around the edge of the lake into croplands by building *chinampas*, very fertile plots of land created by piling up mud and decaying vegetation behind dense wattle fencing secured by trees and stakes. (These are sometimes called "floating gardens," but they were not actually floating.) Stone and adobe walls surrounded the city itself, making it, like Constantinople, highly defensible and capable of resisting a prolonged siege. By the end of the fifteenth century, the urban area on and near the island had about 60,000 households and a total population of around 250,000. These included Mexica, groups who had already lived there at the time of Mexica conquests, emissaries bringing tribute from distant conquered states, traveling merchants, and war captives.

In the many public squares and marketplaces of Tenochtitlan, butchers hawked turkeys, ducks, chickens, rabbits, and deer; grocers sold kidney beans, squash, avocados, maize, and all kinds of peppers. Male artisans sold intricately designed gold, silver, and feathered jewelry, while female artisans offered various items of clothing customarily worn by ordinary people along with embroidered robes and cloaks for the rich. Wood for building, herbs for seasoning and medicine, tobacco for chewing and smoking, honey, chocolate, obsidian knives, jade jars, and many other products added to the array of goods, with both cacao beans and lengths of cloth used as money. Women and men mixed in these public places, for female seclusion was not a gender norm. Other gender distinctions were: girls were given spindles and shuttles for weaving cloth at their birth ceremony while boys were given a shield and four

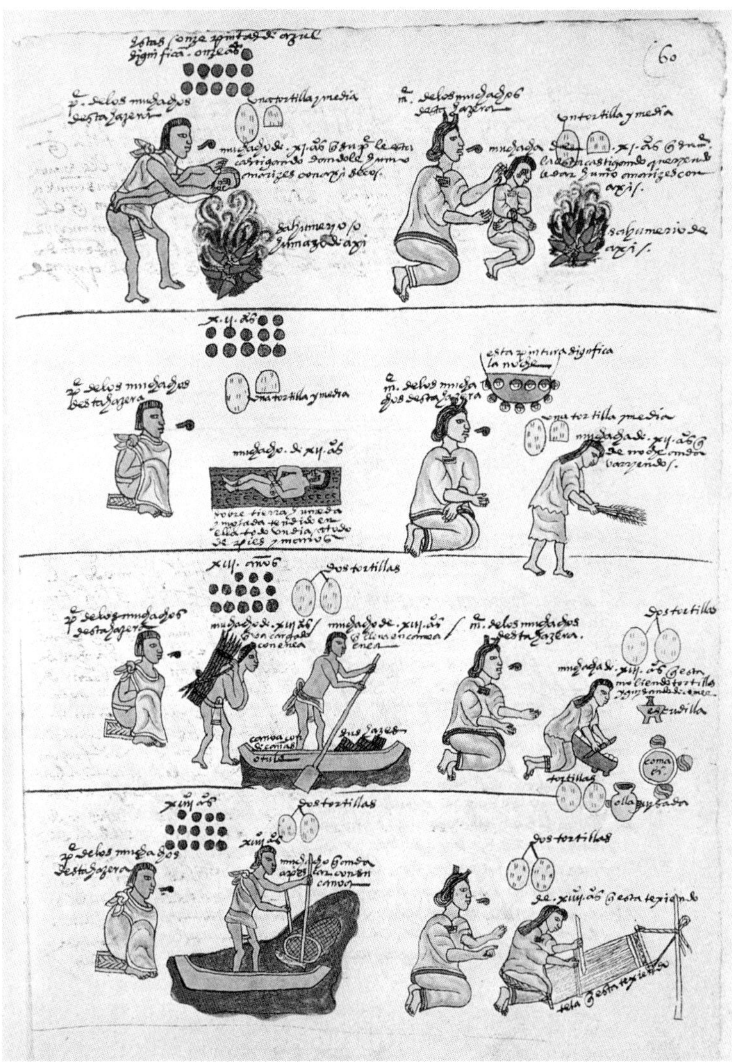

3.6 Punishments and chores of Mexica children of different ages, as depicted in the Codex Mendoza, a book written about twenty years after the Spanish conquest that depicts Mexica history and daily life. At the top, boys and girls of eleven and twelve are disciplined by their parents, and at the bottom adolescents sweep, carry sticks, fish, grind corn, and weave.

arrows, all of these symbols of the activities they would be expected to perform as adults in service to the expanding Aztec state.

Information about the social structure in Tenochtitlan and in Mexica society more broadly comes largely from documents written in Spanish in the first century after the European conquest, augmented by archaeological evidence and ethnographic research. The basic unit was the *calpulli*, which consisted of several interrelated family groups under the leadership of a chief. Members of a calpulli shared religious practices, often lived in the same location, and in specialized economies like that of Tenochtitlan might follow the same occupation. Society was understood to be made up of different calpullis, grouped into noble lineages that controlled most land and received taxes, rents, tribute, and labor services from those living on it, and commoner lineages. Mobility between these two groups was difficult, although occasionally successful commoner warriors could become nobles, and long-distance merchants who brought in the luxuries used by nobles gained some of their social privileges. Commoners (*macehualtin*) worked their own land or did other types of work in the city, and were liable for military duty if they were male, as well as other labor services. Beneath these were landless people and slaves, who included war captives, criminals, and people sold into slavery by their families. As in the Muslim world, slavery was not necessarily a heritable condition; other than war captives destined to be sacrificed to a deity, people moved in and out of slavery and could buy their own freedom. Those war captives became increasingly important in the later fifteenth century, when changes in the Mexica religion led to a greater emphasis on offerings to the sun of human blood as necessary for daily survival and cosmic order. The huge pyramid-shaped temple in the center of Tenochtitlan became the site of regular human sacrifices attended by many observers.

Not every city in this era had a giant church or temple at its center (though many did), nor were they all built to promote imperial power and glory (though many were). Hangzhou began as a rice-growing village in the fertile Yangzi River delta, and grew steadily to become the largest city in China (and perhaps the world) by 1200. During the short-lived Sui dynasty (581–618), residents built the first walls, and the city became the southern end of the Grand Canal system that linked the Yangzi River region with the Yellow River region in the north. Barges on the canals carried rice for tax payments and the feeding of troops to the centers of political and military power in northern China, along with goods imported from Japan, Southeast Asia, and India. This trade continued in the longer-lived Tang dynasty (618–907), when the city became one of many cosmopolitan centers of learning, where Nestorian Christianity, Judaism, Zoroastrianism and Islam brought by foreign merchants joined various branches of Buddhism. Officials selected through the examination system were in charge of the city, and gained renown for their poetry and calligraphy as well as their public policies. The scholar-official Bai Juyi (772–846) expanded the city walls, repaired a collapsing dike to improve irrigation, built a large causeway to assure access to a lake renowned for its peaceful beauty, and also wrote thousands of poems, popular for their simplicity of language. His poems were taken as far as Japan, where they were quoted by characters in Murasaki Shikibu's *Tale of Genji.*

When centralized Tang rule collapsed, Hangzhou became the center of the small independent coastal Wuyue kingdom, continued to prosper economically through agriculture and trade, and exchanged diplomats and Buddhist monks with Japan and Korea. The city was reabsorbed into the expanding Song dynasty in the late tenth century, and in 1132 was made the capital of the Southern Song state when the existing Song capital at Kaifeng was captured by nomadic Jurchens. Immigrants poured into the city from the surrounding countryside and the conquered north, and its population may have reached a million or even a million and a half a century later. Merchants in Hangzhou—and other large Chinese cities—organized themselves into guilds according to the type of product they sold, and used paper certificates of deposit issued by the Song government, the world's first paper money, along with coins for their business. Social hierarchies were somewhat fluid; marriages between social equals were preferred, but wealth gained through new economic opportunities might make up for slightly lesser stature, as would a prospective husband's success in the civil service exams that could lead to an official position.

The city was a center not only of trade and production, but also of culture, entertainment, and education. The scholar-official and scientist Shen Kuo (1031–95) wrote his major works in Hangzhou after political factionalism resulted in his dismissal from court. These included essays on medicine, astronomy, mathematics, civil engineering, archaeology, and geography, and contain the earliest known discussions of the magnetic needle compass, the dry dock for repairing ships, erosion and uplift as geological forces, and climate change, along with plans for improving relief maps, astronomical and surveying instruments, and the cultivation of medicinal herbs. Visitors reported on the city's many markets, bathhouses, silk draperies, painted ships, and brothels. Conquest by the Mongols established a new dynasty, the Yuan (1234–1368), and the capital moved north again, this time to the newly built capital Dadu, but Hangzhou remained an important port and a giant city. Dynasties, states, and empires might rise and fall, and occasionally cities fell with them and completely disappeared. Like Dadu, however, many of the most important cities from this era have endured far longer than the governments that first built them. By 1500, most of the world's largest megalopolises today were already cities, though sometimes with a different name: Tokyo was Edo, Jakarta was the port of Sunda, Mexico City was Tenochtitlan. Seoul was already Seoul, and Shanghai was Shanghai.

ZONES OF CULTURAL AND RELIGIOUS EXCHANGE

Among the many visitors to Hangzhou during the Yuan dynasty were two who came from slightly further away than most, the Venetian merchant Marco Polo (*c.* 1254–1324) and the Moroccan scholar and diplomat Ibn Battuta (1304–68). Polo apparently spent seventeen years in China, primarily as a courtier and official of the Yuan emperor Khubilai Khan, and dictated the account of his travels to a writer of romance stories while they were imprisoned together as war captives after he returned to Italy. Originally written in French—a common language for European merchants traveling east—*The Book of the Marvels of the World* was recopied and translated many times even before the development of the printing press, providing accounts of the riches and splendors of Asia that Polo's contemporaries suspected were exaggerated, but that inspired them nonetheless. Ibn Battuta began his travels with the pilgrimage to Mecca expected of observant Muslims, and then continued on to

Persia, down the east coast of Africa to Kilwa on the Swahili Coast, back north through Syria to the Central Asian steppes, then south again to India, where he became an official of the sultan ruling there. The Delhi sultan sent him as a diplomat to China, and although he was shipwrecked he did make it to the Yuan emperor's court in Beijing, with stops in Bengal, southern China, and various Southeast Asian ports on the way. He returned home to Morocco by way of Mecca, stopped for a bit, and then set out by camel caravan across the Sahara desert to Mali. When he returned from that trip the sultan of Morocco gave him a scribe, and the two together composed a travel book in Arabic, whose formal title reads *A Gift to Those Who Contemplate the Wonders of Cities and the Marvels of Travelling*. A few copies were made, but it was largely unknown until the nineteenth century. Both books relied on memory rather than written notes and mixed in stories of foreign lands from the works of earlier travelers to increase the number of "marvels" they contained. For these reasons there has been some skepticism about both travelers, but the scholarly consensus now is that both were actually in most of the places they said they were.

Marco Polo and Ibn Battuta were not typical travelers—Ibn Battuta may have traveled more than 75,000 miles—but their journeys share features with those undertaken by increasing numbers of men (and some women) in this era. Marco Polo's began as a trading venture and Ibn Battuta's as a religious pilgrimage, but their skills and foreign backgrounds brought them to the attention of rulers, and they became official envoys as well. Religion, trade, and diplomacy (along with conquest) motivated more people to travel after about 1100 than had before. Some wrote about their travels, and people wanted to read what they wrote because *they* thought of traveling. Polo and Ibn Battuta traveled by both land and sea in their journeys from and back to the Mediterranean, along trade routes that had developed in ancient times, but were becoming increasingly active.

Pilgrimage was one of the duties of a believer in Islam, and Buddhism and Christianity also encouraged pilgrimages to holy places, which became scattered all over the map as both religions continued to expand—but also contracted—in this era. Like Islam, Christianity and Buddhism became large zones of cultural exchange through which people, ideas, and objects flowed (see Map 3.4).

The transmission of Buddhism was never undertaken in a centralized way, but itinerant monks and merchants carried Buddhist teachings, texts, relics, devotional objects, and images widely, and by the tenth century Buddhism extended from the western steppes of Central Asia to the towns and mountains of Heian Japan. Buddhist festivals became popular holidays, and rituals marking stages of life incorporated Buddhist concepts, especially funerals, when the deceased moved from one lifetime to a new existence. Thousands of temples and monasteries were built, and many became wealthy as believers gave them land and goods. Communities of nuns were poorer and less popular than those of monks, who were regarded as spiritually superior, but they did offer some women an opportunity to learn to read and write. Monasteries housed literate and numerate men, and merchants entrusted monasteries with money and merchandise for safe-keeping; the monasteries in turn provided loans to merchants and space for fairs and markets. The wealth and power of monasteries occasionally led rulers to suppress them and persecute Buddhism itself—most famously in China under the Tang emperor Wuzong in 845—but Buddhism had penetrated deep into society, and it soon became an important force again. Monasteries ran schools, engaged in charity, provided lodging for travelers, and became major centers of art and learning. The Nalanda monastery in the present-day Bihar state of India developed into the leading center of advanced Buddhist learning, and by the seventh century was attracting students from across Asia and sending out monks to propagate Buddhist teachings. Korean monasteries printed the entire canon of Buddhist texts using woodblocks, while those in Japan produced narrative hand scrolls that conveyed Buddhist ideas about the transience of life and the rewards open to the believer.

The diffusion of Buddhism was a complex process, with ideas sometimes filtering back to places that were the original transmitting centers; multiple strains of doctrines originated in different regions that addressed local situations, but then spread. One of these was Tantra, a body of esoteric beliefs and practices that sought to channel the divine energy understood to maintain the universe in creative ways, often through chants (mantras), diagrams with cosmic meaning (mandalas), gestures, and rituals. Tantrism developed in South Asia in the seventh century and spread rapidly to all parts of the Buddhist realm; it became particularly important

3.7 A wooden figure of Avalokiteśvara, the bodhisattva of compassion who helps all sentient beings, from eleventh- to twelfth-century Tibet. Avalokiteśvara was (and is) widely venerated in different branches of Buddhism, and depicted in an extraordinary variety of forms and manifestations, both male and female.

in Tibet, where in the eighth century King Tri Songdetsen (r. 754–797) converted to Buddhism. He employed Buddhism not only to consolidate and legitimize his political power, but also in diplomatic relations with other states, a pattern seen with new dynasties that emerged across Asia, including the Tang in China and the Koryo (935–1392) in Korea. Tibet also added its own unique features to Buddhism, including the belief in reincarnating *lamas* (religious teachers). Another strain of Buddhism was Chan, which emphasized rigorous meditation, monastic discipline, and direct master-to-student transmission more than the authority of sacred texts. Japanese monks who had traveled to China introduced Chan (or Zen, as it was known in Japan) to Japan in the twelfth century, where samurai were attracted by its emphasis on discipline and obedience to a master. Tantra was also followed at some monasteries in Japan, and Pure Land Buddhism, which venerated the Buddha Amitabha and offered the possibility of reaching paradise through simple devotional practices, was popular among many lay people, who blended this with traditional Japanese religion (termed Shinto). In many other places as well various strains of

Buddhism that had developed locally or were brought in from elsewhere mixed and coexisted.

The polycentric nature of Buddhism encouraged travel in many directions as followers sought to visit holy places and find new teachings and texts. Chinese Buddhists visited the sites of the Buddha's life in South Asia, but Mahayana Buddhist monks from South Asia also went to China to honor celestial buddhas and bodhisattvas purportedly living on Chinese mountains. That polycentric nature also allowed Buddhism to survive the Turkic Muslim conquest of its homeland. In 1193 a Muslim army destroyed the great center of learning at Nalanda, and in general the Muslim rulers of North India were hostile to Buddhism as a rival proselytizing religion. Many monks fled. Buddhism declined in India, while Hinduism flourished, especially in southern areas that had not been conquered by Turkic forces, and often including practices shared with Islam and Buddhism, including mysticism akin to Sufism and esoteric Tantra teachings. Elsewhere Buddhism continued to thrive, however, bonding distant towns, ports, oases, and sacred sites more closely than did mercantile networks alone, and shaping the formation of political/cultural identities throughout much of Asia.

Christianity also expanded and developed variant strains in this era, although these divisions were more clearly geographic than those in Buddhism and only rarely coexisted in one area. The bishops of Rome claimed authority over all Christians, asserting that they had a privileged position because Jesus had given special power to one of his disciples, Peter, and Peter had been the first bishop of Rome. They became known as popes—from the Italian word *papa*, meaning father—and with the collapse of the Roman Empire in the west in the fifth century the popes also took over political authority in central Italy, charging taxes, sending troops, and enforcing laws. Churches in what had been the western half of the Roman Empire and the rest of western and central Europe slowly coalesced into a single hierarchical Roman Church—later called Roman Catholic—with Latin as the official language and periodic councils deciding matters of doctrine and discipline, although with local variations in devotional practice.

The Byzantine emperors in Constantinople and the bishops in what had been the eastern half of the Roman Empire did not accept

Rome's claim to primacy, and gradually the Eastern Christian or Orthodox Church developed, over which the emperor retained some power and which split formally from the papacy in the eleventh century. By the fifth century Christianity had spread beyond the borders of the Roman/Byzantine Empire south to Ethiopia, and east to Persia, Armenia, Parthia, and the southwest coast of India. Churches here generally looked neither to Rome nor to Constantinople as the ultimate authority, but formed their own hierarchical structures of power that split, shifted, and regrouped with changes in the political landscape and doctrinal differences. Some of these churches were in states that were officially Christian, such as Ethiopia and Armenia, but most of them were in states where the ruler was not Christian, which resulted in alternating patterns of toleration and repression. Many of these Churches of the East, as they came to be known, used Syriac as their liturgical language and accepted an interpretation of the nature of Christ based on the ideas of the fourth-century church leader Nestorius, which regarded the divine and human natures in Jesus as distinct from one another, whereas in Catholic and Orthodox understanding they were united. The Nestorian position was declared heresy and outlawed in the Byzantine Empire in the fifth century; many Nestorians moved eastward, spreading this interpretation.

All three of these variants of Christianity—Roman, Orthodox, and Nestorian—sent out missionaries, built churches, established monasteries, gained converts, and acquired land. In the sixth century the pope sent monks to England, which then served as a base for the Christianization of Germany and other parts of northern Europe. In the ninth century the Byzantine emperor sent missionaries to Moravia, and in the tenth to Russia. Nestorian missionaries founded churches in cities along the Silk Roads through Central Asia, and in the seventh century in Chang-an, the capital of Tang dynasty China. Sometimes missionaries worked through established political structures, converting a ruler, who then ordered his people to be baptized and celebrate Christian ceremonies, and to support the church financially. Although there were sometimes spectacular conflicts between rulers and church officials, Christianity also offered kings and emperors a way to enhance their authority above landed nobles and other groups, as it taught that both church and state were responsible for establishing order and maintaining social hierarchy. By the eleventh century all of Europe except southern Iberia and the Baltic region was officially Christian, from Kievan Rus in the east, where in 988 Vladimir I converted to Christianity in order to marry a Byzantine imperial princess and held a mass baptism for the citizens of Kiev; to Norway in the north, where in 1024 King Olaf II introduced Christian law, for which he was later made a saint; to Castile in the south, where in 1085 King Alfonso VI at the head of a Christian army captured the city of Toledo from Muslim forces, part of the movement to expel Muslims from Iberia that Christians later called the *reconquista*. Even Norse Iceland was Christian, after the Althing, the legislative assembly that ruled the country, decided in favor of Christianity over paganism in 1000. Everywhere Christianity assimilated certain aspects of existing religious practice, with churches built at springs, groves, or hilltops that had been sacred to pagan gods, and then consecrated to a local saint.

Along with close links to rulers and the incorporation of local traditions, there were other broad commonalities within Christianity. Virginity was viewed as spiritually superior to marriage, and sexual acts that could not lead to procreation were condemned. Monks and nuns lived communally and took vows of chastity, obedience, and poverty, although monasteries as institutions sometimes became quite wealthy. As in Buddhism, communities of nuns generally received fewer donations than those of men and were poorer, although some were well endowed by wealthy families as a demonstration of their piety and a place to send daughters if they could not afford to make appropriate marriages for all of them. Outside of women's monasteries, all church officials were male, as they were in Buddhism and Islam. Organized advanced theological training was for male students, who in Europe after the twelfth century could obtain this in universities, first Paris and then Oxford and Cambridge.

Christians everywhere were organized in communities for collective worship, under the guidance of a priest or monk, which overlapped with existing villages, urban neighborhoods, and other social structures. Rituals marked the agricultural year and the human lifecycle, with a series of sacraments that expressed core beliefs, beginning with baptism through which an infant became eligible for eternal life, including penance through which people confessed and atoned for their sins, and ending with last rites, funerals, and memorials for the dead in which holy objects, blessings, and the prayers of the living helped to speed the soul to heaven. Rituals celebrated the life of Jesus, his mother Mary, and the apostles, martyrs, and saints. Relics associated with these holy individuals and the churches or monasteries that housed them became sites of pilgrimage, creating a sacred landscape that by the thirteenth century stretched from Santiago de Compostela on the northwest corner of the Iberian peninsula—where the body of Saint James had been miraculously transported, and the most popular pilgrimage destination in Europe after Rome—to Beijing, where the Nestorian monk Rabban Bar Sauma (*c.* 1220–94) visited local Christian holy sites before beginning a pilgrimage to Jerusalem.

Unsurprisingly in a religious system this large, there were enormous variations both between and within variants of Christianity, many of them theological but others social and cultural. Roman Christianity came to require celibacy for priests as well as monks and nuns, although this policy proved difficult to enforce, and for centuries priests and higher church officials simply took concubines. Elsewhere married men could generally be priests, and in some places they could rise higher in the clerical hierarchy. Among lay people divorce was generally prohibited, although annulment provided a practical substitute for those with the financial means to arrange this, and in some places divorce itself was allowed. The Coptic Church in Egypt, for example, came to legitimize divorce in the thirteenth century, within the environment of Mamluk society in which divorce was very common. In Orthodoxy, disputes about the proper role of religious images led in the eighth century to an iconoclastic controversy in which paintings and statues were smashed, monks arrested and executed, and provinces of the Byzantine Empire revolted from the emperors who opposed images. Icons were later restored and became a more important part of religious practice than they were in Roman Christianity, although throughout Christianity wonder-working images became pilgrimage sites.

The expansion of Islam reshaped Christianity as well as Buddhism, separating Ethiopian and Eastern Christians from Roman and Orthodox ones. Many Eastern Christians lived within Muslim states; while the general policy was one of toleration, there were also periods of heightened fervor in which Christian practices were restricted or suppressed. When the Seljuk Turkish rulers of Jerusalem and the surrounding area made Christian pilgrimage more difficult, the pope responded in 1095 by calling on Christians to recover Jerusalem from the Muslims, which he hoped would also allow him to assert his authority over Orthodoxy. He urged a holy war against the infidels, offering spiritual and material benefits, to which thousands of Western Christians responded. They succeeded in taking Jerusalem in 1099 in a bloody siege, and established small states in the area. For several centuries Christian pilgrims and fighters went back and forth by land and sea in a series of papally approved expeditions.

For Jews in Europe the Crusades proved disastrous. Inflamed by preachers, Christian mobs attacked and killed whole communities of Jews in many cities, sometimes burning them alive in their places of worship. Legal restrictions on Jews gradually increased throughout Europe, culminating in King Edward I of England expelling the Jews from England in 1290 and confiscating their property and goods, and Philip IV of France doing likewise in 1306. During the Fourth Crusade (1202–4), armies stopped in Constantinople, and when they were not welcomed they sacked the city and grabbed thousands of relics, which they later sold in Europe. This weakened the Byzantine Empire further, and made the split between the Roman and Orthodox churches permanent. Similar infighting among Muslims had facilitated the initial crusader victories, but in the late thirteenth century the Mamluk armies that were conquering other Muslim states also turned against the Crusader states. Their last stronghold, the port of Acre, fell in 1291, although some Christians, especially merchants, remained. The effects of the Crusades on Christian/Muslim relations is disputed; some historians argue that they left an inheritance of deep bitterness, while others note that this might be a projection backwards of later conflicts.

SHIFTING AND LENGTHENING TRADE ROUTES

For Italian merchants the Crusades were a boon. Venetians and Genoese in particular profited from outfitting military expeditions as well as from the opening of new trade routes and the establishment of trading communities that did not disappear when the Crusader states themselves did. Venetian merchants set up permanent offices in Cairo, where they dealt in spices traded up the Red Sea, while Genoese merchants went to Constantinople and the Black Sea, where they met caravans carrying goods over the Silk Roads. A few Italians went to the coastal cities of western India, which were becoming cosmopolitan mixtures of Hindus, Buddhists, Muslims, Jews, Zoroastrians (termed Parsis in India), and Christians, all intent on expanding their profits.

The rise of Italian merchants was one aspect of a general expansion of trade, invention of more sophisticated business procedures, and development of new forms of credit that historians have labeled the "commercial revolution." Although this term was first proposed for Mediterranean Europe, it actually applies more broadly, as throughout much of Eurasia after about 1100 professional merchants moved larger cargoes of more varied commodities longer distances to more destinations serving a wider consumer base than could have been imagined several centuries earlier. Along with religion, trade created regional and transregional zones of exchange.

Most of these professional merchants were male, as trade requires access to trade goods and the ability to move about, both of which were more available to men. Male heads of household generally had control over the products of their household, including those made or harvested by female family members as well as slaves and servants of both genders. Because of this, and because women's ability to travel was often limited by cultural norms about propriety and respectability, men were the primary long-distance traders, sending or taking items of great value such as precious metals, spices, perfumes, amber, and gems, or large quantities of less valuable goods, such as grain, timber, and metals. In some places women did trade locally, handling small retail sales of foodstuffs and other basic commodities, though in others men handled this small-scale distribution of goods as well. In a few places, including West Africa and Southeast Asia, women were important traders at the regional and even the transregional level, handling both basic commodities such as cloth and luxuries such as pepper, betel, gold, and ivory. In many places, male traders established temporary or even long-term relationships with local women. Through such a relationship, the man gained a sexual and domestic partner and connections with groups who provided supplies and goods to trade, and the woman and her family gained prestige through their contact with an outsider. These marriages or other types of domestic arrangements also served as ways in which religious ideas and rituals or other cultural practices traveled and blended, as husbands, wives, and children converted or mixed elements from different traditions as these proved appealing or useful.

The largest trading network in this era was that across Eurasia, which encompassed Muslim, Buddhist, and Christian ecumenes, and both facilitated and was in turn enhanced by the spread of these religions. At the western end of this network in Europe, long-distance trade nearly died out after the collapse of the Roman Empire, but began to revive in the eighth century when Frisians and other northern Europeans began to transport slaves, wax, honey, and especially furs in return for Eastern luxury goods. They sometimes connected with the Radhanites, a loose network of merchants based in Jewish communities who were regarded as neutral by both Muslim and Christian rulers, so were able to cross hostile religious boundaries. The Radhanites traveled by land and sea routes from the caliphate of Córdoba to India and on to China, buying slaves and furs in the West and spices, perfumes, incense, silk, and other high-end commodities in the East. By the twelfth century Venetians and other Europeans had established large merchant colonies in the Crusader states, Constantinople, and the Black Sea, and the Radhanites declined in importance.

The middle of this trading zone was the Muslim world, where the spread of Islam enhanced a wide network of trade contacts and productive handicraft industries already in place. Commerce was judged to be an honorable profession in Islam, as the Prophet himself had once been a merchant. Islam provided a corpus of commercial law, a common commercial language in Arabic, and an international currency, the Muslim dinar. In the eleventh century trade on the Red Sea became increasingly important, and Cairo soon surpassed Baghdad as the hub of world commerce. Persian and Arab merchants sailed down the East African Swahili coast, establishing fortified, independent, merchant-controled trading towns as far south as Sofala in Zimbabwe, and linking these with those across the Indian Ocean. In contrast to this economic growth, the Turkish military leaders who ruled the smaller states of the Islamic heartland after 1100 tended to impose predatory rates of taxation to support the extravagant lifestyles at their courts; these were often imposed in arbitrary ways on trade and production, and merchants did not have the institutionalized political power to oppose this. The commercial and technological innovation that had earlier been common slowed, and imported goods—including basic commodities such as cloth, imported from Europe and India—became cheaper, which ruined local industries.

Coastal Indian cities, including Muslim ones in the north and Hindu ones in the south, made a profit from trade going in any direction. Ships carried all types of merchandise, but spices from the "Spice Islands" (now the Moluccas, part of Indonesia) and other parts of South and Southeast Asia were the most important luxury product. Spices—pepper, cloves, nutmeg, mace, cardamom, cinnamon, and ginger—served not only as flavoring for food, but also as ingredients in perfumes, love potions, painkillers, and funeral balms. In an era before refrigeration, spices helped preserve meats and masked the taste of meat that was slightly spoiled. Other growth markets were cotton textiles, porcelain, and horses for use in warfare and as symbols of power and status. From India, ships went through the Straits of Malacca, carrying merchants and their products to China, the eastern end of this trading zone, and especially to the growing cities of South China. Here the Confucian value system disparaged merchants as dishonorable parasites, tolerable only because they brought in luxuries desired by elites at court and could be taxed. This attitude prevented merchants from achieving political power the way Italian and Swahili merchants did, but did not prevent at least some from becoming very rich.

Wherever they came from and wherever they went, merchants bought and sold slaves along with other merchandise. Italian merchants bought young women in Russia and North Africa to be household slaves in Venice, Genoa, and other Mediterranean cities. Spanish and Portuguese merchants bought North African men captured in war, and sold them for use as galley slaves to row merchant vessels and warships. Vikings sold captives at slave markets from Ireland to the Volga River. Turkish merchants bought Slavs from Turkish and Mongol forces, selling them for use as household slaves, soldiers, textile workers, or in the palaces of rulers. Arabic and African merchants crossed the Sahara Desert in both directions with slaves—West Africans going to the Mediterranean, eastern

Europeans going to West Africa. Indian and Arabic merchants bought slaves in the coastal regions of East Africa, taking them to the west coast of India or further eastward. The Turkic Muslim rulers of North India—some of whom had been slaves themselves—sold captives as military and domestic slaves into Central Asia, primarily Hindus and Buddhists, but also Shi'a Muslims whom the Sunni Turks viewed as heretics. Because they were often taken far from home, slaves in many places were outsiders, differing from their owners in terms of religion, language, or physical appearance. Such differences did not prevent sexual relations between male owners and their slaves, although the legal status of the children of slave mothers varied. Laws usually forbade owners to kill their slaves, and religious teachings advised owners to treat them kindly, or (in Islam) to free them in their wills, but everywhere slaves were a normal part of the social hierarchy.

The routes that connected this Eurasian trading zone varied in their importance over the centuries depending on their relative safety and security. In the fifth through the ninth centuries the Silk Roads were essential, but the fall of the Tang dynasty in 909 and the subsequent Turkic invasions and splintering of the 'Abbasid caliphate led to unsettled conditions in West and Central Asia and a growing preference for shipping via the Indian Ocean. The Mongols first destroyed ancient trade centers such as Baghdad and Samarkand, but once the conquest was complete they adopted policies designed to foster long-distance trade, chief of which was to secure trade routes so that merchants and other travelers, and their goods, were assured safe passage. Merchants could now better predict their risks and profits. Some of the great caravan cities that had been destroyed were rebuilt, and along the routes way-stations were established. The old network of Silk Roads re-emerged, and a newer route further to the north carried luxuries to the Mongol capital at Karakorum and later to the new Mongol Yuan capital of Khanbaliq.

In the middle of the fourteenth century, these routes also carried the pandemic that became known as the Black Death, which originated in Central Asia and was carried in all directions by the people and rats that were in every caravan and on every merchant ship. This virulent disease, new to the populations to which it spread, is estimated to have killed at least a third of the European population in the years

1347–51, and waves of recurrent plague continued for centuries. How many millions died in other places that it spread is unknown, but everywhere the plague brought a decrease in production, a plunge in demand, and an overall sharp decline in prosperity. Some areas began to recover in the fifteenth century, but the overland caravan routes never regained their importance in long-distance trade.

Sea routes benefited from troubles along land routes. In South China, the Yuan dynasty continued the Song policy of encouraging maritime commerce, and sea routes continued to boom. If we believe his account, Marco Polo traveled to the Mongol court by the northern land route, but returned across the Indian Ocean (actually to bring a new wife from Khubilai Khan to the Ilkhan ruler in Tabriz, whose favorite wife had died); Ibn Battuta traveled by ship in both directions. Building on earlier advances in navigation and maritime technology made by Arabs, Indians, and Malays, the Chinese introduced the magnetic compass, watertight bulkheads for shipping, and giant ships with many mainmasts that carried several hundred tons of cargo.

The Yuan dynasty collapsed in 1368 and was replaced by the native Ming dynasty; the new government refused to negotiate with the Mongols who controlled the central Asian trade routes, and initially paid even more attention to maritime commerce. Between 1405 and 1433, the third Ming emperor sent seven huge naval expeditions into the Indian Ocean and the Persian Gulf led by Admiral Zheng He, a Muslim eunuch from southwestern China. Designed to convince potential vassal states of Chinese power, these expeditions called at all major ports and reached the Philippines, the east coast of Africa, and the Red Sea. They were abruptly stopped in a dramatic reversal of government policy, however. The ships were scrapped, log books destroyed, shipyards closed, and Chinese merchants ordered to come home. Historians speculate about the reasons for this sudden halt and turn inward: the voyages may have seemed too costly, as they cost more than the value of the goods brought back; an anti-commercial Confucianist scholar-official faction may have gained the upper hand at court; border wars with the Mongols and with Vietnam, floods, peasant uprisings, and piracy along the coast may have sucked up all government resources. Whatever the reasons, trade in the Indian Ocean did not decline, as Indian, Arab, Malay, Persian, Turkish, and even a few Italian merchants quickly filled any vacuum left by the Chinese.

The Eurasian trading network was by far the largest and the best documented in this era, but it was not the only one. In West Africa, gold began coming across the Sahara by camel in the fifth century, traded for textiles, warhorses, cowrie shells to serve as currency, slaves, and salt. By the fourteenth century, West Africa was producing and exporting more gold than anywhere else in the world, providing metal for court luxuries and monetary uses in both Europe and the Muslim world. In the western hemisphere, regional networks also carried gold and copper, along with other luxury goods, such as obsidian for blades, cacao, jade, and turquoise. One even carried scarlet macaws, whose feathers were prized for the hats and cloaks of warriors and for religious rituals, from Mesoamerica to the North American Southwest, where they were then bred locally.

A MIDDLE MILLENNIUM

The thousand years from 500 to 1500 is often defined by what came before or what came after, so termed "postclassical," "premodern" or at best "middle." Because the idea that this millennium was a distinct middle age was invented in Europe, it is sometimes rejected as Eurocentric, but for many of the large political divisions of the eastern hemisphere, including the Byzantine Empire, China, and the empires of Central Asian steppe nomads as well as western Europe, this thousand years amounts to a meaningful period. And for the people of the western hemisphere, although 500 may not have marked many new departures, 1500 was perhaps the sharpest dividing line since their ancestors had first migrated from Asia. In both hemispheres, similar processes occurred, as trade networks, agriculture, and cities expanded, and interactions among cultures and religions intensified.

In the eastern hemisphere, Islam began and grew, stretching at the end of the Middle Millennium from the Songhay Empire in West Africa to the sultanates of Brunei and Sulu in island Southeast Asia. Sacred texts, spiritual practices, and legal principles bound the Dar-al-Islam together, but the incorporation of existing cultural forms and social structures led to great diversity and often bitter hostilities between varieties of Islam, interwoven with political conflicts between rival Muslim states as well as with their non-Muslim neighbors. Christianity grew as well, as monks and missionaries built churches and gained converts from Iceland to Beijing, as did Buddhism, carried by monks and merchants to form a polycentric world in which ideas, texts, and practices flowed in all directions. Both Buddhism and Christianity were reshaped by the expansion of Islam, and Buddhism also by a resurgence of Hindu traditions in its Indian homeland.

Whether rulers were Muslim, Christian, Buddhist, Hindu, or something else, royal courts in the Middle Millennium were centers of family and factional intrigue, cultural production, and conspicuous consumption, where rituals, ceremonies, and protocol reminded everyone of their place in the cosmic and social order, and codes of behavior set ideals for elite men and women. Courtly splendor was created by local artisans and by merchants who imported prestige goods from far away, and paid for by the increasingly systematic collection of taxes and rents on villagers, and in some cases by a flow of war booty. Rulers were one force behind the expansion and intensification of agriculture that marked this era, though people also decided on their own to migrate, sometimes sailing across vast distances of open ocean, or sometimes simply walking a short distance, and carving new fields out of forests or marshes. Others moved to cities, which pulled in people from the countryside with the promise of economic opportunity and social mobility, a promise on which they sometimes actually delivered.

Both courts and cities offered imported luxuries to those who could afford them. In the Afroeurasian trading network, the scarlet macaw feathers so valued in the Americas were unknown, but other red and purple prestige items were especially prized, including coral beads, blood-red rubies, lacquerware dishes, and cloth dyed Tyrean purple with the secretions of the murex sea snail or vermilion red with the powdered mineral cinnabar. Just such luxury goods—combined with travelers' tales of foreign lands, marriage to the daughter of a Portuguese sea captain, experience in ports, and a sense of personal destiny—would inspire one Genoese merchant and mapmaker not to head east to make his fortune like most of his fellow Italians, but west, first to Lisbon, then to the Atlantic island of Madeira, and then to the Spanish court. In 1492, several weeks after Spanish armies had conquered the last remaining Muslim state in Spain and the Spanish monarchs had banished all practicing Jews from their realms, he received royal support to head further westward. He took with him a printed version of Marco Polo's *Travels* along with other books, religious objects, red cloth, and other goods, and an Arabic-speaking Jewish convert to Christianity as an interpreter, figuring that someone at the Chinese court certainly spoke Arabic or Hebrew. The network of interaction that resulted from his voyages would be far larger than even Rashid al-Din could have imagined, and his voyages brought the Middle Millennium to an end.

FURTHER READING

The works of Rashid al-Din, Murasaki Shikibu, Marco Polo, and Ibn Battuta are all available in English translation: Rashid al-Din, *Rashiduddin Fazlullah's Jami'u't-tawarikh: Compendium of Chronicles. A History of the Mongols*, trans. Wheeler M. Thackston (Cambridge, MA: Harvard University Press, 1998); Murasaki Shikibu, *The Tale of Genji*, trans. Edward G. Seidensticker (New York: Alfred A. Knopf, 1976); Marco Polo, *The Travels*, trans. Ronald Latham (London: Penguin, 1958); *The Travels of Ibn Battuta*, ed. Tim Macintosh-Smith (London: Macmillan, 2003). For recent works about the two travelers, see Ross E. Dunn, *The Adventures of Ibn Battuta: A Muslim Traveler of the Fourteenth Century*, rev. edn. (Berkeley: University of California Press, 2004); Hans Ulrich Vogel, *Marco Polo Was in China: New Evidence from Currencies, Salts and Revenues* (Leiden: Brill, 2013).

Regional studies with a social and cultural focus include: K.N. Chaudhuri, *Asia before Europe: Economy and Civilisation of the Indian Ocean from the Rise of Islam to 1750* (Cambridge: Cambridge University Press, 1991); Victor Lieberman, *Beyond Binary Histories: Re-imagining Eurasia to c. 1830* (Michigan: University of Michigan Press, 1997); Catherine B. Asher and Cynthia Talbot, *India before Europe* (Cambridge: Cambridge University Press, 2006); Charles Holcombe, *The Genesis of East Asia, 221 BC–AD 907* (Honolulu: University of Hawai'i Press, 2001); S. Frederick Starr, *Lost Enlightenment: Central Asia's Golden Age from the Arab Conquest to Tamerlane* (Princeton: Princeton University Press, 2013); John Haldon, ed., *A Social History of Byzantium* (Oxford: Wiley-Blackwell,

2009); Peregrine Horden and Nicholas Purcell, *The Corrupting Sea: A Study of Mediterranean History* (Oxford: Blackwell, 2000); Chris Wickham, *Framing the Early Middle Ages: Europe and the Mediterranean, 400–800* (Oxford: Oxford University Press, 2007); Steven A. Epstein, *An Economic and Social History of Later Medieval Europe* (Cambridge: Cambridge University Press, 2007); Michael E. Smith and Frances F. Berdan, eds., *The Postclassic Mesoamerican World* (Salt Lake City: University of Utah Press, 2003). On gender, see: Gavin R.G. Hambly, ed., *Women in the Medieval Islamic World* (New York: St. Martin's Press, 1998); Rosemary A. Joyce, *Gender and Power in Prehistoric Mesoamerica* (Austin: University of Texas, 2001); Dorothy Ko, JaHyun Kim Haboush and Joan R. Piggott, eds., *Women and Confucian Cultures in Premodern China, Korea, and Japan* (Berkeley: University of California Press, 2003); Leslie Brubaker and Julia M.H. Smith, eds., *Gender in the Early Medieval World: East and West, 300–900* (Cambridge: Cambridge University Press, 2004).

The expansion of Islam has been examined in: Ira M. Lapidus, *A History of Islamic Societies*, 2nd edn. (Cambridge: Cambridge University Press, 2002); Jonathan P. Berkey, *The Formation of Islam: Religion and Society in the Near East, 600–1800* (Cambridge: Cambridge University Press, 2003); David Robinson, *Muslim Societies in African History* (Cambridge: Cambridge University Press, 2004). On the Mamluks, see Thomas Philipp and Ulrich Harmann, eds., *The Mamluks in Egyptian Politics and Society* (Cambridge: Cambridge University Press, 2007).

Studies of courts and courtly culture include: Jeroen Frans Jozef Duindam, *Royal Courts in Dynastic States and Empires: A Global Perspective* (Leiden: Brill, 2011); Hugh Kennedy, *The Court of the Caliphs: When Baghdad Ruled the Muslim World* (Cambridge, MA: DaCapo, 2005); Joachim Bumke, *Courtly Culture: Literature and Society in the High Middle Ages* (Woodstock, NY: Overlook Press, 2000); Daud Ali, *Courtly Culture and Political Life in Early Medieval India* (Cambridge: Cambridge University Press, 2004); Mikael S. Adolphson, *The Gates of Power: Monks, Courtiers, and Warriors in Premodern Japan* (Honolulu: University of Hawai'i Press, 2000); Mikael Adolphson, Stacie Matsumoto, and Edward Kamens, *Heian Japan: Centers and Peripheries* (Honolulu: University of Hawai'i Press, 2007); Anne Walthall, ed., *Servants of the Dynasty: Palace Women in World History* (Berkeley: University of California Press, 2008). Dorothy Ko, *Cinderella's Sisters: A Revisionist History of Footbinding* (Berkeley: University of California Press, 2007) is the most insightful analysis of this complex issue.

On the expansion of agriculture and the changes this brought with it, see Robert Bartlett, *The Making of Europe: Conquest, Colonization, and*

Cultural Change, 950–1350 (Princeton: Princeton University Press, 1994); Dieter Kuhn, *The Age of Confucian Rule: The Song Transformation of China* (Cambridge, MA: Belknap Press, 2011); George R. Milner, *The Moundbuilders: Ancient Peoples of Eastern North America* (London: Thames & Hudson, 2005); Patrick Vinton Kirch, *A Shark Going Inland Is My Chief: The Island Civilization of Ancient Hawai'i* (Berkeley: University of California Press, 2012). On whether villagers exploited or sustained their environments, see Jared Diamond, *Collapse: How Societies Chose to Fail or Succeed* (New York: Viking, 2005) and Patricia McAnany and Norman Yoffee, eds., *Questioning Collapse: Human Resilience, Ecological Vulnerability, and the Aftermath of Empire* (Cambridge: Cambridge University Press, 2010). James C. Scott, *The Art of Not Being Governed: An Anarchist History of Upland Southeast Asia* (New Haven: Yale University Press, 2010) examines groups that resisted the expansion of agriculture and the state.

On the Mongols, see Thomas T. Allsen, *Culture and Conquest in Mongol Eurasia* (Cambridge: Cambridge University Press, 2001); Peter Jackson, *The Mongols and the West, 1221–1410* (London: Routledge, 2005); George Lane, *Daily Life in the Mongol Empire* (Westport, CT: Greenwood, 2006). The study of the male descendants of Chingghis Khan is Tatiana Zerjal *et al.*, "The Genetic Legacy of the Mongols," *American Journal of Human Genetics* 72 (2003): 717–21.

Several recent works have examined the interplay between myth and reality in cities of this era: Elisabeth Crouzet-Pavan, *Venice Triumphant: The Horizons of a Myth*, trans. Lydia G. Cochrane (Baltimore: Johns Hopkins University Press, 2002); Jonathan Harris, *Constantinople: Capital of Byzantium* (London: Bloomsbury Academic, 2009); José Luis de Rojas, *Tenochtitlán: Capital of the Aztec Empire* (Gainesville: University Press of Florida, 2012). Chiara Frugoni, *A Day in a Medieval City*, trans. William McCuaig (Chicago: University of Chicago Press, 2006) presents a fascinating ramble through Italian cities in this era, with wonderful illustrations.

Richard Foltz, *Religions of the Silk Road: Premodern Patterns of Globalization*, 2nd edn. (London: Palgrave Macmillan, 2010) provides a concise introduction to the transmission and intertwining of many different religions. On Buddhism, see Ronald M. Davidson, *Indian Esoteric Buddhism: A Social History of the Tantric Movement* (New York: Columbia University Press, 2002); Tansen Sen, *Buddhism, Diplomacy, and Trade: The Realignment of Sino-Indian Relations, 600–1400* (Honolulu: University of Hawai'i Press, 2003); Jason Neelis, *Early Buddhist Transmission and Trade Networks: Mobility and Exchange within and beyond the Northwestern Borderlands of South Asia* (Leiden and Boston: Brill, 2011). On Christianity, see James Brundage, *Law, Sex, and Christian Society in Medieval Europe*

(Chicago: University of Chicago Press, 1987); Richard Fletcher, *The Barbarian Conversion: From Paganism to Christianity* (Berkeley: University of California Press, 1998); Michael Angold, *Eastern Christianity* (Cambridge: Cambridge University Press, 2006); Thomas F.X. Noble and Julia M.H. Smith, *Early Medieval Christianities, c. 600–c. 1100* (Cambridge: Cambridge University Press, 2008).

Broad analyses of trade networks include Richard L. Smith, *Premodern Trade in World History* (London: Routledge, 2008); Jerry H. Bentley, *Old World Encounters: Cross Cultural Contacts and Exchanges in Pre-Modern Times* (Oxford: Oxford University Press, 1993); Janet L. Abu-Lughod, *Before European Hegemony: The World System AD 1250–1350* (New York: Oxford University Press, 1989); Kenneth G. Hirth and Joanne Pillsbury, eds., *Merchants, Markets, and Exchange in the Pre-Columbian World* (Washington, DC: Dumbarton Oaks, 2013); Kenneth Pomeranz and Steven Topik, *The World that Trade Created: Society, Culture, and the World Economy*, 3rd edn. (Armonk, NY: M.E. Sharpe, 2013). More specific studies of cultural exchange and trade include: Rosamond E. Mack, *Bazaar to Piazza: Islamic Trade and Italian Art, 1300–1600* (Berkeley: University of California Press, 2001); Pamela O. Long, *Technology and Society in the Medieval Centuries: Byzantium, Islam, and the West, 500–1300* (Washington, DC: American Historical Association, 2003); Ralph Austen, *Trans-Saharan Africa in World History* (Oxford: Oxford University Press, 2010); Valerie Hansen, *The Silk Road: A New History* (Oxford: Oxford University Press, 2012).

Essays on many of the topics in this chapter may be found in Benjamin Z. Kedar and Merry E. Wiesner-Hanks, eds., *Expanding Webs of Exchange and Conflict, 500 CE–1500 CE*, Volume 5 of the Cambridge World History. Richard Smith introduced the phrase "Middle Millennium" in an essay on trade and commerce in this volume.

4

A new world of connections, 1500 CE–1800 CE

In 1503, the Florentine trader and explorer Amerigo Vespucci (1454–1512) wrote to his former employers, the Medici banking family, detailing in vivid language the mapping expedition sponsored by the Portuguese in which he had been involved over the previous several years. This voyage sailed along the coast of a large land mass across the Atlantic Ocean from Portugal, which Vespucci in the opening paragraph of the letter called a "new world, because none of these countries were known to our ancestors" and extolled as "a continent full of animals and more populous than our Europe, or Asia, or Africa, and even more temperate and pleasant than any other region known to us." This letter and a subsequent even longer one were published many times in different European languages over the next several years. Among those who read them was the German map-maker Martin Waldseemüller (1470?–1522?), who in 1507 printed a globe and a giant wall map of the world in which the land mass Vespucci had helped map was not connected to any other. Waldseemüller gave the southern part of this landmass a name: America, taken from the Latin form of Vespucci's first name. He justified this with the comment, "I see no reason why, and by what right, this land of America should not be named after that wise and ingenious man who discovered it, Amerigo, since both Europe and Asia had been allotted the names of women." (Europa and her mother Asia were Greek demi-goddesses.) By just a few years later, map-makers—including Waldseemüller—and others knew this was wrong, and that Christopher Columbus (1451–1506) had reached the continent before Vespucci; they wanted to omit "America" from future maps, but the name had already stuck. The Flemish cartographer, mathematician, and instrument maker Gerardus Mercator (1512–94), who invented the projection most commonly used to show the globe on a flat surface, used the word America on his world map of 1538, and later the designations "North" and "South" were added.

To the people who already lived there, of course, Vespucci's designation of what he had mapped as a "New World" was no more accurate than Waldseemüller's claim that Vespucci was the first European to see it. The idea that any European "discovered" islands and continents that were already full of people is also now seen as silly, and many historians avoid using either "discovery" or "New World." Biologists, epidemiologists, agronomists, and environmental scientists do use "New World" and its counterpart "Old World," however, as spatial terms to designate parts of the globe that had been cut off from each other for tens of thousands of years, so that their biospheres evolved independently. By crossing the Atlantic and then the Pacific, European ships linked the two worlds, which allowed the transfer of plants, animals, germs, and people in new directions over vast distances, with consequences that were both disastrous and beneficial. In 1972 the environmental historian Alfred Crosby termed this process the "Columbian Exchange," and noted it began with Columbus' very first voyage. Columbus took ordinary and luxury goods with him, along with men and boys, a group of whom he left in the Caribbean. (They all apparently died, though there are legends that some did not.) He brought back what seemed most exotic: parrots, feathers, cotton cloth, tobacco, rubber, perhaps the pineapple, and several Taino boys captured on the islands. European mariners and adventurers may not have *discovered* a new world, but they created one.

Thus for the study of human beings, "new world" might best be understood in terms of time rather than space. Although interregional interaction had increased with the expansion of the Mongol Empire and the Indian Ocean trading network, the scale of the contacts between peoples was much greater after 1492 than it had been before. Many historians see this as the beginning of a new era in world history, the "early modern." Like "New World," "early modern" has been criticized as hopelessly Eurocentric, implying there is only one path to modernity, that taken by Europe. And it has been criticized for emphasizing change, when throughout the period 80–90 percent of the world's population remained peasants, who continued to be exploited by their landlords and the state. But for world history "early modern" is useful, as there were parallel and interwoven processes of dramatic change going on in many places.

This chapter surveys some of these developments, beginning with the spread of disease, the transfers of plants and animals that were part of the Columbian Exchange, and the establishment of colonial empires through exploration and war. Trade brought in new types of foods, drinks, and addictive substances, many of which were produced on plantations worked by slave labor. These products were often consumed in new urban social settings and cultural institutions, where men—and a few women—shared ideas as well as commodities. Religious reforms and reinvigorations heightened spiritual zeal and created new arenas of conflict, as well as sharpening those created by rivalries over territory or resources. The early modern world was a new one of global connections, in which goods, ideas, and people—including peasants and slaves—moved and mixed, changing social and economic patterns and creating novel cultural forms.

THE SPREAD OF DISEASE

Prime among the disastrous effects of the Columbian Exchange was the spread of disease, which began with Columbus' second voyage in 1493. This expedition was huge, with about 1,500 men, including adventurers, soldiers, artisans, and farmers who brought with them seeds for European crops and farm animals. This voyage set a pattern that would be followed in many other places. The ships landed on the large island of Hispaniola, which had a population between 400,000 and 600,000 engaged in farming cultivated plots. The Spanish were mostly interested in gold, and they captured, tortured, and killed the indigenous Taino in their search for precious metals. Many went back to Spain disappointed after a few weeks, and many more died of starvation, intestinal diseases from drinking the local water, or diseases they had brought from Europe with them, which most likely included malaria, typhus, influenza, and perhaps smallpox. Taino died even more readily from these, and from other Old World diseases against which they had no resistance, such as measles, mumps, diphtheria, bubonic and pneumonic plague, and scarlet fever. After a particularly virulent outbreak of smallpox throughout the Caribbean in 1518, very few Taino were left on Hispaniola, and the number of indigenous people on other islands had fallen dramatically.

Once Europeans reached the mainland of Central and South America in the early 1500s, diseases often spread ahead of actual groups of soldiers, when just a few native people came into contact with a Spanish force and then returned to their home village. People became sick and died quickly, so that when European troops got to the area later, they no longer found places "more populous than our Europe, or Asia, or Africa" that Vespucci had reported in 1503. Spanish troops led by Hernando Cortés (1485–1547) carried smallpox into Tenochtitlan, the capital of the Aztec Empire, when they were briefly allowed into the city in 1519, and this invisible ally—combined with their very visible allies, the Tlaxcalan and other native peoples who opposed the Aztecs—allowed the Spanish to defeat the weakened Aztecs. Smallpox also killed the powerful Inca ruler Huayna Capac in the mid 1520s, setting off a civil war between his sons that allowed Spanish forces to conquer the Inca Empire.

Explorers, conquerors, and settlers who moved into the Americas traveled under a Spanish flag, and then those of other European nations, but they included people from a variety of places, including free and enslaved Africans, and by the end of the sixteenth century Asians brought by Spanish galleons that took American silver to the Spanish colony of the Philippines and returned with silk and other Asian products. Thus Old World diseases mixed in a deadly stew. Although it is impossible to determine the total population of the Americas in 1492, the best estimates put it between 40 and 70 million; estimates of the total decline within the first century after European contact is about 90 percent. Mexico and Peru, whose combined population was greater than the rest of the Americas all together, suffered the greatest drop. War, famine, labor

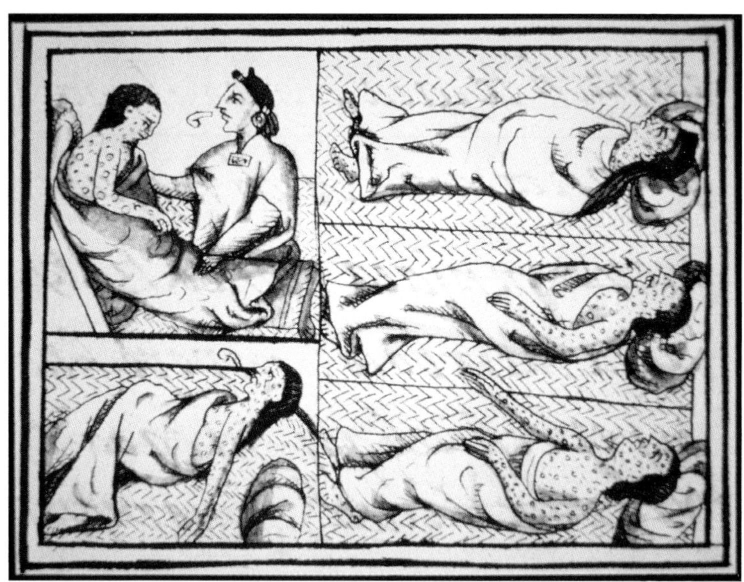

4.1 Aztec people die of smallpox, in an illustration from the *General History of the Things of New Spain*, a 2,400-page book documenting Aztec society, culture, and history written and illustrated in the last half of the sixteenth century by indigenous men under the direction of the Franciscan friar Bernardino de Sahagún. The information in the book came from village and city elders, recorded in Aztec pictorial writing and then expanded in Nahuatl using Latin letters.

exploitation, forced migrations, and enslavement were responsible for some of this, but Old World diseases were the primary killer. In 1650 the majority of people in the New World were still indigenous, but disease and other killers, combined with increasing migration, changed that.

Geochemists and earth systems scientists have recently suggested that deaths in the Americas may have also changed the earth's climate. Wooded areas that had been cleared for agriculture or modified by fire to make hunting better became reforested when no one was left to engage in these tasks. The trees then pulled carbon dioxide from the air—which is traceable in ice cores from Antarctica—reducing the heat-trapping capacity of the atmosphere and cooling the climate, the opposite of what is happening today. Other factors, including reduced sunspot and increased volcanic activity, and changes in the Pacific climatic phenomenon known as El Niño, contributed to the cooling climate as well, and together these created what climatologists have termed the "Little Ice Age," from about 1500 (or perhaps beginning as early as 1300) to about 1850, with several particularly cold periods within this. Evidence for fluctuations in weather and climate comes from the natural world, such as tree rings, volcanic deposits in the polar ice caps, and layers of pollen in bogs and marshes, and from human records, including chronicles, letters, government and business documents, inscriptions, and recorded weather data. Complaining about the weather seems to be a universal human trait, but together these natural and human sources point to a period of unstable climate especially in the seventeenth century, with more extreme cold in the northern hemisphere and more extreme droughts in Africa and in South and Southeast Asia.

Climate extremes contributed to crop failures, which led in turn to increased mortality from hunger and the various illnesses to which malnourished people are more vulnerable. Because grain or other staples were bulky and heavy, it was generally impossible to transport them to a famine-stricken area at a price that people could afford. It was easier for people—even weakened people—to move than for food to do so, so hunger led families and individuals to migrate. Whatever the scale of the famine, governments generally could do little to alleviate them, and often made them worse by prohibiting the export of food or refusing to lower taxes, which peasants paid as a certain amount of their harvest every year. In many parts of Eurasia throughout the early modern period, peasant families paid as much as half of their harvest to their landlords and the state, even in famine years. Famine was thus a social phenomenon as much as it was a natural one.

Famine also led to reduced fertility, as ill-nourished women are less likely to become pregnant, carry a fetus to term, or be able to breast-feed successfully. Nursing mothers need far more calories per day than do other people, and both they and their infants die at a disproportionate rate during times of scarcity. These dismal realities are reflected in death and burial records and in human remains themselves, which can provide information about cause of death, nutrition levels, chronic illnesses, dietary practices, and many other aspects of life and death. Just as archeologists who study the earliest periods of human history are increasingly relying on high-tech methods invented to help solve crimes or make medical diagnoses in contemporary society, such as the analysis of trace elements or DNA, so are historians of the early modern (and modern) period. This frees them from having to rely on written sources alone and allows for comparisons and calculations on a wide scale.

The impact of diseases that went west across the Atlantic is clear, and a few may have traveled in the other direction; historical epidemiologists used to think that one of these was syphilis, which emerged first in Italy in 1493 in an especially virulent form, but now they are less certain about its origins. However syphilis got to Europe, this was an era in which dynastic ambitions and religion combined to provoke nearly constant warfare, which assured it would be spread. Italy was a battleground for the aspirations of many rulers, and decades of war followed a French invasion of the peninsula in 1494. Soldiers fighting in Italy took syphilis with them when they returned home, which the French labeled the "Italian disease" and most of the rest of Europe the "French pox." Armies carried other diseases around Europe as well, including plague, smallpox and influenza, as did migrants and refugees.

Variations in vulnerability to disease also shaped society in China, though this was less dramatic than in the Americas. In the seventeenth century, the leaders of the Jurchens, one of the steppe peoples who lived to the north of China, changed their name to Manchu and began a campaign of conquest. In 1644, after a rebellion had toppled the ruling Ming dynasty, the Manchus captured Beijing, and established a new dynasty, the Qing. Over the next several decades they fought to establish their authority throughout China against Ming loyalists and rebels. Their ability to do so was affected by smallpox, which was endemic in China but to which the Manchus had no resistance. They made efforts to isolate important people from the disease by moving them whenever there was an outbreak, but the second Qing emperor himself died of smallpox in 1661, and his successor was chosen in part because he had already survived the disease. That emperor, the Kangxi emperor, would go on to rule for sixty-one years. Among many innovations, he adopted the use of variolation (from *variola*, the Latin term for smallpox) to inoculate the children of the imperial family against smallpox. In variolation, material taken from the sores of a smallpox sufferer was breathed into the nostrils or scratched into the skin of a healthy person to induce what was hoped would be a mild case of the disease that would provide lifelong immunity. This procedure was used in the sixteenth century in China (and perhaps earlier), and also in West Africa and the Ottoman Empire. In 1721, variolation was brought to England by Lady Mary Wortley Montague, whose husband was the ambassador to the Ottoman Empire and who herself had been scarred by smallpox, but it was greeted with suspicion and never became widespread.

Despite the possibility of preventive measures, however, smallpox outbreaks continued in China and the surrounding areas as well as elsewhere. In the middle of the eighteenth century, for example, the Qianlong Emperor (ruled 1735–96) carried out successful campaigns to incorporate Central Asia into China. One of these, against the Zunghar khanate, was made much easier because a smallpox epidemic had recently wiped out hundreds of thousands of people, perhaps 40 percent of the Zunghar population. The rest either fled or were taken into areas ruled by others, or they were killed by Qing armies, sometimes in an intentional extermination campaign ordered by the Qianlong emperor, who wanted to destroy the Zunghars as a people as well as a state. Zunghar women were given to Manchu soldiers or their allies as bonded servants or concubines.

In major epidemics and in smaller ones, disease killed more women and children than adult men, which meant that population levels were depressed for decades. Disease and famine also made people themselves depressed, or as they termed it in this era before the invention of psychological terminology, distraught, sad, full of grief, miserable, and mournful. Some wrote of their feelings, and others acted on them, committing suicide, giving up their children to monasteries or foundling homes, and marrying late or not marrying at all—which further reduced population levels—all of which were also noted by contemporary commentators. Clergy in Scotland during a famine in the 1630s wrote that some of their parishioners had "desperately run into the sea and drowned themselves," while an official in Shandong province in China wrote in 1670 that "the area was so wasted and barren" that "every day one would hear that someone had hanged himself from a beam." Historians used to think that because so many children died at very young ages people became callous or indifferent to their offspring; that was true in some cases, but there is also evidence that mothers and fathers were deeply saddened, sometimes to the point of madness, by the illness or deaths of their children. Even those forced to abandon children for economic reasons could be torn apart by their decision; a note pinned to a child left at a London foundling home in 1709 read, "I humbly beg of you gentlemen whosever hand this unfortunate child shall fall into that you will take care that will become a fellow creature ... pray believe that it is extreme necessity that makes me do this."

COLONIZATION, EMPIRES, AND TRADE

Soldiers, traders, workers, and settlers traveled the same routes that diseases did as they forged a new world. In the sixteenth century, Spain built the largest colonial empire in the western hemisphere, although Portugal also established a colony in Brazil. The Spanish and Portuguese set up agricultural plantations, built Christian churches, and mined precious metals in empires with mixed populations of Europeans, Africans, and indigenous people. Gold and silver mined in the Americas, especially from the "silver mountain" of Potosí high in the Andes, where tens of thousands of indigenous people were forced to work deep in tunnels, fueled the expansion of global trading. This created enormous profits for European merchants, and contributed to a long period of rising prices economic historians label the "price revolution." Spain also established colonial rule in the Philippines, and Portugal set up small colonies along the west and east coast of Africa and at Goa, Sri Lanka, Malacca,

Macao, and a few other places in Asia. Overseas conquests gave western Europe new territories and sources of wealth, and also new confidence in its technical and spiritual supremacy.

In eastern Europe and across Asia, conquests in the sixteenth century created large land-based empires, many of which also fostered trade. In 1453 the Ottomans took Constantinople (which they renamed Istanbul) and continued to conquer by land and sea in all directions; by the early seventeenth century they were rulers of about a third of Europe and half the shores of the Mediterranean. They became the official Protectors of the Two Holy Cities of Mecca and Medina, and challenged Portuguese control of Indian Ocean trade routes, sending trade ventures across the Indian Ocean down the coast of Africa and eastward to Sumatra. The Shi'ite Safavid dynasty came to power in Persia (today's Iran) in 1501, and under Shah 'Abbas I (r. 1587–1629) built a spectacular new capital at Isfahan, where artisans produced textiles, carpets, and metalwork, and foreign merchants gathered to trade for these. In South Asia, the Mughals, Central Asian rulers who claimed descent from Chingghis Khan ("Mughal" is the Persian word for Mongol), created a huge empire through war and alliances, including alliances by marriage to regional dynasties. India remained the world's largest producer of textiles, and Indian merchant networks stretched from China to Africa. The decline of Mongol power in West and Central Asia allowed the rulers of Moscow to expand their holdings, and they conquered their neighbors to create a vast Russian state under autocratic rulers who called themselves tsars (the Russian word for caesars), a title they adopted to link with earlier Roman emperors. They allied with the high nobles, or boyars, and increasingly imposed serfdom on all peasants, binding them to the land, which also happened in much of eastern Europe. States created in Africa during the sixteenth century, including Songhai, Benin, Buganda, and Kongo, were smaller than these Asian empires, but they also had well-established trading centers. Those on the coasts attracted Portuguese merchants, who often set up their fortified trading posts nearby.

The seventeenth and eighteenth centuries brought the further expansion of empires and new patterns of conquest, colonization,

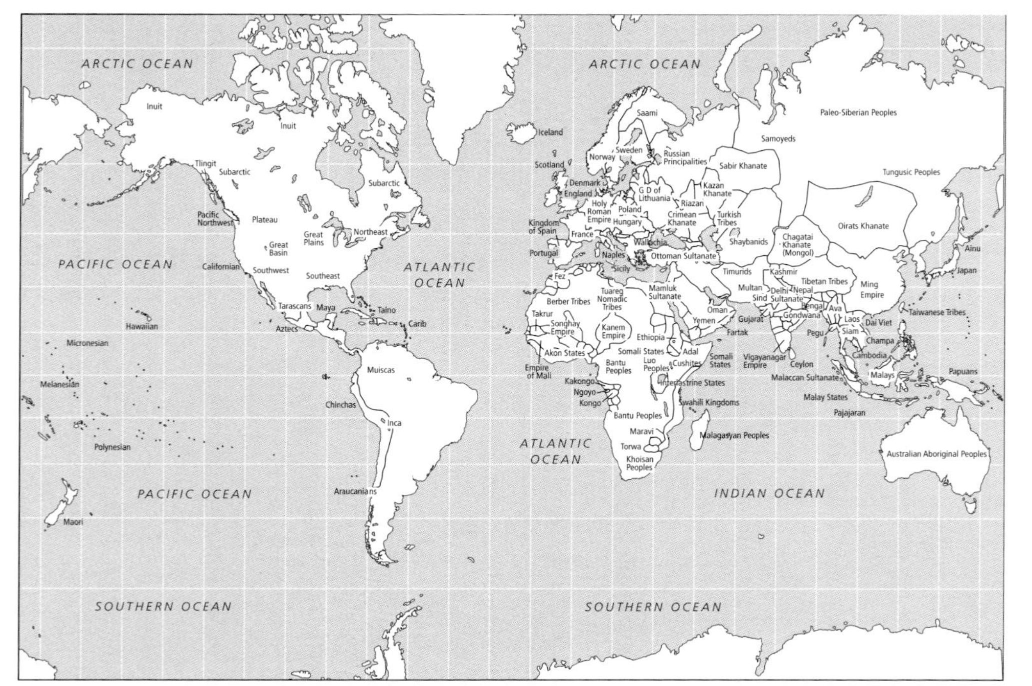

Map 4.1 World map 1500

and trade. Under the Manchu Qing dynasty China expanded into Tibet and Central Asia and asserted its influence over Korea, Vietnam, and Burma. In Japan after a long period of civil war military leaders known as shoguns from the Tokugawa family re-established order and limited the presence of Western merchants, though Japanese silver continued to flow throughout East and Southeast Asia, bringing in silk and other luxuries to growing cities. The Russians expanded across northern Asia into Siberia, an imperialist expansion that brought them great natural resources, and took over the eastern rim of the Baltic from Sweden, where they built a new capital, St. Petersburg. In western Africa, trade in slaves handled by Africans and Europeans grew dramatically, with major consequences for local social and political structures.

In the Caribbean and the lands on its borders, many European powers contested Spanish dominance. Beginning in 1550, the English crown licensed private ships to prey on Spanish shipping and attack Spanish colonies. This government-licensed and-regulated piracy brought glory to successful captains such as Francis Drake and returned a huge profit to the merchants and landowners who invested in it, making them supporters of overseas expansion and naval power. The English, French, Swedes, and Dutch established their own colonies in the Caribbean and along the North American coast in the 1620s and 1630s, and then pushed further inland. Permanent private companies were established in England, the Netherlands, and elsewhere in Europe to support these ventures, which provided financial backing, ships, personnel, and military force, as did similar East India Companies licensed to trade and raid in Asia. They attempted to monopolize trade, although in a place like the Caribbean where colonies were close to one another—often on the same island—smuggling was endemic, and sometimes involved the very government and company officials who were supposed to prevent it. Piracy was also common, conducted both by licensed privateers and by buccaneers, multiethnic groups of former soldiers, escaped slaves, refugees, criminals, and others who attacked silver-laden ships from remote bases.

The Dutch won their independence from Spain through warfare, and established more colonies, trading centers, and plantations in

South Africa and Southeast Asia as well as the Americas, taking Malacca from the Portuguese and much of Java from local rulers to gain pre-eminence in the Indian Ocean basin; in the 1650s they also annexed the Swedish colonies in North America. In the 1660s a second wave of colonies was founded in North America, especially by England. English forces conquered New Amsterdam and the rest of the Dutch holdings, renaming these New York, and founded South Carolina and Georgia to serve as a buffer between existing English colonies in the mid-Atlantic states and New England and Spanish colonies in Florida. The French moved into the Great Lakes and central river valley regions, and in 1699 founded Louisiana at the mouth of the Mississippi to prevent either the Spanish or the British from controlling trade with the interior. French colonies never attracted as many immigrants as did the British colonies, however. By 1750 the entire population of New France probably included only 100,000 Europeans and Africans, while the British North American colonies may have had as many as 2 million inhabitants. Wars in the last half of the eighteenth century gave Britain many of France's overseas colonies, and it became the major power in the Indian Ocean, eclipsing the Dutch. Although Britain lost much of North America with the American War of Independence, in 1787 it established a penal colony in Australia (where it sent convicts because it could no longer ship them to America), and was on its way to establishing the world's largest sea-based empire. Britain maintained a standing navy that now promised to end piracy and smuggling, and claimed the right to board any ship to enforce this. (See Map 4.2.)

Just as land- and sea-based empires expanded, so did global trade, fueling a "consumer revolution" especially in Europe and European households in the colonies, as wealthier households bought imported luxuries and the less well off cheaper imports or locally produced knock-offs. Millions of pieces of Chinese porcelain made in the inland city of Jingdezhen were transported to Guangzhou, carried on ships to Amsterdam and London, and then exported to Jamaica, Boston, Berlin, and Moscow. Calico cloth made by village residents in the Gujarati area of northwest India went to Europe, and also to the Senegambia in western Africa, where it was traded to African merchants for slaves and for the gum of the acacia tree.

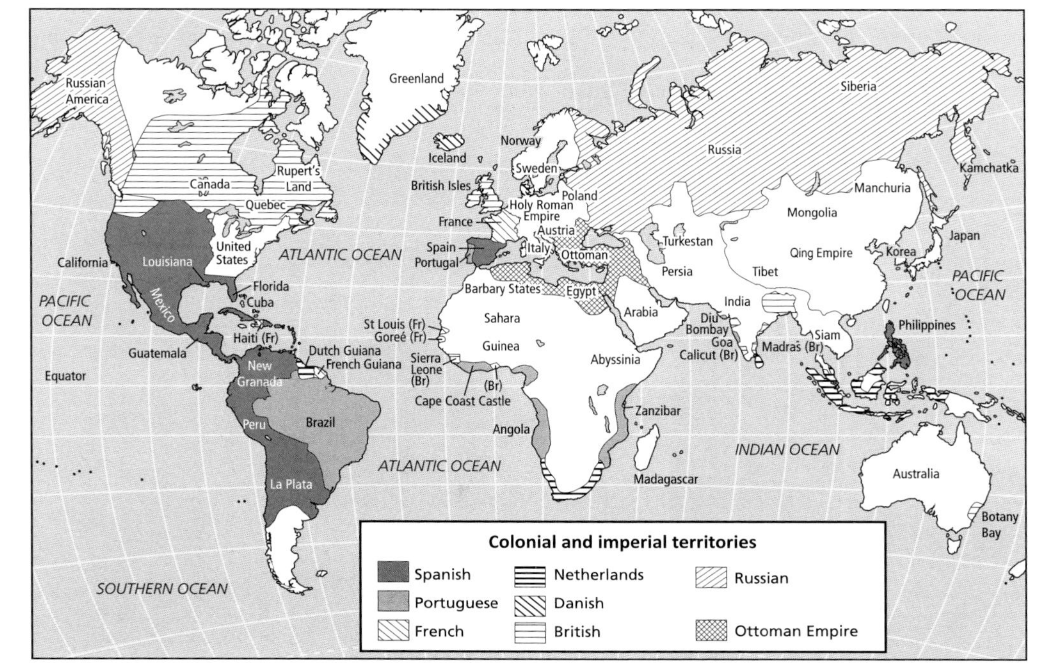

Map 4.2 World map 1783

Acacia gum was used in Britain and France for papermaking and for producing calicoes that Europeans hoped might eventually compete with those of India. These new consumer goods were not worn or used simply by Europeans, however. Wealthy female traders in West Africa combined items of European clothing with their existing dress to create new styles, and calico was one of the many items promised "in perpetuity" to Native American tribes in treaties with British and later American authorities. Tokugawa Japan experienced a similar consumer revolution in its large cities, where imported luxuries from China joined brocade, lacquerware, and porcelain made by local artisans for the wealthy, along with less expensive imitations for those with more style than cash. Prestige goods had separated elites from everyone else since the Neolithic, but now increasing numbers of urban residents could have at least a few of these, and they paid attention to changing fashions in dress and household goods. Commerce in the Atlantic is often described as a "triangle trade" linking Europe, Africa, and the Americas, and that in the Pacific as a line from Mexico to China through the Philippines, but no geometrical figure can accurately capture the many lines of interaction.

Plantations and the global trade network were essential parts of the expanding capitalist economic system. Economic historians often joke about the phrase "the rise of capitalism," as it is invoked to describe quite varied developments over a long period of time. No matter where you look, capitalism always seems to be rising, seemingly independent of human agents, rather like bread dough. Some of this expansionism comes from the elastic meaning of capitalism, which includes investment in property and the materials used to make or provide goods and services (what economists call the "means of production"), wage labor, the use of money to make more money, financial institutions such as banks, and complex forms of economic organization. As we saw in earlier chapters, all of these were present to some degree in many agricultural societies, but they became increasingly important in the trading centers of Europe, China, Japan, India, and parts of the Muslim world during the fifteenth through the eighteenth centuries, with income derived from capitalist business ventures joining landholding as a major form of wealth and creating new avenues for social mobility. Capitalism developed first in long-distance trade—this is often termed "mercantile capitalism" — and then in production.

Trade depends to a great deal on trust, on relying on those who sell, transport, and buy goods, or who borrow and loan money, to act honestly and fairly. Not surprisingly, many firms thus began as family companies or among groups that shared close cultural connections. The word "company" actually conveys this, as it comes from the Italian word *compagnie*, which means "bread together," i.e. sharing bread. In Europe, the Medici family of Florence and the Fugger family of Augsburg became fabulously wealthy as bankers and merchants, with branches in many cities that loaned money to rulers as well as urban residents. Their most prominent members, Lorenzo "the Magnificent" de Medici (1449–92) and Jacob "the Rich" Fugger (1459–1525) were also patrons of the arts, commissioning paintings, collecting sculpture, and supporting musicians and writers. Economic growth laid the material basis for the Italian Renaissance, as rich, social-climbing merchants and bankers joined popes and princes to spend vast sums to glorify themselves and their families, hiring artists, architects, sculptors, furniture-makers, and metalsmiths to create beautiful buildings and objects.

Family connections predominated in business elsewhere as well. In Japan, the family of Konoike Shinroku began as makers of sake, then became rice shippers and bankers, loaning money to local nobles throughout Japan and turning swamps into rice paddies. Armenian Christians in the city of Julfa in the Ottoman Empire (now in Azerbaijan) established family firms that traded across Asia. In 1603, the city was captured by the Safavid ruler 'Abbas I, who decided he could not hold it so burnt it to the ground and deported the Armenians to "New Julfa," a city he built for them right next to his new capital at Isfahan. From New Julfa, the Armenians built even more extensive trade networks that extended from Guangzhou to London, and into the Americas. Here they sometimes settled permanently, building homes and churches, though they returned to New Julfa to marry, and kin networks became denser and more

4.2 This detail from a Chinese porcelain bowl shows a somewhat romanticized view of the manufacturing process of porcelain itself, which involved shaping, painting, glazing and firing. Blue-and-white porcelain using imported Persian or local cobalt came to be mass produced in China, much of it made specifically for the export trade.

interwoven. Most Armenian merchants were multilingual, but they wrote letters and records in a dialect of Armenian that few outsiders could read, thus protecting their trade secrets. Heavily capitalized mercantile firms in India, many from the Gujarat area of the northwest, were also organized along family and caste lines, and those in Chinese cities and among Jews relied on connections among relatives.

The merchants who traveled were almost all men, and the heads of large family firms were as well, although female family members sometimes invested money they had inherited or acquired in business ventures. Occasionally circumstances allowed a widow who did not have adult sons to play a more active role. The Mendes family of Portugal (later known as the Nasi family) was forcibly converted from Judaism by the rulers of Portugal, fled to the Netherlands, and established large-scale banking operations in Antwerp. Gracia Nasi (1510–68), the widow of the firm's founder, ran the family business from Antwerp, Venice, Ferrara, and eventually Istanbul, making an alliance with the Ottoman sultan Süleyman the Magnificent (r. 1520–66) for trading and financial privileges. She reconverted to Judaism, and established an "underground railroad" to get Jews out of places where they were being persecuted by Christian rulers, convincing Süleyman to grant her a long-term lease on property in Greece where these refugees could resettle. Like Lorenzo de Medici and Jacob Fugger, Gracia Nasi patronized learning and the arts, especially the publication of Hebrew books, and her nephew became a close adviser to the sultan and the governor of several territories.

Money made in trade was invested in land in many places, which was expected to make a profit. Landowners encouraged or forced the peasants who farmed their land to raise cash crops alongside or instead of staple food crops, or they switched to raising sheep or other animals if this would generate a higher income. Land that had been held collectively or by customary use became private property, as happened in North America as European settlers moved westward and occupied Native American land and in Central Asia as Chinese settlers also moved west and began farming land that had been the grazing grounds of nomadic pastoralists. This also happened in Europe and other long-settled places as common lands such as forests, meadows, and marshes were enclosed, that is, fenced off into privately owned fields and sheep-runs no longer accessible to poorer people who had used them to raise a few animals or gather firewood. Capitalist trade and production raised overall wealth and brought a greater array of goods to many people, but not everyone shared in these benefits.

Capitalism developed in many places and involved many different groups, but among Europeans it became intimately related to colonialism. Capitalist merchants often provided the impetus and the equipment for colonization, and many colonies were established to be both sources of raw materials and markets for trade goods. Gaining and defending colonies was too expensive for family firms, and large joint-stock companies of unrelated individuals were established, a business form that was later adapted to production as well as trade. Colonies provided income to Europe, which was partly responsible for the divergence in power and wealth between Europe (and its settler colonies) and the rest of the world that would mark the nineteenth and subsequent centuries.

WARFARE

Colonial empires were created by military force, and war was a constant elsewhere as well. Devastating wars, with armies that sometimes numbered in the hundreds of thousands, were widespread across much of the Old World, most fought with gunpowder weapons, which made them more deadly and much more expensive than earlier wars. Military expenditures generally made up the majority of state budgets, and taxes, systems for collecting these, and other apparatus of the state grew, largely to finance war. Some officers were members of traditional elites, but others were professional military contractors, who recruited soldiers and sailors from among the poorer groups in society with promises of pay and bonuses, or forced them into military service by threats or even kidnapping. The demands of war thus shaped all aspects of society, especially for men but also for women.

New military technology—artillery, hand-held weapons, guns on ships—required longer training, so those fielding military forces felt it necessary to maintain at least the core of a standing army from one conflict to the next. Soldiers were often housed with civilian families, with the family expected to provide a place for a certain number of soldiers to sleep and keep warm. In theory the soldiers were supposed to pay for their food, but as their pay itself often remained theoretical, they simply took what they needed by force. Until the development of systems of provisioning in the late eighteenth century, during actual campaigns troops were accompanied by people—sometimes including the soldiers' girlfriends, wives, or other family members—who pillaged the countryside for food and other provisions, as well as food for horses.

Scholars counting wars and their duration and intensity have found that perhaps only one year in ten was war-free in many areas during these centuries. In Europe, there were religious, naval, dynastic, and territorial wars, almost too many to count. Much of continental Europe became involved in the Thirty Years' War (1618–48) that mixed religious and political aims, and in which there were no clear lines of battle. Mercenary armies indiscriminately burned crops and villages, and killed animals and people. Hunger and disease, including dysentery, typhus, plague, and syphilis, accompanied the troops and the refugees who fled from place to place. At least one-quarter and perhaps as much as one-third of the population of the Holy Roman Empire died during the course of the war, civilian losses that would not be matched again until the wars of the twentieth century. The development of colonial empires and international trade meant that European wars in the later seventeenth and eighteenth centuries often spread beyond Europe itself. The Seven Years' War (1755–63) was so global in scope that it could almost be called the first "world war," involving conflict in North America, the Caribbean, the Pacific, and India as well as Europe.

The Ottoman Empire was not a combatant in either the Thirty Years' War or the Seven Years' War, but it was engaged in its own expansionary wars. The Ottomans expanded into Europe and around the Mediterranean, and on their eastern border the Sunni Ottomans engaged in frequent warfare with the Shi'ite Safavids. On *their* eastern border, the Safavids fought with various Central Asian groups, and with the Mughals. These three empires—the Ottoman, the Safavid, and the Mughal—were labeled "gunpowder empires" in the 1970s by the US historian Marshall Hodgson, who saw their ability to use artillery to take stone fortresses as the key to their success in creating and holding large empires. Now historians think a better label might be "empires in the age of gunpowder," as their military success owed as much to their skills at logistics—keeping the armies fed and supplied—and strategies as to the weapons themselves. These three Islamic empires also created relatively effective institutions and bureaucracies to collect taxes and administer their large territories, and ideologies that legitimated their rule in the minds of their subjects, many—and in the case of the Mughal Empire, most—of whom were not Muslim.

The Islamic empires were not always at war with one another or with others of their neighbors, but staying in power required suppressing rebellions and preventing invasions, so they maintained large standing armies, as did the Ming and Qing rulers of China and the states of Europe. Prussia, for example, one of the larger states in a still-disunited Germany, tried in the eighteenth century to sustain a permanent army of about 80,000 troops with a population of perhaps 3.5 million. During war, this army increased to almost 150,000, or about one-quarter of all adult males. The rulers of Prussia expected martial values to influence everything in Prussia, not just the army, demanding obedience from their subjects and supporting compulsory primary education and broadened technical training because these would provide better soldiers. Not surprisingly, observers described Prussia as a state attached to an army.

Military values also shaped Japanese society, even though actual war was rare after about 1600. In the sixteenth century, the regional lords known as *daimyo* built local power bases centered on castles, and used their armies of samurai to fight with one another and seize more territory. Gradually a series of skillful daimyo built up more centralized power, and in 1603 one of these, Tokugawa Ieyasu (1543–1616), defeated most of his rivals and took the title "shogun"; the Tokugawa shogunate, centered in Edo (now Tokyo), lasted until 1867. The Tokugawa shoguns created a rigid class structure, and gave daimyo and samurai special privileges linked to their role as warriors—only they could carry swords, for example, and they could demand deference from commoners. They also stripped them of any real function, however. Daimyo were required to live every other year in Edo, and their wives and children had to live there permanently. Thus the shogun could keep an eye

4.3 Albrecht Dürer's woodcut of the Four Horsemen of the Apocalypse (1498), based on the Book of Revelation in the Bible, shows Death, Famine, War, and Conquest riding across the land; Famine holds a weighing scale, a reference to the high price of food during a famine. This woodcut and accompanying text, part of a series, was published just as many people anticipated the Last Judgment in 1500, and brought Dürer money and fame.

on the daimyo, and they spent much of their time and money moving back and forth to the capital. (King Louis XIV of France and Tsar Peter the Great of Russia would also follow similar policies, requiring their nobles to be at court if they wanted royal favors, which removed them from their local power bases.) Samurai were forbidden to own land or work at other trades, but had to depend on stipends from their daimyo; when death or bankruptcy ended these, they became unemployed *ronin*, scrounging for work as bodyguards, serving as hired muscle, or just stealing. They became enough of a social problem that the shoguns eventually relaxed restrictions on their employment, though gangs of ronin, claiming the samurai code of conduct known as *bushido* ("the way of the warrior") prevented them from engaging in less exalted tasks than fighting, continued to plague the peasants who made up the vast majority of the Japanese population.

Wherever it occurred, warfare was accompanied by diseases carried by the armies and often by famine, a link portrayed visually in images of the Four Horsemen of the Apocalypse described in the Book of Revelation in the Bible, which became a common subject for artists in Europe. More soldiers died from hunger, disease, and infection than from actual battle wounds, and famine and disease killed the general population in war-torn areas as well. War also involved acts of brutality, including beatings, torture, mutilation, and rape, which became common enough that special words were developed to describe this. During the Thirty Years' War, for example, the plundering mob that accompanied troops and terrorized villagers became known as the *Soldateska*, and during the Ming/Qing transition people spoke of *binghuo*, "soldier calamities." Sexual violence had long been part of conquest, of course, with women and girls understood to be among the spoils of war, but the frequency of armed conflicts in this era made this even more common. Some military historians are interested primarily in battles and strategy, but more are now investigating the broader social and cultural forces that led to war, shaped how it was fought, and resulted from it. They also emphasize that discussing war simply in terms of "causes and consequences" misses the point, as this neglects the course of the war itself, which can never be anticipated and is always ghastly.

TRANSFERRING FOOD CROPS

Disease, famine, and war killed huge numbers of people in this era, but the world's total population did not decline. Global population estimates set the world's population in 1500 at about 400 to 500 million, just a bit higher than it had been before the pandemics of the fourteenth century, with more than half of this in South and East Asia. This increased slightly to about 550 million in 1600, as the drastic population decline in the Americas was matched by growth in Europe and Asia. By 1700 world population had increased slightly again, to about 650 million, and by 1800 it had grown at a more rapid pace to about 950 million.

The primary reason for this growth was another consequence of the Columbian Exchange: the spread of food crops, which were taken in all directions. Europeans brought wheat, their staple crop, to the Americas, which did not thrive in the tropical Caribbean, but grew well on the plains of Mexico and South America, and later in North America. Wheat was vitally important to the Spanish; bread was a central element in religious ritual as well as a primary foodstuff, and they thought that if they ate indigenous foods they would turn into Indians. Accounts of the introduction of wheat were thus repeated and written down, which reveal fundamental aspects of Spanish colonial society. In Mexico the first person to plant wheat may have been an African, Juan Garrido, a former slave who had been part of Cortés' conquering forces, while in Peru two widows of Spanish landowners received the first seed grain and oversaw its planting, before they bothered to marry again. Slaves and widows were key to the Spanish colonial economy everywhere. Other crops were not as important culturally, so all we know is that they came: onions, barley, oats, peas, and fruit trees from Europe, and bananas, yams, rice, okra, sorghum, and coconuts from Africa. (The spread of one type of fruit tree later in the United States also has an often-told story attached to it, though the fact that Jonathan Chapman—Johnny Appleseed—planted apple trees in order to have fruit for hard cider is generally left out.)

Tomatoes, chili peppers, sweet potatoes, squash, beans, potatoes, peanuts, maize, manioc, pineapples, avocados, and other crops went from the Americas to other parts of the world, with about

30 percent of the foods eaten in the world today originating in the western hemisphere. Portuguese traders took manioc (cassava), a root crop that was a staple in tropical parts of the Americas, to West Africa, where it became a staple and the basis of what are now seen as national dishes, such as ebà and fufu. Traders took maize to Europe and Africa, where it was first grown as food for animals, and then gradually as food for humans as well, with dishes made of cornmeal integrated into existing cuisines. Peanuts, which the Spanish first encountered in the markets of Tenochtitlan, spread to southern China, tropical Africa, and South and Southeast Asia, as did peppers, becoming essential parts of local foodways. During the seventeenth century, Europeans recognized that the tomato, another New World plant, was not harmful even though it was related to deadly nightshade, and began planting it as a food crop as well as a garden ornamental. This exchange of plants improved nutrition around the world, and allowed the slow increase in total global population, despite the tremendous loss of life because of epidemic disease and war.

Two staple crops had particularly dramatic effects, both good and bad: potatoes and sweet potatoes (which are not related). Potatoes originated in the Andes, and Spanish sailors carried – and ate – them on their way back to Europe. There they met great disdain. Potatoes were not mentioned in the Bible and grew underground, so they were seen as vaguely demonic, and people hated the way they tasted. Potatoes were fine for animals (and slaves in the New World), but not people in Europe. This lack of interest changed slowly when people realized they could be grown on extremely poor soil and were easy to harvest and store. A field planted with potatoes could feed two or three times the number of people that could be fed by the same field planted with grain, and potatoes are more nutritious. The potato crop was also more reliable year to year, as it was less likely to be destroyed by hail, drought, or unexpected early frosts, which evened out the available food supply and lessened the likelihood of famine.

By the late seventeenth century, potatoes were an important crop in the Netherlands, Switzerland, and Ireland, where they fed both animals and people. The rulers of Prussia recognized potatoes would grow well in the cool summers and sandy soil of Prussia, and ordered farmers to plant them, as did the kings of Sweden and Norway. The Qing rulers of China, promoting the westward movement of Han Chinese into high, dry parts of Central Asia where various other ethnic groups lived, offered cheap land and lower taxes for farmers who planted potatoes and other New World crops. Agricultural historians estimate that the cultivated area of China nearly tripled between 1700 and 1850. The War of the Bavarian Succession in 1778–9, between Prussia and Austria, has been nicknamed the "Potato War" because the primary tactic involved gaining the food supply of the opposite side rather than actual battles, and Prussian troops spent their time harvesting potatoes. Antoine-Auguste Parmentier (1737–1813), a French army doctor and agronomist who had been imprisoned by the Prussians during the Seven Years' War—in which France was on one side and Prussia the other—promoted potato cultivation in France, convincing the French queen Marie-Antoinette, so the story goes, to wear potato flowers in her hair and inviting local notables to all-potato dinners. (There are several soups and side dishes named in his honor, all containing potatoes.)

For French nobles an all-potato dinner was a novelty, but for many of Europe's poor it became a reality, as in some places potatoes were the only solid food very poor people ate. Agricultural historians estimate that, for example, the Irish diet in 1800 included an average of ten potatoes per person per day, or 80 percent of people's caloric intake; the rest came primarily from milk and cheese produced by cows fed on potatoes.

On the other side of the world from Ireland, sweet potatoes were another solution for what to grow on poor land. Spanish ships brought sweet potatoes from Central America, where they were native, to the Philippines, and Chinese merchants took them to Fujian province, on the coast of southeastern China, in the late sixteenth century. As the rulers of Prussia had with the potato, the provincial governors supported the growing of sweet potatoes by distributing them to farmers, and they thrived. They also grew well in mountains and dry upland regions, where Hakka people—one of China's many designated ethnic minorities—practiced shifting agriculture on steep slopes, many living in small huts so that others derisively called them *pengmin*, "shed people." The diet of pengmin

4.4 An ink painting by the Japanese artist Ike no Taiga (1723–76) shows a hefty man eating roasted sweet potatoes. Taiga was the son of a poor farmer who had moved to Kyoto, and this painting may be a commentary on gluttony.

and other poor rural people came to revolve around the sweet potato, just as the Irish diet did the potato. But raising crops on steep slopes meant cutting down trees and other natural vegetation, which led to erosion and flooding, destroying fields and drowning rice crops at lower elevations. Officials attempted to stop cultivation in the mountains, but they were unable to do so, and famines and unrest caused in part by flooding would be among the reasons for the fall of the Qing dynasty in the twentieth century. (The communist rulers of China have continued to support the planting of New World crops, and today China grows three-quarters of the world's sweet potatoes, more than a quarter of the world's potatoes, and about a fifth of the world's maize.)

Sweet potatoes also became a staple crop in Papua New Guinea, introduced in the eighteenth century from the Moluccas where they had been brought by Portuguese traders, which led to a change in traditional agriculture and an increase in population. They could also be found across Polynesia and in New Zealand, but here there is a mystery. The route by which sweet potatoes came into China can be traced through written sources, and their introduction occurred after the Spanish were in the Philippines. Sweet potato cultivation in the Pacific began long before this, however. The earliest radiocarbon dating is from about 1000 CE in the Cook Islands, which had been settled by Polynesians coming from Tahiti. The Maori Polynesians who settled New Zealand in the thirteenth century carried sweet potatoes (known as kumara) with them, along with other crops. How sweet potatoes got to eastern Polynesia from Central America is not clear, however. Seeds could not have easily survived floating on the open ocean or in the stomachs of birds, and sweet potatoes are generally cultivated by vine cuttings anyway, not seeds. (This is how they were taken to China.) Many geoarchaeologists thus think that Polynesians at some point reached South or Central America and took sweet potatoes back with them. They thus became part of what might be called a "Polynesian Exchange" that preceded the Columbian Exchange by several centuries. In New Zealand, the Maori adapted their horticultural techniques to raise tropical sweet potatoes in the cooler climate, planting them in sunny places sheltered from the wind and adapting the soil. When the British captain James Cook (1728–79) reached New Zealand on his first voyage in the Pacific in 1769, he reported large fields with sweet potatoes, yams (an Old World crop distinct from the sweet potato), and taro.

Cook's voyage was one of many in the eighteenth century through which much of the Pacific was explored and mapped by Dutch, French, and British ships. Initially they were searching for the huge continent that Europeans expected would be in the southern hemisphere to balance all the continents in the northern hemisphere. This "Terra Australis" (a phrase simply meaning "southern land") showed up on maps before Europeans in 1606 got their first glimpse of what was soon named Australia. Australia was huge, but still not large enough to be the famed southern lands, and eighteenth-century expeditions continued the search. French and British ships reached Samoa, Tahiti, and other island groups, bringing back plants, animals, and often a few residents, along with reports and drawings of what they had seen, just as Columbus had. Naturalists collected specimens for collections—called "cabinets of curiosity"—or for possible use elsewhere. The most important of these Pacific voyages were those under Cook, who landed several times in Australia, and communicated well enough with the indigenous people to adopt an aboriginal word for the most distinctive animal he had seen, a kangaroo. In the 1780s, French and British ships carried breadfruit from the Pacific to the Caribbean, hoping to grow it to feed slaves. One of these ships, the *Bounty*, captained by one of Cook's former officers William Bligh, experienced a mutiny that made it far more famous than its mission. Thus along with the Columbian Exchange and the Polynesian Exchange, what we might call the "Captain Cook Exchange" moved crops and other products around the world.

THE TRADE IN ANIMALS, ALIVE AND DEAD

While crops and soldiers traveled in all directions, animals, like disease, traveled primarily from the Old World to the New. The only New World animal that became a common food in Europe was the turkey, which seems to have acquired its name in English as a result of the new networks of global exchange, as the birds came into England on ships that also carried goods from the eastern

Mediterranean, so the English called them "turkey hens." The transport of animals in the other direction had dramatic demographic and social consequences. Europeans brought the same livestock elsewhere that Columbus had taken to Hispaniola: horses, cattle, pigs, sheep, goats, and poultry. These often escaped into the wild and thrived. Pigs in particular could eat anything and reproduced rapidly, destroying native agricultural plots and making traditional methods of farming with unfenced beds impossible. Cortés established a cattle ranch on his huge estates in Mexico, using African slaves who had familiarity with horses and cattle to work it, while the indigenous people he had enslaved farmed and worked in the silver mines he also ordered built. A herd of a hundred cattle that the Spanish abandoned in the grasslands—called pampas—of the Rio de la Plata area in what is now Argentina grew within several decades to over 100,000. African, indigenous, and mixed race people fleeing Spanish mines and plantations began to herd these cattle from the backs of horses, creating a form of pastoral life new to the Americas but common in parts of Africa (and many other parts of the world). They would later be celebrated as gauchos, the symbol of Argentina.

In the plains and deserts of the North American West and Southwest, horses transformed the economy, as Native Americans gave up sedentary farming and localized foraging for a more nomadic existence hunting vast herds of buffalo and other animals from horseback. The Comanche, Cheyenne, Lakota, and other plains tribes acquired horses from Spanish colonists—and later from each other—through trading and raiding, building up large herds. By the mid eighteenth century tribes from the Rio Grande River north to what is now Saskatchewan depended on horses. They were generally owned by men, and became a prestige item as well as a means of obtaining food. Like all prestige goods, horses appear to have enhanced social and gender hierarchies, as men with more horses married more wives and acquired captives through raiding or purchase, in part to care for their horses. Desire for more horses encouraged warfare among plains tribes and between Native Americans and European colonists, but was also a motivation for trade. Along with horses, indigenous peoples acquired guns and ammunition, woolen and cotton cloth, blankets, metal tools and implements, beads, alcohol, and a host of other goods in a North American consumer revolution parallel to that in Europe and Japan. These were integrated into local cultural forms, as, for example, beads replaced porcupine quills on embroidered clothing. European traders came to recognize that Native American groups had specific preferences in beads and cloth that could change from year to year; writing to their suppliers, they requested certain colors, patterns, and levels of quality, knowing that these would sell while others would not.

European goods were exchanged primarily for furs. Not many live animals were transported from the Americas to Europe, but tens of millions of their skins were. The global fur trade thus altered life in the woodland areas of eastern and northern North America where horses did not become common. Fur had been worn since Paleolithic times for warmth, of course, and the skins or fur of certain animals also had symbolic value. Warriors in many cultures draped lion, leopard, jaguar, or wolf skins over their heads and shoulders to associate themselves with these powerful animals and signify their masculinity. Rulers wore capes or coats of rare furs such as ermine or sable as a sign of high status, while nobles and other wealthy people had their jackets and coats trimmed with fox or lynx. The thickest and softest fur came from mountainous or northern areas where animals built up dense coats to survive the cold; in Eurasia, the vast steppes of Siberia yielded the most highly prized furs, especially as over-trapping and over-hunting had reduced the fur available from other areas. Traders from the city of Novgorod had obtained furs from the indigenous Komi and other Siberian tribes as early as the tenth century, and beginning in the fifteenth century the expanding Russian state with its capital at Moscow conquered much of Siberia, forcing native people—whom the Russians saw as inferior savages—to pay them sable furs as tribute, and spreading smallpox. Russian fur trappers also moved to Siberia to obtain fur directly, particularly as prices escalated in the sixteenth century when wearing fur became even more fashionable and as prices in general went up as a result of New World gold and silver and other global economic developments. Siberian fur traveled south to Persia and China as well as west to Europe, with squirrel fur particularly favored in China because it was durable and relatively inexpensive. At first Russian trappers and traders stayed for a year or two and then went back to Russia, but eventually some stayed in Siberia, often marrying women from among the local tribes.

Siberian fur alone could not meet the demand, and northern North America offered new opportunities for exploitation. In the early seventeenth century, the Dutch, French, and English established inland fur-trading posts as well as coastal settlements. Europeans traders, almost all of them men, brought in goods of interest to both men and women: guns, rum, cloth, kettles, flour, needles, and tea. The Europeans were only interested in fur, however, which came from animals hunted and trapped by men, and not in the products that indigenous women produced, such as crops or clothing. Thus among Native Americans, men's activities often came to be more highly valued as a source of imported goods, in contrast to earlier periods in which men's hunting and women's horticulture had been more equally valued.

French explorers, fur traders, and missionaries moved inland from Quebec on foot and by canoe, founding forts, trading posts, and a few small missions along the coasts of the Great Lakes and the Mississippi River. They did not have the military superiority to demand tribute from indigenous people as the Russians did in Siberia, but traded on terms favorable to themselves for fox, lynx, marten, and especially beaver, whose inner fur was prized by European hat-makers because it was dense and had small barbs, so could be easily felted into the hats that were the height of fashion in Europe. (European beaver had been nearly hunted to extinction by this point.) As in Siberia, French fur traders—called *voyageurs* or *coureurs de bois* ("runners of the woods")—frequently married local women as they traveled further and further west, relying on their wives and their wives' families for many things.

Conflict over the fur trade was one factor in the Iroquois Wars of the seventeenth century—sometimes called the Beaver Wars—in which the nations of the Iroquois Confederacy of the eastern Great Lakes region expanded their area of control west and south, and fought with the French and their Huron and Algonquin allies. The Iroquois appear to have been expansionist before the fur trade gave them an added incentive for warfare, but now the stakes were higher, and the weapons more deadly, as the Dutch and later the English supplied them with guns. The Iroquois may also have been attempting to capture individuals from other tribes to replace the many in their own who had died from warfare or the diseases brought by Europeans, especially smallpox and measles. Taking captives was a common aim in Native American warfare, with the captured sometimes integrated into the tribe through adoption or marriage. Captives occasionally included Europeans taken from isolated farms or villages, some of whom were tortured, but most of whom were simply taken along and later ransomed or escaped. A few of these told their stories in captivity narratives that were published and became best-sellers, shaping colonial and European views of Native Americans.

With the second wave of North American colonization in the 1660s, the English took control of all Dutch territory, and the king granted a new company, The Company of Adventurers of England Trading into Hudson's Bay, monopoly rights to all fur from the area drained by the rivers and streams flowing into Hudson Bay, which turned out to be about 1.5 million square miles, about 15 percent of North America. French claims to this land and other parts of North America ended with a series of defeats at British hands in the eighteenth century, and the Hudson's Bay Company was the de facto government over much of this territory into the nineteenth century, issuing its own money and judicial rulings. In the early nineteenth century the British government gave it monopoly trading rights extending to the Arctic and the Pacific Oceans. Although beaver-felt hats had long gone out of style, furs were still profitable, and the company worked to keep settlers out of the Pacific Northwest through a public relations campaign portraying the area as not suitable for farming. It also banned European women from most fur trading areas until the 1820s, although marriage between English fur traders and indigenous women was less common than marriage between French traders and indigenous women had been. Along the Pacific coast, the Siberian and North American fur economies met, as Russian fur traders captured women and children from Aleut and Kodiak villages along the Alaska coast as hostages, forcing the men to hunt sea otter, which the Russians then sold to British and American merchants, who transported it around the world.

Along with skins, dead animals transported across the Atlantic included fish. Freshwater and saltwater fish were important food items everywhere in the world these were available, providing important sources of protein. In Europe, fishing came to be organized on a larger scale in the fifteenth century, and with the discovery of incredibly rich sources of fish in the Grand Banks of the North Atlantic, fishing fleets soon traveled there. (There is even speculation that Portuguese Basque fishermen landed in what is now Canada before Columbus, but kept this a secret so as not to reveal the location of their source of fish; no archaeological or textual evidence has been discovered to back this theory, but this only proves to its proponents that the Portuguese fishermen were remarkably successful at keeping a secret.) Ever larger fishing fleets, backed by capitalist investors, took several hundred thousand tons of fish annually, especially cod, which was sold fresh, pickled, salted, and smoked, and became a staple food for slaves in the Americas and workers in Europe. European whalers also hunted, killed, and processed tens of thousands of whales, primarily for their oil and bone rather than meat, which was simply discarded.

Fur trapping and hunting, ocean fishing, and whaling were all occupations in which the vast majority of the workforce was male. Like warfare, these took men away from their home towns and villages for extended periods of time into all-male communities, where tasks that were normally done by women, such as cooking and clothing repair, were done by men. These homosocial environments no doubt encouraged the development of same-sex intimate relations, although these have left little trace in the sources, as the men who engaged in these occupations were generally not literate. The absence of men also meant that gender divisions of labor in places they had left shifted, with women and children taking on responsibility for agricultural production and other tasks.

DRUG FOODS AND THE COMMERCIALIZATION OF LEISURE

Hunting, fishing, and trapping communities of men, and villages of women and children they left behind, were not the only type of new social forms that resulted from the global connections of the Columbian Exchange. Various types of pleasurable and addictive products

4.5 In this sixteenth-century miniature of an Ottoman coffeehouse, customers, including a few who appear to be foreign visitors, sip coffee, read, talk, and play backgammon. In the upper left, others queue outside, waiting to enter.

also spread, often consumed in new social settings of commercialized leisure. Among these products were caffeinated beverages. Cacao beans—which the Aztecs believed had been brought from paradise—went to Europe from Mesoamerica, where first the Spanish and then the French and English developed the habit of drinking cups of chocolate. Coffee, native to Ethiopia and grown commercially first in Yemen about 1400, was increasingly drunk throughout the Muslim world, primarily in coffeehouses that served as places of male sociability. Here men gathered with their friends for conversation, business dealings, and sometimes music, although moralists worried that they might be engaged in gambling and other questionable activities, religious leaders wondered whether the addictive properties of coffee might violate Muslim law, and physicians debated whether coffee was harmful to men's health.

Europeans learned of coffee largely from the Ottomans, but it was too expensive for most people until the Dutch began growing coffee on a larger scale in the last half of the seventeenth century in their colonies in Asia and South America. They forced peasants on Java who had been growing rice to provide an annual quota of coffee, and by the early eighteenth century Java was providing much of the world's coffee, as well as a slang expression for the addictive drink. Thousands of coffeehouses opened in Venice, London, Paris, and other European cities, inspiring the French to begin growing coffee in their Caribbean colonies in the eighteenth century. From there coffee cultivation spread to Central America and Brazil, and at the very end of the nineteenth century to East Africa, not far from its place of origin. As in the Muslim world, these cafés and coffeehouses were places where (mostly) men gathered to talk about business, politics, or whatever. Rulers from Sultan Murad IV (r. 1623–40) of the Ottoman Empire to King Charles II of Britain (ruled 1660–85) attempted periodically to close them down as they worried about sedition, but such measures never worked.

In Europe and in larger European colonial cities, coffeehouses were one type of new social and cultural institution where ideas were exchanged, and there were others. Alongside the traditional intellectual centers of courts, churches, and universities, the seventeenth century saw the development of scientific and literary societies, journals and newspapers, and clubs and lodges such as the

Society of Freemasons that one paid to join. Most of these were predominantly male, but first in Paris and then elsewhere elite women also held gatherings of men and women for formal and informal discussions of topics that they chose, holding them in the drawing rooms of their own homes—*salons* in French—from which they take their name. Learned societies, journals, clubs, salons, and other new institutions created what the German philosopher and historian Jürgen Habermas called the "public sphere," and helped create what we now call "public opinion," a force that became more powerful as the eighteenth century progressed.

Public opinion and cultural trends were shaped by the tastes of elites, but also by those of more ordinary people, who purchased specific products, subscribed to certain journals and newspapers, and visited particular cafés and coffeehouses. Gradually, broader groups of people determined which artistic and literary styles would be judged praiseworthy, and which political plans and ideas should be accepted or rejected. Scientific ideas spread beyond scientists themselves to a wider public through these new institutions, as did the self-conscious intellectual movement of the eighteenth century that emphasized the power of reason and called itself the Enlightenment. Groups discussing and advocating enlightened ideas, including lodges of Freemasons, societies devoted to "progress" or the "useful trades," discussion clubs that met in taverns or people's homes, and clubs where people paid a small fee to hear lectures, were founded in many cities across Europe, including Paris, Edinburgh, London, Naples, Rome, and Warsaw, and across the Atlantic in the British, French, and Spanish colonies. Enlightenment ideas flowed not only east to west, but also west to east. Debates about slavery and natural rights going on in the islands of the French Caribbean shaped political discussions in Europe, as people engaged in those debates and newspapers reporting them traveled with Caribbean coffee to Europe. These new ideas were one of the background factors in the Atlantic revolutions, discussed below.

The spread of tea followed a different chronology and path than either chocolate or coffee. Tea originated in southwest China, although exactly when people began to drink it is unknown. By the sixth century CE tea was being grown on many hillsides in south China. The steppe nomads of Central Asia became addicted to tea, traded their warhorses for it, and took it on their conquests of India, Russia, and western Asia. Buddhist monks carried it to Japan and Korea along with texts and devotional objects, where it became a part of quasi-religious ceremonies, with highly ritualized methods of preparation and consumption. Europeans first encountered tea when they reached the Indian Ocean basin, but they thought it bitter and medicinal, not pleasant. Tea drinking did not take off in Europe until the eighteenth century, when sugar produced on Atlantic plantations became affordable to the masses. Tea importation into England grew from one-tenth of an ounce per person to one pound—a rise of 40,000 percent—and the caffeine and sugar combination of sweetened tea allowed for longer work hours as well as new forms of female sociability around a teapot, itself often an import or a cheaper local reproduction.

Tea was also part of less exalted social occasions than Buddhism ceremonies in Japan. During the Tokugawa shogunate teahouses along with theatres and taverns popped up in the districts of major cities set aside for entertainment, termed the *ukiyo* or Floating World, where bored samurai and daimyo, and other urban residents, could find amusement and spend their time. Among the possibilities were geisha, young women who had spent many years of training in singing, storytelling, dancing, and playing musical instruments. Elite men socialized in geisha teahouses and paid large sums of money for their services, which might include sexual services but were often limited to conversation and entertainment. If they preferred, men could instead arrange to spend time with the male actors who played all parts in the wildly popular kabuki theatre performances also found in the Floating World. The shoguns tolerated all this as a way to keep things calm, and the men paid for it by raising taxes and rents on peasants who lived on their lands, or by borrowing. The shoguns did attempt to prohibit peasants from drinking tea or smoking tobacco, as these "take up time and cost money," but most peasants had little disposable income anyway.

As did those in Japan, cities elsewhere in the early modern world also offered an increasingly broad range of places for commercialized leisure. In the larger cities of China and western Europe, people watched plays, operas, and concerts in permanent theatres, and jugglers, acrobats, and storytellers on temporary stages. A resident of Guangzhou or Yangzhou would have found much about London or Paris quite familiar, and vice versa. Among the similarities were brothels—often near the theatre district—that ranged from cheap and rough to sumptuous and very expensive, sometimes licensed and taxed by the city or regional government.

Both work and leisure were accompanied by alcoholic beverages, as every staple crop of the Columbian Exchange was transformed into alcohol somewhere. Grain crops became various types of beers or other drinks made from fermented rice, barley, and wheat, while grapes and fruit were made into wine and hard ciders and drunk at banquets, taverns, festivals, theatre performances, and many other places. People also drank beer, hard cider, and cheap wine as part of their ordinary day, to augment calories provided by other foodstuffs, relieve pain, and partake of alcohol's other effects. Workers in the silver mines of Potosí purchased maize beer (*chicha*) along with potatoes to sustain themselves, and they also bought and chewed coca leaves—which had been used by the Incas in religious rituals and medicinally—to deaden hunger and gain a bit of energy for their grueling work. Coca chewing did not spread beyond the Andes, however; the boom in this drug would come later, after a German scientist discovered how to extract its active ingredient, which he named cocaine.

People sought to create stronger forms of alcohol through freezing off some of the liquid or multiple fermentations. Strong alcohol is produced most easily through distilling, a process that appears to have been invented at least twice—in both China and Italy in the twelfth century—and probably in other places as well. By the sixteenth century every wine-producing area began to distill brandy and sweet liqueurs, while rum poured in from the West Indies and brandy made from fruits such as apples, pears, plums, and cherries was produced and sold locally. Improvements in the distillation of grains helped distilled liquors compete with brandy in terms of price, and whisky, gin, and vodka became more common beverages, especially for poorer people. In England, the government decided that distilling gin was a way to use up poor-quality grain, so let anyone distill and sell it; by 1740, the production of gin was six times that of beer, with thousands of gin-shops in London alone. Gin-drinking was seen as the root of bankruptcy, prostitution, neglect of children and many other social problems, however, and in 1751 the government limited the sale to licensed dealers, although illegal production and sales continued.

Coffeehouses, clubs, taverns, and other centers of commercialized leisure were also places where another new addictive substance was enjoyed—tobacco. Native Americans grew and smoked tobacco long before Columbus, who took some tobacco seeds back to Spain with him, where farmers began to grow it for use as a medicine that helped people relax. The French ambassador at Lisbon, Jean Nicot (1530–1600)—whose name is the origin of the term nicotine and of the botanical name for tobacco, *Nicotiana*—introduced the use of tobacco in France, originally in the form of snuff. In the eighteenth century, using snuff became a marker of sophistication and class status for European men, who carried silver or ivory snuffboxes full of powdered tobacco to snort, which sent the nicotine right into their bloodstreams as they sneezed into lace handkerchiefs. Lesser folk smoked tobacco in pipes, which also became increasingly elaborate for anyone who could afford this. English merchants brought tobacco to the Ottoman Empire, and everywhere coffeehouses became filled with pipe smoke. As with coffee, officials and clerics in the Muslim world debated whether tobacco was discouraged or perhaps even prohibited by Islamic law, and whether it was harmful or beneficial. Sultan Murad IV banned smoking when he shut down the coffeehouses, backing this up with severe punishments, but as the Ottoman official Katib Chelebi commented shortly afterward, soldiers "found an opportunity to smoke even during the executions" of other soldiers for smoking, the next sultan lifted the ban, and "smoking is at present practiced all over the habitable globe." Tobacco was sometimes cut with opium, which had been used medicinally since ancient times, and opium was also smoked on its own, or eaten. In the eighteenth century, the British East India Company began transporting large quantities of opium grown in its Indian colony to China, to pay for Chinese products sent west.

Most tobacco consumed in Europe was grown in the Americas, and during the seventeenth century the Virginia tidewater area around Chesapeake Bay became known for producing the highest-quality tobacco. Tobacco planters contracted their crop to merchants in London—and later in Glasgow in Scotland—who loaned them money to expand their plantations, buy new land and consumer goods, and hire or acquire workers. In the seventeenth century, workers on tobacco plantations included indentured servants from Europe and enslaved persons from Africa, but in the eighteenth century a dwindling number of indentured servants and the push for ever-lower prices led to increased use of slaves, and the slave population of the Chesapeake increased dramatically. Most plantations in this area were small compared to those of the Deep South, although those of George Washington and Thomas Jefferson were relatively large. Tobacco was used as a currency of exchange in the Chesapeake area, and also along the coast of western Africa, where it purchased slaves.

Tobacco was introduced into China in the middle of the sixteenth century, and spread widely by Ming and Qing soldiers. Wealthy people carried pipes and tobacco pouches, or their servants did, with women using very long and slender pipes, as these were seen as more feminine (an aesthetic judgment that carried over into cigarettes designed specially for women in the twentieth-century United States). Gatherings of scholars and aristocrats were times for smoking, and poems in praise of tobacco appeared, extolling the virtues of "the Sage's vapor" and the "golden-thread smoke." Because of the high demand, growing tobacco was more profitable than growing wheat or rice, and Chinese farmers began growing tobacco extensively in the eighteenth century, although it stripped nutrients from the soil and could only be planted for a short period.

SUGAR AND THE SLAVE TRADE

Caffeine and nicotine are powerful drugs, but what led coffee, chocolate, and in the eighteenth century tea to become even more popular was yet another addictive substance central to the Columbian Exchange, sugar. Sugar cane is native to the South Pacific and was taken to India in ancient times, from where it went to southern China and the Mediterranean. The Atlantic islands off the coast of Africa had the right kind of warm, wet climate for sugar, and the Portuguese who established colonies there in the late fifteenth century began growing and processing sugar cane. Producing sugar takes both expensive refining machinery and many workers to chop and transport heavy cane, burn fields, and tend vats of cooking cane juice. This means that it is difficult for small growers to produce sugar economically, and what developed instead were large plantations, owned by distant capitalist merchants or investors. The earliest sugar plantations were worked by both free and slave workers from many ethnic groups, but by the 1480s they were almost all black African slaves.

Columbus saw the possibilities of sugar first-hand when he lived on the island of Madeira, and he took sugar cane cuttings to the Caribbean on his second voyage. The first sugar mill in the western hemisphere was built in 1515 in what is now the Dominican Republic. Brazil also had the right kind of climate, and by the middle of the sixteenth century investors from all over Europe were setting up sugar plantations there. By 1600 Brazil was Europe's largest source of sugar, and sugar was becoming a normal part of many people's diets in Europe and among Europeans in the New World. Per capita consumption in England was several pounds per person per year, still tiny compared to modern sugar consumption (the United States has the world's largest per capita sugar consumption, at about 150 pounds a year), but much more than it had been earlier, when sugar was such a luxury that people thought of it more as a drug than a food. In some ways, sugar is a drug: it may not be physically addictive, but the human demand for sugar seems insatiable, as long as the price is low enough.

Slavery and shipping kept the price of sugar low. Sugar growers in the Caribbean and Brazil first tried to force native peoples to do the back-breaking labor that sugar demands. In the Caribbean, Spanish settlers (*encomenderos*) were given rights to compel native labor in the *encomienda* system, but the native peoples either died or ran away. Few Europeans were willing to wield machetes and haul cane in the hot sun for any amount of wages. The solution was the same one that had worked on the Atlantic islands: import enslaved Africans and set up huge plantations, where large numbers of workers supplied the sugar cane to keep complicated refining equipment running all the time. Slave traders from West and Central African coastal areas went further and further inland to capture, buy, or trade for more and more slaves. Some rulers tried to limit the slave trade in their areas, but others profited from it, and raiders paid little attention to regulations anyway. They encouraged warfare to provide captives, or just grabbed people from their houses and fields. The slave trade grew steadily, and first thousands and then tens of thousands of people a year were taken from Africa to work on sugar plantations. For 350 years after Columbus' voyage, more Africans crossed the Atlantic than Europeans; current estimates of the total are 10 to 12 million, with many more millions dying on the way. Thus, of all the products of the Columbian Exchange, sugar was (and perhaps still is) the most harmful.

The slave trade had dramatic effects in West and West Central Africa, encouraging warfare and destroying families and kinship groups. In these areas women produced the bulk of food, making female slaves often too valuable to sell. Thus two-thirds of the slaves exported to the New World were men and boys, while women were instead retained as farm workers (and wives). The transatlantic slave trade further enhanced women's share of food production, and also increased the trade in slaves within many parts of Africa. Slaves were also transported across the Indian Ocean, both into the Dutch Cape Colony from India, Southeast Asia, and Madagascar, and from East Africa to sugar and other plantations on islands in the Indian Ocean and even to Brazil. Free men and women, ex-slaves, and occasionally even people who were still slaves acted as slave traders in Africa and sometimes in the colonies, responding to the changing demands for labor as the extraction and production for various commodities shifted.

Slavery is not simply a method of organizing labor, but also a method through which a labor force can be reproduced. In Africa, the Muslim world, and Southeast Asia, enslaved women were often part of households, as secondary wives, concubines, or servants. They thus increased the wealth and power of their owner/husbands through their work and their children, although under Islamic law those children would be legally free, as the legal status of children followed that of their father. This was not the case in the slave societies of the Americas, where children inherited their "condition of servitude," as the law described it, from their mothers. In some parts of the Americas, reproduction was not of great concern to slave owners, who simply bought new slaves as others died. In Brazil, for example, conditions on sugar plantations were especially brutal and there were very few enslaved women, so many more slaves died than were born. Slave owners figured that most slaves

4.6 Enslaved workers carry out various steps of sugar processing in this seventeenth-century French engraving. Workers carry cane to the mill at the rear where an ox powers vertical rollers to crush it, juice flows to tanks in the boiling house center-left, and in the front a white overseer supervises.

would live about seven years and calculated the costs of buying new slaves into the price they hoped to get for their sugar. In North America, "natural increase" came to be more important than continued importation in increasing the slave population; of the millions of people who were taken from Africa to be slaves in the New World, only 5 percent went to North America. Evidence from Africa, the Caribbean, and North America suggests that enslaved women sometimes took steps to control their fertility, limiting childbirth through plants and other products that lessened fertility or caused miscarriages. Childbearing, along with agricultural labor, remained a central part of most enslaved women's lives, however, though the number of children who survived to adulthood varied greatly.

By itself, the slave trade did not bring spectacular profits, but the plantation system was an essential part of a capitalist business network that provided steadily increasing wealth for European merchants and investors, who also developed plantations to raise indigo, cotton, rice, tobacco, and other crops. Slavery was a part of many societies around the world in this era—as it had been earlier—but the plantation slavery of the New World was different because it had a racial element that other slave systems generally did not. By linking whiteness with freedom and blackness with slavery, the plantation system strengthened ideas about Africans held by many European Christians and Arabic Muslims, who saw them as inferior, barbaric, and primitive. Plantation owners came to think of their slaves more as machines than human beings; like machines, slaves would wear out and need replacing. Some Christian missionaries objected to this treatment, especially for slaves who had converted to Christianity, but other church leaders praised slavery, saying that although it might make people's lives on this earth worse, it gave them the opportunity of getting into heaven by becoming Christian, so in the long run they were better off.

RELIGIOUS TRANSFORMATIONS AND THEIR CONSEQUENCES

Religion served as a justification for slavery in the early modern period, and also as a justification—and motivation—for conflict and colonization. "God made me the messenger of the new heaven and the new earth of which he spoke in the Apocalypse of St. John," wrote Columbus, a destiny he saw as symbolized by his first name, Christofero, which means "Christ carrier" in Latin. Gold inspired more voyages and conquests than God, but religious aims shaped patterns of expansion and empire-building. This had long been true, but reforms and reinvigorations of existing religions and the creation of new faiths in the sixteenth century led to higher levels of religious zeal. These movements were begun and extended by individuals with a powerful sense of calling, who developed new spiritual practices they believed fit better with divine will. They ultimately gained many adherents because large numbers of people found their message persuasive, or because they saw social, economic, or political benefits in converting (or both). Converts included rulers, who often demanded their subjects adhere to the same religion and used religion as a reason for conquest.

Religious reformers and leaders set out certain duties as incumbent on a believer, often with distinctions between men and women. They viewed everyday activities and family life as opportunities for people to display spiritual and moral values, though at the same time criticized religious practices if they were done without the proper inward belief or faith. Once they were established, these new, reformed, or revitalized religions became part of inherited traditions, as children followed the faith of their parents.

Among these transformations, the splintering of Christianity in western Europe was the most dramatic, and brought the most violence. In the early sixteenth century, most people accepted the Christian church's teachings and found religious activities meaningful, but a significant minority called for reforms. They complained that the church, headed by the pope in Rome, was concerned more with wealth and power than with the spiritual needs of believers. In the 1520s, that group came to include Martin Luther (1483–1546), a professor of theology at Wittenberg University in Germany. Luther wrote and spoke against church teachings, and his ideas turned into a widespread movement that became known as the Protestant Reformation, in part through the new technology of the printing press. Together with Columbus' voyages, the Protestant Reformation has traditionally been seen as marking a sharp break with the past and the beginning of modernity—or at least early modernity—though, like Columbus, on many issues Luther does not seem very modern.

Luther's understanding of essential Christian doctrine, often codified as "faith alone, grace alone, Scripture alone," asserts that salvation comes through faith, which is itself an unmerited gift of God, and that God's word is revealed in Scripture, not in the traditions of the church. Luther translated the Bible into German, and he and other Protestant reformers rejected practices for which they did not see a biblical basis, including clerical celibacy, which Luther thought was a fruitless attempt to control a natural human drive and brought no spiritual benefits. Protestants proclaimed family life in which men were serious, responsible husbands and fathers and women loving, obedient wives and mothers as the ideal for all men and women, and regarded unmarried people of both sexes as suspect. Most Protestant areas came to allow divorce and remarriage for a limited range of reasons, although the actual divorce rate remained very low, as marriage created a social and economic unit that could not easily be broken apart.

The Protestant reformers worked with political authorities, and much of central Europe and Scandinavia broke with the Catholic Church and established independent Protestant churches. Rulers recognized that breaking with the Catholic Church would allow them to confiscate its land and other property, and give them authority over religion as well as other aspects of life. In England, the desire of King Henry VIII (r. 1509–47) for a male heir led him to split from the Catholic Church and establish a separate English church, actions which some people accepted willingly while others resisted. Protestant and Catholic political authorities all thought that their territories should have one official state church, but some individuals and groups rejected this idea, and thought that religious allegiance should be voluntary. These groups also developed ideas that were socially radical, with some calling for pacifism and others common ownership of property, so they were intensely persecuted and often forced to flee from one place to another. Peasants who used Lutheran ideas to justify their demands for social justice were also suppressed with force, a move that Luther supported. The Reformation brought with it more than a century of vicious religious war, beginning in Switzerland and Germany, then spreading to France and the Netherlands later in the sixteenth century.

In the late 1530s, the Catholic Church began to respond more vigorously to Protestant challenges and began carrying out internal reforms as well. Both of these moves were led by the papacy and new religious orders such as the Jesuits, begun by Ignatius Loyola (1491?–1556), a Spanish knight who also thought that Christianity was in trouble, but saw the solution as stricter obedience to the pope and existing practices, not a break from them. By the later sixteenth century, Roman Catholic Christianity was reinvigorated in what came to be called the Catholic Reformation, building stunning churches in which lavish decorations and shimmering frescoes reflected the new dynamic proselytizing spirit. At the same time, the ideas of John Calvin (1509–64) inspired a second wave of Protestant reform, in which order, piety, and discipline were viewed as marks of divine favor, similarly reflected in Calvinist church architecture, which featured white walls, plain windows, and no images. An emphasis on morality and social discipline emerged in Catholic areas as well, however, and authorities throughout Europe sought to teach people more about their particular variant of Christianity in a process historians have termed "confessionalization." This process of confessionalization and the enforcement of social discipline lasted well beyond the sixteenth century, as educating people and encouraging (or forcing) them to improve their behavior took far longer than either Protestant or Catholic reformers anticipated.

Both Protestant and Catholic authorities also arrested, tried, and executed individuals they judged to be heretics or in league with the devil, among whom were between 100,000 and 200,000 people tried for witchcraft. Between 40,000 and 60,000 people were executed for witchcraft in Europe during the sixteenth and seventeenth centuries, at least three-quarters of them women. Misogynist ideas, legal changes, social stresses, religious zeal, and concerns about order all combined into witch panics among learned and unlearned alike, which only abated when the same types of religious and legal authorities who had so vigorously persecuted witches decided that torture would not yield the truth, and that the devil would probably not turn to poor older women if he wanted help.

In the seventeenth century, Calvinist-inspired Protestantism combined with social, political, and economic grievances in England and led to civil war. Some members of the lower-level nobility—usually termed "gentry"—and many urban residents wanted to "purify" the English state church of what they saw as vestiges of Catholicism. These "Puritans," as they came to be known, included members of parliament, the national representative body that had the authority to raise taxes and that opposed an expansion of royal power. Parliament called for legal and religious changes, both it and King Charles I recruited armies, and open fighting began in 1642. Parliament and its army were controlled by a charismatic military leader, Oliver Cromwell (1599–1658), who turned the army into a formidable fighting force and political institution. The army captured and executed the king, to the horror of many English people and monarchs everywhere. Cromwell, who saw himself as called by God, ruled by what was effectively martial law and attempted to maintain order and control in a situation where individuals and groups were promoting (or at least discussing) radical social change, such as communal ownership of property. With Cromwell's death, factions were divided about what to do next, and Parliament backed the restoration of the monarchy in 1660. It was unwilling to see the return of Catholicism, however, so when the restored dynasty became Catholic, Parliament offered the throne instead in 1688 to the Protestant sister of the ruling Catholic king, and her husband a Dutch prince, the joint monarchs William and Mary. This coup, bloodless in England though not in Scotland and Ireland, and later called the "Glorious Revolution," affirmed the power of Parliament even though England was technically a monarchy. It also assured the power of the gentry, that 2 percent of the population perched socially between the tiny group of high nobles and the rest of the population, who along with merchants and professionals who often married into gentry families controlled England's policies and institutions into the twentieth century.

Christianity was not the only religious tradition in which politics and religion became closely intertwined, or in which this led to violence. In 1500, Ismail (1487–1524), a teenager who was the hereditary leader of the Safavid Sufi brotherhood, began assembling an army, asserting power, and conquering territory. He proclaimed himself ruler, or shah, and declared that his subjects would from that point on all accept Shi'a Islam, in a variant known as Twelver. Twelver Shi'a holds that the twelfth and final infallible imam after Ali (Muhammad's cousin and son-in-law) did not die, but went into hiding to escape persecution and will one day return and take over proper religious authority. Many of Shah Ismail's followers, who included large numbers of nomadic Turks, shared these messianic hopes and viewed him as the hidden imam, so they fiercely supported his decisions. Ismail and his successors enforced Shi'ite beliefs through force and through learning. They persecuted Sunni Muslims, many of whom fled to the Ottoman Empire, but also brought in Shi'ite scholars from elsewhere in the Muslim world, who established schools and other institutions. Afghan forces invading from the east ended the Safavid dynasty in the middle of the eighteenth century, but Shi'a religious institutions and leaders grew stronger. Today Iran is the only Muslim state in which Shi'a Islam is the official religion.

As the Safavids were expanding their empire and enforcing Shi'ite conformity, Guru Nanak (1469–1538), a spiritual teacher living in the Punjab area of what is now the India–Pakistan border, added his own insights to elements of Hinduism, Islam, and other traditions to found what was later called Sikhism, a word taken from the Sanskrit word for "learner" or "disciple." His revelations centered on the absolute unity and majesty of God. God is—in words often repeated in Nanak's writings—unseen, infinite, formless, ineffable, and eternal. Salvation can come once one recognizes complete dependency on God, who bestows unmerited grace, an idea that parallels those of Protestants. Nanak emphasized that proper devotional discipline could be done by people living in families and involved with the ordinary things of the world. In fact, service to others was an important part of spiritual life and living in the world with a family was spiritually superior to renouncing family ties, a position very different from that of most Hindu teachers of Nanak's time.

Turning to God is difficult for humans to do alone, Nanak asserted, and in this they often need a teacher, or guru. In Nanak's writings, the word guru usually means the voice of God itself, akin to the Holy Spirit in Christian theology, but gradually it came to be applied to the series of men succeeding Nanak who built on his teachings and transformed his followers into a community. His followers spread the Sikh message, and both Hindus and Muslims converted, though converts included significantly more Hindus. The third Sikh guru, Amar Das (guruship 1552–1574), set up a system for overseeing believers and local leaders, and developed rituals and ceremonies for major life changes, including birth, marriage, and death. The fifth guru, Arjan Dev (guruship 1581–1606) compiled a collection of Sikh sacred writings, the Adi Granth ("first book"), which consists primarily of hymns and prayers written by the gurus to direct believers in their devotions. The Adi Granth contains the writings of Nanak, written in Punjabi, a language spoken in northwestern India, rather than in Sanskrit, the language of the ancient Hindu texts. Like the Protestant reformers who were preaching and translating the Bible in Europe at the same time, Nanak thought it was important that people who were not members of the educated elite have access to religious texts.

During Nanak's lifetime and for several decades afterward, the Sikh community was too small to be viewed with much concern by local Mughal authorities, who regarded Sikhs as simply yet another variety of Hindus or as one of the many movements that blended various traditions common in northern India. By the early seventeenth century this had changed, and intense conflict often erupted. Most later Sikh gurus were military as well as spiritual leaders, but they continued to emphasize that external practices without inner devotion are useless.

Religion and politics were also closely interconnected in Tibet, where nobles along with large Buddhist monasteries were the major landowners. During the Ming dynasty that ruled China after the ousting of the Mongols in the fourteenth century, there were diplomatic relations between Tibetan Buddhist leaders (*lamas*) and both the Chinese imperial government and the Mongols. The monasteries of Tibet followed various schools of Buddhist thought, which vied with one another and sometimes called on Mongol military leaders for assistance against their rivals or against attacks from outside Tibet. In the 1570s, Sonam Gyatso (1543–88), the leader of the quite new Gelug-pa school founded in the early fifteenth century, declared that Altan Khan, the major Mongol lord of the time, was a reincarnation of Khubilai Khan. Altan Khan in turn granted Sonam Gyatso the title "Cosmic Ocean lama," or Dalai Lama, and declared Tibetan Buddhism to be the official religion of the Mongols. The position of Dalai Lama was understood to be handed down through successive reincarnation, and ties between the Tibetans and Mongols were strengthened when at Sonam Gyatso's death divinations and oracles showed that the next Dalai Lama was a great-grandson of Altan Khan. Not all Tibetans were happy with a non-Tibetan Dalai Lama, there was civil war, and he died under mysterious circumstances, but the fifth Dalai Lama, Ngawang Lobsang Gyatso (1617–82) unified Tibet with the assistance of Mongol armies and became its political as well as spiritual leader. Intrigue, civil war, rebellions, and complex foreign relations involving the Manchu Qings, the Mongols, various Central Asian states, Himalayan kingdoms, and eventually European powers continued, but gradually the moral and spiritual authority of the Dalai Lama was accepted by most Tibetan Buddhists. Many of them want the current Dalai Lama, Tenzin Gyatso (1935–)—who fled Tibet in 1949 when the Chinese asserted control and now lives in exile—to have political authority as well.

In the periods in which Tibet was independent, religious and secular authority were fused, which was true for some other early modern states as well. In many more, including every Christian state in Europe, most Catholic colonies, most Muslim states, and initially most British colonies in North America, there was an official religion. Rulers and officials in these places thought it essential that everyone living within their territory follow the same religious tradition, or at least outwardly conform and not engage in practices that clearly aligned them with a tradition the ruler viewed as unacceptable. Those who defied such laws risked penalties imposed by secular political authorities, not simply by religious officials, which could range from fines and confiscation of property to gruesome executions. Those whose religion differed from that of the majority also faced mob violence, which authorities rarely controlled.

There are many examples of religious persecution and religiously inspired violence. In 1492, the armies of King Ferdinand of Aragon and Queen Isabella of Castile conquered Granada, the last Muslim state in the Iberian peninsula, and decided to further enhance religious uniformity by ordering all Jews who had not converted to leave Spain. (Columbus received the support he had been seeking for his voyage from Queen Isabella several weeks later, after he promised to use the wealth gained by the trip to recapture Jerusalem from the Muslims.) About 200,000 Jews left Spain, many to the more tolerant Ottoman Empire, but at the same time Jews who lived in some North African oasis cities were killed by Muslims and their synagogues burned down. The Sunni Muslim Ottomans were relatively tolerant of Jews and Christians, but they arrested and charged people observed performing Shi'ite rituals, accusing them of being sympathizers of the Shi'ite Safavids, with whom they were often at war; conversely, as we have seen, Sunni Muslims were persecuted in the Safavid Empire. In Japan, peasants protesting oppressive taxes revolted on the peninsula of Shimabara on the southern island of Kyushu in 1637–38. Many of the peasants were Christian, and all of them, including women and children, were executed by a huge force sent by the central government, which increasingly viewed Christianity as a threat. Japan had absorbed and blended Confucianism, Daoism, and Buddhism with its own indigenous religious traditions, but Christianity, which demanded sole allegiance and had been introduced by European missionaries, was not to become part of this mixture. Missionaries were expelled, Japanese Christians were tortured and executed, and Christianity in Japan became an underground religion of "hidden Christians" (*Kakure Kirishitan*) in remote fishing and farming villages, in which lay leaders secretly taught and baptized, and people married within the group.

Some rulers and political authorities chose not to enforce specific religious practices. The Manchu Qing patronized Tibetan Buddhism as well as Chinese Confucianism, and allowed Christian missionaries to teach and preach in Beijing and other cities. In the Mughal Empire, the emperor Akbar (r. 1556–1605) built a special building where Muslims, Hindus, Christians, Zoroastrians, Sikhs, and scholars of other faiths could discuss their beliefs and practices. A religious innovator himself, he later developed what he termed the "Divine Faith" that combined ideas and rituals from many religions, although it did not spread much beyond the court or last after his lifetime.

4.7 Scholars from many faiths, including Jesuit priests dressed in black, gather at Akbar's court, in this 1605 illustration by the Sikh artist Nan Singh, from the official history of Akbar's reign. Outside the wall are beggars holding a food bowl and a groom with horses.

Long-distance trade often brought people with different religious traditions together in port cities or other commercial centers, where they lived side by side or even intermarried, creating households that were mixed religiously as well as ethnically. Political authorities seeking to support mercantile ventures and increase the wealth of their territory allowed religious diversity, a strategy that worked well. The Dutch Republic, for example, became prosperous in the seventeenth century in part because of its religious toleration. Jews fleeing the Iberian peninsula, French Protestants seeking refuge from religious wars, and religious radicals from all over Europe settled in Amsterdam and other Dutch cities, where they worshipped openly and established shops and businesses. This diversity in religious ideas created an atmosphere in which new scientific, philosophical, and technical ideas spread as well.

Visitors to places where there was religious toleration often remarked on how unusual this was, however. Rulers of the Ayuthia kingdom of Siam, for example, were strong supporters of Theravada Buddhism, but European traders commented with surprise that Christian and Muslim merchants were always welcome and there was no attempt to convert them. This changed, however, when the Siamese learned that French officials and missionaries were plotting to convert King Narai (r. 1656–88) to Christianity and bring in French troops; they expelled all French and became less open to European merchants in general.

THE EXPANSION AND CREOLIZATION OF CHRISTIANITY

Siam was only one of many places where Christian missionaries and colonial officials attempted to convert a local ruler, for the Reformation in Europe was accompanied by the expansion of Catholic Christianity around the world, a process in which members of new religious orders such as the Jesuits were particularly active. The colonial forces of Spain and Portugal, and later those of France, included Catholic missionaries who worked to convert indigenous people and to establish churches and church institutions for immigrants. They built simple churches and opulent cathedrals, opened monasteries and convents, and extended the system of church courts that handled marriage and morals issues as well as doctrinal ones.

Missionaries also traveled beyond European colonies, although only in Japan and the kingdom of the Kongo did they gain significant numbers of converts. Protestant colonists also included a few clergy who preached to indigenous people, but these were far fewer than among Catholics; intensive missionary work by Protestants would begin in the nineteenth century, with the second wave of European imperialism. Missionaries initially preached to indigenous people in European languages, which few understood, and some missionaries began to learn native languages. Following a pattern that had allowed Christianity to spread in Europe, they often first converted rulers and other members of the elite, hoping they would convince more ordinary people to convert as well.

In the Americas, some missionaries were idealistic, seeing the New World as a place to plant Christianity anew, away from what they saw as the hopeless corruption of European culture. Indigenous religion would also have to be destroyed, however. Ceremonies were banned, religious statuary and objects smashed, temples and other sacred buildings pulled down, and Catholic shrines or churches erected on the same sites. Books were burned by soldiers, officials, and clergy, who could not read them but still considered them "picture-books of the Devil." Along with explaining concepts central to Christianity, missionaries also attempted to persuade—or force—possible converts to adopt Catholic practices of marriage, sexual morality, and day-to-day behavior. Once one was baptized, following Christian patterns in terms of marriage and personal demeanor became a more important sign of conversion than understanding the Trinity or other aspects of Christian doctrine. The same pattern was followed in the Philippines, where the colonial government in Manila gave missionaries great authority. Priests collected taxes and arranged for the selling of crops, and the church became wealthy. In some parts of the Americas and in the Philippines, clergy moved indigenous people into compact villages or towns (termed *reducciones*) for conversion, taxpaying, and cultural assimilation.

Many people resisted Christian teachings and continued to follow their original spiritual practices. In some areas, such as the Andes of South America and the Philippines, women had been important leaders in animistic religions, and they were stronger opponents of conversion than were men; this pattern was enhanced by male missionaries' focus on boys and young men in their initial conversion efforts. Far more people became Christian, however, including women, who sometimes became fervent in their devotions or used priests and church courts to oppose their husbands or other male family members on matters of inheritance or the marriage of children.

The process of conversion used to be described by scholars as a "spiritual conquest," in which indigenous beliefs and practices were largely wiped out through force and persuasion. The spread of Catholic Christianity is now viewed differently, not simply as conquest and resistance—though it was that—but as a process of cultural negotiation and synthesis, during which Christian ideas and practices were selectively adopted, mixed with existing practices, and openly, unknowingly, or surreptitiously rejected, just as they had been when Christianity spread to Greeks and Germanic peoples in Europe. Scholars often refer to this process as "creolization," taking this word from *Crioulo*, the mixture of Portuguese and African languages spoken first in the Atlantic islands. In the Kongo, for example, King Afonso I (r. 1509–1543) supported the development of Christian teachings and practices that blended elements of the existing Kongolese religion with those taught by Portuguese missionaries. Toward the end of the seventeenth century, a religious visionary and reformer, Dona Beatriz Kimpa Vita, went further, saying that the Virgin Mary and many of the saints were Kongolese and she herself was an incarnation of Saint Anthony.

Creolization included the creation of new social and marital patterns. Although officials tried to impose European Catholic patterns—monogamous marriage, male-headed households, limited (or no) divorce—where these conflicted with existing patterns they were often modified and what emerged was a mixture of local and imported practices. The prominent men who missionaries most hoped to convert often had multiple wives and concubines, and missionaries argued about whether they had to give up all but one before Christian baptism, or whether Christian practice would (they hoped) follow baptism. In China the debate centered on rituals venerating ancestors—were these traditional family customs or pagan worship of minor deities?—and on priests touching women on their bare skin during baptism, especially as this involved the priest's saliva along with salt, oil, and water.

Cultural synthesis happened everywhere and involved many aspects of Christianity, but the Virgin of Guadalupe can serve as a good example, particularly because she became so important and also so controversial. In the seventeenth century, published texts in Spanish and Nahuatl told of the appearance of the Virgin Mary in 1531 to Juan Diego Cuauhtlatoatzin, an indigenous farmer and Christian convert, on a hill near Tenochtitlan (now within Mexico City). Speaking in Nahuatl, the apparition told Juan Diego that a church should be built at this site, and her image miraculously appeared on his cloak. Shortly afterward a church dedicated to the Virgin of Guadalupe was begun, named after a monastery in Spain where various miracles associated with the Virgin Mary had been reported, including some involving Christian defeats of Muslim forces. The Mexican Virgin of Guadalupe soon far outstripped her Spanish counterpart in significance. Preachers and teachers interpreted her appearance as a sign of the Virgin's special protection of indigenous people and those of mixed ancestry (*mestizos*), and pilgrims from all over Mexico began to make the trek to her shrine (see Figure 4.8). The Virgin of Guadalupe was made patron of New Spain in 1746 and her banner was carried by soldiers in the Mexican War of Independence in 1810 and in the Mexican Revolution of 1910.

In the twentieth century, however, many scholars, including some members of the Mexican clergy, came to doubt whether the apparition had ever happened or Juan Diego himself had even existed. They pointed out that written accounts were not published until over a century later, and that church officials and missionaries active in central Mexico in 1531 made no mention of the event or of Juan Diego. Specialists in Nahuatl culture note that the hill where the apparition was reported was originally the site of a shrine to Coatlicue, the mother of the most powerful Aztec god Huitzilopochtli, and that aspects of the veneration of the Virgin of Guadalupe were also part of honoring Coatlicue or other Aztec mother goddesses. In their view, the colonial Catholic Church had simply invented the story as part of its efforts to strip Aztec holy sites of their original meaning. The Catholic Church has addressed these doubts resoundingly, declaring Guadalupe the patron of the whole American hemisphere in 1999 and raising Juan Diego to a saint in 2002; he was the first fully indigenous American to be canonized. Many Mexicans have interpreted this canonization, like the Virgin of Guadalupe herself, as a symbol of the place of their heritage within the Catholic Church, while others view Juan Diego and Guadalupe as symbols of the destruction of indigenous culture. Certain recent portrayals of Guadalupe, such as those of the Chicana artist Alma Lopez who depicts her dressed only in strands of roses, have been denounced, but Lopez and other artists have justified their work, noting that through the centuries people have interpreted Guadalupe in whatever way they thought most empowering. The Virgin of Guadalupe, they argue, began as a symbol with multiple meanings, and they are simply continuing the tradition of synthesis that started with the first conversions in the New World.

FAMILIES AND RACE IN THE COLONIAL WORLD

The process of mixture and creolization that marked the early modern world involved people themselves as well as their ideas and practices. Every trade venture, willing or coerced migration, conquest, or any other sort of travel brought individuals who thought of themselves as belonging to different groups together. Despite norms prescribing group endogamy, there were sexual relationships, many of which produced children. Like everything else, the scale of this mixture increased in the early modern period, when the movement of people across vast distances increased dramatically.

As we have seen in earlier chapters, from a very early point in history people developed concepts about human groups—particularly their own—based on real or perceived kinship and shared culture. They used a variety of words to describe these groups; in English these include tribe, people, ethnicity, background, race, and nation. The group was created and maintained by intermarriage, and membership in it was understood to be contained in and passed down through the blood. Religion was also sometimes conceptualized as blood, with people regarded as having Jewish, Muslim, or Christian blood, and after the Reformation Protestant or Catholic blood. European fathers choosing a wetnurse for their children took care to make sure she was of the same denomination, lest, if he was a Catholic, her Protestant blood turn into Protestant milk (the two bodily fluids were seen as fungible) and thus infect the child with heretical ideas.

Describing differences as blood naturalized them, making them appear as if they were created by God in nature, but people often held contradictory ideas about this. Thus the same religious reformers who warned against choosing the wrong wetnurse also worked for conversions, and did not think about whether adopting a new religion would also change a woman's milk. Catholic authorities in colonial areas limited entrance to certain convents to "pure-blooded" white or native women, thus excluding women of mixed background, but were more willing to allow a light-skinned *mestizo* than a "full-blooded" native marry a white person. Such contradictions did not generally lessen people's convictions about the reality of differences and hierarchies, however, and authorities had to decide how to deal with the situation.

In China, the Manchu Qing rulers who assumed power in the seventeenth century initially encouraged Manchu/Han marriages as a way of blending the two cultures, but in 1655 reversed course and forbade them, enforcing this by requiring bannermen to live in separate walled quarters of Chinese cities. There were very few marriages, although Manchu bannermen did buy Han Chinese women as concubines and servants, so there were certainly children.

In the Americas, the Spanish and Portuguese crown first hoped to avoid such relationships by keeping groups—Europeans, Africans, and indigenous peoples—apart. The gender balance among both European and African immigrants made this impossible, and authorities quickly gave up, but they still thought it necessary that people be divided into categories. With each generation, the varieties of possible mixture proliferated, and the response of colonial authorities was to create an even more complex system of categories for persons of mixed ancestry, which were called *castas*. The Catholic Church and Spanish and Portuguese officials defined as many as forty different categories and combinations that were in theory based on place of birth, assumed geographic origin, and the status of one's mother, with a specific name for each one. The various castas and the relationships among them were clearly delineated in treatises and by the eighteenth century in paintings that showed scenes of parents of different castas and the children such parents produced: *India* + Spaniard = *Mestizo*; *India* + *Negro* = *Lobo; Chamiza* + *Cambuja* = *Chino*, and so on. Some of these castas had fanciful names, or ones derived from animals, such as *coyote* or *lobo* (wolf). The casta system built on earlier Iberian notions of "purity of blood," in which descendants of Muslim and Jewish converts to Christianity were viewed as tainted, because their religious allegiance was carried in their blood. In the Latin American colonies, people of indigenous and African ancestry both had lower rank than did those of European ancestry, with blood that was viewed as less pure. New laws passed after 1763 in the French Caribbean colonies set out a similar system, with various categories based on the supposed origin of one's ancestors.

Determining the proper casta in which to place actual people was not as easy as setting these out in theory or in paintings, however. In practice, whether one was a "mestizo" or "mulatto" or "caboclo" or another category was to a large extent determined by how one looked, with lighter-skinned mixed-ancestry persons accorded a higher rank than darker ones, even if they were siblings. Many historians have thus termed the social structure that developed in colonial Spanish and Portuguese America, including the Caribbean (and later in the French Caribbean), a "pigmentocracy" based largely on skin color, but also on facial features and hair texture. Because what category one was in determined one's ability to marry or inherit, enter a convent or the priesthood, attend university, live in certain places, or have access to other advantages, individuals not only passed as members of a higher group, but bought licenses to be considered descendants of Europeans, regardless of their particular ethnic appearance and ancestry. In addition, individuals might define themselves, or be defined, as belonging to different categories at different points in their life, in what scholars have called a "racial drift" toward whiteness.

The granting of honorary whiteness and the difficulty of assigning people to castas points out just how subjective this entire system was, but it was the essential determinant of family life and gender norms in Latin America. For members of the white European elite,

4.8 The Mexican artist Luis de Mena combines a still life, casta painting, and devotional image of the Virgin of Guadalupe on a single canvas, painted about 1750. The racial mixtures he portrays include ones that would have been rare or non-existent, such as that at the upper left showing a light-skinned woman in an elaborate European dress and an indigenous man in a loincloth.

the concern about bloodlines and skin color created a pattern of intermarriage within the extended family, with older women identifying the distant cousins that were favored as spouses. Following the southern European pattern, these marriages were often between an older man and a younger woman, which limited the number of potential spouses for women, and many never married. Most elite men married, and they often also had children by slaves or servants who were part of their household. Rural native people also married most often within their own group, with the extended family exerting control over choice of spouses just as it did for elite whites. For slaves, many persons of mixed ancestry, and poor people of all types, family and property considerations did not enter into marital considerations, and in most cases people simply did not get married at all, though in many cases they did establish long-term unions regarded by their neighbors and friends as stable.

In the European colonies that were established in the seventeenth and eighteenth centuries, patterns were different from those of Latin America and from each other. French authorities, and those of the Dutch and English East India Companies, initially encouraged sexual relations and even marriage between European men and indigenous women as a means of making alliances, cementing their power, and spreading Christianity. In the Dutch East Indies soldiers, merchants, and minor officials married local women, and in French North America fur traders did as well. Attitudes toward this began to change as more European women moved to the colonies, and as it became clear that cultural transformation often went in the other direction, with European men "going native" instead of local women becoming French or Dutch. Hesitation about intermarriage also came from the other side: in much of West Africa, Portuguese men were not allowed to marry local women of free standing, as this would give them claims to land use, while in India, high-caste families were not interested in marrying their daughters to the type of European men usually found in the colonies. In any case, the number of European men in many colonies was small, so European rule did not disrupt existing family patterns to a great extent, and they continued to be shaped by existing social and cultural traditions. In Southeast Asia, these included temporary marriages in which women married men from outside their group in order to create connections and networks of obligations. Merchants from far away had been linked to local families through such marriages for centuries; they ended if the man returned home, but they were marriage, not concubinage or something less formal.

At the same time that the Dutch and English East India Companies tolerated or even encouraged intermarriage, Dutch and British colonies in North America forbade it, with laws that first regulated sexual relations between Europeans and Africans and were then extended to Native Americans. In 1638, the Dutch colony of New Amsterdam forbade fornication (sex outside of marriage) between "Christians" and "Negroes," and in 1662 the Virginia Assembly set double the normal fine for fornication involving people from these two groups. In the very same sentence, the Virginia law declares that "children got by any Englishman upon a negro woman ... shall be held bond or free only according to the condition of the mother." The law makes no distinction for married couples, so reverses normal English practice, in which the legal status of children born in a marriage followed the father, and contrasts with Islamic law, in which the children of free fathers were free. Thus laws about mixing in North America were determined by slavery from the very beginning. A 1691 Virginia law closed any marriage loophole, flatly forbidding marriage between an "English or other white man or woman", and a "negroe, mulatto, or Indian man or woman," with a punishment of banishment. Though such laws were usually gender-neutral, what lawmakers were most worried about was, as the preamble to the Virginia law states: "negroes, mulattoes, and Indians intermarrying with English, or other white women" and the resultant "abominable mixture and spurious issue." Such laws were passed in all the southern colonies in North America and also in Pennsylvania and Massachusetts between 1700 and 1750. (They were struck down by the US Supreme Court in 1967, but remained on the books in some states for decades after that; the last of such "miscegenation" laws was rescinded by Alabama voters in a statewide referendum in 2000.)

The relatively large number of women among European settlers and the declining number of indigenous women in coastal areas where settlements were located meant that marriages or even long-term sexual relationships between white men and indigenous women were rare in the British North American colonies. Government policy toward Native Americans, which increasingly removed them from their original homelands and by the nineteenth century ordered them to live on reservations, disrupted family life along with every other aspect of indigenous society, though extended kin groups retained some voice wherever they could. White families, especially in the north, tended to follow the northwestern European model, with late marriage and a high proportion of people who never married.

Most people of African descent in North America were slaves until the middle of the nineteenth century. Only in New England were marriages between slaves legally recognized, although, as in Latin America, long-term family relationships developed among enslaved people, though these could be easily broken up by the decision of a slave owner. As the slave population in southern colonies increased, sexual relations between white men and black women did as well. White men's fathering of children with their slaves was not recognized legally and rarely spoken about publicly in polite society, though this was so common over generations that by the nineteenth century a large part of the North American slave population was mixed. In contrast to the hierarchy of categories found in Spanish, Portuguese, and French colonies, however, the British North American colonies and later the United States developed a dichotomous system, in which in theory one drop of "black blood" made one black, though in practice lighter-skinned mixed-ancestry individuals may have passed over without notice into the white world.

Laws and norms about sexual relations, and the family patterns that resulted from these, were shaped by changing ideas about the differences between human groups. The Spanish system was roughly based on continent of origin, a schema that was later adopted by European scientists, including the Swedish naturalist and explorer Carl Linnaeus (1707–78), who set down the rules that are still used for naming and classifying all living organisms. Linnaeus classified humans into Americanus, Europaeus, Asiaticus, and Africanus, based on the continents then known, and also on skin color and what he saw as dominant temperament and behavior. Colonial powers also increasingly used skin color. The first New Amsterdam and Virginia laws prohibiting sexual relations mentioned above, for example, distinguished between "christian" and "negroe," but by 1691 Virginia distinguished between "white" men and women and those who were "negroe, mulatto, or Indian." In its use of "white," Virginia picked up language first used in a 1661 census in the British West Indies, and later this language spread throughout the British colonies. Other color designations came later, and in the eighteenth century European natural scientists seeking to develop one single system that would explain human differences settled on the concept of "race" to describe these, with the German Enlightenment philosopher Immanuel Kant outlining these in *Of the Different Human Races* (1775). Intellectual historians disagree about exactly who was the first to use the word "race" in its modern meaning, but Kant is one candidate, and "race" became the primary term for discussing human variety in the nineteenth century and beyond. Today biologists and others who study the human species as a whole avoid using "race," as it has no scientific meaning, but, like Vespucci's labeling of "America," it is an incorrect idea that has stuck.

SOCIAL PROTESTS, REVOLTS, AND REVOLUTIONS

Capitalist enterprises, global trade networks, and colonization made some families and individuals fabulously wealthy—Jacob Fugger is not the only one to acquire the nickname "the rich" in this era—but they were also disruptive. Long-distance trade that brought in foreign goods profited individual merchants and lowered prices for consumers, but also put local artisans at risk, as did larger-scale local production organized by capitalist entrepreneurs through which goods were produced more cheaply. Capitalism thus spawned a variety of social protests. Fugger, for example, established a monopoly of silver and copper mining in Tirol, Hungary and Slovakia, employing thousands of workers, including men who worked underground and their wives, sisters, and children who broke the ore apart and washed it. In 1525, miners discontented with their shrinking wages in an era of rising prices rioted and attacked company officials. Fugger brought in cannon cast from the copper in his mines, defeated the workers, and had their leaders arrested and executed. In England, enclosure and sometimes even the rumor of impending enclosure sparked protests, threats, and occasionally riots.

Famines and food shortages were also important causes for riots and other types of social protests, which numbered in the thousands over the early modern era. Many of these occurred in the countryside, where most people lived. During years with poor harvests, rural crowds tried to prevent grain from being taken away to nearby cities by blocking roads or waterways. This happened in the regions that supplied London in the 1630s and those that supplied Rome in the 1640s; in the latter instance, crowds grew so violent that they killed the local papal governor and burned down his residence. Social protests in cities often centered on food prices. In 1775, a year with crop failures in many parts of France, crowds protesting rising prices gathered in hundreds of towns. They seized wheat, flour, and bread, sometimes for their own use and sometimes to force sales at prices they thought were "just"—that is, lower—what was known as the *taxation populaire*. These violent actions, later called the Flour War, were eventually put down only when the French monarchy brought in troops. In 1787, a year of famine in Japan, poor people in Edo destroyed stores and took rice that was being sold at high prices or dumped it on the ground; in response the government arrested day laborers who did not have families in the city and transported them to work in gold mines, where most died.

Resistance to moves by landlords or the government could also be less dramatic than a riot or revolt. The political scientist James C. Scott has pointed out that foot-dragging, pilfering small amounts of goods, arson, desertion, feigned ignorance, and sabotage are all "weapons of the weak," used by poor people against elites or the state. These do not leave as many traces in the sources as do violent forms of social protest, but we begin to find evidence of them in the early modern period, which allows us to see how ordinary people attempted to shape their own circumstances in a time of rapid social and economic change.

Food and bread riots in Europe were often instigated and led by women, who saw assuring food for their families as part of their role as mothers, but engaged in actions that were not generally viewed as feminine, including shouting, beating drums, carrying weapons, and throwing stones. The women who led such riots were generally older, with reputations for strength and connections to other women in their neighborhoods. Authorities were sometimes more hesitant to use force against women than men, which led in a few cases to men in food riots dressing up as women. Women also participated in other types of popular collective actions and rebellions, but this threatened male authorities and the response could be particularly brutal. For example, English men were horrified at Irish women's support of revolts against English rule in Ireland in the sixteenth century, and saw women's influence over their husbands as yet another sign of Irish inferiority, along with their Catholic religion and "barbarous and brutish" customs. English military actions against the Irish were specifically directed at women as well as men, and included scorched-earth tactics that destroyed crops and villages. Women were not immune from reprisals elsewhere, either. In Japan, women (and children) as well as men were executed as part of the government's response to the Shimabara Revolt of 1637–38. This depopulated the Shimabara peninsula, so the central government gave the land to loyal followers and brought in immigrants from other parts of Japan to farm it.

An increase in rents, government measures to impose new or higher taxes, and the billeting of troops also sparked riots and full-fledged revolts. In southern China, for example, a series of crop failures in the 1560s and again in the 1640s led to attacks on landlords, refusal to pay taxes and rents, an increase in what officials called "roving bandits" who roamed the streets and waterways, and a series of peasant rebellions. These culminated in the capture of Beijing by a coalition of rebel forces led by Li Zicheng and the end of the Ming dynasty in 1644, although the rebels themselves were defeated by Manchu forces several months later and the new Qing dynasty was installed. Government orders requiring troops to be housed and fed by villagers led in 1640 to revolts in Catalonia in northern Iberia and Ulster in northern Ireland. Colonial Mexico experienced hundreds of village riots in the eighteenth century, and changes in Spanish tax policies in the late eighteenth century provoked revolts in northern South America.

In the last decades of the eighteenth century, a series of revolts in the Atlantic world became full-fledged revolutions that ousted or toppled governments. Their leaders were inspired by Enlightenment ideas about freedom, liberty, and rights that circulated in all directions from the new institutions of the public sphere, and also by social conditions and the existing governments' inability to handle economic crises. In political terms they represent a distinct break—some would see the Atlantic revolutions as creating the modern political world—but in many ways they fit with existing patterns of social protest.

In North America, British colonists angry about tax increases and changes in the tea and tobacco trade revolted and declared their independence in 1776, with speeches and documents proclaiming ideals of liberty and equality. They created new ideals of patriotic manliness, telling and retelling stories about freedom-seeking colonists in simple shirts and buckskin jackets shooting from behind trees, while British "redcoats" and German mercenaries stupidly stood in straight lines. (From the British perspective, the colonists were ungrateful vandals and tax-dodgers and the British soldiers models of appropriate military discipline.) France and later Spain and the Netherlands entered the American Revolution on the side of the colonists. Fighting took place in the Caribbean and India as well as North America, which limited British ability to hold territory after military victories or to provide needed supplies. British willingness to engage in harsh repression as they had in Ireland and later would elsewhere was limited by the fact that revolutionaries and loyalists came from the same communities—and sometimes the same families—and that neither ethnicity nor religion separated one side from the other. Disease also played a key role: outbreaks of smallpox convinced General George Washington (1732–99) to have new soldiers into his army inoculated using variolation techniques, thus protecting them. British troops remained vulnerable to diseases, especially malaria, which they contracted when they moved into southern colonies, leaving many too weak to fight. In 1781 British troops under General Cornwallis surrendered at Yorktown, Virginia to a combined American and French army, which was both twice as large and healthier. Two years later Britain recognized the independence of the thirteen British North American colonies that had revolted. Illnesses brought from the Old World as part of the Columbian Exchange shaped conflicts in the New World even when most of those fighting were Old World natives or their descendants.

In France, the enormous expenses of the American Revolution further endebted the government, forcing King Louis XVI (r. 1774–92) in 1789 to call the national representative body, the

Estates General, to try and reform the tax code to prevent bankruptcy. Many middle-class representatives viewed the fact that nobles and clergy held the most power in the way the Estates General voted as outdated, however. They formed a new National Assembly, which the king planned to dissolve by force. But the harvest of 1788 had been meager, so bread prices soared, many people were out of work, and riots broke out in many towns. The most dramatic of these riots was in Paris, where on July 14, 1789 crowds of men and women stormed the Bastille, a fortress and prison in the center of the city, looking for weapons with which to oppose the king. At the same time, peasants in the countryside ransacked the houses of their noble landlords, burned documents that recorded their taxes and dues, and reoccupied common land that had been enclosed. The National Assembly lifted the dues peasants owed to the nobility, and issued a stirring Declaration of the Rights of Man and the Citizen, but it could do little to solve the food or financial crises. In October thousands of women armed with pikes and sticks marched from Paris to the royal palace at Versailles, demanding the king and his family return to Paris. The king vacillated and the Revolution grew increasingly radical. Leaders ousted the king and then executed him and his wife, sent armies against Austria and Prussia, and declared the country a republic in which all men over twenty-one could vote. Women had been active in the Revolution, drafting official grievance lists and forming their own political groups as well as engaging in protests, but the politicization of women shocked both conservatives and revolutionaries, and none of the various constitutions drafted during the Revolution allowed women to vote, though they did allow women some civil rights, such as divorce and property ownership. (These were later rescinded when Napoleon came to power.)

The working poor in Paris, known as the *sans-culottes* ("without knee-breeches") because the men among them wore long pants rather than the knee-breeches of the wealthy, demanded radical action that would guarantee food. As in the American War of Independence, the revolutionaries were seen in contradictory ways: as hard-working people seeking food for their children, or as bloodthirsty fiends shouting "Long live the guillotine!" The government fixed the price of bread in Paris at a point people could afford, and mobilized human and material resources to fight France's enemies by building up a sense of patriotic mission and revolutionary virtue. It also imprisoned and killed its enemies in a Reign of Terror, which in 1794 provoked a reaction; the new middle-class leaders rejected the radicalism of the *sans-culottes*, restricted local political organizations, brought in the army to quell protests, and limited male voting rights. The king was gone, but hunger remained.

In Latin America and the Caribbean, repression of indigenous people and slaves along with social inequality and the spread of new ideals of liberty also led to revolts. By the eighteenth century most of the population of the Caribbean were African slaves, and there were frequent slave revolts. One of these, the Haitian Revolution of 1791 led by a freed slave Toussaint l'Ouverture (1746–1803), ended slavery and established an independent nation, although Toussaint was captured in the course of this and died in a French prison. Haiti became the second independent nation in the Americas, but the first independent nation—the United States—refused to recognize it diplomatically, as its president, Thomas Jefferson, a slave owner himself, feared slave rebellion would spread.

Spanish colonial rule was punctuated by a series of revolts. In the Andean region, 90 percent of the population was indigenous in the eighteenth century, required to labor on European-owned farms and in mines, or taxed heavily. After a major increase in taxes by the Spanish government, Tupac Amaru II (1740–81), a wealthy and well-educated man who claimed descent from the last Inca king, and his wife led a revolt by a coalition of groups that briefly held several provinces of Peru. They were both gruesomely executed by Spanish troops and the rebels defeated. Because the insurrection had identified with the Incas, Inca clothing, language, and other cultural traditions were banned, but revolts continued and became part of a widespread movement for independence from Spain that stretched from Mexico to Patagonia. This was led by locally born men of European background, called creoles, including Simon Bolivar (1783–1830) and José de San Martin (1778–1850), who were successful in ousting the Spanish in the early nineteenth century, but were not able to form representative governments or to incorporate indigenous peoples into the institutions they created.

THE EARLY MODERN AND THE TRULY MODERN

Historians of various world regions begin their accounts of the centuries covered in this chapter at slightly different points—the Ottoman conquest of Constantinople in 1453, the Shi'ite Safavid dynasty's rise to power in Persia in 1501, Luther's first public critique of the Catholic Church in 1517, Mughal expansion into India in the 1520s, the beginning of the reign of Ivan IV (called "the Terrible") in Russia in 1533, the creation of the Tokugawa Shogunate in 1603. In global terms, however, 1492 has few contenders as a sharp dividing line. Although the full impact of the voyages of Columbus would not be felt for centuries, diseases, plants, and animals began to cross the Atlantic immediately, transforming the natural and human worlds on both sides.

In much of the central and southern parts of the New World, mixed populations of Africans, Europeans, and indigenous people mined precious metals and raised crops for export, while in the northern part of the Americas smaller numbers of less mixed people farmed, hunted, trapped, and fished, supplying products for far-flung consumer markets. Most of the millions of people who crossed the Atlantic in these centuries came from Africa, where the slave trade destabilized states and societies, but the ships that carried them along with the products they and others made were owned by Europeans, some of whom made enormous profits from trade. Ships also carried Christian missionaries and officials, and Christianity became a global religion, though it splintered in Europe as a result of the Protestant Reformation and everywhere incorporated local traditions and practices. Ideas also crossed the Atlantic in all directions, exchanged in new urban social settings and cultural institutions, including scientific societies, printed journals and newspapers, clubs, and salons.

Away from the Atlantic, people and products were also on the move: Han Chinese settled in Central Asia with the expansion of the Qing Empire, planting potatoes and sweet potatoes; Russian fur traders moved into Siberia, hunting and trapping sable and mink; Comanche, Cheyenne, and Lakota spread out across the plains of western and southwestern North America, hunting buffalo from horseback; the Ottomans expanded into Europe and around the

Mediterranean and the Mughals into South Asia, spreading Islam and creating new institutions of governance; Dutch and British traders moved into the Indian Ocean basin, gradually taking over more trade. Chocolate, coffee, tea, tobacco, and sugar were increasingly available in cities and larger towns far from any coast, at prices that even servants could sometimes afford. They might be paid for with Mexican silver pesos, which circulated globally, and were especially popular in China, where people thought the hefty rulers portrayed on their faces looked like the Buddha.

In every migration, whether willing or coerced, people carried their customs, languages, religious beliefs, foodways, and other aspects of their culture with them, which blended into new hybrid forms in many places. Groups themselves blended through intermarriage and other sorts of heterosexual relationships, though conquering and colonizing authorities often tried to prevent this. Those authorities created systems of defining and regulating difference, in which a hierarchical system based on "race" became increasingly dominant.

Some aspects of life changed little in these centuries, however. While people and goods moved regularly around the world by water, land transport of bulky goods remained difficult, and local and more widespread famines continued, contributing to infant and child mortality that remained high. War was also a constant, now fought with gunpowder weapons in many places, but continuing to carry disease, hunger, and brutality with it. Cultural traditions and religious ideas were still taught primarily through the spoken word. Wealth created by commerce allowed some individuals and some families to increase their social stature, but did not upset a hierarchy in which being born into the landholding elite was the best assurance of power and prosperity. Hierarchies of wealth and inherited status continued to intersect with hierarchies of gender, for whether one was born male or female shaped every life experience and every stage of life.

Where to set the end of the early modern period—and thus the beginning of what we might call the "truly modern"—for world history is not as clear as where to set its start. The conventional date is 1789, but this privileges the political history of western Europe. Perhaps it should be 1787, when the first fleet of convicts set sail from Britain to Australia, carrying about a thousand people to a new colony on what was not yet designated a continent (that would come about a hundred years later). Or 1791, the beginning of the Haitian Revolution, the only successful large-scale slave revolt in history. Or 1792, the publication of Mary Wollstonecraft's *The Vindication of the Rights of Woman*, the first explicit call for political rights to be extended to the female half of the population. But 1789 was also the date that the English inventor Edmund Cartwright patented his second power loom. Although the loom had serious mechanical problems and creditors repossessed his cotton mill, other inventors quickly improved on Cartwright's design, and mills filled with mechanical power looms soon opened in several parts of Britain. The industrialization that began with those mills created the modern world, so 1789 might be the best date after all.

FURTHER READING

Alfred W. Crosby, *The Columbian Exchange: Biological and Cultural Consequences of 1492*, 30th Anniversary edition (Westport, CT: Praeger, 2003) is a good place to start, as is Crosby's later book, *Ecological Imperialism: The Biological Expansion of Europe, 900–1900* (Cambridge: Cambridge University Press, 1986). Charles C. Mann, *1493: Uncovering the New World Columbus Created* (New York: Alfred A. Knopf, 2011) is an excellent recent survey of the long-term implications of the transfer of food crops and other products, written for a general audience by a skilled science journalist. On disease, see Noble David Cook, *Born to Die: Disease and New World Conquest, 1492–1650* (Cambridge: Cambridge University Press, 1998) and John R. McNeill, *Mosquito Empires: Ecology and War in the Greater Caribbean, 1620–1914* (Cambridge: Cambridge University Press, 2010). A broader study of the environment in this period is John F. Richards, *The Unending Frontier: An Environmental History of the Early Modern World* (Berkeley: University of California Press, 2003). Volume 6 of the *Cambridge World History*, Jerry H. Bentley, Sanjay Subrahmanyam, and Merry E. Wiesner-Hanks, eds., *The Construction of a Global World, 1400–1800 CE*, discusses many of the issues covered in this chapter.

David R. Ringrose, *Expansion and Global Interaction, 1200–1700* (New York: Longman, 2001) and Kenneth Pomeranz and Steven Topik, eds., *The*

World that Trade Created: Society, Culture, and the World Economy, 1400 to the Present, 3rd edn. (Armonk, NY: M. E. Sharpe, 2012) are excellent introductions, designed for students. John H. Elliott, *Empires of the Atlantic World: Britain and Spain in America 1492–1830* (New Haven: Yale University Press, 2006) and John R. Chávez, *Beyond Nations: Evolving Homelands in the North Atlantic World* (Cambridge: Cambridge University Press, 2009) offer comparative studies of Atlantic colonialism. On legal aspects, see Lauren Benton, *Law and Colonial Cultures: Legal Regimes in World History, 1400–1900* (Cambridge: Cambridge University Press, 2002).

For both social protests and warfare, Geoffrey Parker, *Global Crisis: War, Climate Change and Catastrophe in the Seventeenth Century* (New Haven: Yale University Press, 2013) is comprehensive, and Jane Landers, *Atlantic Creoles in the Age of Revolutions* (Cambridge, MA: Harvard University Press, 2010) presents a comparative study of revolution. Marshall Hodgson's notion of "gunpowder empires" was first published in his *The Venture of Islam*, Volume 3: *The Gunpowder Empires and Modern Times* (Chicago: University of Chicago Press, 1975); for a more recent discussion of these empires, see Douglas E. Streusand, *Islamic Gunpowder Empires: Ottomans, Safavids, and Mughals* (New York: Westview Press, 2010). On Chinese expansion, see Peter C. Perdue, *China Marches West: The Qing Conquest of Central Eurasia* (Cambridge, MA: Belknap Press, 2005).

There are many fine studies of the Reformation, among them Peter Matheson, ed., *Reformation Christianity*, Volume V of *A People's History of Christianity* (Minneapolis: Fortress Press, 2006), which includes essays on the religious life of ordinary men and women. R. Po-chia Hsia, *The World of Catholic Renewal, 1540–1770* (Cambridge: Cambridge University Press, 2nd edn. 2005) and Merry E. Wiesner-Hanks, *Christianity and Sexuality in the Early Modern World: Regulating Desire, Reforming Practice* (London: Routledge, 2nd edn. 2010) cover both European and colonial Catholicism. On mixing and creolization more generally, see Serge Gruzinski, *The Mestizo Mind: The Intellectual Dynamics of Colonization and Globalization* (London: Routledge, 2002), James Sweet, *Recreating Africa: Culture, Kinship and Religion in the African-Portuguese World, 1441–1770* (Chapel Hill: University of North Carolina Press, 2003), and John Thornton, *A Cultural History of the Atlantic World, 1250–1820* (Cambridge: Cambridge University Press, 2012).

On the fur trade in North America and its social impact, two classic studies are William Cronon, *Changes in the Land: Indians, Colonists, and the Ecology of New England* (New York: Hill and Wang, 1983) and

Richard White, *The Middle Ground: Indians, Empires, and Republics in the Great Lakes Region, 1650–1815* (Cambridge: Cambridge University Press, 1991). More recent studies of colonial development are Susan Sleeper-Smith, *Indian Women and French Men: Rethinking Cultural Encounter in the Western Great Lakes* (Amherst: University of Massachusetts Press, 2001) and Sophie White, *Wild Frenchmen and Frenchified Indians: Material Culture and Race in Colonial Louisiana* (Philadelphia: University of Pennsylvania Press, 2012). Mark Kulansky, *Cod: A Biography of the Fish that Changed the World* (London: Penguin, 1998) is a lively book for general readers.

On drug foods, see Wolfgang Schivelbusch, *Tastes of Paradise: A Social History of Spices, Stimulants, and Intoxication* (New York: Vintage, 1993) and William G. Clarence-Smith and Steven Topik, eds., *The Global Coffee Economy in Africa, Asia, and Latin America* (Cambridge: Cambridge University Press, 2003). Sidney W. Mintz, *Sweetness and Power: the Place of Sugar in Modern History* (New York: Penguin Books, 1986) is a classic study.

A good brief survey of the slave trade is Herbert S. Klein, *The Atlantic Slave Trade* (Cambridge: Cambridge University Press, 1999), while Jennifer Morgan, *Laboring Women: Reproduction and Gender in New World Slavery* (Philadelphia: University of Pennsylvania Press, 2004) examines gender issues. For a study of Africans more broadly, see John Thornton, *Africa and Africans in the Making of the Atlantic World, 1400–1800* (Cambridge: Cambridge University Press, 1998).

For the development of ideas about race, Ivan Hannaford, *Race: The History of an Idea in the West* (Baltimore: Johns Hopkins University Press, 1996) is a good place to start. On families and race, see Ann Laura Stoler, *Carnal Knowledge and Imperial Power: Race and the Intimate in Colonial Rule* (Berkeley: University of California Press, 2002) and Tony Ballantyne and Antoinette Burton, eds., *Bodies in Contact: Rethinking Colonial Encounters in World History* (Durham, NC: Duke University Press, 2005).

5

Industrialization, imperialism, and inequality, 1800 CE–2015 CE

Writing from prisons in British India where he was imprisoned for political activity in the early 1930s, the Indian independence leader Jawaharlal Nehru (1889–1964) sent a series of nearly two hundred long letters to his teenage daughter Indira, in which he provided her with a sweeping view of world history. Gathered together in 1934 with the title *Glimpses of World History*, the letters range from the rise of the first cities to Nehru's own day. About a third of the way through the book is a letter titled "The Coming of the Big Machine," in which Nehru comments that, more than anything else he has written about, industrialization "changed the face of life ... It was a revolution affecting all the various classes, and indeed everybody. It has made the difference between the luxury of the very rich and the poverty of the poor even greater than it was in the past." These effects were felt around the world, Nehru comments, for "capitalist industry led inevitably to a new imperialism, for everywhere there was a demand for raw materials for manufacture and markets for new manufactured goods ... So there was a wild scramble among the more powerful countries for new territories ... [and then] a new kind of empire, invisible and economic, that exploits and dominates without any obvious outward signs."

Nearly a century later, world historians generally agree with Nehru that industrialization created the modern world, not only that of his day, but our own as well. The use of fossil fuels—first coal and then also oil and gas—allowed a dramatic increase in productivity, as the energy stored over hundreds of millions of years was taken out of the ground and put to human use. Industry transformed the world politically, economically, socially, and physically, and allowed the nations that industrialized to dominate those that did not in a new wave of imperialism through military conquest that began in the nineteenth century. The invisible, economic empire that Nehru alluded to, often called neocolonialism or soft imperialism, also expanded throughout the world. In this new form of empire, multinational corporations and international agencies were often more important than states, shaping society and culture as well as the economy. Together industry and imperialism (both hard and soft) facilitated greater inequality, both within one nation or region and among them.

From the huge amount of information available about the world since 1800, this chapter focuses on these three themes: industrialization, imperialism, and inequality. It begins with the earliest industrialization, which took place in England, and examines the uneven spread of industry around the world. Growing inequality within and among societies was accompanied by the growth of movements calling for social change, some with egalitarian goals, including the end of slavery and rights for women, but others that advocated segregation, racial exclusion, and even selective breeding. Industry facilitated long-distance migration on a massive scale as well as imperial conquests, which simultaneously challenged and reinforced existing social hierarchies and cultural patterns. Moving into the twentieth century, the chapter examines the impact of total war on modern culture and society, and traces processes of decolonization along with struggles for social and political liberation that marked the postwar decades. Developments that lessened some forms of inequality were countered by economic measures that increased disparities of wealth as industrial and postindustrial jobs followed low wages around the world in the ever more connected network of global capitalism. People continued to move as well, transforming cities into megacities and increasing religious, linguistic, social, and ethnic diversity and blending, despite efforts by religious fundamentalists, cultural conservatives, and some political leaders to combat this. The chapter ends with a brief discussion of the still-short third millennium, with the world's population passing the 7 billion mark and both poverty and prosperity on the rise.

COTTON, SLAVES, AND COAL

Because industrialization underlay both British economic and political power and growing Western dominance over much of the world in the nineteenth century, why England industrialized first is a key question in world history. Industrialization began with cotton production, so some of the answer is specific to cotton. Technology is part of this story, but so are the social organization of cloth production and the new patterns of consumption that resulted from global trade outlined in Chapter 4.

By the seventeenth century, cloth production in some parts of the world was increasingly commercialized, but organized in slightly different ways. In China and Japan, peasant households raised silk and cotton, which the women spun and family members wove into cloth, to be worn by the household, used to pay taxes, or sold through networks of merchants. More than half the rural households in China had a loom. In India, cotton and cotton-silk blends were produced in specialized weaving villages by specific castes; generally women spun, men wove, and both sexes finished the cloth, selling cloth not needed by the household to a merchant. In the western European countryside, merchants arranged for wool and flax, and in some places cotton and silk, to be distributed to households and spun into thread by the women of those households, then taken to other households to be woven and finished, and then returned to the merchants for transport and sale. Economic historians have given this system several different names, including "cottage industry," the "putting out system," "domestic industry," and "proto-industry." In all these areas—China, Japan, India, and western Europe—and perhaps in other places that have been less well studied, rural households intensified their labor to produce more cloth in the seventeenth century, what the economic historian Jan de Vries has called the "industrious revolution."

Silk retained its status as the most luxurious fabric, but Indian cotton was the most widely traded, exchanged for slaves on the West African coast, gold and silver in South America, spices in Southeast Asia, and other goods elsewhere. When the Dutch and English East India Companies began to import cotton cloth from India into Europe in the later seventeenth century, consumers there slowly learned its benefits: it was lightweight, felt pleasant against the skin, and could take vivid colors when dyed, printed, or painted. Contemporary commentators noted that the demand for Indian textiles became a "calico craze," and complained that women of all classes were wearing them or decorating their houses with them, so that differences between social classes were not as evident. Debates raged in coffeehouses and in the new print venues such as newspapers that shaped public opinion over whether Indian cottons encouraged poorer people—especially women—to spend money on imported frivolities. Weavers in London protested, attacking the headquarters of the English East India Company, and tearing the cotton clothes off women in the streets or throwing acid on them. Between the 1680s and the 1720s, the English, French, Spanish, and Prussian governments limited or banned the import and wearing of Asian cotton cloth. The enforcement of these laws was feeble, however, and because they did not also ban the re-export of Indian cottons to colonial or African markets, they put no dent at all in the trade.

What changed this global pattern was not better law enforcement, but a process of import (and re-export) substitution through imitation, borrowing, experimentation, and mechanization, first in printing cotton fabric and then in spinning and weaving it. Armenian artisans who had learned cloth-printing in India brought this to Europe, and both they and local artisans opened large-scale "manufactories," where hundreds of male and female workers used hand tools or hand-powered machines to print cloth. Entrepreneurs and tinkerers seeking to increase cloth production experimented with machines that would allow women to spin more than one thread at a time, sometimes applying mechanical principles they had learned from reading scientific works. By the 1760s several types of these machines could produce thread that was strong and thin enough to make acceptable cotton cloth. Some of these machines could be powered by hand, but others needed an external power source, which was provided by falling water; spinning mills grew up along streams and rivers, first in the British countryside and then in other parts of Europe and North America.

Machines and their inventors generally dominate the story of the Industrial Revolution, but existing marriage patterns and gender norms were also significant factors. Northwestern Europe had a distinctive marriage pattern, with both men and women generally waiting until their mid or late twenties to marry, and then setting up an independent household immediately rather than living in an extended family. The late age of marriage for women was especially unusual, for this was long beyond the age of sexual maturity generally favored as the proper age at which women should marry. Women themselves contributed wages they had saved or goods they had made to establishing the household, often working outside the supervision of their father or another male family member, which was culturally unacceptable in many other parts of the world. Many people never married at all—between 10 and 15 percent of the population, and in some places perhaps as high as 25 percent. In the seventeenth century unmarried women in England acquired a name that also reflected their most common occupation: spinster. Thus, when spinning mills opened, young women were often the first to be hired, because they had been spinning anyway, and also because they were viewed as more compliant, willing to take lower wages, and better able to carry out the repetitive tasks of tending machines.

Mechanized spinning eventually allowed a young woman or girl to spin about a hundred times more than she could by hand, and inventors then turned their attention to mechanical looms, which became practical in the early decades of the nineteenth century. Anti-industrialization activists known as Luddites, mostly male skilled hand-weavers, wrecked machinery in mass protests, but, as with many other social protests, they were suppressed by the army, and destroying machinery was made a capital crime. Cities located in areas with favorable river systems became centers of cloth manufacturing, and output soared; in 1750, Britain produced about 50,000 pieces of printed calico (a piece was about 28 yards long), and in 1830 over 8 million. Urban populations also soared: Manchester in northwestern England, for example, one of the main centers of British cotton production, grew from 17,000 in 1760 to 180,000 in 1830. Conditions in the mills were unpleasant and unhealthy, with cloth fibers filling the air and a work day that stretched thirteen or fourteen hours, six days a week. Workers included migrants from the countryside and immigrants from further away. Many of these came from Ireland, where population growth and worsening economic conditions led many young people to seek jobs elsewhere. When a blight destroyed the potato crop on which people depended in the 1840s and more than a million people died of hunger and disease, even more Irish people moved to English industrial cities, or to those in the northern part of the United States that were also industrializing.

British industrialization thus depended on the labor of migrants, and not simply those in Britain itself. The explosion in production required a vastly increased supply of raw materials, which would not have been possible with linen or wool, because that would have taken far more land devoted to flax or sheep than all of the land in Britain. (The fact that Chinese peasant households raised their own cotton is one reason that large machines did not gain favor there.) But cotton was imported, and in the late seventeenth and eighteenth centuries Britain gained colonies in the Caribbean and North America, places where cotton could be cultivated. The organization for doing so was already in place: the plantations discussed in Chapter 4, worked by African slave labor. New plantations were established across the Caribbean, attracting capital and people, both slave and free. Cotton is extremely hard on the soil, however, and the land was quickly exhausted in the type of boom-and-bust cycle common in the exploitation of commercial crops and natural resources. Cotton production shifted, especially to the southern United States, where the invention of the hand-powered cotton gin (short for "engine") in 1794 had just substantially lowered the amount of labor needed to clean cotton.

Slavery expanded geographically and numerically with cotton. In the 1790s, there were perhaps 700,000 slaves in the American South, most in Maryland and Virginia, and some commentators predicted slavery might die out because it was not economically viable. By 1850, the number had instead increased to 4 million, the majority in the new states of Alabama, Mississippi, Tennessee, and Louisiana, where "King Cotton" ruled. They produced nearly two-thirds of the world's cotton, which accounted for half the worth of all US exports. Enslaved people worked under harsher conditions in cotton plantations than they had earlier, with longer daily working hours in gang labor that moved across vast monocultural cotton fields in lines rather than tending more varied crops. (The work day was slightly shorter than that in textile mills, but longer than the normal workday of peasant farmers.) Like factory workers, slaves had a continually intensive work year, as cotton was picked three times a year and cleaned and processed during the winter, and as slaves also manured fields and cut down forests for new plantations. The USA had outlawed the importation of slaves in the early nineteenth century, so the older slave states supplied them through a network of companies and independent traders. Hundreds of thousands of people were forcibly migrated, usually with no concern about family relationships; the threat of being sold to a cotton state served as a means of controlling slaves' behavior throughout the American South.

The increasing productivity of slave labor, along with decreasing shipping costs because of steamships and better packing methods, kept the price of raw US cotton low. Other than a brief period during the American Civil War (1861–65), when hundreds of British factories closed because they could not obtain raw cotton, US cotton dominated the market. Cotton picked and cleaned by American slaves (or, after the Civil War, by former slaves who were now sharecroppers and tenant farmers), bought, sold, and financed at commodity exchanges in New York, New Orleans, London, and other cities, and spun, woven, and finished in European (especially British) factories, clothed the world. During the War of 1812 between Britain and the United States, patriotic campaigns in the USA promoted the production and use of homespun, but British manufactured cloth was cheaper as well as better, and it remained a standard item for shopkeepers in towns and peddlers on the frontier, sold to Native Americans as well as immigrants. By 1850 Britain was producing half the world's cotton cloth, and exporting more than half of this, including to India. Millions of people in India lost their livelihoods, and from 1750 to 1850 manufacturing cities such as Calcutta shrank, with people migrating to villages in a process of de-urbanization. Industrialized cotton thus shaped family life for weavers in India just as it did for factory workers in Britain and slaves in the USA.

Industrialization was initially powered by water, but because water-powered machinery could be interrupted by drought or freezing weather and was geographically limited, strong impetus emerged to search for other sources of power, which could also address shortages of wood for heating and cooking in large cities such as London. The solution was coal, available in certain parts of Europe, most plentifully in England and Wales. British toolmakers and engineers invented and then improved steam engines to pump water out of ever-deeper coal mines. Carts full of coal were pushed and pulled along rails first by human and animal power, and then by coal-powered steam engines. Steam technology spread out from the coalfields to steamships, steam locomotives that ran on iron tracks, and other uses. Steam-powered transport allowed the faster and cheaper movement of people, goods, and ideas, thus thickening networks of connection.

Coal went hand-in-hand with iron. The spread of gunpowder weapons increased the demand for iron astronomically, and in the early nineteenth century British ironworkers developed coal-powered steam blowers and other equipment that allowed new iron- and steel-making processes. Many machines and machine parts that had earlier been made out of wood were increasingly made of the much more durable iron or steel, and iron began to replace stone as a construction material. In the periodization of human history into eras developed at roughly this time, the Iron Age began in the second millennium BCE, but in terms of iron's impact on everyday life, the Iron Age really began in the nineteenth century.

Early steam engines were so wasteful of energy that they only made economic sense where fuel was cheap and did not need to be transported very far, so the iron industry grew up in coal-mining regions, and cities such as Newcastle and Liverpool expanded at an amazing rate. They were filthy and lacked enough housing, clean water, or sanitation services for their residents; diseases such as typhus and tuberculosis spread easily. Work was structured by the need to use machines efficiently, so tasks became more routinized and the work day even longer and more regimented in coal-fired factories than it had been in water-powered ones, and far more so than in household forms of production. Wages were low, but often higher than those in the countryside, and the opportunities to escape parental and family control were greater, so the new industrial cities sucked in young people, as cities always had. The British state supported industry through tax policies that favored investors, high tariffs or outright bans on manufactured goods from elsewhere, and naval power that could enforce laws requiring colonies to trade only with Britain. In 1750, Britain accounted for less than 2 percent of production around the world, while in 1860 its share was more than 20 percent, including two-thirds of the world's coal and more than half of its iron.

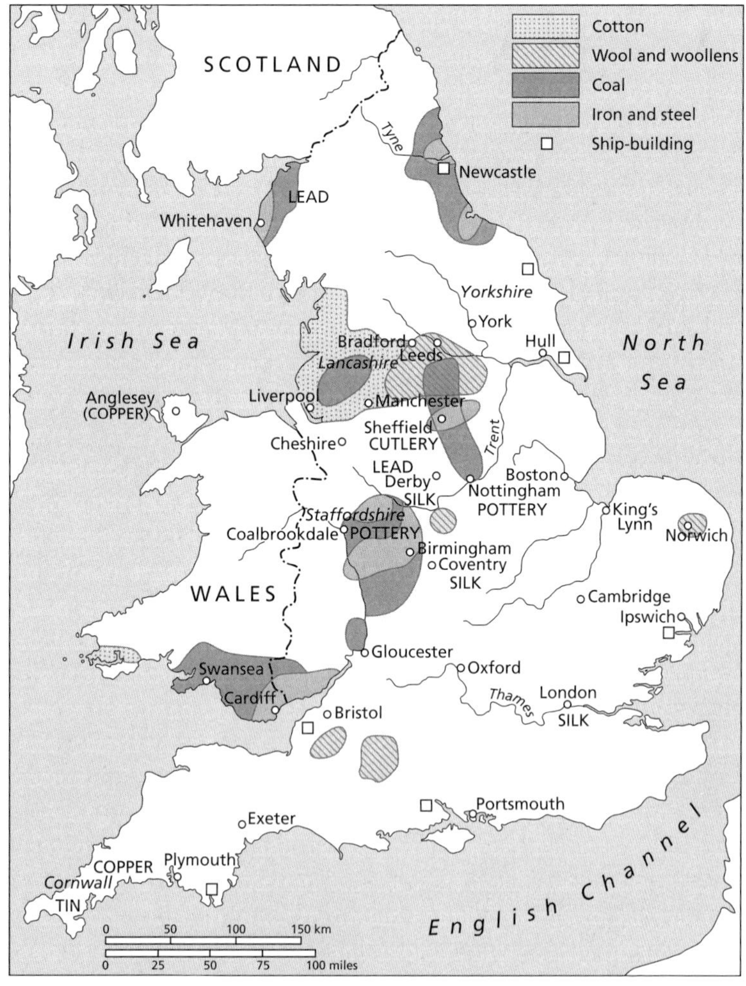

Map 5.1 Industrial development in England and Wales

Thus many factors, some local and some global, led industry to develop first in Britain: the stimulus provided by Indian cotton; a growing and geographically mobile population that provided a broad-based market for consumer goods; marriage patterns and gender norms that provided a cheap workforce already accustomed to cloth production; access to essential raw materials and markets for manufactured products provided by colonial possessions that were growing more extensive through war; a raw material produced elsewhere, so that the environmental and social effects of intense monoculture were not experienced locally; navigable rivers and abundant natural resources such as coal and iron ore located in easy-to-reach places; a culture of innovation in which entrepreneurial artisans could sometimes make a profit from their inventions; a relatively broad-based political system that supported commercial interests and innovation; a lack of warfare in Britain itself, at a time when continental Europe was disrupted by the French Revolution and the conquests of Napoleon. The coincidental interdependence and interaction of these factors set Britain on what the economic historian Joel Mokyr has called the "peculiar path" toward industrialization. Its ultimate implications were only recognized later, of course, not foreseen by a few people with a telescopic vision of the future. No one set out to develop an industrial society, because in 1750 no one knew what that meant.

THE EXPANSION AND TRANSFORMATION OF INDUSTRY

After relative peace returned to Europe with the final defeat of Napoleon in 1815, other countries attempted to follow the English path. Although Britain forbade skilled workers to leave or to export machinery, many slipped out and introduced new methods abroad. Continental and American industrial spies roamed England, and returned home with memorized plans for machines and techniques, receiving awards from their governments. The governments in France and Prussia helped pay for railroads, and established protective tariff barriers against British goods that allowed infant industries to develop. In these measures, they were motivated by nationalism, a new ideology that built on the very old idea (discussed in Chapter 1) that each people has its own culture and identity, expressed through language and reinforced by marriage within the group. European nationalists—and later nationalists around the world—sought to make the territory of each people coincide with the boundaries of an independent nation-state. They developed symbols and ceremonies that expressed this conscious common identity, such as ethnic festivals, flags, foods, costumes, and parades. Many of these claimed to draw on traditional ethnic forms, but were in fact invented in the nineteenth century.

Nationalist political leaders also began to spread standardized national languages through mass education. Mass schooling developed earliest in Prussia and Sweden, where it was explicitly linked to obedience to political authorities, religious orthodoxy, and the development of a modern army, in which soldiers not only would have the technical expertise to handle modern weapons but also would have learned from an early age to follow instructions and orders without question. Early industrialism did not require formal schooling, and, in fact, often relied on the labor of children, but as industrial processes became more complex, those countries in which a large share of the population could read and write had an advantage. More schools were opened for boys than for girls in the nineteenth century, but educational reformers regarded the schooling of girls as important, for these girls would eventually become mothers, and thus responsible for the early upbringing of future soldiers and workers. Women's education came to be linked with the good of the state, part of creating a strong nation in which people understood their proper roles.

In the nineteenth century, nationalism sometimes combined with liberalism, an ideology that grew out of the eighteenth-century revolutions and that advocated individual liberty, political equality, representative democracy, and individual rights. Or it combined with socialism, an ideology that advocated greater economic and social equality and the common or public ownership of institutions. Nationalism also became increasingly aggressive, as nationalists emphasized the superiority of their nation over inferior others, and built up armies that could—and did—enforce this superiority through war in Europe and empire-building in Africa and Asia. Nationalists of all types regarded economic growth as essential to a strong nation, so advocated for the development of industry.

Across the Atlantic, the new United States expanded steadily, through a combination of land purchases from and wars against other countries, along with manipulation, theft, fraud, and violence against Native Americans (and the bison on which some of them depended). The Native American population in the United States declined to slightly over 200,000 by 1900. The same thing happened in Canada, which became a self-governing nation in 1867, bought the vast territory of the Hudson's Bay Company, and annexed other provinces shortly after this to stretch coast to coast. The US version of nationalism became one of "manifest destiny," a phrase invented by a newspaper editor to convey the idea that God had foreordained the United States to spread across and rule the continent. This territorial expansion and the growth of industry were both backed by government action, including the construction of a heavily subsidized rail system that connected every part of the nation, built largely by immigrants from Europe, Mexico, and China. The expansion westward exacerbated tensions between the North and the South in the United States over whether new territories would allow slavery, which erupted in the Civil War (1861–65) that ended in Northern victory and a prohibition of slavery throughout the United States, although this fell far short of creating equality for people of African descent.

Beginning in the 1870s, the newly reunited United States and a newly unified Germany joined Britain in leading what has been termed the "second industrial revolution." Chemicals, electrical goods, pharmaceuticals, food, military technology, and the automobile joined textiles and iron as key industrial products and factory production was speeded up through the use of the assembly line. Industry became increasingly dominated by giant business enterprises and conglomerates, such as those of the Krupps in Germany or the Rockefellers in the United States, that could afford the huge capital investments needed to open a factory using the latest technology and weather boom and bust business cycles. These included a severe economic depression in the 1890s, in which the politically well-connected factory and mine owners slashed wages, laid off workers, and fought the organization of labor unions, often hiring private military contractors to enforce their aims. In the United

States, this was most often the Pinkerton Private Detective Agency, which at the turn of the twentieth century had more employees than there were soldiers in the US army.

Outside of western Europe and the United States, industrialization proceeded fastest in Japan, where a long political crisis beginning in the 1850s ended with reform-minded local aristocrats (samurai) seizing power in the name of the emperor (the "Meiji Restoration"). They decided to make Japan a "rich nation, strong army," by following Western models. Various class privileges were abolished, property rights and the tax system were radically altered, and commoners were drafted into a new national army. Thousands of schools were opened where students were expected to learn discipline and patriotism as well as reading and arithmetic; by 1910, 98 percent of school-age boys and girls were enrolled in elementary school. Meiji reformers explicitly rejected China as a political and cultural model, and urged Japanese to become Western, or to combine Western and Japanese values in a new and stronger synthesis. Men, and some women, began wearing Western clothes and eating beef, increasingly available in restaurants and praised as the "prince of foods" responsible for Western success. Using taxes gained from agriculture, the government invested in railroads, mines, and factories, though most of the latter were later privatized.

Beginning in the 1880s, the Japanese government increasingly modified Western capital-intensive models of industrialization to the Japanese situation, and developed a more labor-intensive type of industrialization that relied less on the replacement of labor by machinery and often combined machine and hand production. Light industry such as textiles and later toys quickly became globally competitive. By 1933, Japan was the world's largest cotton textile exporter, and a new agricultural extension network helped silk—Japan's largest single export until well into the twentieth century—flourish. But heavy industry, such as steel and chemicals, which required more capital and energy and were less able to use cheap rural labor, remained uncompetitive, and depended heavily on close ties to the government, especially the military. At one end of the Japanese economy, large conglomerates (*zaibatsu*), with strong political ties, predominated, in a pattern that has continued

5.1 Women reel silk using large machines in a Japanese silk mill, 1921. Sorting and unwinding the cocoons was done by hand in the same factory, and sometimes weaving was done by hand as well in the Japanese pattern of labor-intensive industrialization.

to today. At the other, small, often family-based firms relied on cheap but relatively skilled labor, and developed networks with each other to duplicate some of the economies of scale created by big firms elsewhere, sustaining a much higher level of self-employment than in any Western country with a similar level of income and industrialization. The distinction between management and labor was smaller than it was in larger Western companies, with more (male) members of the firm retaining managerial aspects of their work.

In several other states, including Russia, Egypt, Persia, the Ottoman Empire, and the new countries of Latin America, political leaders and ambitious entrepreneurs also sought to promote industry in the nineteenth century, but with less success. They could not compete with cheaper European or US imports, and the governments were not powerful enough to enforce high tariffs like those that had protected German and US industries as these were getting started. European and US governments acted to keep markets open for their own industrial products, and to ensure the steady flow of raw materials and agricultural commodities from weaker nations.

In Latin America and the Caribbean, indigenous people were not pushed off their land as they were in the United States and Canada, but instead were kept in place and their land was taken from them through laws that favored the tiny elite of wealthy landowners. Huge estates came to be owned by a few private individuals, who paid those who worked the land not in money, but in vouchers redeemable only at company stores. Those stores used high prices and fraud to keep workers permanently in debt, a system of debt peonage that was also common in cash-crop plantations, mines, and extractive industries such as lumbering in other parts of the world. In the second half of the nineteenth century, businessmen and bankers from Europe and the United States established or expanded plantations in Latin America that grew cash crops for export, including coffee, hemp, sugar, cotton, bananas, beef, and rubber, along with mines for the tin, copper, nitrate (used in fertilizer, explosives, and pharmaceuticals) and other minerals used in industrial processes. European and US governments used investments, loans, technology, and military actions to support this neocolonial system of Western economic domination and maintain friendly governments. Commercial agriculture for export, and mining, employed many more men than women; men migrated to large plantations, cities, or even other countries in search of paid labor, and women remained in villages to care for children and the elderly and to engage in unpaid agricultural work, or traveled to cities and mining areas to work as barmaids, laundresses, and prostitutes. Rural impoverishment led to social protests and local revolts, such as a revolt in Cuba against Spanish colonial rule in 1895 and the Mexican Revolution in 1911–20. Most people remained poor, however. Latin American economies expanded somewhat in the early twentieth century as a result of industrialization, but social inequalities also expanded, and the region's reliance on extractive industries and monoculture left it economically vulnerable and environmentally degraded as native forests were chopped down for their timber or to make way for plantations and ranches.

Industrialization was thus an uneven process. In many parts of the world, subsistence agriculture remained the primary means through which families supported themselves well into the twentieth century, and even in the most industrialized countries non-industrial work remained important throughout the nineteenth century. In the 1880s, only 44 percent of the British, 36 percent of the German, and 20 percent of the US labor force was in industry. But by harnessing power that was not produced by humans, animals, wind, or water, and by using machinery, industrial production allowed workers to produce far more than they would have been able to otherwise, created opportunities for great wealth for those who owned this output, and eventually raised the standard of living for most people in industrialized countries when compared with those who lived in non-industrial ones. From 1820 to 1913, Asia's share of world Gross Domestic Product (GDP) declined from 60 to 25 percent, while that of western Europe rose from 20 to 31 percent, and that of North America from 2 to 20 percent.

Industrialization also spurred new technologies, such as the steamship and railroad, which allowed products to be shipped long distances fairly cheaply and dominate the global marketplace. New tools included new weapons, including the repeating rifle and the machine gun, through which a few industrial states were able to conquer many others. Just as the increase in productivity that resulted from the domestication of crops in the Neolithic generally allowed agriculturalists to dominate their non-agricultural neighbors—although the Mongols are a significant counter-example—so the explosion in productivity created by the harnessing of fossils fuels allowed industrial states to rule much of the world directly through global empires, and to dominate the rest through their control of the economy.

In a very influential conceptualization, the sociologist Immanuel Wallerstein termed the hierarchical set of global relationships that developed in the nineteenth century the "modern world system" in which economic growth in western Europe and the USA (the core) was achieved by dominating partially industrialized independent states (the semi-periphery) and especially by using—and exploiting—the raw materials and people of colonial and other non-industrial areas (the periphery). World-systems theory has been criticized as overly monolithic and materialist, and as putting too much emphasis on the West and ignoring the activities of people elsewhere, especially in Asia. Even its critics, however, view industrialization as the foundation of what the historian Kenneth Pomeranz has called the "great divergence" —the gap in income and material well-being between the West and the rest of the world that marked (and continues to mark) the modern world.

CLASS, GENDER, RACE, AND LABOR IN INDUSTRIAL SOCIETIES

Industrialization was facilitated by existing social and gender structures, but it then changed these significantly, and also led to new understandings of how society operated. Hereditary aristocracies did not disappear (other than in political revolutions in which they were ousted) but social elites increasingly included families that had made their wealth in production, banking, and commerce, rather than through land ownership. They understood themselves to be "middle class," set apart from those beneath them by education, culture, and habits. Those beneath them included not only rural villagers—who remained the bulk of the population throughout the nineteenth century, even in industrializing countries—but also a new social group created by industrialization, the "working class" made up of wage-laborers. Thus, along with a sense of group cohesion (and distinction from others) that came from language, ethnicity, nation, race, and religion, industrialization created a new type of group identity and consciousness: class.

Reflecting on what he saw around him, the German philosopher Karl Marx (1818–83) theorized that all history was class struggle, and that just as the industrial middle class—the bourgeoisie—had triumphed over the aristocracy, in the future the working class—the proletariat—would conquer the bourgeoisie in a violent revolution, after which all would share the wealth and exploitation would end. Marx thought that everything in society arose from material conditions, including religion, laws, family relationships, ideas, and culture. He criticized capitalism for the extremes of wealth and poverty it had created and for its separation of workers from ownership of the means of production, and opposed nationalism, asserting that working people everywhere had common interests.

Marx's ideas shaped socialism (though he called himself a communist rather than a socialist, as he saw socialism as too naïve and utopian) and attracted a wide following. Socialism was instrumental in a series of (ultimately unsuccessful) popular revolutions that swept Europe in 1848. In the later nineteenth century, socialists founded political parties, which grew to millions of members and focused more on improvements in working conditions through labor unions, elections, and laws than on revolution. More radical communist ideas would lead to social revolution not in industrialized countries as Marx had expected, but in the largely agricultural societies of Russia and China.

Ideas about the power of class distinctions were also held by those who regarded Marx and socialism as dangerous and misguided. In industrializing countries, successful businessmen and their wives—and those who hoped to become these—created standards of dress, household furnishings, cuisine, decorum, and behavior that marked their middle-class status. Ironically but unsurprisingly, many of these were derived from earlier aristocratic conventions of behavior, as now middle-class people were expected to behave like ladies and gentlemen, and to employ at least one servant girl if they could afford it. The middle class was extremely diverse, ranging from wealthy industrialists to the owners of tiny shops, but shared a code of behavior that for men involved hard work and discipline and for women ladylike gentility. Respectability meant more elaborate meals of several courses that were different depending on the time of day, often using industrially made products. In Japan, for example, factory-made miso, wheat noodles, and white rice allowed middle-class women to spend more time on other aspects of the meal, including elaborate presentation. In Europe and among European-background people elsewhere, women followed recipes in cookbooks or women's magazines to make sweet cakes and puddings using mass-produced white flour, sugar from sugar beets, and canned condensed milk. Canning was invented in the early nineteenth century to provide food for armies and navies, and men simply opened the cans with their knives and bayonets. Increasing safety and reliability in industrial canning processes and the invention of the can opener in 1870 led urban households to begin using canned foods, dramatically increasing the range of foodstuffs available.

In the later nineteenth century, opinion-leaders, including some women, emphasized the propriety of a distinction between the "private" world of home and family and the "public" world of work and politics for middle-class families, what became known as a doctrine of "separate spheres." Married women were encouraged to avoid work outside the household and make their homes a "haven in the heartless world" of industrialism and business. Europeans and Americans often criticized the societies they were colonizing for requiring women to be secluded in the home, but at the same time they created a stronger ideal of domesticity for women in their own societies. The Meiji reformers of Japan similarly stressed the importance of women's domesticity; "good wife, wise mother" (*ryosai kenbo*) became a standard government slogan defining women's proper roles.

Middle-class ideals emphasized the mother–child bond, and also stressed the importance of children in general, in what some historians have dubbed the "discovery of childhood." At the same time, however, working-class children were hired in factories and mines at very young ages, and rural children worked as soon as they were able. Concerns about the effects of factory work on children's health, the opening of free public schools, and the enforcement of mandatory schooling laws began to reduce child labor in the factories of some industrialized countries in the early twentieth century, but children continued to work in home-based production and on the plantations and farms that produced the raw materials for industry. Throughout the world, children continued to work in rural and urban family enterprises, just as they had for millennia, for their labor was vital for family survival, and working alongside parents, relatives, or older siblings was how they learned necessary skills.

5.2 Breaker boys, whose job was to break the coal into uniform pieces and pick out impurities, work in the Kohinore Coal Mine, Shenandoah, Pennsylvania, 1891; most worked ten hours a day, six days a week. Technological improvements, the enforcement of compulsory education laws, and union actions led to a decline in child labor in European and American mines by 1920.

Women also continued to make up a significant share of the workforce in many industries despite the ideology of separate spheres. In Japan, for example, though women were urged to stay home as "good wives, wise mothers," their lower wages made them attractive to factory owners; in 1909, 62 percent of the factory labor force was female, working primarily in silk production. In the United States, more than a million women worked in factories in 1900, with similar large numbers elsewhere. Most of these were unmarried women, for the separation of workplace from home made it difficult for women with infants or small children to combine factory work with their responsibilities of feeding, clothing, and caring for the family. They often continued to engage in paid labor at home, however, sewing clothing, making hats, or doing other types of piecework for very low wages, what is often termed "sweated" labor, or they took in boarders. For married working-class women home was a workplace, not a haven.

Supervisory positions in factories everywhere were reserved for older men, who were sometimes expected to oversee the morals and leisure-time activities of their workers as fathers had been expected to earlier. Middle-class officials worried about promiscuity among unrelated young people who worked together, and this, combined with a sense that mines in particular were dangerous for women's health, led to laws prohibiting underground work in mines for women, and later to restrictions on the hours of work by women in factories. In some heavy industries, such as steel and machine production, almost all of the workers were male; work was thus segmented by gender both within factories and across industries. In some areas segmentation by race or national origin was added to that of gender and marital status; by the 1880s, in the tobacco industry of North Carolina, for example, black men handled the bales of tobacco, black women stemmed tobacco leaves, white women operated cigarette-making machines, and white men repaired machinery and supervised the entire operation. In the gold and diamond mines of South Africa, where after the 1880s heavy machinery and a huge labor force were needed to extract deep deposits, white men held all skilled positions and lived with their families in subsidized housing, while African men did all actual mining and lived in police-guarded dormitories. Labor force segmentation limited the range of jobs available, and helped keep wages low. Prostitution increased as cities grew and women's wages remained low, and sexually transmitted diseases, especially syphilis and gonorrhea, spread widely.

Industrialization involved de-skilling, as work that had traditionally been done by high-status skilled artisans was subdivided and made more monotonous with the addition of machinery, and was redefined as "unskilled," with a dramatic drop in status and pay. In some cases there really was less skill involved, but the definition of "skill" is often gendered and racialized. For example, women had been excluded from certain crafts, such as glass-cutting, because they were judged clumsy or "unskilled," yet those same women made lace, a task that required an even higher level of dexterity and concentration than glass-cutting. Thus in a circular process, jobs at which women came to predominate were viewed as less skilled and lower status, and they paid less, which meant that men avoided them if they could, thus further lowering their status and pay. This happened in weaving and shoemaking, and also in work outside of factories. Secretarial work changed from a male profession to a female job in the late nineteenth century with the introduction of the typewriter, as did teaching when the governments implementing mandatory schooling recognized that female teachers would work for far less than male. Schoolteaching came to be seen primarily as an occupation for young women; though male schoolteachers could marry, female schoolteachers who married were fired, a practice that continued until the mid twentieth century in many areas. Defenders of this practice argued that a woman's teaching continued, of course, after marriage, with her most precious pupils—her own children. They provided books of instruction for mothers based on contemporary educational theories in what some historians have termed the "professionalization of motherhood."

The second industrial revolution created technologies of communication, transportation, and computation, including the typewriter, telephone, telegraph, dictation machine, automobile, airplane, and adding machine, that allowed the development of a new sector of the economy in cities and larger towns in the early twentieth century, often termed "postindustrial." In the postindustrial sector, service, sales, and information transfer played a more important role than production, with the store or office rather than the factory the primary place of work. Employees were expected to maintain certain standards of dress and decorum; their jobs were "white-collar," though often the only way those collars (and the white cuffs that went with them) could be kept clean was by making them detachable and washing them after every wear. A white-collar job became a mark of middle-class status, although many paid far less than did blue-collar jobs in factories or as skilled tradesmen. Post-industrial workplaces also had their own gender expectations: Male managers and salesmen were celebrated for both competition and teamwork, and women were hired for their appearance and pleasing demeanor as well as their abilities.

By the end of the nineteenth century, unions and social reformers had succeeded in shortening the work day and work week in many places, and industrial cities became places of leisure as well as labor. Downtown department stores, the first of which was Bon Marché in Paris, offered a staggering variety of consumer goods with fixed, marked prices, and free returns and exchanges, completely new practices in retail trade. To entice customers, department stores spent millions on illustrated newspaper advertising showing goods that were stylish and chic, innovations such as electric lighting and escalators, and elegant fixtures and decorations. They hired female salesclerks to attract middle-class women to the center city and because their wages were lower than those of their male counterparts. From Buenos Aires to Tokyo, shopping became a pastime as well as a necessity. Middle-class urban men and women also attended concerts, theatre and operas, and visited cafés, tea-shops, museums, and in many cities open-air beer gardens, where they drank lager beer made in industrial breweries established by German migrants. Working-class men (and some women) spent time in pubs and taverns, watched spectator sports such as soccer and racing, and went to music halls and vaudeville theatres. Working-class families rarely had much kitchen space, so purchased prepared food from shops and street vendors. In Europe and among European migrants this was primarily white bread, augmented by warm takeout foods such as the frankfurter (served on bread), meat pies, and in the British Isles fish and chips, served with mushy canned peas. By the 1920s, there were 30,000 fish and chip shops in Britain, which used half the fish caught in British waters.

Many middle- and working-class people also attended church, although in Protestant or largely Protestant countries these became increasingly divided by social class and in the United States by race as well. The nineteenth century is often described as a time of growing secularism, when religion became less important in people's lives in Christian areas. This is true for some individuals, especially among educated elites, but for many people religion became *more* important, something to be expressed through daily individual actions and not simply communal worship. The charismatic English religious reformer John Wesley (1703–91), for example, advocated personal regeneration and sanctification through study, prayer and Bible-reading. His followers, known as Methodists, became the largest Protestant denomination in the English-speaking world, and provided strong support for missionaries active everywhere, who built churches and schools and sought converts. Some union leaders opposed the Methodists and other evangelical Protestants for emphasizing holiness and personal morality instead of social change, which they saw as placating and patronizing workers, but many Methodists also came to support humanitarian social causes, including the abolition of slavery, temperance, prison reform, and public education.

MOVEMENTS FOR SOCIAL CHANGE

Problems created by the growth of industry combined with liberal and socialist ideologies advocating greater political and social equality to inspire movements for social change. In crowded industrial cities, workers lived in narrow houses built wall to wall as close to factories as possible, separated by streets and lanes with open sewers and drains. In many Asian cities, human and animal excrement was used as fertilizer on fields and so taken out of the city quickly through an organized system of collectors, but in Europe human excrement was never used in this way, so piled up in communal outhouses until it overflowed and joined the rest of the garbage and animal dung in the streets. Medical reformers increasingly viewed this filth as a source of disease, and advocated the construction of underground systems for sewage and clean water, thus returning to ideas that had been practiced millennia earlier in the ancient Indian city of Mohenjo-Daro and classical Rome. Public health boards were established in the late nineteenth century, and built sanitary systems in many of the cities of Britain, France, Germany, and the United States. Death rates declined dramatically, as outbreaks of typhus, typhoid, cholera, dysentery, and other diseases decreased. In Paris, shoddy slum housing was torn down and new wider streets were laid out, with parks, open spaces, sewers, and fresh water pipes. Paris became the model for other cities, including Mexico City. The destruction of housing meant workers had to live further away from factories, but mass public transportation made this easier: first horse-drawn streetcars that moved on steel tracks, and after the 1890s, electric streetcars, powered by coal-fired power stations. Power stations only increased the amount of coal smoke in the air, and cities were often blackened by smog, but otherwise they slowly became healthier places to live.

The conditions of work under early industrialism were horrendous, with twelve-hour days and dangerous machinery and chemicals. Such conditions led workers beginning in the 1820s to form labor organizations that sought shorter hours, better wages, and safer working conditions. Initially governments outlawed unions and strikes, but workers organized anyway and engaged in actions and collective bargaining. Unions and other labor organizations pushed for an eight-hour work day and a five-day work week instead of the twelve-hour, six-day work schedule that was common; the eight-hour day became law in most industrialized countries in the first quarter of the twentieth century. Unions also pushed for an expansion of the right to vote, which was limited by property restrictions, and by 1914 universal male suffrage among white men was the norm in most countries that chose their leaders though voting. (Indigenous First Peoples were granted voting rights in Canada only in 1960 and Aboriginal peoples in Australia only in 1962, and in many places certain groups were kept from voting by discriminatory practices or violence long after they had officially been granted the vote.)

Unions were predominantly male organizations. Women were harder to organize than men, as their wages were often too low to pay union dues, their family responsibilities prevented them from attending union meetings, and they had been socialized to view their work as temporary and not to challenge male authorities. Women made up a much smaller share of union membership than they did of the workforce, though they often participated with men in strikes, demonstrations, and protests for better conditions, even if they were not members, just as they had in earlier food riots. Separate women's unions were formed in some countries, however; by 1900, for example, women's unions in the tobacco, coffee, and textile industries in Mexico and Puerto Rico were demanding recognition and the right to bargain collectively.

As had working men, women also began to demand the right to vote. The "woman question" was an international issue in the late nineteenth and early twentieth centuries, though with different emphases in different parts of the world. Reformers in India urged an end to female infanticide, the prohibition of widow remarriage, and the practice of *sati*, a widow's self-immolation on her husband's funeral pyre; those in Europe worked for women's rights to own property and control their own wages; those in the United States worked for temperance and women's greater access to education; those in Latin America sought improvements in working conditions, and a restructuring of the civil codes that limited women's land ownership and economic rights. In most parts of the world, reformers did not dispute ideas about the centrality of marriage and motherhood in most women's lives, but used the notion of women's responsibility for home and family as the very reason that women should have an equal voice with men, often intertwining this with ideas about what would make their nation stronger. Women, they argued, needed the vote to assure the well-being of their families and children, and would clean up corrupt politics in the same way that they cleaned up their households. A Japanese suffrage song from the early twentieth century called on women to "Be wise mothers and sisters to our people, and spread women's love throughout the land. Let us scrub away the age-old corruption of politics run by men and for men."

Groups specifically devoted to women's political rights began to be established in many countries of the world; they organized petition drives, letter-writing campaigns, demonstrations, marches, and hunger strikes, communicating with each other in what became an international feminist movement. Suffragists were initially ridiculed and attacked physically, and in many countries anti-suffrage groups were formed whose tactics paralleled those of the suffrage groups; such groups included women as well as men, for women have been the only group in history to mobilize both for and against their own enfranchisement. The efforts of suffragists, combined with international events such as World War I, were ultimately successful, however, and suffrage rights were gradually extended to women over the twentieth century.

Both women and men became involved in movements for other types of liberal social change along with those for better working conditions and broader political rights, including prison reform, temperance, the extension of free public schooling, and the protection of animals. The abolitionist movement, inspired by the published writings and speeches of former slaves such as Olaudah Equiano (1745–97), and led by activists in Christian churches and advocates of human rights, called for an end to slavery and the slave trade. The revolutionary governments of France and Haiti outlawed slavery, although that of the United States did not. Britain and the USA banned the transatlantic slave trade in 1807, though Britain did not end slavery itself in its colonies until 1833 and the USA only in 1865, as a result of the Civil War. The new independent nations established in Latin America in the early nineteenth century outlawed slavery, as did France in its colonies in 1848, and finally Cuba and Brazil in the 1880s.

The end of slavery did not bring dramatic change for most people of African descent in the Americas, however. In Latin America and the Caribbean, the multi-category racial hierarchies that had developed in the colonial period provided some social and economic mobility for mixed-race people with lighter skin. Those with darker skin remained on the bottom. Former slaves generally became sharecroppers or tenant farmers, or workers in mines and factories, as did indigenous people. In the United States, after a brief period following the Civil War in which former slaves voted and a few were even elected to office, white Southerners reasserted their power, passing so-called Jim Crow laws to keep blacks from voting through literacy tests, poll taxes, and property restrictions, and

5.3 A woman dominates her tiny (and drunken) husband in this anti-suffrage postcard from early twentieth-century England. Suffragists and their opponents waged their battle in all available media.

enforcing rigid racial segregation in schools, housing, employment, and every other aspect of life. Most former slaves became sharecroppers on white-owned land, paying landowners about half a year's crops in return for seed, mules, a cabin, and tools. Black domestic servants were found in many white households, but otherwise even brothels, taverns, and toilets were supposed to be racially segregated. In the dichotomous racial system that had developed in the United States, even a small amount of "black blood" made one black, an idea reaffirmed with a vengeance in the 1896 US Supreme Court case Plessy vs. Ferguson, which upheld a lower court case requiring a New Orleans man who was one-eighth black to ride in a "colored" railway car. This "separate but equal" doctrine made racial segregation legal, and was enforced in all Southern states; in reality segregated schools and other facilities were never equal.

Racial segregation and discrimination in the late nineteenth and twentieth centuries were bolstered by new ideas about the reasons for differences among groups of people understood as grounded in science. In *On the Origin of Species by the Means of Natural Selection* (1859), the British scientist Charles Darwin proposed that all life had evolved from a common origin through the process of natural selection, by which small differences within individuals in one species had given them advantages that allowed them to gain more food or better living conditions. This made them more successful in reproduction and allowed them to pass on their genetic material to the next generation. Because Darwin included humans in his conceptualization, this idea provoked furious controversy, although today evolution by natural selection is one of the fundamental principles of biology. The English philosopher Herbert Spencer (1820–1903) and others applied evolutionary thinking to human society, arguing that history was a "survival of the fittest" in which the strong were destined to triumph and prosper and the weak be conquered or remain poor. This "Social Darwinism"—a term coined later by its opponents—built on existing ideas about qualities passed on in the blood and about ethnic superiority, which were being enhanced at just this point by the growth of nationalism. "Survival of the fittest" was applied to every sort of difference: nation, ethnicity, race, gender, class. European and American scientists and physicians, along with scholars in new fields such as anthropology and psychology, sought to provide proof of these differences by measuring skulls, brains, facial angles, forehead height (the origin of the terms highbrow, middlebrow, and lowbrow), and other features, publishing their findings in scholarly and professional journals and in books and articles for a more popular audience. Unsurprisingly, their findings supported the idea that whites were more intelligent than other races, what the black American historian and activist W.E.B. Dubois (1868–1963) called in 1910 "this new religion of whiteness." Whiteness also had gradations of fitness, however, as scientists, thinkers, and political leaders sought to prove the existence of a northern European "Nordic race" or "Aryan race" superior to southern Europeans, identified Jews as a separate "Semitic race," and asserted that criminals and the poor were anatomically different.

These ideas led to calls for social and political changes, as groups advocating change in this era included many that wanted less equality, not more. In the western United States, hostility toward Chinese workers led to riots and other types of violence, and to restrictions on immigration by place of origin. These began with the Chinese Exclusion Act of 1882, which forbade Chinese laborers from entering the country and prohibited those already in the USA from becoming citizens. The world was divided, as one US Senator put it, between beef-eating men and rice-eating men, and the beef-eating men needed to protect themselves from what was regularly referred to across the English-speaking world as the "yellow peril." In the eastern United States, worries centered on immigrants from southern and eastern Europe, often Catholics or Jews, which Senator Henry Cabot Lodge, the leader of the Senate and a close friend of President Theodore Roosevelt, described as "removed from us in race and blood." (By "us" he meant Anglo-Saxons, also viewed as a race in this era.) In 1894, three recent Harvard University graduates established the Immigration Restriction League, which pushed for literacy tests as a requirement of immigration; these became part of a comprehensive Immigration Act in 1917. This act also banned "homosexuals, idiots, feeble-minded persons, criminals, professional beggars," and others judged "mentally or physically defective," along with all immigration from an "Asiatic Barred Zone" that stretched from Turkey to New Guinea. The subsequent

Immigration Act of 1924 continued these bans, and sought to freeze the existing ethnic distribution by introducing nationality quotas set according to the census of 1890, thus before most eastern and southern Europeans had immigrated. National quotas remained the basis of US immigration policy until 1965. In Australia, which became self-governing in the 1850s, the Commonwealth Immigration Act of 1901 closed immigration to Asians completely and established a "white Australia policy" that remained on the books until the 1970s. Similar measures were passed in New Zealand and Canada in the 1920s. Governments of industrialized countries thus acted to assure the free flow of capital and commodities, but prohibited that of people.

In Brazil and Cuba, measures were passed to encourage immigration from Europe, not only to bring in labor for plantations and factories, but explicitly to "whiten" the population through intermarriage with people already there. In many parts of the world, color lines were drawn around territories, districts, and neighborhoods to separate white from non-white spaces. Documents identifying race, place of birth, parents, and other personal characteristics were developed and required, part of an increasingly routine surveillance and management of human life that the French social theorist Michel Foucault has called "biopower."

For some, "survival of the fittest" was not to be left to natural selection or immigration restrictions alone, but should be shaped by the intentional selective breeding of certain types of people and the prevention of breeding among the unfit. This idea was promulgated in the eugenics movement, which gained broad acceptance around the world in the first third of the twentieth century, with financial support from governments, universities, foundations established by major industrialists such as the Carnegie and Rockefeller Foundations, and civic groups. Laws ordering sterilization of criminals, the "feeble-minded" or others viewed as genetically undesirable were passed in the United States, Canada, Japan, Brazil, and most of the countries of Europe, and tens of thousands of people were sterilized. People applying for marriage licenses were required to have medical certifications, and laws added eugenics language about "racial integrity" and "racial hygiene" to prohibitions on marriage between certain groups. Various positive measures were also adopted,

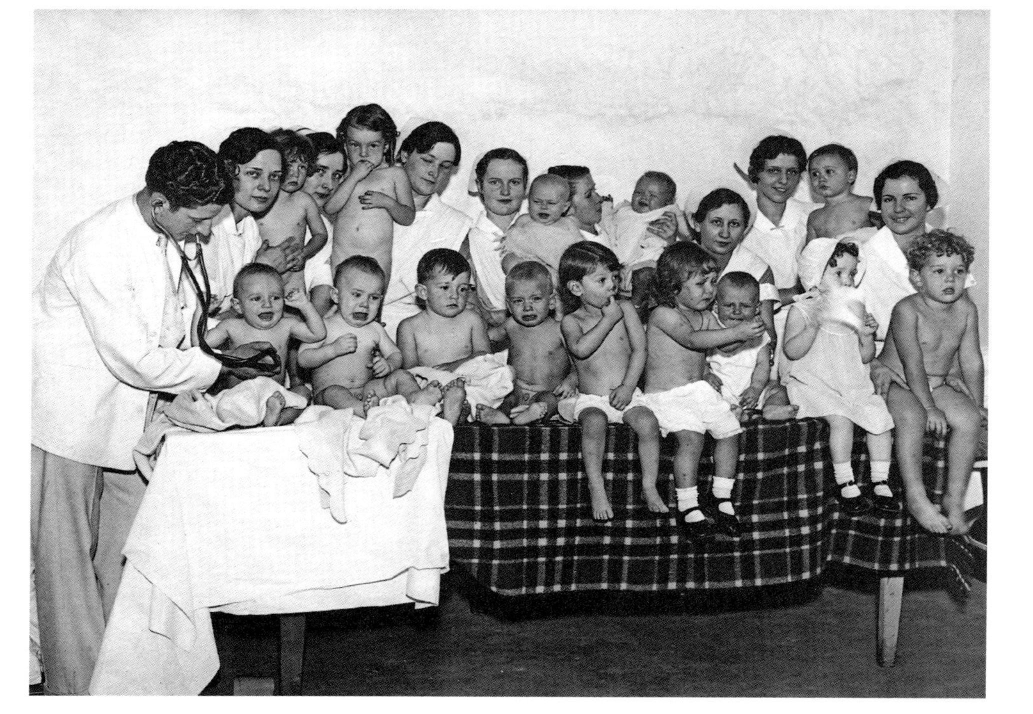

5.4 Better Baby Contest, sponsored by the Kallpolis Grotto Masonic Lodge, Washington, DC, 1931. The original newspaper caption commented that a staff of forty physicians and nurses was "faced with the stupendous task of examining 983 children between the ages of 2 months and 5 years," and that "at least 8 hours will be required to inspect all the youngsters."

including payments or tax breaks for couples who had the appropriate type of children, and "better baby" and "fitter family" contests that presented awards to children and families with certain physical and behavioral characteristics. Both negative and positive measures used elsewhere were adopted by Nazi Germany, and carried to extremes, as hundreds of thousands of people viewed as physically or mentally unfit were forcibly sterilized or simply killed, experiments were conducted on children to test genetic theories, marriages between "Aryans" and "non-Aryans" were declared "racial defilement" (*Rassenschande*) and prohibited, and awards were presented to women who bore many "Aryan" children. Eugenics was discredited by its association with Nazi racial ideology, although forced sterilization programs of mentally handicapped individuals continued at least into the 1960s and perhaps longer.

POPULATION GROWTH AND MIGRATION

Eugenics and other racial ideologies developed in a world in which not just the fittest were surviving. As a species, humans were showing amazing evolutionary success, reproducing and passing their genetic material to the next generation very well. Despite continued famines, war, and epidemics, beginning about 1700 global population began to go up, and especially after 1750 to go up at a steadily increasing rate. Without significant immigration from other parts of the world, and despite fairly substantial emigration to the Americas, the population of Europe nearly doubled from 1750 to 1850, from about 140 million to about 270 million, and that of England tripled. Public health measures, especially water and sewer systems that lessened contagious and intestinal diseases, were one important factor. Contagious diseases tend to hit infants and children particularly hard, so that a slight reduction in their occurrence decreases infant and child mortality faster than the mortality of adults, which has a multiplier effect, as those children grow up to have their own children. Draining swamps and marshes—done to increase agricultural land, not as a public health measure—reduced the fly and mosquito population, which lessened outbreaks of malaria and other insect-borne diseases. Climatic conditions improved slightly after the cooling trend in the seventeenth century, which brought increases in food production and fewer disastrous harvests. Food could be transported on canal and railroad systems, lessening localized famines. Eighteenth- and nineteenth-century armies were larger and their weapons were deadlier, but they were generally provisioned rather than living off the land, so they confiscated less food and supplies than had earlier armies. Historians and demographers debate exactly which of these factors was the most important, but there is no debate about the actual trends.

In Europe, the decline in death rates and consequent population growth accompanied industrialization, which also happened in Japan, where population grew from 33 million at the time of the Meiji Restoration in 1872 (about the same as the population of the United Kingdom at that point, and somewhat less than the population of the United States or France) to 69 million in 1935. By this time about a third of the Japanese people lived in cities, including 6 million in Tokyo. Rice production increased with the use of new varieties and techniques, and public health measures improved sanitation and the water supply. Railroads constructed in the last part of the nineteenth century carried rice and other foodstuffs to the growing cities from rural areas, and ships brought food from overseas.

Elsewhere the decline in death rates occurred without high levels of industrialization. In China, population began to grow steadily in the eighteenth century as well, in part because of the increased food supply that resulted from New World crops such as corn and the sweet potato, but also because of the Qing government's measures to improve transportation networks and distribute food or adjust taxation (paid in grain) during shortages. Estimates of the population of China place it at about 150–200 million in 1700, and 400 million in 1900. In India, the population grew from about 100 million in 1700 to about 300 million in 1900, aided by expanded irrigation systems and a rail network that carried food to famine-struck areas.

Declining death rates had other effects besides increasing the total population. They gradually regularized the process of life, and death became associated with aging, rather than being something that occurred randomly. Infant and child mortality slowly declined, so that the most perilous years of life—the period in which the greatest percentage of the population died—were no longer the first five. Even more dramatic was a decrease in mortality among older children and adolescents. In 1750, a ten-year-old child in France had a one in four chance of dying before his or her mother; by 1850 this had declined significantly (and today it is about one in sixty).

Most leaders and opinion-shapers who were aware of the growing population of their own nations in the eighteenth and nineteenth centuries saw this as a cause for celebration, as they regarded a large population as essential for a strong country. A few did worry that the growth in population might outstrip any surplus, however. The Qing scholar Hong Liangji (1746–1809) and the English clergyman and economist Thomas Malthus (1766–1834) both argued that population increases geometrically while food supply increases arithmetically, so that population will always outstrip food supply. They looked to history as well as mathematical models for their proof, noting the many times that famine, disease, and war had served as a check on population growth. They wondered when their societies would reach what later economists called the "Malthusian limit" and suffer a catastrophic collapse, and suggested measures that might delay this, such as emigration. Malthus also suggested moral restraint might lower the birth rate, as would what he termed "vice," by which he meant contraception.

For working-class families, lower child mortality was both joyful and burdensome, and the demand for contraception grew in the late nineteenth century. The same leaders who described the family as a private haven viewed birth control as a highly public issue, however, passing laws that prohibited the distribution of birth control devices, and arresting those who disseminated birth control information, especially when this was to working-class women. Religious authorities also made pronouncements on this issue; Pope Pius IX, for example, declared in 1869 that the fetus acquires a soul at conception rather than at quickening, which had been the standard Western opinion before that point. (Quickening is the point when a mother feels movement, usually about the third or fourth month; the word "quick" is an old word for alive, as in the phrase "the quick and the dead.") Any postconception methods of contraception would thus be considered abortion, whereas until this point they had been viewed as contraception, a lesser sin. Birth rates did begin to go down slightly in industrialized countries in the first half of the twentieth century, but not until birth control became culturally acceptable, more reliable, and more widely available in the 1960s did families grow significantly smaller.

The other option suggested by Malthus and Hong Liangji for overpopulation—migration—was a far more common solution than contraception to population pressures and poverty, and also to religious persecution, war, political turmoil, family stresses, and other problems that pushed migrants from their homelands. Migrants were pulled to certain parts of the world by the hope of a better life, often influenced by agents, labor brokers, and advertisements that promised land, high wages, or easy riches. The hysteria about immigrants in the early twentieth century was fueled by racism, but also by the fact that steamships had made long-distance migration much easier and cheaper, and millions of people moved.

In the century before the outbreak of World War I in 1914, 50–60 million Europeans emigrated, with the crest coming in the first decade of the twentieth century. Some of these eventually returned to Europe—no statistics were kept on return migration, so it is impossible to know how many did—but most stayed. More than half went to the United States, including 4 million Irish, which together with the potato famine cut the Irish population by half. Two million British and Irish people moved to Australia and New Zealand, beginning in 1787 when a thousand convicts were sent to a penal colony established at Botany Bay (today's Sydney) after the American War of Independence made transporting British convicts to North America no longer feasible. Australia was already populated by 300,000–800,000 Aborigines, but the British simply ignored this, declaring the land empty. The white population of Australia—most of whom were actually voluntary migrants, not convicts—remained small until gold was discovered in 1851, when it ballooned, some coming from California, which had experienced a similar gold rush two years earlier. The gold rush also brought in Chinese workers, who as in the USA built railroads, which carried settlers in and wool and wheat from Australia's expanding sheep ranches and farms out. Also as in the USA, racist hostility to Asians led to riots and legislation increasingly limiting Asian immigration.

Many southern Europeans moved to South America, where they formed the majority of the population in rapidly growing cities such as Buenos Aires and Rio de Janeiro. Here they worked twelve-hour days in meatpacking, food-processing, wool production and other industries that processed South American raw materials, but had a better chance of upward mobility than they would have had in Europe and gradually came to dominate certain industries and move into the middle class. In contrast to European immigrants to North America, who generally went as family groups, most European immigrants to Latin America and the Caribbean were young single males. They married indigenous, African-background, or mixed-race women, further increasing the ethnic and cultural mixture. That pattern can now be traced through genetic evidence. In Brazil for example, around 75–80 percent of the gene pool in the early twenty-first century comes from Europe, around 15 percent from Africa, and around 10 percent is indigenous, with most people having a mixture of all of these, no matter what their classification on the national census or outward appearance; almost all of the African and indigenous genetic material comes from their mother's side. This mixture was reflected in new musical forms that blended African and European traditions, including the tango in Argentina and the samba in Brazil, which were then carried around the world through further immigration or by traveling bands and singers who entertained at clubs and dance halls. In part to counter eugenicist ideas about "racial hygiene" that were gaining an audience in Brazil, the Brazilian sociologist Gilberto Freyre (1900–87) developed the idea that blending such as this gave Brazil an edge economically as well as culturally. That idea was later extended to Portugal and all of its colonies in an ideology known as Lusotropicalism, though Freyre was criticized for ignoring the very real racial and social hierarchies of Brazil and creating a myth of racial harmony and democracy.

Asians also migrated in unprecedented numbers in the nineteenth and early twentieth centuries. Chinese had long emigrated from southern coastal regions to Southeast Asia, where they established mercantile communities, sometimes marrying local women in long-term temporary marriages, and sometimes forming separate ethnic enclaves. When these areas became part of European colonial

5.5 Indentured plantation workers from India arrive in Port of Spain, Trinidad, in 1891. More than 130,000 immigrants from India came to Trinidad between 1845 and the official ending of the indentured labor system in 1917, and many stayed.

empires, Chinese immigration increased, ranging from wealthy merchants who established tin mines to penniless laborers who worked in them, or on sugar, tobacco, cocoa, rice, tea, and rubber plantations alongside local people. Contractors traveled to China to recruit laborers for mines and plantations elsewhere as well, including Hawai'i, South Africa, Brazil, and the Caribbean, where the end of the slave trade had created a labor shortage. Most of these were indentured laborers, hired under five- or eight-year contracts, paid almost nothing, fed badly, and placed in chains if they tried to flee. Japanese people migrated to Hawai'i, California, Peru, and Brazil to work on plantations and produce farms. The USA banned further Japanese immigration in 1924, a move that politicians advocated in Brazil as well, as Japanese and other Asians did not fit with their policy of racial whitening. Indentured laborers were also recruited in India, and hundreds of thousands migrated to the Indian Ocean island of Mauritius, South and East Africa, Malaya, Fiji, British Guiana (now Guyana) and Dutch Guiana (now Suriname) in northern South America, and the Caribbean, especially Trinidad; here they worked on plantations, built railroads, and opened shops. Some Indians returned home, but many stayed, expanding trade, business, and social networks based on kin and caste ties around the world in a global diaspora. The first wave of Indian migrants was often young, unmarried men, but they tended to arrange for women to be sent from home to marry rather than marry local women. Today people of Indian or mixed-Indian ancestry make up at least half of the population in Fiji, Mauritius, Trinidad, Guyana, and Suriname, and are significant minorities in Kenya, South Africa, Burma, Malaysia, and Singapore.

THE NEW IMPERIALISM

The migration patterns and social systems of the nineteenth and early twentieth centuries were shaped by population increase and racial ideologies, and also by the establishment of global European empires made possible, as Nehru asserted, through industrial technologies. They often built on or began as informal commercial empires run by companies, and then became formal political empires run by civilian or military officials. The social structures of these empires were different from those of the early modern period in several ways: gradually more women joined their husbands and fathers, and sexual relations involving European men and local women were generally seen as prostitution rather than marriage or another type of recognized relationship. European families attempted to recreate life "at home" as much as possible, eating imported industrially produced foods and wearing clothing dictated by European norms and weather. European families included those of Christian missionaries, now Protestant as well as Catholic, who attempted to model proper family life as well as convert and "civilize" the people among whom they worked.

Imperial power was explicitly and implicitly linked with cultural constructions of masculinity and femininity for both colonizers and colonized. European (and later American) officials, merchants, and missionaries often viewed women's less restrictive dress in tropical areas as a sign of sexual looseness, men's lack of facial hair or trousers as a sign of effeminacy, and any marital pattern other than permanent monogamy as a sign of inferiority. They sought to impose their own views of proper gender relations on their far-flung colonies, establishing schools to teach Western values and using taxes, permits, and registration documents to impose Western family structures.

In South Asia, largely independent regional governors and external enemies weakened the Mughal Empire in the eighteenth century, and the British East India Company (EIC) came to govern more and more territory in alliance with local princes. The EIC exported Indian cottons by the boatload, but there was little demand for these in China, nor for anything else the EIC brought in except for silver. That changed when English merchants began to smuggle increasing amounts of opium grown in India into China. When in 1839 the Chinese government attempted to stop opium importation in order to halt the spread of addiction, the British responded with warships, took over key coastal cities, and forced the Chinese to agree to open ports to European trade (including opium). That still was not enough to solve the growing European addiction to tea in this era of industrialization, so the EIC sent a botanist to China, where he stole tea plants and the techniques of processing tea. Tea-growing was introduced to

British-ruled Ceylon, Dutch-occupied Java, and then to Assam, a thinly populated forested region of northeast India. European planters who promised to grow tea were given land to cultivate, and the indigenous population was forced either to move or to work on tea plantations through methods similar to those used in the United States and Mexico, including military force, debt peonage, and the criminalization of hunting and foraging.

Although the British government regularly supported the EIC, it also increasingly thought the company was corrupt, and in 1857 decided to rule India directly through a civil service, transforming an informal empire into a formal one. The upper echelons of the civil service were all white, and they created a lifestyle more luxurious than would have been possible back in England, with cooks, chauffeurs, gardeners, and maids instead of the one servant-girl common in most middle-class households. Because there were only a few thousand to govern a population of several hundred million, they depended on Indian officials and bureaucrats. Missionaries and social reformers opened thousands of English-language schools, where high-caste Hindus and well-to-do Muslims learned Western curricula; many went on to colleges and universities to study law and other advanced subjects. The British built railroads and irrigation systems to aid the expansion of agriculture, particularly plantation agriculture that raised cash crops such as coffee, sugar, cotton, opium, and tea.

In the last half of the nineteenth century, the British expanded their territory to include Burma, Malaya, and parts of Borneo, bringing in indentured laborers from India and China to harvest timber, mine tin, and grow rubber and rice. At the same time the French seized Vietnam, and then Laos and Cambodia, to form French Indochina in 1887, and the Dutch government took over direct control of Java and other islands from the Dutch East India Company, leaving Siam as the only independent state in Southeast Asia. Colonial regimes often required rural people who were unable to pay taxes to work on plantations or in mines, or to purchase certain items from government monopolies. In Vietnam, for example, French authorities required all villages to buy a designated amount of opium and alcohol from government authorities, which increased opium addiction and alcoholism.

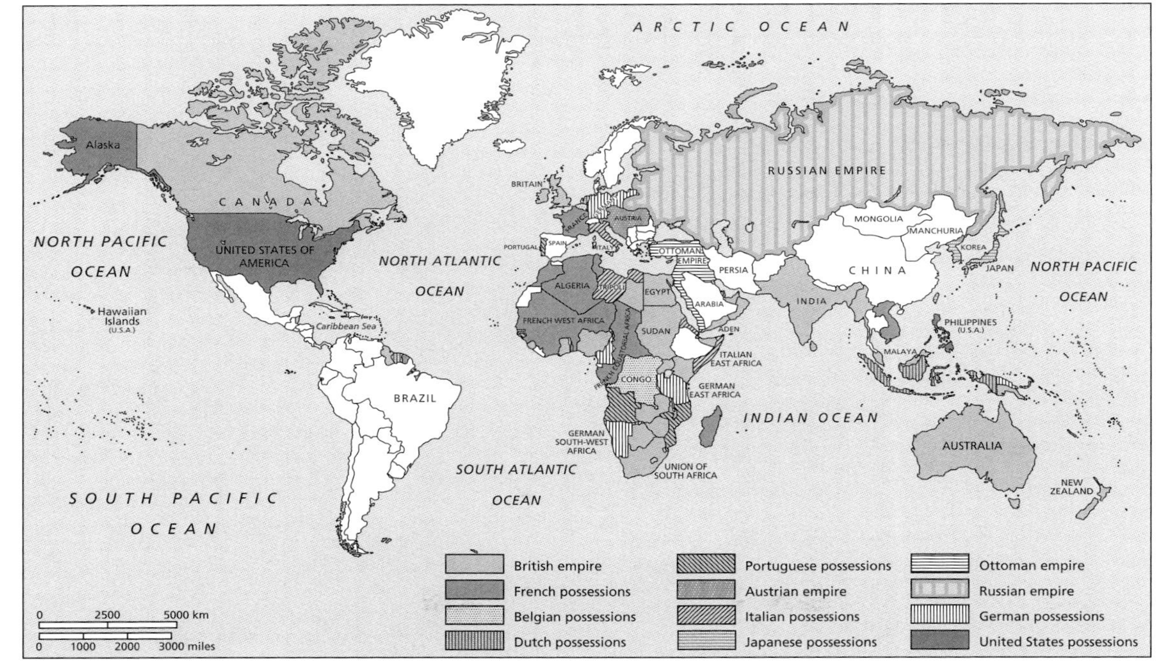

Map 5.2 Major overseas empires, 1914

Imperialism followed a different course in Africa. The transatlantic slave trade slowly declined beginning in the 1830s, and small settlements of freed slaves shipped from British colonies and the USA emerged in Sierra Leone and Liberia. European colonies were limited to tiny areas along the coasts, for malaria and other diseases killed Europeans who ventured inland. In searching for an export good to replace slaves, British, US, and local merchants established palm tree plantations in West Africa, where workers harvested palm oil for lubricating machinery and manufacturing cosmetics and soap. (The brand Palmolive is a vestige of this, although now soaps and detergents are made from petroleum products.) Such plantations encouraged slavery rather than ending it, however, as local warlords continued slave-raiding, now sending men they had captured to grow crops, mine gold, and transport goods locally instead of to the Americas, while women were retained as workers and secondary wives, as they always had been. Some of these plantations were in states such as Sokoto (part of today's Nigeria) where charismatic Muslim religious leaders had recently attracted broad followings by calling for a purer Islam purged of animist practices and local customs. A more orthodox Islam, including regular worship and the veiling of women, was becoming a vital cultural force, but this also contributed to the continuation of slavery, as Islam allowed the enslavement of non-Muslims. Slavery continued in East Africa as well, as Arabs built a commercial network centered on the island of Zanzibar, shipping slaves, ivory, and other natural products taken from the East African interior across the Indian Ocean.

These patterns changed abruptly and dramatically in the period 1880–1914, when Britain, France, Germany, Belgium, Spain, and Italy scrambled to take what King Leopold II of Belgium called "a piece of that magnificent African cake." European armies pushed insistently into the African interior, and by 1914 controlled almost all of the continent except Ethiopia and Liberia. The causes of this new imperialism were intertwined, just as were the causes of the Industrial Revolution, and many of them were directly related to industrialization. European companies sought direct access to raw materials and agricultural products and did not want African intermediaries. Once one nation began to grab territory, others worried that they would erect tariff barriers and lessen future opportunities, so grabbed their own. Industrially produced weapons, especially the Gatling gun, a hand-cranked machine gun that could fire 1,000 rounds a minute, and the Maxim gun, an automatic recoil-operated machine gun, allowed the easy slaughter and defeat of people armed with spears, swords, or at best rifles. As the Anglo-French writer, soldier, and historian Hilaire Belloc (1870–1953) put it, speaking as the voice of Blood, in his poem "The Modern Traveller": "Whatever happens, we have got / The Maxim gun, and they have not." Newly discovered quinine proved effective in controlling malaria, and steamships and later the railroad allowed medicine, manpower, weapons, and supplies to be delivered quickly. Agents of European governments preferred to acquire land by peaceful means such as treaties and bribes rather than have to waste manpower on war, but African leaders knew that resistance would be met with force. Despite this, political and military resistance, sometimes led by Muslim or animist religious leaders, in Sokoto, the Ashante kingdom (today's Ghana), among the Mandinka people of western Sudan and the Shona and Ndebele in southern Africa, slowed down the process of conquest.

Ideas as well as technology played an important role in imperialism. In an atmosphere of nationalist rivalry and "survival of the fittest," no nation wanted to appear weak or unmanly. Journalists and political leaders whipped up popular support for conquests, arguing that colonies benefited local people as well as European plantation and mine owners. Christian missionaries published accounts of the horrors of the slave trade, and Europeans and Americans came to believe they had a sacred mission to bring, in the words of the Scottish medical missionary and explorer David Livingstone, "Commerce, Christianity, and Civilization" to "Darkest Africa." The English poet and official Rudyard Kipling referred to this as "the white man's burden," a phrase that was later used to sell Pears' Soap, which its advertisements proclaimed as "a potent factor in brightening the dark corners of the earth as civilization advances." There were critics of imperialism in Europe and the USA, but they were few.

This new imperialism changed Africa dramatically. Government authorities and private companies used violence to appropriate land, retain control, and force Africans to work long hours at demanding and dangerous jobs. European powers established strong authoritarian control in the name of "good government," building up armies and police forces of Africans to protect property and put down revolts, and bureaucracies to collect taxes. In the early twentieth century they built railroads to get raw materials from the interior to ports, and then roads for trucks. Slavery ended slowly, replaced in many places by a system of forced labor in which Africans worked for wages or exchanged their labor directly to pay taxes and purchase goods. Commercial agriculture for export and mining both employed many more men than women, and men left their villages for years at a time to grow cocoa, mine diamonds or gold, or build railroads, leaving women to continue subsistence agriculture, a gendered labor pattern similar to that of Latin America. Where the climate was cooler, such as British East Africa (today's Kenya) and southern Africa, settlers from Europe and from India immigrated in substantial numbers, and formed the bulk of the urban professional and mercantile class. In other places, such as the Gold Coast (today's Ghana), there was less immigration and a westernized African elite of lawyers, businesspeople, civil servants, and professionals educated in missionary schools and sometimes European universities gained some control over economic resources. As in South Asia, imperial power was maintained by giving some individuals and groups from among the subordinated population special privileges, and convincing them the new system was beneficial or preferable, a system referred to as hegemony.

The new imperialism of the late nineteenth and early twentieth centuries was primarily a European venture, although the USA and Japan acquired overseas territories as well, with opinion leaders in both countries arguing that expansion was essential for a strong, manly nation. American settlers led by sugar planters and US troops overthrew the ruling queen of Hawai'i in 1893, and the USA annexed the islands as a territory. In the Spanish-American War (1898–1902), the USA coopted revolutions against Spanish rule in Cuba and the Philippines, transforming them as well as Guam and Puerto Rico into formal colonies or effectively colonies. Japan successfully fought China over influence in Korea and Taiwan, and in 1910 took over both as outright colonies. Opposition to Japanese rule and attempts at cultural assimilation in Korea took widely varying forms, including political demonstrations, conversion to Christianity, and the growth of a strong ethnic nationalism emphasizing the purity of the Korean "race" or bloodline (*minjok* in Korean).

TOTAL WAR AND MODERN CULTURE

Nationalism led European states into a frantic rush to plant their flags over as much of the globe as possible, and it also led to a war of unprecedented scope, which strengthened anti-imperial nationalism around the world but also spurred the creation of authoritarian regimes that sought to create completely new types of societies. World War I (1914–18) was sparked by nationalists in the Balkans who wanted to carve their own countries out of the multi-ethnic Austro-Hungarian and Ottoman empires, and was prefaced by a series of Balkan Wars. It eventually pitted most of the countries of Europe, including Russia, against one another in a war that was enormously destructive. Nationalistic propaganda encouraged young men to enlist and whipped up support, portraying the outbreak of war as a great heroic moment, when "the flashing of the unsheathed sword" could lift men from their "wish for indulgence and wretched sensitiveness." Both sides fielded huge armies that fought in trench or battlefield warfare in which millions were killed, wounded, or taken prisoner. Their weapons and supplies included all the newest products of industry: heavy artillery, giant battleships, poisonous gas, canned food, mass-produced uniforms, synthetic rubber. The British poet Wilfred Owen, who was killed in battle a week before the war ended, captured the effects of gas on a soldier who did not get his gas-mask on in time: "Dim, through the misty panes and thick green light, / As under a green sea, I saw him drowning / … the white eyes writhing in his face, / … the blood come gargling from the froth-corrupted lungs." Nations mobilized their populations to be part of the war effort, rationing food and other goods, organizing production, allocating labor, setting wage rates, and encouraging more women to join the paid labor force with facilities such as child care centers. More than a million conscripted or recruited colonial troops fought in Europe and in European colonies around the world, often very successfully, destroying the impression that Europeans were somehow superior and creating resentment at the tens of thousands of wasted lives.

After three years of slaughter on the eastern front, a revolution of soldiers, peasants, and city residents overthrew the tsarist government of Russia in 1917, and in the disorder that followed the communist Bolsheviks under the leadership of Vladimir Lenin (1870–1924) came to power. Renaming their nation the Union of Soviet Socialist Republics, Lenin and other Communist Party leaders asserted that imperialism was the direct result of industrial capitalism and that communist revolution would bring an end to colonial exploitation, an idea that proved attractive around the world but also provoked anti-communist "Red Scares" of government crackdowns on labor leaders, immigrants, and advocates of civil rights.

The United States entered the war shortly before Russia left it, and this tipped the balance of power in the favor of the Allies. The Treaty of Versailles negotiated in Paris in 1919 declared Germany and Austria were responsible for the war, demanded they pay reparations, and transferred Germany's colonies to France, Britain, and Japan (an ally of Britain), denying Germany an empire. The Austro-Hungarian and Ottoman empires were dissolved and the League of Nations was established as an attempt to prevent future wars, although the USA refused to join and retreated into formal political isolationism. World War I allowed the USA to leap ahead of Europe economically, and by 1919 it was producing 42 percent of the world's industrial output, more than all of Europe combined.

Britain and France had made vague promises of self-government, independence, land, and jobs to gain support for the war from their colonial subjects, but at the Paris Peace Conference would not even listen to proposals for national self-determination from individuals such as the Vietnamese leader who would later take the name Ho Chi Minh (1890–1969). The victorious allies made independent nations out of Austro-Hungarian and Ottoman territories in Europe, but they refused to extend this to Asia or Africa, which they defined as "peoples incapable of governing themselves." Instead the "well-being and development of such peoples" would be assured by "developed nations" until some unspecified point in the future. Disillusioned with democracy, Ho became one of the founders of both the French Communist Party and the Indochinese Communist Party.

In the former Ottoman Empire, France ruled Lebanon and Syria under a mandate system, and Britain Jordan, Iraq, and Palestine, in which it promised to establish a Jewish national homeland. Many European Jews migrated to Palestine. Arabs gradually won control over internal political affairs, but Western powers retained control of much of the economy, including the newly discovered oil fields. Europeans also occupied parts of Turkey, but a revolution led by Mustafa Kemal (1881–1938) threw them out, deposed the Ottoman sultan, and established a secular state in which law codes influenced by Western models replaced Islamic law, including that governing marriage, and secular schools expanded literacy, now in a new Turkish script instead of Arabic. As in Meiji Restoration Japan, dress was westernized, with government employees ordered to wear suits and women to appear in public without veils. Arabia moved in the other direction, when the powerful tribal leader Abdul Aziz Ibn Saud (1902–69), whose forces were conquering the Arabian peninsula, accepted the puritanical and anti-Western version of Islam known as Wahhabism. Saudi authorities strictly enforced what they saw as an uncorrupted version of Islam, prohibiting alcohol, tobacco, and women appearing in public unveiled or without a male escort, though they welcomed material innovations, which flowed especially to the royal family and its allies after the world's richest oil reserves were discovered in Saudi Arabia in 1935.

In South and Southeast Asia, educated elites increasingly demanded the self-government that nationalists claimed in Europe, along with the political rights that working-class men had gained through union activism. Among these was Mohandas Gandhi (1869–1948), who studied law in England, led a campaign for the rights of Indian immigrants in Natal in South Africa, and then in 1920 launched a non-violent campaign against British rule in India, among other things urging people to spin and weave their own cloth and not buy imported British goods. The nationalist independence movement grew into a mass movement, supported by people of all castes as well as the outcaste "untouchables," whom Gandhi welcomed. Gandhi and other leaders, including Nehru, were arrested and imprisoned off and on through the 1920s, 1930s, and most of

World War II for sedition and fomenting rebellion, but the British began to negotiate. In French Indochina, colonial authorities repressed all nationalist groups in the 1930s, and only the communists survived. In Vietnam, they waged war against the French, Japanese occupiers during World War II, and ultimately the USA, linking themselves in poems, songs, speeches, and images with long traditions of Vietnamese resistance to foreign conquerors. In the Dutch East Indies, nationalist leaders sought freedom from Dutch control, transforming Malay, which had been a language of trade across much of this huge culturally diverse area, into a unifying national language, which they called Indonesian. Some adopted a more conservative Islam and wanted to rid Indonesia of anything un-Islamic, whether Western or pre-Muslim local traditions, while others adopted Marxist ideas, or blended all these in a distinctive Indonesian nationalism.

As World War I sparked political and cultural nationalism in colonial areas, it also led to dramatic cultural change in the West. Young people turned against what they saw as the values of an older generation that had led to the unprecedented carnage of industrial warfare. They listened to new types of music, including jazz, either live or on wind-up phonographs, wore less restrictive clothing, and watched motion pictures with internationally known stars such as Charlie Chaplin or Rudolph Valentino at movie houses in cities. They even rejected their parents' notion of the ideal body type; wealth and social prominence were now to be shown through a slender figure rather than the bulky body of prewar "men of substance." Bicycles allowed young people, including women, to travel without parental supervision and for wealthier people automobiles further increased mobility for work and leisure. Writers and creative artists rejected old forms and values in favor of ones designed to shock, challenge, and perhaps foment radical social change, but also to strip things to their basics, a movement that came to be called "modernism." Modern architecture and furniture used straight lines with no ornamentation, and modern art, music, and literature sought to express anxiety, multiplicity, irony, and dissonance rather than heroism, glory, harmony, and unity, as these seemed absurd. Art in particular often incorporated Europeans' growing familiarity with non-Western art as artists traveled in colonial empires or

5.6 Poster for the French bicycle company De Dion-Bouton, 1921. Advertisements for bicycles, cars, and other consumer goods in the 1920s often showed young people in fashionable modern clothing, and emphasized mobility and freedom.

objects were shipped back to European museums for display. In Paris, for example, the Spanish artist Pablo Picasso (1881–1973) drew on the ways African masks portray faces to create cubist forms of zigzagging lines and angled overlapping planes. Artists and writers were also influenced by the ideas of Sigmund Freud (1856–1939), an Austrian neurologist and inventor of psychoanalysis, who argued that human behavior was guided in part by reason, but also by powerful subconscious desires such as aggression and pleasure-seeking that people repressed in order to live peacefully in society.

Freud's ideas were an important part of what historians have called "modern" sexuality—by which they mean modern Western sexuality. Sexual desires and activity that deviated from the expected norm were increasingly viewed not as sin, but as "degeneracy" or as "perversion" to be corrected or prevented by scientifically trained professionals, especially physicians. Commentators in this era often used industrial or mechanical metaphors when talking about sex, describing sexual drives as surging through the body in the same way steam did through engines or water through pipes in a "hydraulic model" of sex. Western leaders sought to promote a healthy society as a way of building up national strength, and anything that detracted from this became a matter of official and often public concern. Robert Baden-Powell (1857–1941), a British officer who had served in Africa and India, founded the Boy Scouts in 1908 explicitly to teach British boys what he regarded as the right sort of manly virtues and keep them from masturbation, effeminacy, physical weakness, and homosexuality, which he saw as especially prevalent among the non-white subjects of the British Empire and British men who lived in cities. Efforts were made to "cure" people of homosexuality and other types of "deviant" sexuality through drugs, surgery, or psychological treatments. At the same time, however, same-sex desire became something that linked individuals in homosexual subcultures and communities, a matter of identity rather than simply actions. "Heterosexual" became an identity as well, and the idea that people had a permanent "sexual orientation" eventually became a central part of modern Western notions of the self.

The experimentation of the 1920s included financial speculation. Bankers, investors, and even people of modest means bought stocks with borrowed money in a speculative bubble, and the crash of the New York stock market in 1929 triggered a global financial crisis that led to declining productivity, plummeting trade, mass unemployment, and a long and severe economic depression. The Great Depression shattered fragile political stability in Europe, and made people in many places willing to put their trust in authoritarian leaders. These emerged in Germany, Italy, Spain, Portugal, the Soviet Union, most of eastern Europe, Latin America, and Japan, developing in many places into totalitarian regimes that asserted a complete claim on the lives of their citizens, and demanded popular support for their ambitious aims, which they expected would be achieved by war.

In the Soviet Union, Joseph Stalin (1879–1953) emerged triumphant from an intense power struggle during the 1920s, and under his direction the Communist Party began a series of five-year plans that sought to expand and transform the Soviet economy from one of peasant farmers to one of state-controlled agriculture and industry. Peasants were ordered to give up their land and animals and become members of collective farms; if they resisted, they could be arrested and sent to forced-labor prison camps, and millions were, along with other opponents of Stalin, including artists, intellectuals, journalists, union leaders, army officers, and lesser party officials. Collective farms were supposed to increase output, but they did not, and there was mass famine, particularly in Ukraine, where Stalin used forced collectivization as a tool to destroy Ukrainian opposition to Soviet rule. Peasants were also sent to the factories opened as part of the five-year plans, or moved to cities for work; during the 1930s, more than 25 million people became industrial workers in the Soviet Union, increasing industrial output by about four times. The Party opened schools and universities to train engineers, skilled workers, and managers, and a technical elite developed. Stalinist propaganda, expressed through posters, government-commissioned music and art, and the government-controlled press, constantly proclaimed the superiority of communism to Western capitalism and highlighted socialist achievements.

In densely populated Japan, as the world economy collapsed, necessities like food and fuel grew scarcer, and the leadership became increasingly aggressive. Following a pattern of imperial expansion begun several decades earlier, Japan invaded the Chinese province of Manchuria in 1931 to gain its coal, iron, and land, and then took over eastern China in brutal conquests that involved mass murder. The military imposed authoritarian rule, repressing dissent, organizing production, glorifying martial honor and sacrifice, and promoting notions of the sacred origins of the emperor and the Japanese people. In Germany, Adolf Hitler (1889–1945) and the Nazi Party used discontent at the humiliation of World War I and the Versailles peace treaty, combined with economic insecurity, constant propaganda, and racist sentiments to develop a broad base of popular support and take over control of the government. Hitler supported the Italian Fascist totalitarian attack on Ethiopia—the last independent state in Africa—in 1935 and sent troops to aid Fascist forces in Spain.

Hitler first cloaked his plans for expansion in claims about the rights of ethnic Germans living in non-German states, but in 1939 his attack on Poland made his true intentions clear, and the British and French declared war. Nazi armies seized Belgium, the Netherlands, and France, and then turned east and attacked the Soviet Union. He intended to create a New Order across Europe based on racist imperialism, in which a "master race" of German "Aryans" would rule inferior Latin peoples and even more inferior Slavs, and in which Jews and others the Nazis declared undesirable, such as Jehovah's Witnesses, Roma (Gypsies), socialists, and communists, would all be killed. Systematic extermination began in 1941 as the Nazis sought what Hitler termed "the final solution to the Jewish question," resulting in mass deportation to concentration camps, where Jews and others were shot or killed by poison gas. About 6 million Jews were murdered in this Holocaust, along with millions of others, in a process that involved the cooperation of many German and non-German officials and ordinary people, and provoked little protest from either inside or outside the Nazi empire.

Japan allied with Germany and Italy, invaded mainland and island Southeast Asia, claiming it was creating a Greater East Asia Co-Prosperity Sphere, but in reality confiscating raw materials and drafting local people for military and labor services, including "comfort women" forced to provide sex for Japanese soldiers. In 1941 Japan attacked the American naval base of Pearl Harbor, and the United States entered the war. The industrial capacity and large population base of the USA, combined with those of the Soviet Union, Britain, and the other Allies, ultimately defeated Germany and Japan, the latter in part because of the use of the atomic bomb, an outgrowth of the second industrial revolution. Thus the needs of the military had served as an important impetus to the Industrial Revolution, and the expansion of industrialism ultimately determined the outcome of what is, to date, the most deadly war in world history, with 50 million soldiers and civilians killed.

World War II was a total war just as World War I had been. Governments directed the economy and intervened in education, culture, and family life in totalitarian regimes, but also in democracies. They used new means of mass communication, especially radio and movies, as tools to bolster support for the war, broadcasting speeches and sending filmmakers to shoot actual battles for newsreels, documentaries, and feature films. The Nazis were particularly hostile to modern art, viewing it as Jewish-influenced and "degenerate" and in some cases destroying it. They favored heroic realism, as did their Soviet enemies, in which soldiers, workers, and mothers gazed into the distance at a brighter future. In Germany, Italy, and Japan, birth control was prohibited and large families were rewarded among groups judged to be desirable; those judged undesirable were sterilized or executed. Among the Allied Powers, women were recruited to work in munitions and aircraft factories, join the nursing corps or auxiliary armed forces, raise money for war bonds, and plant "victory gardens" to raise home-grown food to replace that sent to troops; by the end of the war one-third of the vegetables consumed in the USA were being grown in private gardens. Women's factory work allowed astounding increases in the production of weapons and military equipment, but after the war a similar marketing campaign urged the return to "normal" gender roles, women's paid employment declined, and the birth rate soared in a postwar "baby boom."

DECOLONIZATION AND THE COLD WAR

World War II left Europe, Japan, and other areas where there had been air bombardment and ground fighting physically shattered, and also left the Allied Powers in deep disagreement about the shape of the postwar world. The USA demanded free elections in eastern Europe and refused to negotiate with Stalin. In response, Soviet occupying forces installed pro-Soviet communist leaders in eastern Europe, including the eastern zone of a divided Germany. The United States and its allies reacted with a policy of "containment" that tried to stop any further expansion of communism. For forty years after the end of World War II, political, economic, and even cultural life in much of the world was shaped by the geopolitical and military conflict known as the Cold War that pitted the Soviet Union and the United States against one another. Each side saw itself as the defender of what was good and pressured other countries to follow:

the Soviet Union supported Marxist-inspired nationalists who sought to end colonialism or Western economic domination and create new social orders with a more equitable distribution of resources, while the United States supported leaders who promised to fight communists, maintain free trade and private property, and hold democratic elections. Commentators used this division to create a conceptual scheme of the entire world: a First World of wealthy industrial democracies; a Second World of communist nations; a Third World of poor, non-industrialized nations with economies shaped by colonialism or neocolonialism, which in the 1950s meant most of Africa, Asia, Latin America, and the Caribbean; and sometimes a Fourth World of the absolute poorest nations with few exploitable resources, such as Haiti and Mali. The schema ignores differences within nations, as in every Third and Fourth World country some people have led First World lives, but it came to be widely used as a shorthand.

Both superpowers built up huge arsenals of conventional and nuclear weapons and formed military alliances, sending large-scale military and financial aid to their allies, no matter how repressive or corrupt. This enhanced regional conflicts into larger "proxy wars" that substituted for direct conflict between the two superpowers, which might have escalated into nuclear war. Military expenses made up a large share of the budgets of many nations, leaving little for other uses, as US President Dwight Eisenhower (1890–1969)—the general who had led the defeat of the Nazis—noted in 1953: "Every gun that is made, every warship launched, every rocket fired signifies, in the final sense, a theft from those who hunger and are not fed, those who are cold and are not clothed. The world in arms is not spending money alone, it is spending the sweat of its laborers, the genius of its scientists, the hopes of its children . . . This is not a way of life at all, in any true sense." Eisenhower described the growth of what he termed the "military-industrial complex," and warned of its power.

Conflicts between the superpowers played out on a global stage of decolonization, in which people around the world sought political self-determination; between 1945 and 1965, almost every colonial territory gained formal independence. This process was supported by the United Nations, the intergovernmental organization formed in 1945 to mediate international conflicts. The General Assembly of the UN became a forum where nationalist leaders condemned colonial powers and neocolonial economic domination. The UN also established agencies and bureaucracies to promote economic development, improve health and nutrition, and eradicate disease, and sent military forces to serve as peacekeepers in various conflict zones around the world. As empires and protectorates across Asia, Africa, and the Middle East were transformed into independent nations, religious and ethnic conflicts complicated the struggle. Thus cultural and social issues had a deep impact on decolonization.

In South Asia, Gandhi hoped for a united independent India, but Muslim leaders worried that the majority Hindus would dominate, and pressed for a separate state, arguing that Hindus and Muslims were "two different civilizations" that each deserved its own nation. The British proposed partition, and in 1947 India and Pakistan gained political independence, with Pakistan divided into two provinces. The "two civilizations" actually lived intermingled in many areas, especially in Kashmir, the Punjab, and Bengal, and independence was followed by bloodshed and mass expulsions, as each side tried to create a more homogenous state. Millions of people became refugees or were forcibly relocated. Political, economic, and ethnic conflicts between East and West Pakistan led to further violence and more refugees, and East Pakistan won its independence in 1971 as Bangladesh. Bangladesh was (and is) an extremely densely populated country centered on the low-lying Ganges Delta, often subject to natural disasters such as floods and typhoons. It was also very poor, although programs to help lessen poverty, such as expanded elementary education, very small loans to help people establish village businesses, and rural cooperatives, slowly brought improvements for some people.

Nehru became India's first prime minister, establishing a political dynasty in which his daughter Indira Gandhi (no relation to Mohandes Gandhi) and his grandson Rajiv Gandhi also became prime ministers. He was one of the leaders of the Non-Aligned Nations Movement, through which some recently independent nations in Asia and Africa hoped to find a "third force" that was neither Soviet nor US, and promoted industrial development and agricultural innovation through a system that blended capitalism and socialism. The Indian state was officially secular and democratic, although traditional attitudes toward women and untouchables changed very slowly. Most people in India lived in villages, and irrigation projects plus new high-yield wheat and rice introduced as part of what was known as the Green Revolution of the 1960s increased agricultural output significantly. This was paralleled by population growth resulting from the spread of vaccines that lowered the death rate among children, the use of antibiotics, DDT spraying to reduce insect-borne diseases, and other public health measures.

Religious conflicts were even more explosive in the Middle East. In the 1940s, France and Britain granted independence to most of their mandate-held countries, and the British dumped the problem of what to do in Palestine in the lap of the United Nations. The UN proposed a two-state solution—a Jewish Israel and a Muslim Palestine—which the Jews accepted and the Arabs rejected. Jews then proclaimed the state of Israel, which they enforced through military victories over coalitions of Arab countries in 1948, 1967, and 1973. Many Palestinians fled Israel or were expelled, becoming refugees in surrounding Arab countries who sought to return to their homeland. The Arab defeat led to a nationalist revolution in Egypt, which emerged as the leader of the Arab world. Egypt received significant financial aid from both the Soviet Union and the United States, but a series of authoritarian leaders, ruling through emergency laws that suspended rights, extended police powers, and limited freedom of expression, funneled this into the military or the hands of corrupt officials, and the economy stagnated. Corruption, one-party dictatorships, and great disparities in wealth and poverty marked many other Middle Eastern countries as well, including Iran, where in the 1950s the hereditary ruler, known as the shah—restored to power with the help of secret US forces after he had been thrown out in an election—set out to modernize the country using Iran's gigantic oil revenues, which were controlled by US companies. The shah and his officials opened secular schools, proclaimed women's rights, and promoted a market economy, but also tolerated no dissent and siphoned off much foreign aid and oil revenue for themselves, living extravagantly while most peasants remained poor and landless.

In Africa, resistance to colonialism combined with nationalism to create new nations after World War II in processes that ranged from largely peaceful to extremely violent. In the first half of the twentieth century, many educated Africans and people of African descent who lived elsewhere were pan-Africanists, who sought cultural solidarity among black people everywhere, combined with an "Africa for the Africans" in which all Africans would form some sort of united government for the whole continent. Some articulated the idea of *negritude*, a sense of racial identity and pride in black creativity and African cultural traditions to counter the prevailing Social Darwinist notion that Africans were at the bottom of a hierarchy of races. Postwar leaders, many educated in Europe or the United States, tended to accept existing political boundaries as a practical matter that would allow them to gain independence as soon as possible. This came first in the Gold Coast, where Kwame Nkrumah (1909–72) organized a mass political party that staged strikes and political actions until the British agreed to an election. Nkrumah's party won a huge majority, and he headed both a transitional government and the new nation of Ghana. Independence for most other British and French African colonies and the establishment of democratic constitutions followed fairly quickly, with extensive bloodshed only where there were large numbers of white settlers, such as Kenya, Algeria, and Rhodesia, and in the Congo. The political boundaries established by European imperial powers had not followed the lines of earlier African kingdoms or ethnic divisions, however, and political parties and rival factions often coalesced along regional or ethnic lines, which led to violence. Many leaders decided that authoritarian rule and a one-party state were the only way to assure order, and in some countries the army—the institution that had been the best developed under imperial rule—seized power.

Because cash crops took the best land in Africa, food imports brought in as aid or purchased were often necessary for survival. Child mortality remained much higher than in industrialized countries, though some improvements in health care lowered the death rate, which led to a rate of population increase that far outstripped economic growth. Most postcolonial states provided more access to education than the colonial governments had, and literacy rates slowly began to rise during the 1960s, with those for girls lagging behind those for boys, as girls generally attended school less often and for a shorter period than boys. Women were also often excluded from development plans, as international development agencies assumed—based on Western practices—that men were the primary agricultural producers. They thus often sought to "modernize" agriculture by teaching men new methods of farming or processing crops in cultures where these tasks had always been done by women.

Although most of the countries of Latin America and the Caribbean had gained political independence in the nineteenth century, their economies were similar to those of Africa, in that they often depended on the export of one or two crops or natural products, which regularly suffered price collapses that brought unemployment, social unrest, and sometimes starvation. Economic nationalists sought to free their countries from US and European domination and expand the economy through industrialization in the same type of important substitution strategy that had sparked the Industrial Revolution in Britain. This began in Mexico, where in the 1930s President Lázaro Cárdenas (1895–1970), from a poor and indigenous family, nationalized the oil industry and promoted industrialization. Brazil and Argentina followed a similar pattern, with populist leaders such as President Juan Perón of Argentina promising rapid industrialization and higher wages. The communist Cuban Revolution in 1959 led conservative political and business leaders and the military in much of Latin America to fear a further spread of communism and the redistribution of wealth this might bring. As in Africa, coups and armed interventions undermined or overthrew elected governments, and right-wing military dictators came to hold power, often backed covertly or openly by the United States government, which saw everything through a Cold War lens.

China also experienced the establishment of an authoritarian one-party state, in which party leaders sought to revolutionize social structures and cultural forms. Nationalists opposed to Japanese and other foreign imperialism had established a republic before the war, but the Chinese communists, led by Mao Zedong (1893–1976), defeated the nationalists in a civil war that ended in 1949. The nationalist leadership and about 2 million refugees fled

5.7 In a scene staged for the photographer, young men read *Quotations from Chairman Mao Tse-tung* while waiting for transport during the Cultural Revolution, 1968. The book, known in the West as the "Little Red Book" because of its small size and red cover, became required reading in schools, workplaces, and military units; more than a billion were printed.

to Taiwan. The communists distributed land confiscated from landlords and richer peasants to hundreds of millions of poor peasants, and looked to the Soviet Union for inspiration, beginning to collectivize agriculture and developing a five-year plan for growth that would allow China to compete with the West. China became a second major communist power, sending troops to fight the USA and its allies in the Korean War (1950–53), one of the Cold War's proxy wars that ended in a truce and a divided Korea. In 1958, Mao broke with Soviet patterns and proclaimed a Great Leap Forward, in which industrial growth would be centered not in large factories, but instead in small backyard workshops and mills run by peasants living collectively. This was a disaster, as people who were not skilled workers attempted industrial production instead of farming, and there was widespread famine in which as many as 30 million people died. Further chaos resulted from Mao's Great Proletarian Cultural Revolution of the 1960s, a purge of the Communist Party in which young people organized themselves into revolutionary cadres known as Red Guards and denounced those they thought were insufficiently loyal to Mao's ideas. Anything that represented "feudal" or "bourgeois" culture was suspect, and art and books were destroyed. The universities were closed, and millions of people were sent to rural forced-labor camps.

While communism triumphed in China, capitalism triumphed in Japan. Japan was occupied by US forces from 1945 to 1952, who dictated a new constitution that abolished the armed forces but left the emperor as a symbol of the state. The Americans also left Japan's bureaucracy and large corporations in place, and they continued the policy of close cooperation that had characterized earlier industrial development in Japan. Japan served as a military base for the USA during the Korean War, and was increasingly seen as an important ally in the fight against communism. The Japanese economy grew at a breathtaking pace from the 1950s through the 1980s, the fastest economic growth in world history. "Salarymen" were hired for life, and their social lives came to revolve around the company, with long hours of work followed by long hours of drinking while their wives remained at home.

As Japan rebuilt, so did western Europe. Economic aid provided by the United States and hard work by local people and migrants from the Mediterranean basin who filled labor shortages led to an amazing recovery from the war's devastation. Housing was reconstructed, productivity and wages rose, and new factories opened, now often using oil imported from the Middle East by European or American corporations such as British Petroleum or Standard Oil instead of coal. Many jobs in newer industries such as chemicals, pharmaceuticals, and electronics were increasingly managerial, and required higher levels of education than blue-collar jobs in mining and heavy industry had. Expanding government-financed higher education allowed some young people from working-class backgrounds to move into these positions, but older and less-educated workers were vulnerable. Seeking to prevent the dislocation that had led to fascism and war, and often led by moderate socialist political parties that responded to labor interests, western European governments created a social safety net for workers and families, with unemployment insurance, family allowances, old-age pensions, government-supported health care, and inexpensive public housing, building what was termed the "welfare state."

As the dominant power in the First World, the USA experienced a postwar boom similar to that of Japan and western Europe, becoming the world's largest economy. Despite a growing population, per-worker productivity and real wages increased steadily from 1945 to 1975 as people built houses (often in suburbs around cities), bought cars to take them from work to home and on vacations on the nation's new interstate highway system, and filled their houses with consumer goods. Consumer spending became the driver of the US economy, and to a great degree of its culture, and has remained so, with global implications. Well-paying industrial jobs drew African Americans into northern cities from the South in what is often termed the "Great Migration." Here as well as in the South they confronted segregation and discrimination, and beginning in the 1950s black leaders began a civil rights movement that challenged this. They often looked to Gandhi and other anticolonial leaders for inspiration and tactics, and worked for greater equity in schools, voting, housing, employment, and every other aspect of life. In the mid 1960s, laws prohibiting discrimination were passed and programs created to lessen poverty and provide a social safety net, although these never went as far as those in western Europe, as health care remained a matter for employers or individuals, and much of higher education was private.

In the Soviet Union and the rest of the Second World, communism prescribed social egalitarianism, and education and health care became more widely available to all social groups. Party members and officials had easier access to housing and consumer goods, however, both of which were in short supply, as planners concentrated on heavy industry, not consumer products. Communism also prescribed gender egalitarianism, and women entered occupations that had been previously limited primarily to men, including engineering and medicine. Women continued to do almost all of the household tasks, however, and shortages in foodstuffs and household goods meant that they had to spend hours each day (after their paid workday was done) standing in lines. Because of this "second shift," women were not free to attend Communist Party meetings or do extra work on the job in order to be promoted. In the 1970s Soviet Union, for example, though women made up over 50 percent of the paid workforce, only 0.5 percent of managers and directors were women, about the same as in Western democracies at that time.

Immediately after World War II, the Soviet-dominated states of eastern Europe adopted the Stalinist system, nationalizing industries, collectivizing agriculture, limiting religious worship, and controlling the media and education. The communist regime established in Cuba in the 1950s as a result of the Cuban Revolution similarly abolished private property and repressed opposition to the government. Party control over cultural and intellectual life in communist states waxed and waned. Periods of liberalization were followed by crackdowns when reformers, students, workers, or opposition leaders voiced protests too loudly, or when eastern European countries attempted to leave the Soviet sphere, as they did in Hungary in 1956.

Cold War conflicts and anti-colonial struggles came together in many parts of the world in the decades after World War II, including Guatemala and the Congo, and especially in Vietnam. In 1945, Ho Chi Minh declared Vietnam an independent country after the Japanese occupation ended. The French attempted to continue their colonial rule instead, but were defeated in 1954. A national election was supposed to be held, but the USA, worried that Ho would win, backed his non-communist opponents in South Vietnam, while Russia and China supported North Vietnam. The USA sent massive military aid, and then hundreds of thousands of troops, who bombed North Vietnam and engaged in a ground war. Support for the war in the USA was initially strong, but an anti-war movement grew in the 1960s, particularly on college campuses. Protests on campuses and in cities, some of which were put down violently, denounced the war as criminal, and despite a large loss of life on both sides US military victories were inconclusive. The USA withdrew from the war, and Vietnam became a unified communist nation in 1975.

Protests against the Vietnam War, which occurred in many other parts of the world along with the USA, were part of a global youth movement among the unusually large and prosperous cohort of young people born in the postwar baby boom. Young people in the late 1960s, much like those of the 1920s, renounced what they saw as the militaristic and conformist values of their parents' generation, wore clothing and hair styles that signified their countercultural values, and listened to new types of music—now rock 'n' roll and folk music rather than jazz. Anti-war protests combined with other demonstrations: for women's rights and the rights of racial minorities in the USA; against right-wing governments in Argentina, Brazil, and Mexico; for students' and workers' rights in France; against nuclear proliferation in Australia and western Europe. Even the Catholic Church saw calls for dramatic change emerge from within its ranks, as Latin American theologians and clergy created liberation theology, a movement that called on religious and political leaders to address the suffering and oppression of the poor and move toward greater social justice. Mass communication and cheap youth travel facilitated contacts among politically active students, who often idealized Marxist leaders such as Mao or Ho for their emphasis on social equality and revolutionary change. But calls for dramatic change occurred in the communist world as well, especially in Czechoslovakia in 1968 where reformers within the Czechoslovakian Communist Party calling for "socialism with a human face" eased civil rights and press restrictions.

LIBERATION AND LIBERALIZATION

The protests of the late 1960s suggested the possibility of revolutionary social transformation, but this was not to be. Soviet tanks rolled into the streets of Prague, crushing the reform movement and reintroducing rigid one-party rule. The Mexican government shot student protestors, as did police on several US university campuses. Advocates of liberation theology, including priests and nuns, were killed by repressive regimes and the movement itself was condemned in the 1980s by the Catholic Church's Sacred Congregation for the Doctrine of the Faith (led by Cardinal Joseph Ratzinger, later Pope Benedict XVI) for its use of ideas taken from Marx. The military government in Brazil imposed martial law, and the military government in Argentina carried out what became known as the "dirty war," imprisoning, torturing, and killing its opponents. In many newly independent African nations civil war, corruption, and ethnic tensions limited stability.

Movements for greater social egalitarianism continued, however. The student and civil rights movements of the 1960s led to a renewed women's rights movement in the 1970s, when women around the world organized, marched, and mobilized to achieve what was termed "women's liberation" and full political, legal, and economic equality. They opened rape crisis centers and shelters for battered women, pressured for an end to sex discrimination in hiring practices and wages, pushed for laws against sexual harassment, and called for better schools for girls and university courses on women. The reinvigorated feminist movement sparked conservative reactions in many countries, with arguments often couched in terms of "tradition," and "women's libbers" accused of causing an increase in the divorce rate, the number of children born out of wedlock, family violence, and juvenile delinquency. Such arguments were effective in stopping some legal changes, but the trend toward greater gender egalitarianism in political participation, education, and employment continued in most parts of the world. In many countries, gay and lesbian rights activists also organized beginning in the 1970s, and worked to end discrimination on the basis of sexual orientation, including the right to marry.

In southern Africa, white minority rule slowly crumbled. Portugal had resisted decolonization, but armed guerrilla movements defeated colonial forces and new nations were established. Their leaders were generally Marxist, and experimented with central planning or combining socialism with African traditions of sharing resources. In South Africa, the Afrikaner-dominated government had limited black ownership of land to native reserves that formed a tiny share of the poorest land in the country and held none of its mineral wealth, and after World War II created an increasingly more stringent system of white supremacy and racial segregation officially known as apartheid. Protests against the system were put down with brutal police actions, and many leaders, including Nelson Mandela (1918–2013), were jailed, along with thousands of others. Global sanctions and local actions combined to force negotiations; Mandela was freed from prison and in 1994 became South Africa's first black president.

Women had been active in opposition to imperial rule, but their roles in the new African nations were frequently limited. Young male nationalists were often successful at changing traditions through which older men had held power over them, such as painful initiation rituals and unfavorable inheritance practices, but viewed traditions though which men held power over women or that restricted women's actions positively. Carmen Pereira, an independence leader who fought the Portuguese in Guinea-Bissau in the 1970s, recognized this tendency, and noted that women were "fighting two colonialisms"—one of nationalist struggle and one of gender discrimination. In the 1990s, women became more prominent in formal political processes, part of a trend toward reform and broader democracy in much of Africa. Urban middle-class male and female professionals educated at new universities in their own countries generally led such movements against the privileges and corruption of the elites. Similarly in Latin America, women led public protests against the actions of military dictatorships. The most famous of these, the "Mothers of the Plaza de Mayo" in Argentina, gathered weekly wearing white headscarves embroidered with the names of the "disappeared" and painting their silhouettes on walls. Public pressure combined with military leaders' inept decisions led to the return of democratic elections and civilian governments in most of Latin America during the 1980s.

These shifts toward greater political and social liberation and more egalitarianism occurred within a climate of economic liberalization, however, which generally increased disparities of wealth and power rather than lessening them. Economic liberalization, often termed "neoliberalism," favors the free circulation of goods and capital, deregulation, the privatization of state-run enterprises, and reductions in government spending, generally through cutting social programs. Its proponents have included leaders regarded as politically conservative as well as politically liberal. Such measures were sparked in part by the oil crisis of the 1970s. Seeking to gain control of their resources from Western corporations, many oil exporting countries nationalized their industries and formed a cartel—the Organization of Petroleum Exporting Countries (OPEC)—which in 1973 placed an embargo on oil exports during the Arab-Israeli War, and the price of oil quadrupled. Productivity declined worldwide as industries cut back to deal with higher energy prices, while unemployment and inflation rose. In western Europe the welfare system prevented mass suffering, but taxes did not rise to match increased government spending, and leaders increasingly introduced austerity measures to deal with the recession. OPEC countries deposited their money in international banks, often headquartered in the United States, which then loaned this money, dubbed "petrodollars," to governments to build infrastructure, deal with fluctuations in the prices of raw materials and agricultural commodities (still the primary export of many countries), purchase military equipment, line their corrupt and authoritarian leaders' pockets, and other uses. Nations trying to industrialize thus faced both higher energy costs and a mounting public debt. Debt obligations became crushing for many poor countries, but as a condition of receiving further loans or a cancellation of some of their existing loan obligations, the International Monetary Fund (IMF), World Bank, and other financial organizations imposed neoliberal policies throughout the world in a process of structural adjustment that required countries to open their economies to private and foreign investment, lessen their foreign debt obligations, and reduce government spending on social programs.

5.8 Mothers of the Plaza de Mayo protest against the 1986 "law of full stop." (Punto Final), which halted investigations and prosecutions of people accused of political violence and violations of human rights during the military dictatorship in Argentina. The law was repealed in 2003, and the government reopened some cases of crimes against humanity.

Throughout the West, employers responded to the economic downturn by slowing the pace of wage increases, and from that point real wages of both white- and blue-collar workers have been largely flat. Productivity has continued to rise, but the profits from this have gone to stockholders and corporative executives, as income inequality has again risen to late nineteenth-century levels. Families responded to this situation by borrowing, as credit became easier to obtain, and by working more hours. They also sent more family members into the labor force, as the paid work of two people was increasingly essential to achieving and maintaining a middle-class lifestyle or simply keeping the home bought on credit. Married mothers with children became the fastest-growing group within the paid labor force in many countries; their labor force participation in the USA, for example, more than tripled from 1950 to 1995, from less than 20 percent to more than 60 percent. The growth in women's paid employment was largely concentrated in lower-paying service jobs such as office work, retail sales, child care, hairdressing, and cleaning (dubbed the "pink collar ghetto"), so that women's average full-time earnings were less than those of men. The movement of women into the labor force was thus a result of both women's liberation and economic liberalization policies.

Economic liberalization, particularly the development of free markets, spread into communist countries as well as capitalist ones. After the disaster of the Cultural Revolution, leaders in China during the 1970s and 1980s allowed peasants to farm land in small family units again, which increased food production significantly. Although most large-scale industry remained state-owned, factories owned by foreign capitalist investors were permitted in southern China. Young workers flowed in from the countryside, as they had in early nineteenth-century England or early twentieth-century Japan, but on a far larger scale. Because many of these factories used coal, the environmental degradation was just as awful as it had been in industrial cities in Britain, or perhaps worse. Greater economic freedom was not accompanied by greater freedom in other realms of life, however. Chinese leaders worried that population growth would overtake economic expansion, and called for a "one-child" policy in which families who had more than one child were penalized by fines and the loss of access to opportunities. The policy was strictly enforced in urban areas, and though the government tried to minimize gender differences in its effects, because the value put on having a son was higher, the sex ratio—the number of males for each female in a population—slowly became higher, though whether this was the result of sex-selective abortion or the under-reporting of daughters is disputed. The leaders of China cracked down on a wave of political dissent and student-led demonstrations in 1989, arresting, jailing, and sometimes executing critics of the regime. They continued to open the economy, however, and encouraged consumerism and private enterprise. Giant factories producing electronics, clothing, chemicals, toys, and other products for a global market were opened, the standard of living rose, and in 2011 China replaced Japan as the world's second-largest economy. As in China, during the 1980s the leaders of Vietnam began to move away from a planned economy toward open markets and private ownership, transforming Vietnam into a capitalist economy in which communist leaders hold political power.

In South Korea, and also in Taiwan and Singapore, nationalist anti-communist authoritarian political leaders worked with multinational capitalist corporations, banks, and conglomerates to transform the economies from agricultural to industrial, specializing in high-tech and electronic products and with a pace of growth so fast they were dubbed the "Asian tigers." Singapore created a distinctive mixture of free-market practices, economic planning, public order, and social engineering. For example, the government became concerned that men who were college graduates were marrying women who were not, leaving college graduate women unmarried and childless, with negative effects on the national gene pool. In 1984 the government established a special dating network for graduates and gave college graduate mothers tax rebates and other benefits, although the birth rate for all women remains among the lowest in the world.

During the 1980s, economic crisis spread to eastern Europe, with dramatic political and social as well as economic consequences. This began in Poland, which had been the most resistant to Soviet efforts at collectivization and where the Catholic Church remained strong. Economic turmoil led workers to form an independent and democratic trade union they called Solidarity. Its leaders were initially arrested, but continued economic decline, non-violent protests, and strong popular support from workers, students, intellectuals, and church leaders led the Communist Party in Poland to allow free elections to the Polish Parliament, and the communists were voted out of power in 1989. A series of largely peaceful revolutions overturned the other communist regimes in eastern Europe and brought in democratic elections. In the early 1990s the anti-communist movement swept into the Soviet Union itself, which was also in the midst of severe economic troubles caused in part by continued high military expenditures. In contrast to China, the government was not able stop change, and the Soviet Union broke apart into separate states, each with its own leaders, goals, and policies.

The end of communism in the Soviet Union and eastern Europe brought greater personal freedom, but also more economic disparity and social dislocation. As state monopolies became private companies, a few of their owners became fabulously wealthy, especially through oil, sometimes intimidating their rivals through physical force as well as economic pressure in what has been called a "plutocracy," or government by the rich. For most people, the end of communism meant soaring prices, food shortages, a decline in health care and public services such as government-supported day care centers, a drop in income, increased alcoholism and street violence, and, for women, a huge growth in prostitution. Average life expectancy for a Russian man dropped from 69 years in 1991 to 59 in 2007, with some commentators describing this as Russia's becoming a Third World nation.

Ethnic and religious conflicts flared up in many parts of what had been the Second World, most devastatingly in Yugoslavia, a federation of regions under communist rule that broke into states hostile to one another in the 1990s. The resultant war brought murder, rape, brutal cruelty, and concentration camps, along with forced migration and genocide—especially of boys and men— described by its practitioners as "ethnic cleansing" that would rid an area of unwanted groups. Military intervention from Western nations brought this civil war to an end, and some of its leaders were tried for crimes against humanity by a war crimes tribunal in the Netherlands, but tensions remained.

RELIGIOUS FUNDAMENTALISM AND DIVERSITY

Conflicts in the former Yugoslavia point toward another global force that along with economic liberalism became more powerful in the later twentieth century: religious fundamentalism. The word "fundamentalism" comes from a movement within Protestant Christianity in the early twentieth century that downplayed complex doctrines in favor of what were described as fundamental teachings, opposed the cultural changes of modernity, and advocated a conservative social agenda. It is now used for similar movements in all religions. Within most religions, including Judaism, Christianity, Islam, and Hinduism, the last half of the twentieth century saw disagreements and conflicts between a fundamentalist wing that advocated a return to what were viewed as core texts, patriarchal gender norms, and a rejection of secular values, and a more liberal wing that advocated greater gender egalitarianism, toleration of other faiths, and an emphasis on social and economic justice. Fundamentalism combined with nationalism, ethnic identity, anti-colonialism, and economic grievances as a motivation for action, which sometimes included violence and extremism.

In Iran, an economic slump in 1979 led to strikes and protests; the shah fled, and leadership in Iran was increasingly assumed by fundamentalist Shi'ite Islamic clerics led by Ayatollah Ruhollah Khomeini (1902–89). They overturned the shah's modernization and replaced secular law with the Islamic Shari'a, forbidding alcohol, requiring women to wear veils and forbidding them from public socializing with men, censoring the media, and jailing or executing their opponents. The Iranian Revolution alarmed Western powers, and also Iran's neighbors, most of which were led by Sunni Muslims. Iraq launched a war against Iran in 1980, which drew in outsiders but was ultimately inconclusive, and then itself became the target of two wars led by the United States, a brief but very bloody one in 1991 and a much longer one that began in 2003. In Saudi Arabia, modernization and religious fundamentalism have coexisted rather than conflicted, as the Saudi royal family has used oil money to build schools, hospitals, and shopping malls, but has also continued to support Wahhabism. Although the royal family has a close relationship with US leaders, Wahhabists often oppose US military bases on Saudi soil, and in some cases their opposition has led to violence. Most of the young men who carried out the September 11, 2001 attacks on the USA were well-educated, middle-class Saudis, who described their motivation primarily in religious terms; the letter they wrote on the night before the attack explaining their action mentions God more than a hundred times.

The movement of fundamentalist activism within Islam—often termed Islamism—has made conservative gender patterns a primary symbol of Islamic purity against Western cultural imperialism and commercialism. In part because of this, the movement of women into the paid labor force has been the slowest in Muslim countries of the Middle East, where in 2000 it was generally only between 2 and 10 percent, with many of these highly educated professionals such as teachers and health-care workers, trained to assist other women in sex-segregated settings. Young women in Muslim countries outside the Middle East, such as Malaysia, were caught between two sets of expectations and values. Their labor in factories was essential to their families' survival, as they sent the majority of their wages home, yet they were also criticized for flouting Muslim norms. Women's dress has often been a flashpoint: Muslim women in many parts of the world have adopted the veil or other types of covering dress as a way to affirm their religious devotion, express their social and moral values, and travel outside the home without being subject to male harassment. They regard Muslim dress as a means of empowering themselves, while others—both Muslims and non-Muslims—have viewed it as an example of women's oppression, and in some cases prohibited head- and body-coverings. As with other types of religious symbols, the veil clearly has multiple meanings that vary with the individual and with the political setting.

Islamic fundamentalism has had the most widespread political and social impact, but fundamentalism in other religions has also become more powerful, and has sometimes contributed to violence. In the 1990s the power of conservative Hindu nationalist parties in India began to grow. They argued that India's schools, legal system, culture, and other aspects of life should be more clearly Hindu, and that both Western and Muslim influence should be rejected. In Israel, a right-wing Jewish extremist assassinated Prime Minister Yitzhak Rabin in 1995 for signing a peace agreement with the Muslim Palestinians. Strictly orthodox Jews, known as Haredi,

5.9 A small group of Ugandans take part in the 3rd Annual Lesbian, Gay, Bisexual and Transgender (LGBT) Pride celebration in Entebbe, Uganda, in August of 2014. This was the first public event after a Ugandan court invalidated a draconian anti-homosexual law.

who represent perhaps one-tenth of the population of Israel, have successfully pressured bus companies not to include any women in their bus advertising, and until recently many public buses were gender segregated, with men in the front and women in the back. Incidents of harassment involving female bus passengers who refused to move back led to a court decision in 2011 ruling mandatory gender segregation in buses illegal, though it continues at the Western Wall, the holiest site in Judaism, and in the public spaces of Haredi communities in the United States. Christian extremists in the United States have shot abortion providers and bombed clinics, and in Nagaland of northwest India have forced conversions through violence. A bill to drastically increase punishments for homosexuality was introduced in Uganda shortly after US Christian fundamentalists held an anti-gay conference there, and became law in 2014, though the final version dropped the death penalty. Buddhist monks have led attacks on mosques in Sri Lanka and burned Muslim homes in Burma, killing their residents; displaced Rohingya Muslims have fled into neighboring countries or refugee camps. Religious violence is often directed not only at those of a completely different religion, but also at those of a different variety of one's own, who are perceived with even more hostility. Sectarian violence between Protestants and Catholics tore Northern Ireland apart for many decades, and hostility between Shi'a and Sunni Muslims continues to erupt in many countries.

Religious fundamentalism and hostility to those of other faiths has been accompanied (and in part caused) by increasing religious diversity as migration brings those of different religious traditions together, missionaries gain converts, and individuals blend elements of different traditions in new ways. In Africa, indigenous religions remain widely practiced, including Vodun across much of coastal West Africa and the Yoruba religion in Nigeria, both of which center on spirits that govern the natural world and human society, including the spirits of the dead, which can be approached for assistance in life. Christianity and Islam have also expanded in Africa. In the immediate postcolonial period, Christianity was often rejected as a remnant of the colonial past, but this began to change in the late twentieth century, and Africa now has the world's fastest growing Christian churches, many of them nondenominational and fundamentalist rather than more traditional Catholic or Protestant. Christianity has expanded elsewhere as well; in 2000, nearly two-thirds of the world's Christians lived outside Europe and North America, with churches incorporating local cultural values on such issues as marriage and female clergy.

Religious life in Latin America also became more diverse in the later twentieth century. Until then, most people were baptized as Catholics, and, as we saw in Chapter 4, practiced a creolized Catholicism centered on religious festivals, the veneration of the saints, and family altars in which indigenous and African traditions were blended with European ones. Catholicism has remained strong, but evangelical Protestantism, especially pentecostalism, in which worship involves speaking in tongues and faith healing, has grown rapidly as a result of extensive proselytization efforts, initially by missionaries from the United States and now largely by local missionaries. New religions, especially those created in the Caribbean, have also gained adherents. These include Vodou, a religion created by slaves in Haiti that blended elements from West African Vodun with Christianity, and involved rituals common to both, including offerings, personal altars, and elaborate ceremonies of music and dance. They also include Rastafari, a religion created by poor people in Jamaica in the 1930s whose adherents regard Emperor Haile Selassie of Ethiopia (1892–1975), at that point the leader of the only unconquered, non-colonial state in Africa, as a messianic figure. Rastas called for a redistribution of wealth, and a return of black people to Africa, in spirit if not in body. Migration has taken both Rastafari and West African Vodun around the world, and transported other religions as well. Hmong shamans now conduct healing rituals in hospitals in Minneapolis, Sikh temples (known as gurdwaras) can be found in Montevideo, Montreal, and Mannheim, and new religions centered on more recent charismatic leaders and their ideas, such as Mormonism or Scientology, gain followers and build places of worship across the globe. In contrast to native language, skin color, or ethnic background, religious adherence is to some degree changeable and chosen, with converts often the most vocal advocates of their new faith. The contemporary religious picture is thus very complex, with variety and conflicts within groups and among them.

POST-INDUSTRY AND POVERTY

In the later twentieth century, many older industrial centers declined, transformed into "Rust Belts" of aging machines and aging workforces, as new giant factories were built in China, Bangladesh, Vietnam, Puerto Rico, Mexico, and wherever else wages were low. As in the early Industrial Revolution, women and girls make up a large share of the workers in these factories. The postindustrial service economy expanded, often decentralized, for computer and communications technology allows many employees to work from their own homes or in small sweatshops rather than in large factories. Like the domestic production of earlier centuries, such work is often paid by the piece rather than the hour, which allows for greater flexibility but also greater exploitation as there is no limitation of the workday and benefits such as health care are often not included. A few of those who work at home are highly educated and highly paid "tele-commuters" in the burgeoning information industry, but most home or sweatshop labor involves routine data processing and other forms of computerized office work or more traditional jobs such as making clothing or shoes. Along with the computer and the cell phone, the sewing machine continues to be an effective tool of decentralization, and cotton clothing remains an important product. Work at home, whether using a sewing machine or a computer, is sometimes included in official statistics, but often it is not, and it shades into what economists term the informal or underground economy. Such work off the books is an important part of the economies of many countries, including highly industrialized ones; estimates from Italy judge that the unrecorded exchange of goods and services is probably equal to that of the official economy, and essential for survival. The increasingly global nature of business and dramatic cycles of boom and bust has led men's work in many areas to become feminized, that is, lower-waged and not bound by long-term contracts or providing much job security. Union membership has dropped significantly from mid twentieth-century highs, and threats to move jobs elsewhere have been successful in preventing unions from being formed or limiting their effectiveness.

Gender and racial segmentation and ideas about the value of certain types of labor continued to keep wages low in teaching, nursing, institutional child care, and other jobs in which women made up a majority of the workforce, and also low in jobs in which non-white men predominated, such as lawn care and custodial work. The gender wage gap has decreased over the last several decades, but as of 2010 across industrialized countries men's median, full-time earnings were 17.6 percent higher than women's. The gender wage gap was highest in Japan and Korea—more than 30 percent in 2010—a situation that has caused many highly educated young Japanese women to leave Japan. Gender and race intersected to keep wages especially low in jobs in which non-white and immigrant women predominated, such as domestic service, in-home child care, cleaning offices and hotels, manicuring, and sex work. The opposite happened when tasks were redefined as male. Using a typewriter was gendered female, but working with computers has been gendered male and accompanied by an increase in pay and status. This regendering of work on a keyboard has been accomplished by associating computers with mathematics, machinery, and warfare, typically viewed as masculine. Thus it was called "data processing" instead of "typing," and advertisements in computer magazines as the field was developing generally portrayed women at the keyboard only when they were emphasizing how easy a computer system was to use. Computer and online games of combat have played a significant role in this masculinization of computers, as warfare itself has become more technical, but such "militainment" has also provoked criticism by those concerned with the growing militarization of popular culture. Because East and South Asians are associated with high technology, the racialization of computer work is more complex in Western societies than a white/non-white dichotomy, but a similar masculinization of work on a keyboard occurred in Asia as well. Currently high-tech companies are far less diverse than other corporations, especially in upper management, despite rhetoric about meritocracy.

By the end of the twentieth century, most of the world's industry, and even more of its postindustrial economy, was part of the connected network of global capitalism. Neoliberal policies triumphed. Open markets, free trade, privatization, and a reduction in government expenditures became a condition of joining the European Union (EU), the economic alliance and monetary union that some hoped might be a step toward political union, which many former members of the Soviet bloc also sought to join after the end of communist systems in eastern Europe. Deregulation and privatization led to economic expansion in some places. For example, several Indian cities became high-tech centers of global communications networks, and some educated middle-class Indians living in North America and Europe have returned to India, moving into new suburbs similar to those built around American cities. This boom has not been experienced in the villages where three-quarters of the Indian population live, however. Globally, measures reducing social benefits to shrink government budgets have had a disproportionate impact on children, women, and the elderly, often resulting in what economists term a "feminization of poverty."

Increasing poverty has also been the result of a population explosion in Asia, Africa, and Latin America after 1950, largely because of medical advances such as vaccinations that lowered the death rate among children dramatically. (World population was 2.5 billion in 1950, and passed the 7 billion mark in 2012, with most of the increase in the world's poorer countries.) This growth threatened to outpace economic gains, putting pressure on every institution, from the family to the nation, and also led to a population skewed toward the young. Children were desired for their labor and as caregivers for their parents in later life, and contraceptives were not available, too expensive, or seen as socially unacceptable. Population growth has been reduced in some quite poor countries through strict government policies or subsidized contraception, but international aid programs have also been hampered in this by stringent limitations on the types of birth control they are allowed to provide that result from the moral and religious concerns of political pressure groups in wealthier countries. Aid agencies have also discovered that the most effective means of decreasing the birth rate is to increase the level of basic and technical education for girls and women, while providing small loans for sewing machines, farm flocks, or even cell phones so that women could gain some economic independence. In the 1980s, development programs did shift somewhat to smaller-scale projects directed at women, such as small irrigation systems, improvements in stock-raising techniques, credit associations, and micro-loan programs, but warfare, environmental crises, declines in funding, and cultural attitudes about women's proper role have limited such measures.

The dramatic growth in population has occurred despite the emergence and spread of new diseases, some of which have had significant social and cultural as well as health consequences. In the 1980s, the emergence of a new sexually transmitted disease—Acquired Immune Deficiency Syndrome (AIDS), caused by the Human Immunodeficiency Virus (HIV)—shaped both sexual behavior and opinions about it around the world. AIDS is transmitted by the exchange of bodily fluids, and is extremely contagious. Its initial victims in the West included many homosexuals and intravenous drug users, who were seen by some as meriting their fate. Extensive medical research led to antiretroviral drugs in the 1990s, and, for those who could afford these, HIV/AIDS became a chronic condition rather than a death sentence. In poorer parts of the world, AIDS spread first among prostitutes and their clients, and its rapid transmission around the world was related to an explosive rise in international sex tourism. Drugs were far too expensive and many men objected to using condoms, which would have slowed its spread. Eventually huge numbers of people were infected, particularly in southern Africa, where having multiple sexual partners concurrently was common, especially for men, and population displacements resulting from conflict and drought hastened the spread. AIDS lowered life expectancy in South Africa and neighboring countries by more than a decade in the 1990s, and, according to the World Health Organization, is currently the leading cause of death among women aged 15–44 worldwide.

The world's villages had few prospects for the growing numbers of young people, and they went where they always have—to cities, which expanded at an astonishing rate, sometimes doubling or tripling in a single decade. As of 2000, Latin America was the world's most urbanized region, with 75 percent of the population in cities. Lagos, the former capital of Nigeria, grew from less than a million in 1965 to an estimated 20 million today, making it Africa's largest city. Here and in other megacities such as Nairobi, Dakar, Mexico City, and Rio de Janeiro, water and sewage systems, electric power, police and fire services, housing and even streets could not (and cannot) keep up with the explosive growth. Cities such as these have a small group of wealthy and middle-class people, who live in pleasant apartments or suburban mansions and work in offices in skyscrapers, but most people live in crowded apartments or make "self-help" housing on land they do not own out of cardboard cartons, plywood, packing crates, fabric, and other scavenged materials. Most people survive through the type of economy of makeshifts that has always been the situation for poor urban dwellers, selling commodities and labor services—including sex—on a very small scale. Cities bring people of different backgrounds and traditions together, creating new cultural mixtures but also fostering hostilities, both of which are enhanced by modern media technologies including the loudspeaker, the cell phone, and the internet.

Moving takes young people away from their extended family, which weakens lineage ties and allows them to be more independent. Most urban households are much smaller than those in villages, with marriages decided upon by the individuals rather than arranged by the family. Moving also leaves people vulnerable because they do not have a lineage to support them economically or emotionally. Voluntary associations, youth groups, churches, and women's clubs established in urban neighborhoods have tried to help migrants adjust, but their employment prospects remain limited and they have only a small chance of escaping poverty.

INTO THE THIRD MILLENNIUM

At the beginning of the third millennium, the most common buzzword for the current situation of the world is "globalized," in which the regions of the world are integrated into a single system. Some commentators, including many world historians, see globalization as a very long process, beginning with the Columbian Exchange, or with travel along the Silk Roads across Asia, or even with the initial migration of *Homo sapiens* around the world. More often, globalization is seen as a product of advances in transportation and telecommunications over the last several decades, which have allowed international business and financial institutions, along with international agencies and organizations, both governmental and nongovernmental, to become increasingly important. Large multinational corporations now know more and determine more about

2012 DHL Global Connectedness Index, Top 20 and Bottom 20 Countries

Country	Total Connectedness Index	Country	Total Connectedness Index
1 Netherlands	89	121 Bosnia and Herzegovina	28
2 Singapore	83	122 Niger	26
3 Luxembourg	82	123 Uzbekistan	25
4 Ireland	81	124 Kyrgyz Republic	25
5 Switzerland	80	125 Bolivia	24
6 United Kingdom	78	126 Iran	24
7 Belgium	76	127 Syria	23
8 Sweden	75	128 Venezuela	23
9 Denmark	74	129 El Salvador	23
10 Germany	73	130 Benin	22
11 Norway	71	131 Lao PDR	22
12 Hong Kong	71	132 Tajikistan	22
13 Malta	69	133 Nepal	21
14 South Korea	69	134 Botswana	21
15 Thailand	67	135 Paraguay	20
16 Malaysia	66	136 Burkina Faso	18
17 France	65	137 Myanmar	15
18 Israel	65	138 Rwanda	14
19 Austria	65	139 Central African Republic	12
20 Iceland	64	140 Burundi	10

Pankaj Ghemawat and Steven A. Altman, "DHL Global Connectedness Index 2012," Deutsche Post DHL, November 2012

more people's lives than was imaginable earlier, including people who live in the very few nations where those corporations are not active, such as North Korea, where private corporations are prohibited, or Burundi, in 2014 the world's poorest and hungriest nation and thus not of much interest to international business. According to the Global Connectedness Index developed by DHL, the world's largest logistics company, in 2012 Burundi was the least globalized country in the world. The Netherlands was the most globalized, dozens of times more connected than Burundi in terms of the depth and breadth of the flows of trade, capital, information,

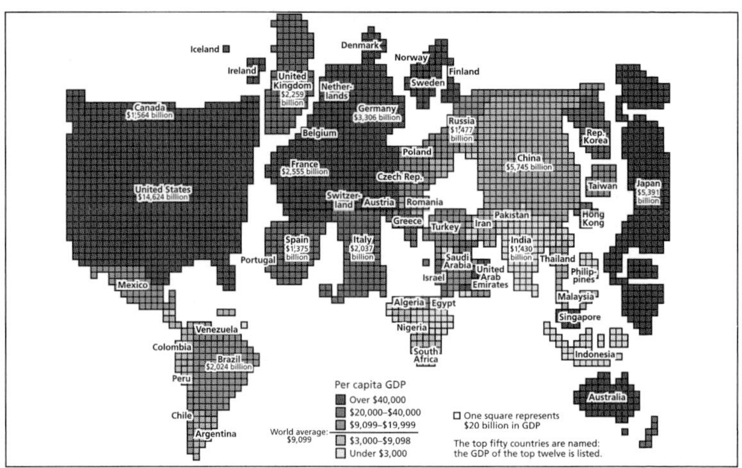

Map 5.3 Global distribution of wealth, 2010

and people that DHL chose to measure. It was also one of the world's wealthiest countries (seventeenth in per capita GDP, according to the UN), with a level of hunger so low it was not even measured in the Global Hunger Index prepared by the International Food Policy Research Institute.

Analysts of all political persuasions see these three statistics—global connections, wealth, and hunger—as causally related, with the lines of causation flowing in all directions. Burundi is poor and hungry because it lacks global connections, and it lacks global connections in part because it is poor. That poverty is itself in part a result of the two processes traced in this chapter, industrialization and imperialism, as is the wealth of the Netherlands. The movement of some of the world into a postindustrial economy and the waning of political imperialism have enhanced this inequality rather than lessening it. In general, in terms of standard of living, access to health care, child mortality, life expectancy, literacy rates, political stability, freedom from violence, and other measures of the quality of life, the regions of the world that were highest in 1950 are still highest today. Inequalities within nations have also continued. In Latin America, for example, although Mexico celebrates its *mestizo* heritage and Cuba, Brazil, and other nations proclaim themselves racially egalitarian, light-skinned people dominate the top income brackets and dark-skinned the bottom. Individuals classified as white on the 2007 Brazilian national census had an income twice that of those classified as black or mixed race.

Demographic trends are also both a cause and a result of inequality. New birth control methods introduced in the 1960s, particularly "the pill" but also new types of intrauterine devices (IUDs), proved very effective, and by 2000 roughly two-thirds of the world's population appeared to have been practicing some kind of birth control. Fertility rates remain high in the world's poorest countries, however; the total fertility rate for women in Burundi in 2009 (according to UN estimates) was 6.8 children, fourth highest in the world, while in the Netherlands it was 1.7, 155th in the world. Since 2005, birth rates have actually fallen below replacement levels in many places. In China, the one-child policy has been so effective that officials are now worried about too low a birth rate—often called the "graying" of a population—and are granting more exemptions. The expenses of a second child and a shortage of housing mean that few urban couples choose to have a second, however. The Chinese population is still expanding because a large share of the population is in its childbearing years, but in Japan birth rates are so low that the population is declining. Japan is culturally homogenous and government policy has never favored immigration—the solution to a shrinking population elsewhere—so various high-tech methods including robots and electronic monitoring systems are currently being proposed to address such issues as care for the elderly. In India, middle-class urban families have access to contraception and thus have smaller families, while families in villages remain large; demographers predict that as of 2050 India will pass China as the world's most populous country, with 1.5 billion people. Today the world's lowest fertility rates are in the wealthy, heavily urbanized, and crowded states of East Asia, including Singapore, Hong Kong and Macao as well as Japan, and in eastern Europe and the former Soviet states, where what sociologists term "partner instability" and other uncertainties have led women to decide not to have children. France, Italy, Germany, Poland, Russia, Taiwan, Singapore, and some other countries have adopted policies to encourage couples to have more children, and there has been a slight uptick in some places, but the increased cost of living, especially in cities where most of the world's population now lives, women's participation in the paid labor force and the social acceptability of small families mean that low birth rates in industrialized societies will no doubt continue. All of these trends make it very difficult to predict what will happen to global population levels over the next century, and estimates range from a near flattening-out at current levels to growth at an even faster pace.

Migration and travel were responsible for the global spread of AIDS—along with other, less devastating new diseases—and are also among the factors creating changes in family structure. Despite continued ethnic and religious tensions and violence in many areas, in some parts of the world marriage or cohabitation between individuals of different races, ethnicities, and religions has become increasingly common, challenging centuries-old boundaries and definitions of who is family and who is kin. Long-distance migration and urbanization account for most of these inter-group relationships, but many also result from internet-based sex, dating, and marriage services, which involve thousands of agencies. In some situations the internet also enhances endogamy, however; high-caste Hindus and orthodox Jews now search for appropriate spouses through internet ads as well as traditional marriage brokers and matchmakers, and people in various new sorts of clan groups—fans of Star Trek, birdwatchers, gay police officers—can find like-minded partners through the web as well.

Households today are less likely to consist only of a married couple and their children than they were fifty years ago. Effective contraception has meant that sexual activity is separated from its reproductive consequences for people in many parts of the world, and sex before marriage with a variety of partners has become more widely accepted, even for women. Since 1970, marriage rates have steadily fallen in most of the world, as the increasing social acceptability of cohabitation and childbearing outside of marriage has led many people not to marry until quite late in life or never marry at all. Divorce rates have simultaneously risen: in the United States in the 2000s one out of every two marriages ended in divorce, and in the Arab world one out of every four. Many families include the children from several different relationships, thus returning to an earlier pattern when spousal death and remarriage had created such "blended" families. To this variety are added households in which children are being raised by their grandparents, by gay, lesbian, and transsexual individuals and couples, by adoptive parents, by single parents (most often the mother), and by unmarried couples who have no intention of marrying. Statistics from the USA provide evidence of all these trends: in 2013, 15 percent of new marriages were mixed race, 19 percent of households consisted of a married couple and their children, 51 percent of adults were married (down from 72 percent in 1960), and 41 percent of children were born to unmarried women.

The transportation and communications systems that have allowed globalized banking and dating have also allowed a spread and blending of cultural forms on an unprecedented level, as music, movies, television programs, websites, radio stations, internet-based social networks, classrooms, and everything else can now reach a global audience. Prophets of the new information technologies also predict that older cultural forms—the university, the gallery, the book, the musical recording—will disappear in the near future, replaced by computer or cell phone based forms of training, display, and distribution. Advocates of these developments praise the possibilities, arguing that this will democratize culture, making it open to anyone with creative ideas and access to digital technology. Critics highlighting a "digital divide" note that most of the world's population still does not have access to computers, and though more and more people each year have cell phones, this is leading to commercial globalization and cultural homogenization rather than a flourishing of individual local cultures.

The last letter in Nehru's collection was written in August 1933, in the midst of a worldwide economic depression when the Japanese army was advancing in China and the Nazis had just come to power in Germany. It is not surprising that Nehru comments: "our age ... is an age of disillusion, of doubt and uncertainty and questioning." He might have been speaking of the early third millennium, and now access to a television, a computer, or a cell phone allows people all over the world to see the affluence or misery of others on a regular basis, rather than simply during a royal procession or a visit to a capital city, as was the case in earlier centuries. Inequality has been a central feature of human society since the Neolithic (or perhaps earlier), but within the last several centuries ideologies of egalitarianism have said this is wrong, and people have worked to lessen it, in some cases successfully. Whether this will be true in the future—whether Burundi and the Netherlands will move together or further apart in their connectedness, wealth, and hunger—remains to be seen.

FURTHER READING

General introductions to the modern era abound. Among the best, with considerations of social and cultural history as well as political and economic, are Christopher Bayly, *The Birth of the Modern World, 1780–1914* (Malden, MA: Wiley-Blackwell, 2004) and Eric Hobsbawm, *The Age of Extremes: A History of the World, 1914–1991* (New York: Pantheon, 1994). Volume 7 of the *Cambridge World History: Production, Destruction, and Connection, 1750–Present*, edited by J.R. McNeill and Kenneth Pomeranz, has many relevant chapters. Books that examine transformations in key social structures across the modern period include Joan Smith and Immanuel Wallerstein, *Creating and Transforming Households in the World Economy* (Cambridge: Cambridge University Press, 1992); Susan Bayly, *Caste, Society, and Politics in India from the Eighteenth Century to the Modern Age* (Cambridge: Cambridge University Press, 1999); "Forum: Transnational Sexualities," *American Historical Review* 114/15 (2009): 1250–1353.

Regional histories that pay attention to society and culture include: Sugata Bose and Ayesha Jalal, *Modern South Asia: History, Culture, Political Economy* (London: Routledge, 3rd edn. 2011); Norman Owen, ed., *The Emergence of Southeast Asia: A New History* (Honolulu: University of Hawai'i Press, 2004); James L. Gelvin, *The Modern Middle East: A History* (New York: Oxford University Press, 3rd edn. 2011); Teresa A. Meade, *A History of Modern Latin America: 1800 to the Present* (Malden, MA: Wiley-Blackwell, 2009); Richard Reid, *A History of Modern Africa: 1800 to the Present* (Malden, MA: Wiley-Blackwell, 2nd edn. 2012).

On the role of cotton in sparking and sustaining the Industrial Revolution, see Giorgio Riello, *Cotton: The Fabric that Made the Modern World* (Cambridge: Cambridge University Press, 2013), which has wonderful color illustrations, and Prasannan Parthasarathi, *Why Europe Grew Rich and Asia Did Not: Global Economic Divergence 1600–1850* (Cambridge: Cambridge University Press, 2011). On the development of industrialism more broadly, see Jan de Vries, *The Industrious Revolution: Consumer*

Behavior and the Household Economy, 1650 to the Present (Cambridge: Cambridge University Press, 2008), Robert C. Allen, *The British Industrial Revolution in Global Perspective* (Cambridge: Cambridge University Press, 2009), Joel Mokyr, *The Enlightened Economy: An Economic History of Britain* (New Haven: Yale University Press, 2010), and Jack A. Goldstone, "Efflorescences and Economic Growth in World History: Rethinking the 'Rise of the West' and the Industrial Revolution," *Journal of World History* 13:2 (2002): 323–90, which has a huge bibliography. Jordan Goodman and Katrina Honeyman, *Gainful Pursuits: The Making of Industrial Europe, 1600–1914* (London: Edward Arnold, 1988) and Joyce Burnette, *Gender, Work and Wages in Industrial Revolution Britain* (Cambridge: Cambridge University Press, 2008) examine social changes that accompanied industrialization in Europe. On industrialization outside of Europe, see Tessa Morris-Suzuki, *The Technological Transformation of Japan: From the Seventeenth to the Twenty-first Century* (Cambridge: Cambridge University Press, 1994), Atul Kohli, *State-Directed Development: Political Power and Industrialization in the Global Periphery* (Cambridge: Cambridge University Press, 2004), and Marcel van der Linden, ed., *Workers of the World, Essays toward a Global Labor History* (Boston, MA: Brill Academic Publishers, 2008). On the role of large corporations, see Geoffrey Jones, *Multinationals and Global Capitalism: From the Nineteenth to the Twenty-first Century* (Oxford: Oxford University Press, 2005). Immanuel Wallerstein's classic work is *The Modern World System* (New York: Academic Press, 1974, 1980, 1989), and a more recent discussion with Wallerstein is "Globalization or the Age of Transition? A Long Term View of the Trajectory of the World System," *International Sociology* 15:2 (2000): 251–67. Kenneth Pomeranz's major study is *The Great Divergence: China, Europe, and the Making of the Modern World Economy* (Princeton: Princeton University Press, 2000).

Benedict Anderson's *Imagined Communities: Reflections on the Origin and Spread of Nationalism* (London: Verso, 1983) has been extremely influential in highlighting new developments in the eighteenth century that led to modern nationalism, but Azar Gat, *Nations: The Long History and Deep Roots of Political Ethnicity and Nationalism* (Cambridge: Cambridge University Press, 2013) has countered that political nations are very old. On inclusions and exclusions in ideas about the nation, see Ida Blom, Karen Hagemann, and Catherine Hall, eds., *Gendered Nations: Nationalisms and Gender Order in the Long Nineteenth Century* (Oxford: Oxford International Publishers, 2000); Andreas Wimmer, *Nationalist Exclusion and Ethnic Conflict* (Cambridge: Cambridge University Press, 2002); Martin Manalansan and Arnaldo Cruz-Malave, eds., *Queer Globalizations:*

Citizenship and the Afterlife of Colonialism (New York: New York University Press, 2002); Rogers M. Smith, *Stories of Peoplehood: The Politics and Morals of Political Membership* (Cambridge: Cambridge University Press, 2003); Don H. Doyle and Marco Antonio Pampalona, eds., *Nationalism in the New World* (Athens, GA: University of Georgia Press, 2006). For nationalism today, see Craig Calhoun, *Nations Matter: Culture, History, and the Cosmopolitan Dream* (London: Routledge, 2007).

Every movement for social change has a deep bibliography. The books of the Oxford University Press Very Short Introduction series are good places to start, including Michael Newman, *Socialism* (2005), Leslie Holmes, *Communism* (2009), and Manfred B. Steger *Neoliberalism* (2010). On women's movements, see Estelle Friedman, *No Turning Back: The History of Feminism and the Future of Women* (New York: Ballantyne Books, 2003). On immigration restrictions, see Marilyn Lake and Henry Reynolds, *Drawing the Global Colour Line: White Men's Countries and the International Challenge of Racial Equality* (Cambridge: Cambridge University Press, 2008). On eugenics, see Alison Bashford and Philippa Levine, eds., *The Oxford Handbook of the History of Eugenics* (Oxford: Oxford University Press, 2010).

Dirk Hoerder, *Cultures in Contact: World Migrations in the Second Millennium* (Durham, NC: Duke University Press, 2003) is an excellent overview of migration. More detailed studies include: Pamela Sharpe, ed., *Women, Gender, and Labour Migration: Historical and Global Perspectives* (New York: Routledge, 2001); Philip A. Kuhn, *Chinese among Others: Emigration in Modern Times* (London: Rowman & Littlefield, 2008); Tony Ballantyne and Antoinette Burton, eds., *Moving Subjects: Gender, Mobility, and Intimacy in an Age of Global Empire* (Urbana: University of Illinois Press, 2009); Marjory Harper and Stephen Constantine, *Migration and Empire* (Oxford: Oxford University Press, 2010).

On European imperialism, the best place to start is Eric R. Wolf's classic *Europe and the People without History* (Berkeley: University of California Press, 1982, reissued 2010). H.L. Wesseling, *The European Colonial Empires, 1815–1919* (London: Routledge, 2004) is a good introduction to European colonization in the nineteenth century. Philip D. Curtin, *The World and the West: The European Challenge and the Overseas Response in the Age of Empire* (Cambridge: Cambridge University Press, 2000) offers a comparative analysis of reactions to European colonialism, and Tony Ballantyne and Antoinette Burton, *Empires and the Reach of the Global, 1870–1945* (Cambridge, MA: The Belknap Press, 2014) provides a comparison of the British, Japanese, and Ottoman imperial systems, and their racial, gendered, and economic forms. A few of the many books on empire that focus on issues discussed in this chapter are: Daniel Headrick, *The Tools of Empire: Technology and European Imperialism in the Nineteenth Century* (Oxford: Oxford University Press, 1981); Ann Laura Stoler, *Carnal Knowledge and Imperial Power: Race and the Intimate in Colonial Rule* (Berkeley: University of California Press, 2002); Catherine Hall and Sonya Rose, eds., *At Home with the Empire: Metropolitan Culture and the Imperial World* (Cambridge: Cambridge University Press, 2006); Mrinalini Sinha, *Specters of Mother India: The Global Restructuring of an Empire* (Durham, NC: Duke University Press, 2006); Rachel Laudan, *Cuisine and Empire: Cooking in World History* (Berkeley: University of California Press, 2013).

The total wars of the twentieth century have been examined from every possible perspective. Studies that examine their cultural impact include Paul Fussell's classic, *The Great War and Modern Memory* (Oxford: Oxford University Press, 1970, reissued 2013) and Modris Ecksteins, *Rites of Spring: The Great War and the Birth of the Modern Age* (Boston, MA: Houghton Mifflin, 1989).

Raymond F. Betts, *Decolonization* (London: Routledge, 2nd edn. 2004) provides a brief overview of the process of decolonization. Prasenjit Duara, ed., *Decolonization: Perspectives from Now and Then* (London: Routledge, 2013) is an excellent collection of articles by prominent historians of decolonization and writings by some of its architects, including Nehru, Ho Chi Minh, and Kwame Nkrumah. On the Cold War, see Odd Arne Westad, *The Global Cold War: Third World Interventions and the Making of Modern Times* (Cambridge: Cambridge University Press, 2005).

Gabriel A. Almond, R. Scott Appleby, and Emmanuel Sivan, *Strong Religion: the Rise of Fundamentalisms around the World* (Chicago: University of Chicago Press, 2003) traces fundamentalism in seven different religions, and Mark Juergensmeyer, *Terror in the Mind of God: The Global Rise of Religious Violence* (Berkeley: University of California Press, 3rd edn. 2003) analyzes religious extremism.

On neoliberalism and economic developments, see Vito Tanzi and Ludger Schuknecht, *Public Spending in the Twentieth Century: A Global Perspective* (Cambridge: Cambridge University Press, 2000); Alfred D. Chandler and Bruce Mazlish, eds., *Leviathans: Multinational Corporations and the New Global History* (Cambridge: Cambridge University Press, 2005); Maxine Molyneux and Shahra Razavi, eds., *Liberalism and its Discontents: Gender Justice, Development, and Rights* (New York: Oxford University Press, 2002); Kevin Bales, *Disposable People: New Slavery in the Global South* (Berkeley: University of California Press, 2nd edn. 2012). On cities, see David Clark, *Urban World/Global City* (London: Routledge, 2003).

The cultural and social effects of globalization have been examined in Ulf Hannerz, *Transnational Connections: Culture, People, Places* (New York: Routledge, 1996); Saskia Sassen, ed., *Globalization and its Discontents* (New York: The New Press, 1998); Pierre Hamel *et al.*, eds., *Globalization and Social Movements* (London: Palgrave Macmillan, 2000); Frank J. Kechner and John Boli, *World Culture: Origins and Consequences* (Malden, MA: Blackwell, 2005); Jennifer Cole and Deborah Lynn Durham, eds., *Generations and Globalization: Youth, Age, and Family in the New World Economy* (Bloomington: Indiana University Press, 2007); Will Kymlicka, *Multicultural Odysseys: Navigating the New International Politics of Diversity* (Oxford: Oxford University Press, 2007). The latest comments, research, and reflections on these issues (and on everything else in this book) are available on the various forms of modern media that have made this globalization possible, on a device that is most likely within your easy reach, if it's not how you are reading this book.

INDEX